Bonds of War

CIVIL WAR AMERICA

Peter S. Carmichael, Caroline E. Janney, and Aaron Sheehan-Dean, *editors*

This landmark series interprets broadly the history and culture of the Civil War era through the long nineteenth century and beyond. Drawing on diverse approaches and methods, the series publishes historical works that explore all aspects of the war, biographies of leading commanders, and tactical and campaign studies, along with select editions of primary sources. Together, these books shed new light on an era that remains central to our understanding of American and world history.

DAVID K. THOMSON

Bonds of War
How Civil War Financial Agents Sold the World on the Union

The University of North Carolina Press *Chapel Hill*

This book was published with the assistance of the Authors Fund of the University of North Carolina Press.

© 2022 The University of North Carolina Press
All rights reserved
Set in Arno Pro by Westchester Publishing Services
Manufactured in the United States of America

The University of North Carolina Press has been a member of the Green Press Initiative since 2003.

Complete Library of Congress Cataloging-in-Publication Data is available at https://lccn.loc.gov/2021054797.

ISBN 978-1-4696-6660-0 (cloth: alk. paper)
ISBN 978-1-4696-6661-7 (pbk.: alk. paper)
ISBN 978-1-4696-6662-4 (ebook)

Cover illustration: 1862 $500 twenty-year coupon "five-twenty" bond. Courtesy of Joe I. Herbstman Memorial Collection of American Finance™, https://www.theherbstmancollection.com.

To Mom, Dad, Patrick, Ellen, and Katie

If it succeeds the bonds are good, if it fails they are worthless, that is the war.

—Thomas Haines Dudley, United States consul to Liverpool, to Secretary of State William Seward, December 5, 1862

Contents

Acknowledgments xi

Introduction 1

CHAPTER ONE
Freedom of Debt: The Lessons of
Government Financing before the Civil War 11

CHAPTER TWO
A Thousand-Dollar Breakfast: The Limits of
War Financing by Elites 22

CHAPTER THREE
Patriotism and Profit: Jay Cooke and the Democratization of Debt 55

CHAPTER FOUR
The Sale of American Stocks Constitutes the Chief Business
at the Bourse: Foreign War Finance 85

CHAPTER FIVE
Like a Cord Through the Whole Country:
Nationalizing the Economy 121

CHAPTER SIX
A Permanent National Debt Is Not an American Institution:
Postwar Debt 157

Conclusion 194

Appendix. Supplementary Tables 205

Notes 209

Bibliography 247

Index 263

Illustrations and Tables

ILLUSTRATIONS

"Jackson Slaying the Many Headed Monster" 16

Assay office 38

Jay Cooke 43

Philadelphia offices of Jay Cooke & Co. 45

1861 bond 48

Female employees of the Treasury Department 60

Jay Cooke & Co. flyer 62

German 5-20 ad 67

August Belmont 91

George Peabody 95

Night offices 147

Rothschild ad 175

TABLES

1.1 Mexican War long-term bond issues 20

6.1 Public loan transactions of the U.S. Treasury, 1865–1869 183

A.1 New York banks, their operating capital, and their subscriptions to the initial $50 million installment 205

A.2 5-20 Primary sales by subtreasury region 207

Acknowledgments

This book, much like the debt it traces, was a product of many cross-country and transatlantic trips. The travel not only enabled some of the vital research for the book, it provided planes and trains as both modes of transit and precious space to write the book itself. While this work stresses the power of debt during the bloodiest conflict in American history, I must also take time to thank those to whom I owe a great debt for their faith in me throughout the duration of this project that spans a longer period of time than I care to note. The debt that I owe many can never be fully repaid, but it is my hope that I can begin the process here.

Great teachers fostered my love of history through the years. My high school history teacher, Mr. Eugene Beliveau, well and truly made history come alive for me, and I'll never forget the opportunities he put before me, such as teaching a Civil War lecture to a group of high school students as a fifteen-year-old sophomore. To this day I likewise will never forget his ability to make the intricate developments of the French Revolution accessible and interesting to that very same sophomore. Mr. Beliveau introduced hundreds of students to history during his tenure at St. Thomas Aquinas and those who were able to take a course with him were better off for it. I am sorry that Mr. Beliveau will not be able to see the final iteration of this manuscript, but I would hope that it would have met with his approval, accompanied by a wry smile as he leaned back in his desk chair.

There is not an institution of higher education in Maine more closely tied to the Civil War than Bowdoin College. As a self-identifying Civil War nerd by the end of high school, I had the great opportunity of attending Bowdoin College as a young and earnest undergrad and it was there that I had the privilege to take numerous courses with Professors Patrick Rael and Jill Pearlman. Patrick served as my adviser from my first day at Bowdoin and I had the opportunity to take courses with Patrick on the Civil War era and Reconstruction. Not only that, Patrick also supervised my senior thesis work on Oliver Otis Howard that resulted in my first publication and furthered my interest in pursuing a doctoral degree. (It is worth noting that the research into Howard would not have been realized without hitting the work-study lottery with a job in the archive—so thank you, Richard Lindemann and

Caroline Moseley.) Patrick always pressed me to become a better writer and instilled that desire in me from the time I set foot on the campus. While I know there is still some ways to go to reach Patrick's level of proficiency, I hope he will take this offer of gratitude from a former student whom he provided so much to in a four-year period. Patrick's voice is frequently in my head as I sit down to write and I hope that he will approve of this work. I also appreciate the opportunity that Patrick provided when he extended an invitation to present an early version of this work at Bowdoin in the fall of 2016. His thoughts helped me to reframe and sharpen the focus of the work. Additionally, I must thank Jill Pearlman for pushing my abilities as a writer and for opening the world of urban history to me, fostering a deep love for so many cities in Europe. Jill's courses at Bowdoin are some of my fondest memories and a shining example of the benefits of a liberal arts education. For Patrick and Jill, I must offer my sincerest thanks for their willingness to put up with an overanxious undergraduate and push him to develop better writing skills, better argumentation skills, and confidence in his own abilities. Truly, this project could not have been possible without the groundwork that they helped to lay.

This project began at the University of Georgia. I must thank, first and foremost, the University of Georgia's History Department, and especially the travel funds endowed by Greg and Amanda Gregory that proved instrumental in facilitating the research for this project—especially the research conducted abroad. I truly believe this story cannot be told without the European narrative incorporated, and to move beyond mere newspaper articles and online source materials, it required access to archives in Europe. The Gregorys helped to facilitate travel to London, Paris, Amsterdam, Brussels, and Frankfurt to research the scope of American Civil War bond sales abroad. To them I owe a tremendous debt of gratitude. I also want to thank the History Department at UGA for signing off on said travel and for having faith in me to conduct this research. Thanks are also in order to the University of Georgia graduate school, which helped facilitate travel to England as part of a doctoral exchange with the University of Liverpool.

There were many at the University of Georgia and beyond who aided this project that resulted in this book. First and foremost, I must thank Stephen Berry. Steve took an eager student under his wing and pressed me with my writing and exploring new topics of interest that culminated in an exploration of Civil War debt. I must also thank Stephen Mihm, Daniel Rood, and Julia Ott. It was a privilege to work with a quartet of such knowledgeable historians.

All four helped in various ways to refine the project as it evolved by offering strong commentary, feedback, and probing analysis of what I was trying to accomplish. The "two Stephens" continue to influence my writing and work to the present day and I am truly in their debt. It is my hope that they have learned something in this process about the subject matter as a small repayment for all the assistance they have offered to me. I earnestly look forward to calling these individuals colleagues as I move forward with my professional career.

As I have shifted from a completed degree into a tenure-track position at Sacred Heart University, I have become greatly indebted to research funds that have been afforded to me by my institution. On several occasions I have received support from my then dean, Robin Cautin. Successful applications to the University Research and Creativity Grant Committee were essential to completing the research for this project. I thank these colleagues on the committee who have enabled the research in archives domestically and abroad—it has proven vital to the end product here. I've had the opportunity to work with some wonderful colleagues in the History Department and beyond. Many thanks to Jennifer McLaughlin, David Luesink, Kelly Marino, Charlotte Gradie, John Roney, Brent Little, Charlie Gillespie, Christine Susienka, Jennifer Trudeau, June-Ann Greeley, and Michael Gorman for all they have done to make work more rewarding and simultaneously feel less like work at times.

I am also indebted as well to numerous institutions for their travel grants and residential fellowships that enabled prolonged stays in locations that proved of tremendous importance to my research. These include the Library Company of Philadelphia, the Huntington Library, Harvard Business School, the Rothschild Archive, New York Public Library, Gilder Lehrman Institute of American History, the Harvard Center for History and Economics, Obama Institute for Transnational American Studies at Mainz University, and Indiana University. On many occasions, specific archivists were of great assistance to this project. I would especially like to thank Melanie Aspey, Martin Mueller, Justin Cavernelis-Frost, Clara Harrow, Sabrina Sigel, Anne-Lise Ducoroy, Hugo Bänziger, Natalie Attwood, Sylvia Goldhammer, Ariane Huber Hernández, Geert Leloup, Kathrin Enzel, Martin Luepold, Steve Smith, Julia Mayle, Bart Schuurman, and Daniel Frankignoul. There are countless other archivists and individuals at the various archives within the United States and abroad who were of great assistance. To these individuals above and those I have accidently neglected to mention, I offer my sincere thanks for assisting me with this project. Archives can be incredibly difficult to navigate—especially when they are not in your native language—and so for these international archivists I am eternally grateful.

The world of academia is strange at times, but it does nevertheless foster an atmosphere that I am proud to call "home" and enabled me to forge friendships that move beyond professional responsibilities. I am grateful to many individuals who have provided commentary, encouragement, or pushback on this project, all in an effort to make it better. Many thanks to Bill Blair, Brian Luskey, Martha Hodes, Jim Marten, Sharon Murphy, Jason Phillips, Julie Mujic, Ryan Keating, Megan Kate Nelson, Sven Beckert, Nicolas Barreyre, Jay Sexton, Scott Nelson, Seth Rockman, Andrew Popp, Steve Soper, Alex Finley, John Inscoe, Jim Cobb, Mandy Cooper, David Sim, Susannah Ural, Lesley Gordon, Diane Summerville, Jonathan Jones, Kevin Waite, David Silkenat, David Gleeson, Sarah Handley-Cousins, Noam Maggor, Hilary Green, the late Chris Kobrak, Marc Flandreau, Ralf Banken, Sebastian Jobs, Mira Wilkins, Michael Caires, Robert Wright, Gary Gallagher, Elizabeth Varon, Franklin Noll, Peter Carmichael, Don Doyle, Anne Sarah Rubin, Sarah Gardner, Carole Emberton, Jim Broomall, Torsten Kathke, Joost Jonker, Guus Veenendaal, Rachel Shelden, Carrie Janney, Aaron Sheehan-Dean, Laura Mammina, Megan Bever, Lauren Thompson, Ann Daly, John Handel, Lindsey Peterson, and Jim Downs. For those who I may have missed or accidently omitted, please know that I am eternally grateful. All of these individuals helped to make the graduate school journey possible and have become colleagues and friends as I have entered the profession following the completion of my degree, and for that I am forever grateful for their assistance. I am sure I have omitted several names here and for that I must offer my sincerest apologies.

I also appreciate the opportunity through invited lectures, workshops, and conferences to share some of this work with colleagues who have helped to improve it markedly. This includes guest lectures and workshop presentations at the University of Zürich, University of Edinburgh, Freie Universitat Berlin, University of Virginia, University of Liverpool, Brown University, Bowdoin College, Gettysburg College, Sacred Heart University, Pandit Deendayal Energy University, European University Viadrina, Johann Wolfgang Goethe University, Newberry Seminar in the History of Capitalism, German Historical Institute, and the Treasury Historical Association. I have also valued the feedback I've received while presenting this work at the Business History Conference, Society of Civil War Historians, British American

Nineteenth Century Historians, Southern Historical Association, and the European Association for Banking and Financial History.

This project would not have come to fruition without the support of friends and colleagues who offered words of wisdom, encouragement, and advice during periods where it was needed the most. I am grateful to David Sokolow, Oliver Radwan, Lexie Radwan, George Radwan, Stephanie Greene, Sabrina Correll, Maxwell Palmer, Cori Palmer, Kathleen Shea-Porter, Michael Stubbs, Elisabeth Conroy, Brandon Mazer, Bernardo Guzman, Hilary Lewis, Bennett Lewis, Nathan Elder, Griffen Stabler, Melanie Haas, Robin Warner, Drew Boudreau, Jess Rodriguez, Amy Rosania, Rashni Grant, Kaitlyn Hennigan, and Kate Lebeaux for all they have done the past few years to help encourage me in the completion of this work. I must also thank fellow history doctoral students Robby Poister, Trae Welborn, Kylie Hulbert, Matt Hulbert, and especially Angela Elder for their tireless support during my time at the University of Georgia. Angela has remained a sounding board for my work in the subsequent years and I cannot thank her enough for her counsel as a colleague and friend.

The University of North Carolina Press has embraced this project from the start. My editor Mark Simpson-Vos welcomed this project and has helped move it to publication. He has patiently answered many questions during the process and helped to reframe some crucial components of the work. The Civil War America Series is one of the standards in Civil War–era studies and I'm thrilled to be a part of it. Many thanks to series editors Caroline Janney, Peter Carmichael, and Aaron Sheehan-Dean for taking this project on with great enthusiasm. In particular, I wish to express my sincere thanks to Aaron for such a close read of the manuscript and offering edits on multiple occasions that have significantly improved the manuscript. I must also thank María García from the Press, as well as Mary Gendron and Brett Keener, who helped shepherd this through production. I must also thank Cate Hodorowicz from the Press, who played such a crucial role in matters of presentation and style. Finally, I must thank the two anonymous readers for the Press who helped to significantly strengthen the final product.

Portions of this book appeared in previously published journal articles and book chapters. Chapters 3 and 5 expand on arguments introduced in "'Like a Cord Through the Whole Country': Union Bonds and Financial Mobilization for Victory," *The Journal of the Civil War Era* 6, no. 3 (September 2016). Some ideas in chapters 4 and 6 can be found in "Reorienting Atlantic World Financial Capitalism: America and the German States," in Klaus

Weber and Jutta Wimmler, eds., *Globalized Peripheries: New Approaches to the Atlantic World 1680–1860* (Suffolk: Boydell UK, 2020); "'The National Debt May Be a National Blessing': Debt as an Instrument of Character in the Civil War Era," in Caroline Janney and James Marten, eds., *Buying and Selling Civil War Memory in Gilded Age America* (Athens: University of Georgia Press, 2021); and "Financing the War," in Aaron Sheehan-Dean, ed., *The Cambridge History of the American Civil War*, 3 vols. (Cambridge: Cambridge University Press, 2019). I am grateful to the publishers for allowing some of this material to be reproduced here.

The greatest debts are of a personal nature and to family. I must offer thanks to my extended Thomson and Kelley families who endured many holiday conversations about this project and my general passion for the Civil War, only to ask for updates during the next visit. I assume for all their enthusiasm they are grateful they no longer have to ask the dreaded question, "So, when's the book coming out?" For my cousins, aunts, uncles, and grandparents no longer with us, I am deeply indebted to their love, support, and assistance in shaping who I am today. Their support has been more than I could have ever asked for and enabled me to pursue this passion into a career.

To my brother Patrick, I must thank him for his hospitality (and air mattress) on numerous early research trips and understanding of his "weird" brother's passion for the Civil War, even if it is not as wonderful as the world of economics. Patrick's partner, Jenna, and my precious niece, Charlotte, have provided amazing support. Charlie's smile and barrage of daily photos provide a welcome respite from nineteenth-century finance and she is so beyond adorable (a statement of fact in no way biased by my self-declared status as favorite uncle). To my sister Ellen, I am grateful for her love and support throughout this entire process, especially the many car rides to battlefields and historic sites when we were younger—something she endured with virtually no complaint. A special thanks to Ellen as well for a last-minute trip on my behalf to research at the Library of Congress. Alongside her partner Phil and their wonderful cats Ash and Bridge it was always a treat to make it to Washington, D.C., and the bed they provided for some much-needed time at the College Park branch of the National Archives. Their support has been immeasurable.

To my mother and father, Coralee and Jeffrey, I cannot properly articulate in words what their love and support has meant to me. For introducing me to history at such a young age and encouraging my pursuit of this hobby, I offer my sincerest thanks. The early trips to battlefields, historic sites, and historical events significantly outnumbered the solo trip to Disney World, and

I cannot thank them enough. They provided access to an exceptional education that opened doors to help me get to where I am today. For their patience and understanding as this hobby became a passion and future career, I can never express enough gratitude. Alongside their feline friends Abby, Sam, Makenzie, Riley, and Finnegan, they've cheered me on. They have been my advocates and counselors through the years. This unyielding faith in me to succeed has truly made all the difference.

I must also thank my partner, Katie Straw, for her support of this project. Katie has fully embraced this nerd whose love of history I'm sure has been overwhelming at times. While this project began before Katie was in my life, as she came to realize the scope of this project she has supported me and the time spent time away from her and the four-legged center of our life, Oliver. These research trips and presentations were so important to this work and at times were weeks long, but undoubtedly the thing I looked forward to the most was the return home. As the final stages of this book came together in the midst of a global pandemic, Katie provided all the necessary support and invaluable time in order to ensure the book crossed the finish line (often with Oliver purring right along on my lap). I am forever grateful for your love, companionship, selflessness, and patience for my other passion in life. Thank you for everything, Katie—I look forward to continuing our journey together.

Bonds of War

Introduction

In July 1894 financier Jay Cooke ruminated on his professional career. Cooke had started as a simple clerk in a Philadelphia banking house and in short time climbed the financial ladder in the city to run his own firm. In fact, Cooke rose all the way to the top of American finance in the Reconstruction era, only to lose it all. Although infamous for his role in the Panic of 1873, in the initial pages of his memoir he focused on another experience: his service to his country during the American Civil War. "Like Moses and Washington and Lincoln and Grant," Cooke proclaimed, "I have been—I firmly believe— God's chosen instrument especially in the financial work of saving the Union during the greatest war that has ever been fought in the history of man." Cooke continued, "I absolutely by my own faith and energy and means saved the nation financially . . . the public should know even at this late period the unselfishness and sacrifice made by myself and [my] firm." Not one for subtlety or modesty, Cooke's analysis of his role in the bloodiest war in American history staked a claim to the vital importance of his work as part of the larger Union war effort. Cooke looms large in understanding the story of finance during the American Civil War, but a more detailed analysis of his position reveals a far more nuanced series of events and deeper understanding for this moment in American financial history. For as much as Cooke and his traveling agents revealed a dynamism within the Northern bond market, it remained predicated on international bond sales.[1]

Sovereign debt—an interest-bearing financial instrument that served as an IOU for the government—enabled the United States government to pay soldiers and contractors. Equally important, bond sales to the public during the war democratized debt during the conflict. Cooke's "army" of financial partners and traveling salesmen sold well over $1 billion in federal debt alone. The selling of U.S. public debt across the Union and parts of the Confederacy by war's end was instrumental in keeping soldiers equipped, fed, and mobilized against the various Confederate armies. By Appomattox, the public and press alike recognized Cooke as "the Napoleon of Finance" and "Our Modern Midas." The Philadelphia banker rose in acclaim and the national spotlight, all through the sale of a standard financial instrument of the nineteenth century.[2]

On May 10, 1863, just days after the Army of the Potomac's disastrous defeat at the battle of Chancellorsville at the hands of Robert E. Lee's Confederate Army of Northern Virginia, *Harper's Weekly* wrote about the financing of the war. "When the history of this war comes to be written," remarked the author, "no part of it will attract more attention or command more admiration than the chapters which relate to finance." Yet, for all the ink spilled regarding the American Civil War, few historians have addressed how the North financed the war effort. The cause of Union and emancipation relied upon a triumvirate of financial instruments: bond issues (more than $2 billion worth), the issuance of a new currency backed by the United States government referred to as "greenbacks," and a new taxation policy centered on the first federal income tax all paved the way for Union financial success. Despite the necessity of these instruments and their recognized importance during the war itself, little has been written on the topic. This is a crucial gap, because these financial stories come with repercussions for our understanding of the Civil War and the postwar United States. Of these three financial legs that the Union utilized, none proved more critical than the various bonds and Treasury notes issued by the federal government during the war. These war bonds provided nearly two-thirds of the $3.2 billion in funding for the Union cause—and in doing so helped keep the country afloat financially.[3]

"The Yankees did not whip us on the field. We were whipped in the Treasury Department," quipped one perceptive Confederate after Appomattox. While military historians continue to argue that Generals Grant, Sherman, and Sheridan surely had something to do with it, I will argue that the war's "financial soldiers"—especially the employees of the large financial house of Jay Cooke & Company, their subcontracting agencies, and the thousands of traveling agents who canvassed far and wide to sell U.S. securities—won the financial war for the Union. Through exhaustive marketing campaigns tailored to a wide class of investors, these financiers and their salesmen instilled in many everyday Americans what proved to be a self-fulfilling faith in Union victory. In selling confidence, they created confidence, not merely in Union armies but in a Union "way of life." Such confidence in the imperiled American Union via investment reflected a deviation from antebellum concepts of investment. While popular support for savings banks grew in stature in the late antebellum period, "popular" investment in financial instruments on such a large scale even in such mundane products as bonds reflected a new line of thinking in the United States. The results profoundly impacted American finance in this era. The marketing of Union bonds on such a widespread, democratic basis constituted a critically important episode in the long-term evolution of capital markets.[4]

Union financing via bond issues ran up against recent challenges in the United States to effectively honor debt instruments. The country had to contend with a legacy of state debt defaults in the antebellum period. In the early 1840s, a series of states in the North and South defaulted on their debt payments. While some states only threatened to default, and others defaulted only briefly, some fully repudiated their debts. This action threatened the prospects of federal debt issuance. This proved especially important with international financiers in important cities such as London and Amsterdam. The 1849 repudiation by Mississippi was especially concerning to British, Dutch, French, and German bankers. The issue, when raised on the floor of the House of Representatives, even led former president John Quincy Adams to declare that such a state could not rely on federal military protection if it did not honor its debts. According to Adams's logic, the United States was under no obligation to defend Mississippi or any other state from a theoretical attack by a foreign power. Future Confederate president Jefferson Davis's defense of Mississippi's repudiation proved additional fodder for the Union cause during the Civil War. Wartime finance, therefore, found itself deeply entwined with the financial instruments of the antebellum period and the lasting legacies of state impropriety.[5]

By the time of the American Civil War, the United States joined the long list of nations opting for bond issues to finance its conflicts. The Bank of England financed debt issuances for British wars of the eighteenth century. Moving into the early nineteenth century, the Napoleonic wars forced many European nations (including the French) to market public debt on a large scale to keep up with the costs of war. By the 1850s, France had marketed several different bond issues among its populace—a fact not lost on those planning to sell Union debt during the American Civil War. In fact, many nineteenth-century states often struggled with budget deficits and relied on public debt to cover these shortfalls. Such acts only accelerated when preparing or directly engaged in war—an all too frequent occurrence for nineteenth-century states. European investment banks worked extensively to market this debt throughout Europe and eventually across the Atlantic, drawing in American financial houses. Such financial assets became a defining characteristic of European (and even American) portfolios. The fixed interest rates of these transferable bonds that were also liquid in nature proved highly desirable to the wealthy elites on both sides of the Atlantic.[6]

The American Civil War, though, became far larger than anyone had anticipated or experienced. Union officials recognized that the financial support of northeastern elites would not be enough to keep the Union war machine alive. As the Union armies expanded in the first months of the conflict, this meant hundreds of thousands of soldiers to clothe, feed, and supply as they fought the Confederacy. To that end, reaching out and selling the war's financial burdens via bond issues to larger swaths of the Northern public was a necessity. As Civil War debt made its way throughout the United States and pulled in investors from across the socioeconomic spectrum, Cooke and his army pitched investing as a form of patriotism. More specifically, patriotism became conjoined with self-interest. Investment as a patriotic notion in the war became one example of what historian Melinda Lawson describes as the "diverse and at times contradictory ideas about the meaning of patriotism and of the American nation." By making investment and self-interest ideologically virtuous, Cooke and his network of financial surrogates transformed the bond market landscape in America.[7]

Substantive discussions of finance and the American Civil War are long overdue. Some historians have explored various components of Civil War finance. Heather Cox Richardson and Jane Flaherty have both analyzed bond issues as well as taxation during the war. Max Edling has explored Civil War bond sales as part of the larger conversation surrounding American war financing since the country's inception. Richard Bensel's *Yankee Leviathan* likewise offers readers an important assessment of war financing as critical to the cause of the Union. While other scholars like Michael Caires are now demonstrating the importance of greenbacks in a more holistic context, so too must bonds and other federal financial instruments be put under the microscope. Bonds, especially during the Civil War, became a more democratic instrument in which increasingly larger segments of the U.S. population came to invest. War finance ensnared more than just the well-to-do in its web; it also attracted some of the more marginalized members of American society, with consequences that outlasted the war.[8]

Civil War bond drives represented a shift in popular investing strategies. As excess capital grew out of the market revolution and the rise of wage-earning professions during the first half of the nineteenth century, everyday Americans—largely but not exclusively white—shifted funds into savings accounts. As the Civil War moved into its second year and a new phase, many Americans shifted these funds into the bond market. Such a deliberate action represented a way not only to pursue their own self-interest (with higher interest rates in bonds compared to their savings accounts) but also as an appeal to the patriotic calls of the federal government. Whereas other wartime appeals focused on individual self-sacrifice and struggle for the common good as inherently patriotic, bond purchases and broader investment allowed individuals to pursue profit in the name of a patriotic act. Only after the war and the drastic drawdown of the debt did these same Americans revert to savings accounts. Northern financial elites used the war as a means to concentrate their power by working in close coordination with the expanding American state. Thus, the "democratic" pursuits of Northerners led to a greater concentration of wealth and power in the hands of the financial elites—especially those located in New York City. The city witnessed tremendous growth in the number of bankers within its borders, and those bankers took an increasing interest in selling these bonds.[9]

Bond sales did more. They also provided an opportunity for marginalized groups in the United States to assert a newfound civic inclusion. Bond purchases in the hands of women, immigrants, African Americans, and even native peoples revealed the possibility to expand this civic identity during the war—if only for a brief time. Such an act reflected a hope and belief that the federal government could mobilize the American populace during the war, even those who did not hold full political rights. As historian Julia Ott cogently describes, during World War I mass investment in federal debt reflected "a means of encouraging a widespread sense of identification with the war effort and the nation itself." By incorporating such an array of the American population in these sales, it brought them in as part of a national war effort. In the confluence of governmental legislation, Wall Street action, and democratic investment, the war ushered in a fleeting financial moment in which investment shifted away from financial elites to everyday investors.[10]

Financing the war required a degree of state-led financial innovation utterly at odds with American antebellum financial culture. The moral hazards of the anonymous marketplace from the antebellum era found themselves replaced by a statist response that called on the citizenry to embrace an evolving financial world punctuated by wartime exigencies. Historians of the nineteenth-century state have explored different institutions as reflective of a burgeoning American state, while others such as Brian Balogh demonstrate that in time some public-private partnerships rather than unilateral state power provided another path for depicting the American state in the nineteenth century (despite the fact it may not be particularly visible to the American public). So, too, did bond sales of the Civil War reflect such a state dynamic and, in the process, increase the clout of the wartime Republican Party.[11]

Everyday Americans who in the late antebellum period had increasingly found a home for excess capital in savings institutions now migrated that capital into the market as a whole. Such an act placed a new trust in financial instruments that offered greater uncertainty than most of these investors' traditional savings accounts. But if the war offered this moment for financial democratization, the postwar period witnessed the concentration of these financial instruments in the hands of the wealthiest of Americans and a return for other Americans to the greater comfort of savings banks. Additionally, such acts also pushed the marginalized groups back out of the fold—investors asserting a new form of civic identity were once more expelled. The moment proved brief, but it allowed American financiers greater influence over the federal government moving forward on all elements of fiscal policy. Such actions also led to an undeniable concentration of wealth and subsequent exacerbation of class tensions.[12]

More than any other financial instrument, the sales of Northern bonds during the war and Reconstruction offers a window into an evolving financial world. The war fostered a new world of American investment banking, where firms came to focus on specific investments such as government bonds and later railroad stock while also underwriting major bond and rail issues. This represented a demonstrable shift away from the joint merchant/broker world that prevailed before the war. This was also a marked deviation from the antebellum world of American merchant finance, in which bonds and stocks comprised part of a larger portfolio that relied on the trade of goods. Such actions paved the way for more widespread investment beyond the war and even into popular culture. The world of popular fiction and things like Wall Street board games reveal the financial hold that gripped the Northern community at large as a result of Civil War finance. Modern American finance—from highbrow financiers to everyday speculators—grew out of government-issued bonds and greenbacks. The world of finance and speculation that emerged in Reconstruction and carried forward into the latter part of the nineteenth century foreshadowed the popular investments of World War I and corporate stock ownership of the 1920s. In short, modern American finance materialized out of the Civil War.[13]

But if the story of United States debt is rooted on one side of the Atlantic, it is equally important to understand how those outside the country viewed and interacted with the debt. The story of Civil War–era finance contains transatlantic, even global dimensions. The literature on Civil War–era finance has long told a story of a massive repatriation of American debt from major financial powers such as Britain and France. These nations, closely tied to the cotton-growing American South, wanted to err on the side of caution as they attempted to remain neutral in an increasingly expanding conflict. While some foreign investors did shift their money from American to European financial instruments at the war's immediate outset, the interest in American bonds quickly returned. Investors exhibited such interest not only among the normally cautious financial powerhouses of London and Paris, but increasingly in the more pivotal markets of Amsterdam and the German states. Amsterdam had long been a financial center, but its level of interest in American debt during the war and beyond far exceeded its antebellum investment. Furthermore, Frankfurt became a vital financial center for American debt during the war—faith and kinship networks serving as key conduits for this financial exchange. In the case of Frankfurt, financiers in this city also leveraged anticompetitive market practices and a relative lack of transparency to fuel bond sales by major banking houses. The size and scope of investment during the war reveals the diplomatic and transatlantic elements of the war itself. Whereas histories of the Civil War focus on the neutrality of European nations and the inability of either the Union or Confederacy to raise meaningful funds through direct foreign loans (with the exception of the Confederate Erlanger Loan), they miss the significance of private foreign investment in the Union bond issues.[14]

In the Reconstruction period American bond sales spread across the globe, reaching every inhabited continent by the late 1860s. In doing so, these sales reflected a shift in American investment banking. American banks bypassed traditional relationships with the long-established banks of London and created relationships in other established as well as emerging markets. Networks based on faith and familial relations were essential to understanding the shift in international financial dynamics that came about during and after the Civil War. By 1869, half of all American national debt could be found abroad (mostly in Europe) and among a widespread group of financiers and their respective clients, revealing a globalization of the American financial world and a greater integration with global financial markets. This shifted the financial balance in American capitalism moving forward. American banks no longer served at the behest of London banks alone, but projected a newfound confidence and financial weight that underpinned the world's strongest economy by the turn of the century. In the end, these actions represented an important moment in the history of the fiscal state during a particular era of financial globalization.[15]

Bonds of War examines how, precisely, these bonds were marketed and sold, how the bond markets evolved domestically and overseas, and with what long-term consequences for American and world financial systems. Additionally, it uncovers what the bond drives suggest about the version of the war the Union public was willing to buy and to buy into. Following tremendous difficulty on the part of the Treasury to raise capital in the wake of the Union defeat at Bull Run in July 1861, Philadelphia financier Jay Cooke received exclusive rights from Secretary of the Treasury Salmon Chase to sell the $500 million "5-20" bond issue of March 1862. This subscription met with wild success and the federal government followed up with the 1865 "7-30" Treasury note issue (with a bond convertibility option) of $800 million. Because these bond issues were critical to Union finance, Cooke's Philadelphia bank is often at the center of this study. However, this is not a biography of Cooke. Rather, it extends to the thousands of smaller agents and subagents who canvassed the North, the western territories, and even parts of the Confederacy to market these bonds to millions of subscribers by war's end.[16]

While several factors played to Cooke's advantage, it is undeniable that Cooke understood that what mattered most was confidence. Like an evangelist spreading the gospel of capitalism and Union, Cooke trafficked in faith. How else can one explain Cooke's abilities to convince some four to five million individuals of various racial and gendered backgrounds to subscribe over two billion dollars (1865 dollars) to the various loan subscriptions in a manner that exuded confidence to a skeptical populace—less than 1 percent of whom had invested in the antebellum period? Perhaps New York City financier Joseph Seligman put it best: "Now I confess that altho' I know the U.S. to possess unparalleled resources, I sometimes doubt whether any people in any nation can successfully go on for years adding 1000s of millions to their National debt. If such a nation however does exist, there is no doubt but that the U.S are that nation." This was confidence made manifest as a market, and Cooke represented the apostle of that experience. As historian Stephen Mihm has noted, "Confidence was the engine of economic growth, the mysterious sentiment that permitted a country poor in specie but rich in promises to create something from nothing." Confidence, *Bonds of War* argues, became a sort of emotional commodity, ultimately providing a more durable basis for the Civil War economy than the antebellum one of cotton and the enslaved.[17]

The sale of Northern bonds and the evolution of finance during this period centers on three key ideas. First, bond sales were not restricted domestically. The marketing of such securities crossed the Atlantic to buyers in England, France, Belgium, Ireland, Russia, Malta, Switzerland, Spain, the Netherlands, the Italian states, and the German states and helped ensure that foreign countries, through their citizens, had a vested interest in the Union's success. These bonds also gained traction in Cuba as many prominent members of the Cuban elite purchased bonds. International sales accounted for at least $400 million of overall Civil War sales (almost a quarter of those produced) and in turn had tremendous influence over domestic markets and performance on Northern exchanges. Secondly, bonds found their way throughout the nation. Agents sold bonds in virtually all parts of the country, including Confederate states, as Union forces advanced into these areas during the course of the war. These purchases offered Unionists a chance to demonstrate their loyalty and wavering Confederates a chance to hedge against their own cause. From the small farmer in Maine to the New Orleans Unionist, Northern bonds offered an outlet for support of the government and in the process reconstituted how individuals related to the war, the federal government, and the new economy.[18]

Third, this is also a book about marketing. Newspapers served as the primary advertisement mechanism for salesmen, as newspapers published lists of subscriber names and quantities from various regions as measures of loyalty and a stimulus to patriotic competition. Ministers too thundered to their congregations that they should invest in the holy cause of Union, in the form of Treasury securities. One minister, George Ide, preached that Northerners possessed a "Christian Duty" to buy war bonds. Other prominent Northern financiers organized societies in cities such as Boston, New York, and Philadelphia for the purpose of promoting the Union cause and its capitalist institutions. The Loyal Publication Societies that sprang up in Northern cities published volumes such as "The Maintenance of Union: A National Economic Necessity," to reinforce the importance of the capitalist system among the Northern population. Bond purchases became an embodiment of and essential to the success of that capitalist system.[19]

Bond drives funded the daily operations of the war at its most basic level. More than that, they served as both cause and effect of a new economic order. The traveling agents that came knocking on doors and tent flaps, the advertisements plastered across the country's newspapers, and the efforts of German-speaking bankers to sell bonds all effectively spread a new gospel: the idea that one of the key rights of citizenship entailed the right to invest in a modern economy rooted not merely in commodities but in confidence—we invest, more than anything else, in the nebulously awesome "future of America." The bond drives gave all Americans an opportunity to literally buy into the Union cause, their country, and themselves. And buy they did, opening a new chapter in American financial history—one that extended the sale of financial instruments and securitized debt to a global community.

CHAPTER ONE

Freedom of Debt

The Lessons of Government Financing before the Civil War

In January 1790, Secretary of the Treasury Alexander Hamilton produced his infamous *First Report on the Public Credit*. One of several reports of consequence issued by Hamilton as treasury secretary, the ambitious plan posited several key areas where the United States could tackle its outstanding debt from the Revolutionary War. The report called for critical policies of "redemption" and "assumption" of debt. Redemption referred to full federal payment at face value of government securities and "assumption" enabled the federal government to assume state debts tied to the Revolution. While many often associate the passage of these key provisions with the accompanying compromise to relocate the federal capital along the Potomac River, the policies debated and subsequently enacted served as the first deliberation in the United States around the country's war debt and how it should be resolved following its sale during the war itself.[1]

Despite Hamilton's efforts, questions lingered about various financial instruments, perhaps none more important than bonds. Government-issued bonds acted as fixed-income instruments and served as a loan made by an investor to the borrower—in this case the government. In return for laying out an initial investment for the principal amount of the bond, say $50, the investor received interest payments of varying percentages. In the antebellum era, these often involved semiannual payments—that is, two interest payouts a year. More often than not, governments issued the interest in notes backed by specie. At some future date, bonds reached maturity and the issuing body returned the principal to the bondholder—although by that stage the initial bond purchaser may have sold the bond itself.

While the American Civil War called for unprecedented financial resources on the part of the government, it did not serve as the first such experience for the United States. The American Revolution, War of 1812, and Mexican War all relied on varying degrees of war bonds and closely related Treasury notes to finance the operations of the United States. Yet in each of these conflicts, American financial participation remained mostly restricted to the more well-to-do in society and a small amount of international support. The issuance of non-war debt at the state level also proved of consequence in the antebellum period. While most state bond issues centered on internal improvements and the financing of new banks, the slew of state bond defaults in the 1840s had a lasting impact on international support during the Civil War itself. By the end of the antebellum period, various financial issues plagued the United States. The Lincoln administration waded into this financial environment and considered how to fund its modern war.

Revolutionary War Finance

The American Revolution introduced the new nation to the importance and challenges of war finance. Robert Morris was the key actor in supporting the financial efforts of a new Congress and a struggling Continental Army. Morris famously spearheaded $2.5 million in loans from wealthy elites during the American Revolution. Foreign loans from the French and the Dutch financed portions of the Revolution as well. The United States also introduced a fiat currency of "continentals" that generated severe inflation as the war progressed. The war effort also comprised a small-scale introduction of war bonds (known at the time as "loan certificates"). Totaling some $6 million in specie—a rather modest sum compared to later American wars prior to the Civil War, even when adjusting for inflation—it nevertheless represented an important first step in American war finance. Historians such as Woody Holton have even gone so far as to postulate that bond issues helped lay the groundwork for the transition to a Constitutional form of governance.[2]

A fiat currency, continentals represented the immediate solution for war finance at the outset of the conflict. As the war escalated to become a struggle far exceeding the expectations of both sides, the currency likewise expanded, leading to rampant inflation. British forgeries of continentals exacerbated the situation. What began as a small trickle of currency rapidly spiraled out of control by the late 1770s. In January 1777, one needed $1.25 in currency to purchase $1 in specie; in 1779, $8 in currency; and by January 1781, $100 in continentals purchased $1 of specie.[3]

Between 1778 and 1781, individuals subscribed some $60 million in currency to bond sales, but because the Congress paid bond interest in currency, the value of the bonds varied widely and became increasingly negligible as the months progressed. Furthermore, merchants and suppliers of the armies represented the majority of the holders increasingly being paid in this format. In addition to domestic bond sales, a series of foreign loans brokered by various American agents also defined Revolutionary War finance. Some foreign merchants purchased the bonds or brokered deals with the American government in bonds. France, Spain, and the Netherlands all served as crucial financial partners to the new nation as it fought a war against the British.[4]

War of 1812 Finance

From a war finance perspective, the War of 1812 represented the most important of the three major wars of the antebellum period. While creating a debt equal in size to that from the American Revolution, the financing of the War of 1812 under Secretary of the Treasury Albert Gallatin (and to a lesser degree his successor, Alexander Dallas) represented the United States' first foray into conventional long-term bond issues. Entailing some $73 million in bonds (and a total of $37 million in Treasury notes, although never more than $17.1 million in circulation at any time), the effort to sell these in the United States signaled a major shift in American war financing. A sharp contrast to the continental fiat currency days of the Revolution, the implementation of these bond issues—admittedly to varying degrees of effectiveness—represented a strong shift toward adopting more traditional efforts of war finance modeled after the British. During the European wars of the early nineteenth century, Britain also sold financial instruments to fund its conflicts—chiefly 3 percent British consols. As was often the case in wartime, these bonds sold at a significant depreciation averaging in price of £61 for a £100 consol between 1812 and 1815. In peacetime in the latter part of the eighteenth century, the same securities ranged between £90 and £106. By avoiding a rash repayment of debt in the postwar period through high taxation, the United States acted in a similar manner to her European counterparts that shouldered—and to a certain degree, embraced—a national debt as part and parcel of being a country.[5]

The willingness to accept long-term debt through bond sales emerged as the norm for all future war financing. At the time of the War of 1812, Secretary Gallatin served at the helm of U.S. finances. A firm opponent of war (owing to the financial burden it imposed), Gallatin nevertheless undertook his work with gusto. Gallatin preferred to raise funds through taxation and pursued taxation tolerable to the general public without evoking the popular uprisings of the 1780s. Additionally, Gallatin also had to contend with selling War of 1812 bonds before the country had even really advertised any sort of loan. In true Jeffersonian fashion, there existed a deep distrust of a long-standing public debt. In part to alleviate these concerns over long-term bonds, Gallatin also issued shorter-term instruments known as Treasury notes, which often had maturity dates of a year or less. They afforded Gallatin and the

Treasury the opportunity to finance the war in a piecemeal fashion while avoiding the Jeffersonian critique that such instruments would balloon the debt. Usage of Treasury notes also enabled a stronger market for the long-term bond issues. In the fifteen years prior to the War of 1812, the United States halved the remaining public debt from the Revolution, which proved that the country could repay its obligations. But Gallatin feared that the war debt from 1812 would prolong fully eliminating the public debt by another fifteen years.[6]

The failed renewal of the Bank of the United States in 1811 proved consequential to the financing of the war. Since the inception of the bank twenty years earlier, it had played a key role in financing government debt. It also featured prominently in extending the government credit. Without the Bank of the United States, Gallatin realized he needed to find a market for the securities in the country and he found them (despite the use of short-term Treasury notes) in long-term interest-bearing bonds. While the bonds did not sell at face value at any point during the war (and the legislation did not mandate this to be the case), they still represented a significant increase in long-term securities issues compared to the American Revolution. Ensuring, in Gallatin's words, that "neither a perpetual and increasing public debt nor a permanent system of ever-progressing taxation shall be entailed on the nation" drove his actions and the Treasury Department as a whole. Thus, Gallatin found himself navigating challenging waters in the buildup to a war with Britain—one that he did not want, but nevertheless needed to properly finance. Gallatin's work during the War of 1812 therefore entailed financial struggles in a politically challenging conflict. Nevertheless, the actions of Gallatin and the Treasury Department reflected a continued evolution in the development of American war finance.[7]

Debt, Default, and Repudiation: Antebellum American State Bond Issues

The challenges of war finance in the antebellum period were intertwined with domestic financial policy. State bond issues during this period and the subsequent default of many states' debt soured international investors on future American debt. In antebellum America, northern and southern states leveraged the increasing importance of canals, railroads, and cotton to pursue economic growth. Because state leaders needed to finance internal improvements but opposed excessive taxation, they pioneered new financial entities to underwrite debt. State debt underwritten by state banks proved the most consequential of these financial instruments at the time. In 1820, American state indebtedness totaled some $12.7 million. By 1830, that number rose to $26.4 million and by 1835 it reached $66.5 million. The years 1835–40 witnessed an even greater expansion of state-issued debt to more than $170 million.[8]

By the 1830s, American state securities were a valuable commodity in Europe. The fact that the United States completely retired its national debt in 1835 made other American investment opportunities desirable for European investors. The British and Dutch investor class in particular demonstrated an interest in these state securities. Amsterdam-based Hope & Co. and Crommelin & Sons marketed bonds of various American states and municipalities such as New York City, Boston, and even Mobile, Alabama. In London, American state securities found interest among the banks of Baring Brothers, Frederick Huth & Co., Gurney & Co., and N. M. Rothschild. While most American securities sold abroad in the 1830s initially operated through London, by decade's end these bonds could be found among the Dutch, French, Portuguese, and increasingly the Germans and Swiss. In the summer of 1838, Congressman James Garland placed the amount of debt held abroad at $65 million.[9]

In 1836, President Andrew Jackson issued his infamous Specie Circular. This executive order required payment for government land in gold or silver. This act was significant in scaling back the concentration of gold and silver in eastern banks and its gradual accumulation in western banks. The fears over this accumulation led many eastern banks to cut back on lending and contributed to a credit crunch in America and a corresponding real estate crash. The lack of credit sunk many merchants who could not function without that level of liquidity. The panic extended beyond the United States, as Great Britain placed what one historian has referred to as "a stranglehold on international lines of credit." The Bank of England grew concerned over the credit liabilities in the United States in the summer of 1836 because of the array of state-chartered banks in existence. The Bank of England likewise worried about the Coinage Act of 1834 in the United States, a piece of legislation that helped transition the United States from silver to gold. The increase in the Bank of England interest rate to 5 percent marked a significant rise from the 4 percent established in July 1827. This led to gold fleeing the United States for Britain, which exacerbated the availability of specie in the United States. Crises among New Orleans merchant houses and banks made their way up the Atlantic seaboard to New York City, leading to the full suspension of specie payments in the United States. The Panic of 1837 ushered in a financial crisis with transatlantic ramifications. As noted by historian Peter Austin, Jacksonian

GENERAL JACKSON SLAYING THE MANY HEADED MONSTER.

This 1836 caricature of Andrew Jackson depicts his fight to revoke the charter of the Second Bank of the United States. Of note are the twenty-four heads of the snake representing the twenty-four state branches of the bank. Fittingly, the largest head belongs to Jackson's primary financial foe, Nicholas Biddle of Pennsylvania. (American Cartoon Print Filing Series, Prints and Photographs Division, Library of Congress, LC-USZ62-1575)

policies on the domestic front coupled with monetary issues including "specie and money flows" facilitated the Panic. The subsequent depression lasted into the middle part of the 1840s. Additionally, the depression initiated by the Panic of 1837 resulted in many American states looking to Europe to hawk their high-interest bond issues in order to pursue new lines of capital.[10]

From 1837 to 1839, American state debt increased by more than 40 percent and some $100 million of stocks and bonds found their way to London alone. This level of debt worried many European investors, however, and by the fall of 1839 the market for American state debt constricted across much of Europe. In fact, the Panic of 1837 and its fallout proved to be one of the first real challenges for German investors in American indebtedness—but only after a flurry of increased debt sales abroad. The panic, coupled with the failure of the

Second Bank of the United States (operating under a state charter in Pennsylvania after it failed to receive a renewal of its federal charter by 1836) resulted in a new, smaller panic in the fall of 1839. There was a quick rebound, however, and American state securities continued to flood markets throughout Europe—reaching the point by 1840 that every major European financial center had several financial houses selling American state securities. But the ongoing depression left many states cash-strapped, and they began to signal an inability to meet these debt obligations. By 1841, many European banks (and politicians) grew wary of language surrounding the reluctance of many states to honor their debts and called on the federal government to assume state debts. Such a practice, inaugurated by Hamilton after the Revolution, led many in Europe to logically assume that the federal government would not risk default on the part of numerous states within the union. Missouri senator Thomas Hart Benton, however, conveyed the domestic concern surrounding state debts. Benton worried that a federal assumption would be "to the enormous and undue advantage of foreign capitalists." Based on a letter between a London bank and the state of Missouri over debt, Benton boldly asked on the Senate floor, "Have foreigners interfered in our election?" Part of the 1840 presidential election, after all, entailed charges by the Democratic Party that a Whig victory would amount to foreign financiers taking over the federal government. Benton's proclamation and the anxiety on the other side of the Atlantic further fueled concerns over debt repudiation.[11]

By 1842, eight U.S. states and one U.S. territory (the future state of Florida) defaulted on bond interest payments. While some state officials assured foreign investors that such actions reflected a temporary measure, others doubled down on the default as a way to "punish" foreign investors. Governor Alexander McNutt of Mississippi specifically targeted the Jewish Rothschild family who invested heavily in Mississippi debt via the Frankfurt branch of their financial house. "The blood of Judas and Shylock flows," proclaimed McNutt, as he warned of a conspiracy on the part of the German family to "mortgage our cotton fields and make serfs of our children." By 1843, concerns over the level of American indebtedness in the hands of foreign creditors led to a congressional investigation of the matter. The publication of a report on foreign debt estimated $279 million in total liabilities, of which $150 million was held in Europe; of that $279 million, $231 million took the form of state debt. The possible default of such a massive quantity of debt pushed European financiers to stabilize said credit in their own self-interest. While almost every state began to resume its interest payments by the middle part of the 1840s, the actions of southern states in particular made some Europeans reticent to invest in the United States moving forward—not even in federal debt or the emerging market for U.S. railroad stock.[12]

Financing the Mexican War

In the aftermath of state debt repudiations, the Mexican War drew the United States into conflict with its southern neighbor. A perceived border dispute between recently annexed Texas and Mexico prompted U.S. forces to invade Mexico, taking on the Mexican republic in the name of American expansion amid sectional fights over the future of U.S. slavery. Known for the training it afforded to junior army officers who would later play large roles in the Civil War, the war likewise initiated instruction in a new wave of war finance for northeastern financiers. The administration of James Polk opted to pay for the war largely via bonds as opposed to taxation. George Beckwith, the chairman of the American Peace Society, commented, "The war system with its debts and its current expenses, has become a mammoth incubus on the bosom of all Christendom." During the Mexican War, bond sales amounted to slightly less than $43 million. Most bond sales originated with a syndicate organized by Philadelphia-based Drexel & Co. and Washington-based Corcoran & Riggs. These firms won the role of sellers through a system that involved financial firms offering sealed bids to Congress indicating how much they would pay relative to par for the bonds and detailing their ability to sell the bonds on the secondary market.[13]

As the war began, Congress and the Treasury worked to finance the military operations through three separate war loans (Loans of 1846, 1847, and 1848). Secretary of the Treasury Robert J. Walker worked closely with Congress for the 1846 Loan Act to ensure flexibility in the funding of the war loan in either short-term Treasury notes or longer-term bonds. The bill set an interest ceiling at 6 percent and, because many assumed the war would be a brief one, the Treasury preferred notes that could be repaid in one or two years' time once the government again ran a surplus. The hope to finance the war largely through Treasury notes, however, quickly fell apart. Walker's personal negotiations in New York City, Boston, and Philadelphia for a Treasury note sale proved fruitless, and subsequent attempts to advertise the sales in prominent northeastern newspapers confirmed the difficulty in selling the issue.[14]

In addition to the first loan, Congress permitted the Treasury to issue one- or two-year Treasury notes totaling $23 million for the 1847 Loan. The language of the bill also permitted the Treasury (with official permission from the president) to issue twenty-year bonds at a maximum of 6 percent interest for any portion of the $23 million issue. The bill incorporated language wherein the conversion option could also be extended to any remaining unsold Treasury notes from the July 1846 loan (totaling somewhere in the neighborhood of $5.37 million). After very brief debate and minor amendment, both houses of Congress passed the legislation—the most consequential amendment being that any Treasury notes (but not bonds) could not be sold below par— and President Polk signed the bill into law on January 28, 1847. Any parties interested in the subsequent $18 million issue of February had to submit their bids by April 10.[15]

On April 12, 1847, Walker and several Treasury officials opened the sealed bids. Widespread efforts to combine on the bids among different financial houses proved wildly unsuccessful. In fact, several financial firms bid for the entirety or large percentages of the loan. These firms, based out of Boston, Washington, and New York, predictably followed the map of war finance to date. Because legislation prohibited the issue from being sold below par (at least as long as it was initially issued as notes) it led to bids well above par. Institutions placed slightly over $21 million in bids at 100.125 or above for the particular issue. Corcoran & Riggs received the entirety of its bid ($14.7 million). After Corcoran & Riggs was a significant drop-off to other large-scale purchasers, including John Thompson (New York City, $500,000), the Bank of North America (Philadelphia, $200,000), and the Bank of the Metropolis (Washington, $100,000). Corcoran & Riggs therefore found itself in an incredibly favorable position on the secondary market to sell significant amounts to firms in Boston, Philadelphia, and New York who had been shut out. Corcoran & Riggs's notes at several points became liabilities in the summer of 1847, as the bank borrowed money to carry the inventory of unsold notes and promises made regarding delivery of funds to the Treasury.[16]

Despite the success of the $18 million issue, the federal government still needed additional funds. In lieu of any sort of additional legislation from Congress, Robert Walker used authority granted under the Act of January 1847 to issue a supplementary $5 million in Treasury notes in February 1848. Once again the notes (duration of one to two years) had the convertibility option. Once again, Corcoran & Riggs emerged as a sizable purchaser in the remaining issue, albeit this time in a joint venture with the illustrious Rothschilds. Another successful bidder of note was Philadelphia-based E. W. Clark, which procured $350,000 of the February 1848 note issue in conjunction with broker Charles Macalester. While E. W. Clark became a successful syndicate member and aggressive actor on the secondary markets, the firm's senior

TABLE 1.1 Mexican War long-term bond issues

Issue	Amount authorized	Amount issued
July 22, 1846	$10 million	$4,999,149.45
January 28, 1847	$23 million	$28,230,350
March 31, 1848	$16 million	$16,000,000
Total	$49 million	$49,229,499.45

Data compiled from Bayley, *History of the National Loans*, 364–67, 437–42.

partner did not take the leading role. Rather, the new junior partner, Jay Cooke, took on the responsibility of selling the issue. Cooke took the $350,000 of notes and successfully sold it on the secondary market. Such an aggressive pursuit of sales on the part of Cooke foreshadowed his central role in financing the American Civil War some fifteen years later. All told the 1847 loan totaled $26,122,100 when it formally closed on November 30, 1848. The federal government subsequently converted nearly the entirety of the issue into long-term bonds, totaling close to $24.7 million.

The end of the war brought with it a sale of $49 million in bonds and $33 million in Treasury notes (see Table 1.1). The Mexican War increased the national debt from approximately $15.5 million in 1846 to $63 million by 1849. The obligations tied to the Mexican War loans totaled $48,661,073. The Franklin Pierce administration subsequently reduced the Mexican War debt by $26.8 million via bond redemptions. The Panic of 1857 and ensuing sectional tensions made future liquidation on a sizable scale impossible, and at the onset of the Civil War slightly less than $18.5 million of the Mexican War debt remained. While the government redeemed some of the debt in the late 1860s following the maturation of the bonds, the remainder of the Mexican War debt was absorbed into the larger financial obligations tied to the Civil War.[17]

As James Polk submitted the Treaty of Guadalupe Hidalgo to Congress for ratification in 1848, he emphasized the importance of retiring the national debt. According to Polk, the national debt operated "against sound policy and the genius of our institutions of the Treasury." Similarly, Polk spoke in his final annual address about the importance of paying off the national debt. For the United States, it was "our true policy, and in harmony with the genius of a great Republic, possessing vast resources and wealth, wholly exempt from public indebtedness. This would add still more to our strength, and give us a still more commanding position among the nations of the earth." While Polk spoke optimistically that such results could be easily attained and the

United States could once more zero the national debt as it had done in the 1830s, the reality proved far different. Never again would the national debt be discussed merely in millions of dollars. By the time of the Civil War an unprecedented military action on an incomparable scale would require massive efforts of public finance. While drawing on past wars, the Civil War would represent a wholly new experience in war finance.[18]

Antebellum Americans transformed their financial infrastructure prior to the Civil War. As America evolved from an infant nation-state with no national credit to an established new-world power, the ability of the country to solicit funds from the general populace (and eventually foreign investors on a large scale) reflected the changing power of America from a financial standpoint. It also demonstrated the evolution of war finance. In particular, long-term bond issues featured more prominently in American finance. While lip service to a democratic issue of these bonds emerged in each of these wars, the bonds still found their way largely to northeastern banks and financial elites even as late as the Mexican War. It would take a seismic event like the Civil War to fundamentally upend American finance.

CHAPTER TWO

A Thousand-Dollar Breakfast
The Limits of War Financing by Elites

So the case stands, and under all the passion of the parties and the cries of battle lie the two chief moving causes of the struggle. Union means so many millions a year lost to the South; secession means the loss of the same millions to the North. The love of money is the root of this, as of many other evils. The quarrel between the North and South is, as it stands, solely a fiscal quarrel.
—Charles Dickens (1861)

As Confederate forces fired upon Fort Sumter in Charleston Harbor in April 1861, the saber-rattling of war that permeated the halls of Congress and taverns of the United States in the secession winter of 1860 became a full-blown reality. Abraham Lincoln's subsequent call for 75,000 soldiers to put down the Southern insurrection pushed several more Upper South states to secede—including the pivotal states of Virginia and North Carolina. The prospect of civil war left the Lincoln administration with many questions moving forward. For now, Lincoln and Republicans in Washington promoted a war to preserve the Union and sidestepped the question of slavery. In 1861, uncertainty prevailed over the future of the "peculiar institution," but the notion of emancipation remained far on the horizon for many in the North and South alike as well as those anxiously watching the impending conflict from across the Atlantic. Anxieties also ran high over whether the U.S. government could meet its debt obligations and fund a standing army in the field. Others contended that the war would pull men out of the "real" economy and trap them in armies of physical and fiscal destruction. Indeed, one Republican bemoaned, "All this immense Army add nothing by their labor to the wealth of the economy. What a mighty drain this war is upon the productive energies and resources of the country." But with this anxiety came a great patriotic sentiment among the Northern people to rally behind the grand cause of Union.[1]

Perhaps one of the greatest examples of early Northern support for the war occurred on April 20,' 1861, in New York City. By various estimates, as many as 250,000 people crowded Union Square and its environs to voice their support for the Northern cause as they prepared for the conflict. High-profile entities such as the New York Stock and Exchange Board closed in order for their members to attend the rally. "Union Square was a red, white and blue wonder," declared the *New York Times*, as speeches directed at the massive crowd included "tones of thunder for the Union, the Constitution and the enforcement of the laws." But while the crowd size in and of itself proved remarkable, so too was its composition: Prominent citizens from various walks of economic life spoke in favor of the Union, and these upper-class New Yorkers bridged partisan divides as Democrats and Republicans alike voiced support for the Union cause. Merchant Hiram Ketchum proclaimed, "We must resist to the death, if necessary, all who attempt to destroy the principle of popular liberty." At the same time Senator James Dixon wrote to James W. Beekman echoing the sentiments of many wealthy New Yorkers when he declared, "I am for using every means in the power of the Government to crush the rebellion . . . Let it cost what it may, in blood & treasure." Such bold declarations on the part of New York's merchant and financial classes in the early days of the war foreshadowed the desires of the Lincoln administration to lean heavily on New York's financial soldiers to underwrite the war itself.[2]

Alongside the logistical and political questions associated with secession and war came the very real issue of funding such a conflict. Presumably once again the U.S. government would have to go to the well of the northeastern elites to shoulder the financial burden of waging a war. While most hoped for a brief conflict in the early months of 1861, the ultimate reality was more sobering: some 750,000 deaths and over a million men forever scarred (not including families left behind) in four years of warfare. Aside from the casualties of the war came billions of dollars (1865 dollars) that fell on a federal government that viewed national taxation and deficit spending as anathema to the founding principles of a democratic republic.[3]

The four-year war therefore came at an enormous cost, despite Lincoln's aspirations that the war be a "short and decisive one." In his initial address, Lincoln called for $400 million in war funding to fund a 400,000-man army. As historian Max Edling notes, this initial estimate would be enough to pay for four Wars of 1812 and five Mexican Wars combined. And this proved to be just a fraction of the actual total cost of the war. All told, the war generated a forty-two-fold increase in the national debt of the United States. The level of mobilization for this war challenged U.S. finances to a degree never before seen. In fact, the Civil War represented a conflict that the modern Western world had never encountered in terms of size or scope.[4]

From a war finance standpoint, no one realized in the war's early months what lay ahead. Many approached the Civil War as part and parcel of prior military conflicts for the United States. Newly minted Secretary of the

Treasury Salmon Chase professed to follow previous financial plans in the mold of Albert Gallatin and his efforts to finance the United States preceding and during the War of 1812. In particular, Gallatin's efforts at crafting a short-term Treasury note as a hybrid instrument of currency and debt management became an early element of Civil War finance under Secretary Chase. The Treasury previously utilized these kinds of notes for decades to help pull the United States through times of emergency, and once again Chase relied on this instrument in order to bridge the financial chasm. But who would purchase these and future financial instruments? According to precedent, Chase and other administration officials assumed that elites in New York, and to lesser degrees those in Boston and Philadelphia, would serve as the primary source of funding for the Civil War. Such an approach reflected a close private-public partnership that enabled such financial actions to occur and in part defined elements of the American state in the antebellum period. Yet the troubles that emerged with such an approach revealed the limits of loyalty and confidence on the part of Wall Street financiers. Most of these Northern capitalists held financial interests deeply entwined with the Confederate states' cotton production and distribution. Lincoln's pick for secretary of the treasury further complicated matters. A fierce antislavery lawyer from Ohio, Salmon Chase had no experience in the world of finance. While Chase's position served political ends, he remained a tremendous liability in the crucial position, and his brash demeanor turned off the financial elites who assumed they knew better than a political appointee and financial novice. In the wake of the Union defeat at the battle of Bull Run in July 1861, and the suspension of specie payments by December 1861, it became clear to Chase and the Lincoln administration that the war would require heretofore unseen levels of funding that elites proved unwilling to meet.

While Wall Street financiers and their Boston, Philadelphia, and Washington counterparts financed earlier American wars, the Civil War represented a new era. The impressive advancements made in agriculture, transportation, manufacturing, and communication (even in the thirteen years since the end of the Mexican War) made possible the fielding of truly vast armies. The sheer volume of funds required by the government and the limitations on the part of many New York banks to contribute in the war's first year meant that Union finances required a new approach. In time, widespread democratic funding of the war shouldered by the people of the Union at large would emerge. First, however, the Lincoln administration and Treasury Department in particular needed to grasp the limitations of elite financial support in 1861 and the underlying threat this posed to the Union's quest for financial solvency.

The failures and doubts on the part of financiers to cover all costs would spur a new method of public war financing on a monumental scale by 1862.[5]

Finance under a Cloud of War

The United States on the eve of the Civil War had been coming off decades of economic growth—the likes of which have not been replicated to the present day. Built largely on the backs of enslaved labor, the production of cotton in the United States propelled the nation onto a transatlantic, if not global stage. Northern financiers who underwrote such propositions benefitted alongside Southern enslavers by financing the production of cotton and even the enslaved labor that proved integral to this growth. Northern states enjoyed the robust antebellum economy as well, as banks financed capital works projects with the issuance of state bonds.[6]

But in the years leading up to the war, the financial prospects of the United States took a turn for the worse. These concerns largely emanated from the actions of the Buchanan administration. In his 1857 inaugural address President James Buchanan proclaimed, "No nation has ever before been embarrassed from too large a surplus in the Treasury." On the surface, evidence would support Buchanan's assertions. On July 1, 1857, the national debt stood at approximately $29 million, with a cash balance in the Treasury of more than $17 million. But economic fortunes soon soured. The Panic of 1857 and the looming specter of a sectional crisis initiated a sharp decline in the federal government's financial prospects. Debates over tariff policy, government corruption, and an increasing reliance on Treasury notes to fund the government increased the national debt by July 1, 1860, to nearly $65 million with only $3.6 million in cash reserves—a remarkable gain of $50 million in peacetime financial liabilities for the modest nineteenth-century federal government. By the time Abraham Lincoln took office in March 1861, this debt had expanded to $76.4 million. The fraught election of 1860 depressed sales of Treasury notes in June and December 1860. By January 1861, New York financiers stepped in to purchase enough treasuries and public lands so that the government could make an interest payment on the public debt. Treasury Secretary Howell Cobb's address to Congress in December 1860 in his last days in the position revealed a deep concern on the part of the Treasury to garner enough interest in the loans to even meet interest payments. Such words did not satisfy Republican critics. On the Senate floor, Zachariah Chandler of Michigan responded to Cobb's address by leveling a diatribe at Democrats. "Had there not been traitors in your Cabinet and imbeciles in your presidential chair," exhorted Chandler, "your credit to-day would have stood as high as it ever stood." In addition, the unwillingness of Southern ports to forward import duties to the Treasury Department in Washington reduced federal coffers. As secession loomed the financial picture looked bleak.[7]

Buchanan's fourth secretary of the treasury, John Dix (who assumed the role on January 15, 1861), shared little hope of regaining public confidence in the midst of the secession crisis. In February 1861, Dix declared to Congress that only "superadding to the plighted faith of the federal government that of the individual states" would bring New York bankers back into the fold. New York City financiers remained skeptical of engaging further with the Treasury. In essence, there proved a limit to how far the men of Wall Street would extend their faith to the federal government. One newspaper reacting to Dix's financial plans claimed, "Money lenders entertain so little confidence in the future of the United States that in order to secure loans for the use of the government its bonds must be endorsed *by the individual states*." The end of Buchanan's tenure marked a clear decline in financial prospects for the country and left Lincoln the task of righting the economic ship.[8]

In March 1861, Salmon Chase assumed the role of secretary of the treasury. Chase had earned a national profile as an antislavery lawyer defending fugitive slaves in Ohio, and then as a leader of the Free Soil and Republican Parties. Chase had previously served as governor of Ohio in the antebellum period and was subsequently elected to the Senate. Many found Chase a difficult individual to contend with. His most prominent biographer described him as "a majestic figure with an air of conscious superiority that many found repellant." One of Chase's colleagues even said, "He [Chase] thinks there is a fourth person in the Trinity." Despite this reputation, Chase (at least privately) questioned his appointment to office. Confident "his education and habits had not fitted him to the duties of the place," he hoped that the president would relieve him of his post. What Chase could not comprehend were the larger political games at work that lay behind his appointment to the cabinet seat, and the need for Lincoln to appease various factions of the Republican Party in the process. Indeed, the Ohioan had been the presidential choice of some at the 1860 Republican convention in Chicago, and like fellow Lincoln rival William Seward, Chase found his way into Lincoln's cabinet in part so he could be closely watched. Perhaps Jay Cooke said it best when he uttered, "I see Chase is in the Treasury, and now what is to be done?" Cooke, a fellow Ohio native, hoped to leverage their shared heritage in the financial battles to come.[9]

Chase inherited a Treasury in dire straits. The federal government faced a $65 million shortfall with several Treasury notes issued in the wake of the

Panic of 1857 coming due. To make matters worse, the federal government relied almost entirely on customs duties for its revenue and a significant portion of these duties came via Southern ports. With the refusal of Southern (and later Confederate) ports to pass along customs duties, the government needed to address the issue to stay afloat fiscally. Chase presented the financial situation to Lincoln shortly after the president's inauguration in March 1861. The ports of Boston, Baltimore, New York, and Philadelphia produced $1.5 million in import duties for the two weeks beginning March 1, 1861, and Chase projected receipts for these ports would amount to $11 million in total by July 1. There remained the matter of some $41 million in loans that Congress had originally authorized in 1860 but had yet to place on the market. Conversely, Chase estimated the government's expenditures prior to April 1, 1861, would run to as much as $3 million. Furthermore, Congress adjourned on March 3, 1861, prior to the new Congressional session starting March 4. Despite a special Senate session that ran from March 4–28, 1861, Congress stood in recess from late March until Congress reconvened on July 4. In the interim, Chase could rely only on undersubscribed loan measures passed under the Buchanan administration. The situation was very clear: the federal government did not have enough funds to meet basic operating expenses, not to mention any possible rise in expenses related to a war.[10]

But where would the revenue come from? A national income tax did not exist and the erratic state-based banking structure spread across the United States made any attempt to swiftly transfer money cumbersome. Perhaps the biggest hindrance remained a deep aversion to national indebtedness. The American people worried that the rise of a substantive national debt akin to the sizable British debt would inevitably lead to taxation borne on the backs of the poor while the wealthy would profit from egregiously high interest rates for any bond issues. "An encumbrance upon the national estate" that was "anti-republican" in nature, according to one newspaper, would never gain traction among the general populace. Such a line of thinking encouraged Chase to push for lower interest rates on bond issues to appease the bulk of the citizenry—while also desperately avoiding the image of a wealthy class of war profiteers.[11]

Chase originally pursued a widespread use of short-term Treasury notes to meet the initial financial crunch for the federal government. As early as March 1861, Chase began to pay government contractors with already approved Treasury notes. Chase emphasized to Secretary of War Simon Cameron that the notes should be used "without publicity, and only in the largest contracts." Chase demonstrated his apprehension with the arrangement when he later commented in the same letter, "It is a dangerous experiment for a Government to pay in anything but money." And yet he viewed Treasury notes as an indispensable tool for the Union war effort.[12]

Chase's endorsement of Treasury notes as a short-term financial instrument initially received a warm reception. The act garnered some support within the Northern press. The *Boston Daily Advertiser* suggested that such a "national loan" would help mobilize popular support among a large swath of the people without relying solely on the power and influence of bankers in New York, Boston, and Philadelphia. Likewise, the *New York Times* supported the Treasury note, indicating its dual power to pay the debt as well as act as "a sound, reliable currency, and its shape may be that of an investment as well as a currency." While these articles and letters emphasized the dual ability of Treasury notes to cover debts as well as to act as a de facto national currency, they realized that a long-term fix on the part of Congress would be necessary to resolve the fundamental fiscal issues at hand for the federal government. Such congressional action also served the purpose of reaffirming among the public that the note operated as a sound instrument.[13]

The importance of Treasury notes to the early war effort also centered on the importance of small denominations. Although initial drafts of the legislation in 1860 promoted $100 notes, Republicans successfully lowered the notes to $50 denominations in December and (then) Senator Simon Cameron even advocated for a $20 denomination to encourage investment by those of "small means but thrifty habits." In the middle of a floor debate, Cameron had even gone so far as to muse on the difference between $20 and $50 notes (about $600 versus $1,500 in 2020 dollars). "Is there any difference in principle," Cameron asked, "between issuing a twenty-dollar note and a fifty-dollar note? The only difference is, that practically the one becomes a currency for the rich and the other a currency for the poor." In part, this currency would allow those of lesser means to have access to the money supply. Likewise, this pursuit of small-denomination notes as early as the secession winter of 1860–61 played an important role in laying the groundwork for future small-denomination operations.[14]

While hoping for widespread adoption of the Treasury notes, time constraints to finance government operations dictated that Chase had little choice but to raise funds in March 1861 through the sale of government Treasury notes directly to financiers through a bidding process. The U.S. government had pursued similar strategies in previous wars. The large amounts of capital concentrated in these Northern metropolitan centers afforded Chase the opportunity to appeal directly to investors. These influential men held millions in gold specie—gold the government desperately needed. While these financiers absorbed the bonds initially, they would then sell them to investors in a more convoluted and profitable secondary market. With this in mind, Chase traveled to New York in March 1861 and offered to the bankers of that city an $8 million loan at 6 percent interest. It was a relatively meager sum (albeit at a high interest rate), but at this point the cannons pointing at Fort Sumter remained quiet and a future conflict was uncertain.[15]

Chase's travels to New York reflected the primacy of that market to dictate Northern finance. While Wall Street had advanced in the previous decades and recovered from panics in 1837 and 1857, it grew dramatically over the next decade starting with the Civil War. The scene in 1861 reflected a bustling and relatively chaotic environment as one author depicted life on the Street:

> The tide of humanity that pours down Broadway, is dashed against the bulwarks of Wall Street, and whirled to the eastward, between the mighty walls of granite and sandstone, which line that renowned thoroughfare. Through two mouths, New Street and Broad Street, it is sucked into that seething, whirling, roaring maelstrom—the stock-market. Speaking in the language of the common-place, these two streets are merely avenues in the lower part of the city for the passage of men and loaded wagons, and for the transaction of business; but these streets also form the environs of the Stock Exchange, which as from the focus of a gigantic parabolic reflector, throws a light, more or less lurid, over the whole financial community.[16]

Wall Street served increasingly as the most important hub of finance in the United States. The chaotic nature of the city reflected an evolving New York financial market. The prospect of war ran counter to the interests of many New York City bankers, and the sooner the war reached a conclusion, the sooner the bankers could again facilitate financial transactions of cotton and resume prewar levels of foreign currency exchange. But these initial efforts on the part of Chase and Wall Street financiers revealed the emergence of a close but contentious relationship between Treasury officials and New York City financiers for the duration of the Civil War.[17]

Despite disagreements among various wings of the Republican Party (and a sizable Democratic Party presence among certain New York City financiers), Northern capitalists initially demonstrated sympathy and unity with the federal government, as exemplified just a few weeks later in Union Square. On April 2, 1861, Chase opened $30 million worth of bid letters he had received for the aforementioned $8 million in Treasury notes. The bids Chase obtained ranged between ninety cents on the dollar and par. Chase wrote encouragingly to the president regarding the "decided improvement in finances"; the press shared in the optimistic mood. The *Philadelphia Inquirer* detailed that the bids were "the subject of much congratulation, not only among the money Kings of Wall street, but by people elsewhere, who were gratified to see the Government credit thus handsomely sustained." The optimism, however, obscured an underlying fracturing of trust on the part of Wall Street elites in the federal government and federal securities. Only 10 percent of the $30 million in bids came in at $0.94 or higher—an indication that many New York City financiers lacked confidence in federal finances. Despite the optimism that permeated the financial world, press, and Treasury alike, Chase had made a fatal error in believing that the initial faith of bankers would translate into a blind following on their part of any and all monetary policies emanating from the Treasury, especially those pertaining to future war financing. As such, Chase only accepted bids at $0.94 to the dollar and above, funding a portion of the $8 million issue. Chase erred mightily; the various financiers of the Northeast, but especially New York, believed the secretary's actions constituted a slap in the face to those who had acted in good faith by leaping to the patriotic defense of their country. For many financiers, Chase's refusal of bids under $0.94 proved arbitrary and bordered on collusion, as one bank received over half the bids. Rumors ran amok through Wall Street, State Street, and Chestnut Street that some financiers were reticent to ever trust Chase again. Many declared such a position untenable for the federal government, for traditional Treasury logic held that financial support from the private banking sector was the sine qua non for fiscal survival of the Union.[18]

Chase Battles New York City Financiers

Anxieties intensified following the firing upon Fort Sumter in April 1861. It was in this environment that Chase returned to the New York financiers in an attempt to elicit their support. Yet, by law Chase could offer only $14 million in new bonds—and all at face value. This caused great concern among Northern bankers. Chase's assurances that any losses on the secondary market should the bonds sell below par would be offset by "patriotism" did not dissuade the concerns of New York's financial elite. The New York Chamber of Commerce refused to accept such terms. Similar efforts to elicit investors in Philadelphia, Boston, and Providence likewise met with demurred indifference.[19]

By early May 1861, it became apparent to Chase that his belief in patriotism trumping self-interest among New York financiers was unfounded. In an effort to regain some trust with the financial elite, Chase followed up with a bid for $9 million in bonds with no par restriction. The banks purchased $7.5 million in bonds and another $1.5 million in Treasury notes. Yet such acts on the part of Chase were too little, too late. The government projected it would run an $11 million deficit by August 1. The situation remained dire, and the financial uncertainty that persisted required a special session of Congress.

The special session presented Chase with the challenge of laying out a clear and coherent financial strategy. Chase's initial report to the session convened in July 1861 called for a clear plan of war finance, consisting of, among other measures, a foreign loan and a popular loan. It called for the government to raise a sum of $318 million. While taxation only comprised $80 million of this request by the secretary, even this proved to be a tall task. Chase ran out of avenues to raise these revenues through the existing tax channels and called on "the superior wisdom of Congress" to identify new taxes in order to raise the requisite $80 million. While Chase suggested a property tax, he made it clear that the source of revenue via taxation could only occur with new funding sources.[20]

The remainder of the war funding centered on a $250 million loan, composed primarily of three-year Treasury notes bearing 7.3 percent interest. One-year Treasury notes represented a smaller segment of the loan. These short-term notes served primarily as a means to pay contractors and salaries for government employees. Chase made it clear that he wished to disseminate this loan widely though both domestic and foreign sales, although he provided few if any details as to how that might be accomplished. Yet spreading the sales beyond elites featured in his plan. Chase called on the "people" in conjunction with "capitalists" to invest in this bond issue. According to Chase, such widespread investment in these bonds would "reward those who come forward in the hour of peril."[21]

Chase used this occasion to attempt to speak to the great challenge the nation faced from a war finance standpoint. "It needs no argument," Chase declared, "to work the conviction that, under the existing laws, little or nothing of the required sum can be realized. The magnitude of the occasion requires other measures." Chase continued:

> As the contest in which the Government is now engaged is a contest for national existence and the sovereignty of the people, it is eminently proper that the appeal for the means of prosecuting it with energy to a speedy and successful issue should be made, in the first instance at least, to the people themselves. And it is highly desirable, in order that the

circle of contribution may be widely extended, to make the burden press as lightly as practicable upon each individual contributor, and, if possible, to transmute the burden into a benefit.[22]

Chase made his case clear. In order to win the financial (and military) battles to come, it would require the entire Northern populace to sustain the war effort. In total, Chase's speech to Congress provided a blueprint for funding the basic needs of the government. He based his initial proposal to Congress on the assumption that governmental operating costs would be the remarkably specific sum of $318,519,581.87 for the next year. The secretary's efforts called upon a loan unprecedented in the nation's history. Chase finished his segment regarding domestic bond sales by emphasizing the power of a democratic loan among the people. "The Secretary cannot doubt that for a loan so beneficial and so advantageous, secured, both as to interest and principal, by adequate provisions of revenue, an appeal to the people will be answered with promptitude and liberality." Chase proposed loans issued in denominations as low as $50 and purchased on payment plans that could break down to ten installments over a five-month period (due on the 1st and 15th of the forthcoming months). Chase voiced support to expand the number of financial institutions that could receive payment in an effort to make the bond sales as widely accessible as possible throughout the North. In the summer of 1861, Chase proposed selling these financial issues to the populace at large, facilitating payment structures that enabled larger swaths of the population to participate. Chase also spoke at length about the importance of an international dimension of the loan, hoping to place up to $100 million with foreign investors. Yet despite this vision, a discussion of marketing and raising awareness among broader swaths of the public to garner interest in the drive did not figure prominently in Chase's proposal.[23]

The press endorsed the notion of a popular loan supported by the people. The *Philadelphia Inquirer* argued that to tap the "great mass of the people of the country" would serve the country well. Another newspaper editor noted that a popular loan was "probably the happiest and shrewdest mode of strengthening and consolidating a government that ever was adopted." By the summer of 1861, even the manager of the New York Clearing House for Wall Street Banks, George Lyman, wrote to Chase urging an investment strategy predicated on small-scale investing from the Northern people. "Let . . . the government debt be distributed among them [the general populace] in small amounts," Lyman beseeched. "They will show the world that a government dependent upon the people may be as strong and as rich in resources as it is free." Indeed, it was no coincidence that some of the earliest bond issues contained the image of Alexander Hamilton, a man who believed that citizens of the United States should be linked to a common investment in the solvency of government (and thereby, themselves). Unionism as proposed by Chase no longer represented just a patriotic feeling, it symbolized a new kind of ownership in the United States, spread across the land and supported by all classes.[24]

Congress reacted swiftly to Chase's call for financial support. In July 1861, Republican Thaddeus Stevens, chair of the House Ways and Means Committee, put forward H.R. 14 authorizing the borrowing (as Chase requested) of up to $250 million via long-term bonds, Treasury notes, or demand notes within a year of the passage of the act. In keeping with Chase's proposal, the bill authorized a portion of the loan (up to $100 million) could be sold in any foreign country. The interest rate on the loan could be as high as 7.3 percent (equal to one cent daily interest on $50 bonds). Originally covered by import duties, the Senate rewrote this portion in committee to indicate that the "faith" of the country would repay the debt—in other words, taxation in some shape or form would cover the repayment of the debt. The measure quickly passed Congress despite the concern of some members of the press. "Measures which involve millions of men and money, which inaugurate or abolish systems of revenue and administration, which create armies and navies, and give to the Executive the plenary powers requisite in such grand National emergencies" remarked the *New York Times*, "are hastened from committee-room to the engrossing clerk with a rapidity which in ordinary time, would suggest the idea of the Legislature having surrendered all but the formal exercise of its constitutional functions." Despite such concerns, the measure passed both the House and Senate by overwhelming margins, with only some Democrats opposing. Democrat Clement Vallandigham remained the most vocal opponent of the measure, viewing the bill as part of a "consolidated monarchy or vast centralized despotism" concocted by the Lincoln administration. Lincoln signed the act into law on July 17, 1861, just days before the full outbreak of hostilities some thirty miles away at Bull Run. Thanks to the rapid nature of the congressional process during the special session, the financial crises appeared to abate for the time being.[25]

Confederate Bonds and Their Financial Limitations

The U.S. government was well behind its Confederate adversaries in terms of financing. Two days after the convening of the (then) six seceded states in

Montgomery, Alabama, in February 1861, the Confederate States of America Provisional Government accepted a $500,000 loan from the state assembly of Alabama. This initial loan was the first of many arranged by the Provisional Government in 1861. By the end of February, the Provisional Congress passed "An Act to Raise Money for the Support of the Government and to Provide for the Defence of the Confederate States of America." Through this legislation, the Confederate Congress enacted its first loan—a $15 million loan based on certificates of stocks or bonds bearing 8 percent interest with semi-annual interest payment in specie. The Confederate Congress issued bonds in denominations as low as $50 and supported these bonds through a small export duty on cotton. Confederate Secretary of the Treasury Christopher Memminger worked tirelessly in the early stages, even before the firing on Fort Sumter, to finance the new government. On March 16, 1861, Memminger released a statement reiterating to the people of the Confederacy, "Five millions of this most advantageous investment will be offered to the public ... and every citizen throughout the Confederate states will have the opportunity of taking a share of the benefit, and at the same time of sustaining the cause of the country." Just a few years removed from James Hammond's famous declaration, "You dare not make war on cotton," the Confederate bond issue represented a new financial world for the South.[26]

Mirroring future Union financial efforts in extending popular loans, the Confederacy opened subscriptions in major cities and towns in order to reach "the people." Only 6 percent of the amount subscribed needed to be paid in specie at the time of purchase, with the remainder produced by May 1, 1861. Memminger and the Davis administration hoped for a vast oversubscription of the loan domestically in order to draw European interest to the loan. Memminger even went so far as to hope that upward of a million dollars of the loan could be placed in New York so as to make the Northern financial situation even more untenable.[27]

Memminger's overconfidence in the issue became readily apparent as Confederate citizens across all walks of life struggled to produce the 6 percent specie down payment requirement. Most Southern banks had, in fact, suspended specie payments in the early months of 1861, meaning they no longer would pay out coin for bank notes. Such an act made it remarkably difficult for individuals to get their hands on the valuable specie. Once banks agreed to accept demand notes (a form of non-interest-bearing Treasury notes) in lieu of specie for the loan, the subscriptions again picked up. Boards of commissioners emerged in the various Confederate states, led by prominent businessmen, that became responsible for all purchasers in their respective states.

The opening of the loan on April 17, 1861, covered the initial $5 million loan and then some (perhaps as high as $8 million of the loan subscribed on the first day). Although subscriptions for the balance of the loan lagged after the initial interest, by October 15, 1861, the entire $15 million loan had been subscribed—largely owing to a push by Memminger's treasury department to travel throughout the Confederacy and meet in person with financiers in the various states. A loan subscription largely shouldered by banks in the Confederacy inevitably led to a subsequent drawdown in specie, making future subscriptions all the more difficult. When coupled with a bond valuation that never reached par during the course of the war (peaking in the low 90s in the spring of 1862), it would seem on the surface that the Confederacy's finances were virtually doomed from the start. But a Confederate treasury department that had started from scratch and had closed a $15 million loan in the span of ten months was nothing to scoff at, and it only fueled the fire for the Union to improve its financial organization from Washington on down.[28]

Owing to the specie shortage throughout the Confederacy in 1861, the second major financial measure put through the Confederate Congress, known as the "Produce Loan," permitted investors in Confederate bonds to pay with goods that could be sold by the Confederate government (chiefly cotton, despite the misleading name of "produce" loan). The government would receive funds for its sales largely outside the Confederacy, and the investor would receive specie from the Confederate government in due course. The Confederate Congress authorized such a loan of $50 million in 8 percent bonds in May 1861, while the initial $15 million loan was still being subscribed. The Confederate Congress later extended the loan on August 19, 1861, to $100 million. Although interest in the loan waned by the end of 1861, such efforts on the part of the Confederacy revealed a gulf in organization when compared to Secretary Chase and the Union financial machine in the middle of 1861. Although Confederate states issued their own cotton bonds and further complicated the issue, and rampant currency inflation played a large role in hampering the effectiveness of Confederate finances, the relative success of the Confederacy in 1861 made it readily apparent why foreign markets in part looked more favorably on Confederate finances.

The War Loan Association and the Limits of Financial Patriotism

While Chase eagerly awaited the prospects of the loan, the realities of a shooting war brought on by the battle of Bull Run on July 21, 1861, required Chase to once more reach out to the bankers of New York, Boston, and Philadelphia to provide advances of the funds—funds that exceeded the capital reserves on hand at the various banks in those cities. It remained Chase's intention to receive three $50 million advances worth of the loan at par. While the need remained urgent for the first $50 million, the second and third options of $50 million were dated October 15 and December 15. Congress selected later dates to ensure that the banks could replenish their gold reserves through funds from Europe and California. As bonds sold among the populace (by the government and by the firms), the Treasury would reimburse the banks for their advances that covered the 7-30 Treasury notes (and later 6 percent bonds). If the popular sales never materialized, the Treasury would compensate the banks in the bonds themselves. These loans, however, required the physical transfer of specie from the various banks to the New York subtreasury building, and in the process had the potential of contracting credit in New York and thus creating the real possibility of a massive financial panic in the days following Bull Run.[29]

To fulfill the $50 million advance, the close coordination of the Treasury and northeast financiers in the late summer of 1861 relied upon a newly formed organization in New York City known as the War Loan Association (later the Associated Banks). Prominent financiers and merchants joined this committee, which had no state or federal charter but merely a desire to assist the federal government with finances in the war's nascent months. The association included banks from all three main northeastern financial centers. It was led by John Austin Stevens of the Bank of Commerce and George S. Coe of the American Exchange Bank, two financiers primarily responsible for providing some form of funding for the federal government. The association also worked on a structure in New York to ensure financial liquidity. On August 9, 1861, Chase met with War Loan Association representatives in New York as they presented their view of how to stave off financial collapse. In a unique arrangement, the association's member financial institutions wanted to unite as a single entity for the sake of any loan negotiations to conduct government business, while at the same time being able to act independently when it came to their own commercial (i.e., nongovernmental) transactions. Such an action reflected once more the public-private partnership that several historians have emphasized as essential to the structure of the federal government in the nineteenth century, as well as the foundation to Union success in the war itself.[30]

On August 15, 1861, Stevens addressed Chase in a letter on behalf of the "officers of banks" of New York, as well as delegations from Philadelphia and Boston. Stevens wrote to Chase "respectfully to express to the President of the United States its confident expectation that the Government will, without respect to party or personal considerations, so conduct its affairs in every department of administration as to ensure vigor, integrity, economy, and efficiency to the triumphant termination of the war." Laced with patriotic verbiage, the message was clear: the northeast bankers would be there for the Lincoln administration, but only if Secretary Chase played by the rules—*their* rules.[31]

Initially, Chase refused to conduct business on such terms. According to Chase, he left the bankers with a threat that presented little option for the Associated Banks: "Gentlemen, I am sure you wish to do all you can, and I hope you will find that you can take the loans required on terms which can be admitted. If not, I must go back to Washington and issue notes for circulation; for gentlemen, the war must go on until this rebellion is put down, if we have to put out paper until it takes a thousand dollars to buy a breakfast." Chase's threat reverberated throughout the room—if need be the government stood prepared to flood the market and upset the American financial system as they knew it in order to achieve ultimate victory in the war over the Confederacy. The battle lines had been drawn between Chase and the financial elites of the Northeast. Representing a marked departure from previous war finance arrangements between banks and the Treasury, Chase threatened to push the banks to their breaking point.[32]

Amid such hostile rhetoric, Stevens and Coe worked out an arrangement to cover the first $50 million advance for the Treasury of 7-30s at par. According to the deal (see Appendix), $29.5 million of the advance came from New York banks, while the remaining $20.5 million came from Boston ($15.5 million) and Philadelphia ($5 million). In actuality a grand total of $35 million in New York funds came from a total of fifty banks with an operating capital of $68.5 million—thereby easing the requirements on banks in Boston and Philadelphia. Thus, the New York banks put forth 51 percent of their operating capital in the initial advance. The banks retained the option for two other $50 million 7-30 issues in October and December. Jay Cooke reminisced on the events surrounding the initial $50 million advance: "I went to New York with [Chase] and was present at all the meetings with the presidents of the Associated Banks, giving him my advice and all the aid I could in that transaction. In those days this was a negotiation upon a gigantic scale and, being successfully accomplished, greatly cheered and comforted all the friends of the government and I have always contended that the Associated Banks deserve lasting gratitude for the support they then gave the Treasury at a most critical period." Cooke viewed the Associated Banks as a tremendous asset in the early months of the war. The first $50 million tranche certainly

This print, showing a busy office where citizens have come to loan money to the war effort, appeared in the September 7, 1861, issue of *Frank Leslie's Illustrated Newspaper*. (Prints and Photographs Division, Library of Congress, LC-USZ62-133075)

seemed to indicate this fact, but trouble brewed beneath the surface. For despite Cooke's praise, real challenges remained for federal financing.[33]

The political games between Chase and the New York elites continued following the initial advance. As the summer wore on in 1861, it became readily apparent that New York financiers were growing more hostile to Chase and the Lincoln administration's plans. In one case, Chase alleged that John Stevens proclaimed, "You have now received from the Associated Banks the vast sum of $50,000,000. We all earnestly hope that this sum will be sufficient to end the war. Should it not prove enough we wish to notify you that you cannot depend upon further aid from the Associated Banks. We are glad that we have decided to come thus to the support of the government but we owe a duty to our stockholders and dare not encroach further upon their rights. . . . Therefore husband the resources under your control for this is all that can be expected of us." It appeared that Chase's threat of the thousand-dollar breakfast had done little to dissuade northeastern financial leaders regarding their bearish approach to dictating war policy. Politicians in Washington looked on with some trepidation as the subsequent advances approached. Northern bankers did pick up the second $50 million option despite the combativeness of the Associated Banks. The banks ran into significantly more difficulty in trying to offload the Treasury notes onto a secondary market, however.[34]

The Associated Banks moved beyond mere correspondence, however, and took a rather proactive stance to dictate and impact war policy to protect their pecuniary interest. Although their statement of August 15, 1861, expressing their confidence in Washington to adjudicate war matters implied a laissez-faire approach, it became readily apparent that the Lincoln administration's war policies did not meet their expectations. A delegation of bankers subsequently arrived in Washington to voice their displeasure in the wake of the Bull Run fiasco and urged Lincoln to alter his war policies in order to facilitate a quick end to hostilities and a resumption of a vibrant business between New York City financiers and their Southern clients. The press responded to this move with indignation. "The fact that these gentlemen represent the fifty million which the banks have subscribed to the national loan gives them no prescriptive right to obtrude their views upon the government," the *Philadelphia Inquirer* declared. It did not, however, prevent the bankers from expressing their clear thoughts on the matter. This manifested itself most forcefully through John E. Williams, president of the Metropolitan Bank of New York (a holder of some $2 million of the initial advance), who expressed the belief of many New York bankers. It is "our surprise that you should not take our judgment in this matter," Williams stated, "but rather argue on the supposition that we do not understand the legitimate operations of our own business so well as you do." He claimed that "but for the banks, the Government could not pay at all. It would have been bankrupt six weeks ago." Williams added that "Congress meant something" when passing the act of August 5. An "increase in the Sub-treasury's coin weakens us and the Government too," Williams declared, and he earnestly hoped that Chase comprehended his actions by hoarding so much coin and the probable suspension of specie it would initiate. Williams's harshest critique addressed Chase's perceived lack of understanding when it came to financial matters. "While you speculate as to what is best for sound banks," Williams declared, "they think, with practical experience, they *know* what is best for their institutions." Such patronizing commentary from the New York financial institutions not only reflected a dissatisfaction with the administration, but a sincere desire to force its hand in an evolving American political economy.[35]

Yet Chase remained optimistic and attempted to ease tensions. He wrote to John Austin Stevens on August 22, 1861, "I am told that the associates are already receiving offers for the notes they have subscribed for in large amounts. I devoutly hope this may be true and that they may thus reimburse themselves without calling on the Government." The *Boston Daily Advertiser* echoed similar sentiments a week later. "We are glad to learn that by the united and harmonious action of the Boston banks they will be able to take their portion of the fifty millions, which is ten millions, without disturbing the financial movements of this city. This unanimity, we are glad to say, reflects the public sentiment of Boston." Senate Finance Committee chairman William Pitt Fessenden concurred, declaring the initial $50 million loan as an act that "has given confidence to all who have money to invest." Yet popular financing remained tenuous at best, reflecting the larger struggles of the Union in 1861. An initial $50 million issue hardly covered some of the pressing financial matters facing the country. As questions remained over the war and battles to come, the Union likewise remained concerned about meeting its financial obligations.[36]

As much as Chase relied on Northern financial institutions, he believed that a popular loan could take flight if given enough support and pitched properly. Chase assumed, however, that initially he could "sell" the war himself—or at the very least via the Treasury Department. But a popular loan relied upon a willing populace and in that vein Chase reached out to the public directly on September 1, 1861, with an "Appeal from the Secretary of the Treasury" detailing the three-year loans at 7.3 percent (known as 7-30s) with a promise to open subscriptions to the general public very soon. The Treasury Department hired agents to facilitate these sales, Jay Cooke among them. Cooke threw himself into the effort, selling over $5 million of the loan himself—compared with the other 147 agents who sold slightly less than $25 million worth. But while agents were utilized for the sales, above all else it was the hope of Chase and the Treasury Department that the loan would resonate with the public. Calls arose for loan subscriptions "not to the capitalists of the great cities only but to the people of the whole country." Despite the hopes of Chase and Co. to sell this loan to the population writ large, sales proved slow—especially once one left the major urban centers. The *Boston Daily Advertiser* summed it up most appropriately when it remarked "a United States loan has never hitherto been heard of far outside of the larger cities." The article spoke to the fact that local banks issued bonds to fund improvement projects during the previous decades. Despite such actions, however, many Northerners did not have the financial literacy to understand the workings of bonds during the period. Perhaps a more pressing difficulty facing "the public" was the fact that they were required to purchase said notes in specie and few everyday consumers had enough gold on hand to purchase the notes, nor with great ease actually obtain the necessary gold—especially as they moved farther away from northeastern urban financial institutions and the crucial year of 1861.[37]

One of Chase's colleagues from Ohio, Judge Simeon Nash, warned Chase as early as July 1861 that the very nature of a national loan sold among the people would fall flat if provisions to purchase the notes with something other than gold did not emerge. "I wish you could receive bank paper for the popular loan and then the *people* could take a part of it," Nash declared. "Now it is limited to monied men living in towns and cities. The coin is not in the country." Nash repeated this concern in November 1861. Still another associate in Cincinnati wrote, "If the law would permit and your instructions to the United States depository had allowed him to receive bankable funds for subscriptions to the loan, the amount of them here would have been greatly enlarged. Many persons have small sums of money they would gladly invest but know nothing about exchange, have no correspondents in the eastern cities, and do not know how or where to buy gold." James Gordon Bennett, the publisher and editor of the *New York Herald*, lamented Chase's poor timing and fundamental lack of marketing acumen. "I wish I could do more for your department," Bennett exclaimed, "but the iron should have been struck when it was hot. All the newspapers here and in Boston and Philadelphia should have prepared for this loan weeks ago and the movement would have been more successful." While Bennett's comments ring hollow given the monetary constraints of the Union throughout 1861, they still reveal the challenges of widespread financing of a war increasing in scope.[38]

Some newspapers stressed a democratic bond drive. They hoped that "the people" would invest, and in doing so, become deeply entwined with the interests of the federal government—a government that most had little prior contact with in the antebellum era. One newspaper encouraged people to take their savings from wherever they might be stashed—be it "broken crockery or old stockings"—in order to invest. One letter to the editor tried to alleviate the concerns of investors by noting that a bond "is as accessible to *ladies* as gentlemen, and no one need for application, and not the least 'red tape' or hindrance of any kind." Emphasizing that bonds bridged the gender divide became a recurring theme for the popular loan issues and as early as 1861 many financiers and publishers alike began to lay the groundwork. Political organizations passed resolutions praising the financial instruments and even Salmon Chase's law partner noted the secretary would gain support "from the pockets and stockings of the poor." The 7-30s gained traction in the West as well, where in one Ohio town "many persons called to see them, and with glad hearts rejoiced at the event." One Republican senator reportedly quipped to another, "I never doubted but you fellows out West would *take* anything you could lay your hands on." Yet although the democratic emphasis on bond sales existed in these early phases of the war, it crucially lagged behind the needs of the government.[39]

Jay Cooke Emerges

In the midst of the tensions between Chase and the New York City elite, a lesser-known financier inserted himself into the debate. Philadelphia's Jay Cooke started to raise his profile on the national stage by conversing with the secretary directly regarding the various bond issues. Cooke was a partner in the financial house of Jay Cooke & Co. established in 1860. Formerly an employee of E. W. Clark & Co. out of the same city, and someone who had met with great success selling Mexican War bonds as part of a larger syndicate, Cooke viewed the Civil War as a tremendous financial opportunity. Though an Ohioan like Chase, the two had never met. Shortly after the attack on Fort Sumter, Cooke wrote to Chase asking whether Philadelphia banks could negotiate directly with the secretary on future Treasury issues. Cooke assured Chase that such an effort would meet with success, especially because "capitalists and banks should become more interested in government loans than they have been—a large debt will not hurt the cause of the Union." Cooke wrote to his brother Henry in the summer of 1861, "Can't you sell out the papers & open a Banking house in Wash & be something respectable, or at least can't you inaugurate something whereby we can all safely make some Cash?" By the summer of 1861, Jay Cooke offered to move to Washington to open a "first class banking establishment" that would act with the interests of the Treasury at heart. However, Cooke also made sure to qualify his statement by noting, "We could not be expected to leave our comfortable homes and positions here without some great inducement and we state frankly that we would if we succeeded expect a fair commission from the treasury." Chase already held Cooke in high regard, for at this point he even offered him the assistant treasurer position in Philadelphia—a position Cooke subsequently turned down, but which nevertheless predicted the future close relationship between the two men. Cooke became a household name by the later bond drives and did more than any other individual to ensure their success. In 1861, however, he represented one of many financiers positioning themselves to be in the good graces of Secretary Chase.[40]

Jay Cooke attempted to seize the moment as early as April 1861 by selling Treasury notes—having won a bid for $200,000 worth. Cooke continued with an early bond issue in the spring of 1861, working in concert with the

A photograph of Jay Cooke taken after the Civil War. (Image courtesy of Rutherford B. Hayes Presidential Library & Museums)

much more established Philadelphia banking house of Drexel & Co. The firms only procured $141,000. Cooke remained frustrated by the small number of sales on the table for his firm and began to conceive of an alternative to the financial efforts of Chase. Cooke's brothers Henry and Pitt reiterated such sentiments. Henry, in Washington to lobby Congress, counseled patience for his brother. "We are just beginning to get 'inside the ring,'" relayed Henry, "and there are several 'good things' in prospect which a little management and patience will bring out all right." Pitt, on the other hand, promoted the idea that Jay Cooke could take on a role that would cement him as the financial figure of the Civil War. "'Morris of Philadelphia' was the back bone of the Revolution," Pitt proclaimed. "He was their only financier that could always do something for the cause in the Sinews of war & now Cooke of Phila must not forget his financial patriotism. His mantle has fallen on the right shoulders." Jay Cooke just looked for his opening.[41]

While Cooke became known for his work on the federal level, his leadership in a Pennsylvania state bond issue first put him on the national radar in Washington. The commonwealth decided in the early spring of 1861 to put out a $3 million loan for subscription. Pennsylvania, being one of the states that had defaulted in the recent past, remained pessimistic about what it might be able to attain—perhaps as little as seventy-five cents on the dollar. Jay Cooke thought otherwise. To that end, he suggested to Governor Andrew Curtin (a staunch advocate of the war and stalwart Republican) that the loan would be attainable on par, but only if there was a massive campaign to sell the bonds to the general public by pulling at their patriotic heartstrings. The governor consented to Cooke's plans and Cooke & Co., in conjunction with Drexel & Co., found themselves appointed general subscription agents to execute Cooke's theory. Cooke set to work to appeal to the patriotism of the people of the Keystone State. In one advertisement Cooke and Drexel called on "the patriotism and state pride of Pennsylvania in this hour of trial, that they come forward and manifest their love of the old Commonwealth by a prompt and cordial response to her call."[42]

Like future national drives, Cooke sent agents throughout Pennsylvania to solicit sales. Citizens from all walks of life oversubscribed the state loan. The tremendous success of the loan paid great dividends for Cooke on a national scale. The state treasurer even went so far as to write Salmon Chase telling him that if he entrusted Cooke with a national agency, it would meet with equal success. Cooke also made the success of the loan well known to others, writing not only to Chase, but also oddly Jefferson Davis and the *Times* of London.[43]

This Frank H. Taylor lithograph depicts the Philadelphia offices of Jay Cooke & Co. at 114 South Third Street. From this office Cooke orchestrated his national bond strategy and kept in close coordination with partners in New York City and Washington. (Image courtesy of The Library Company of Philadelphia)

By the fall of 1861 Cooke endeared himself enough to Chase to be granted an agency to try to sell Northern bonds on behalf of the government. While state banks acted as most of the agents with highly capitalized financiers in major cities, Cooke took his responsibility seriously. On September 5, 1861, Cooke opened his doors at 114 South Third Street in Philadelphia as an official government agent. Cooke quickly developed the tactics that defined his approach to war finance—he advertised in local newspapers, and he published the names of those who subscribed, using the power of patriotism to motivate small-scale investors. Just two days later, Cooke wrote to Chase regarding the success of the loan so far:

> This has been a hard day. I have been at it from 8 a.m. till after 5—a continual stream, clergy, draymen, merchants, girls, boys and all kinds of men and women. Some of our citizens who came in—I mean those of

mark—went out almost with tears in their eyes, so overjoyed at the patriotic scene. We gave the day almost exclusively to small subscribers, 106 subscribed today and it's no small job to explain to so many ignorant people the whys and wherefores. I am glad to say that they all went away happy and delighted and we bagged over 70,000 as the days work.[44]

The *Philadelphia Inquirer* also commended Cooke for his actions that day, noting "All classes may at last congratulate themselves that they have here found a stock that will be perfectly safe. This especially to persons of small means who have lately been victims of swindling institutions, is a great mental relief." The *Findlay Jeffersonian* likewise championed the "banks & c" who supported the Union cause. It became readily apparent that Cooke wished to center a strategy on small-scale investors.[45]

Cooke continued to refine his approach and explored tactics that would later become the norm for his national agency. Cooke undertook deliberate actions, some tangible and some symbolic, to frame his sales and identity. Early in the process Cooke extended the hours at his Philadelphia office to nine in the evening to enable "the workingman" to purchase the notes. Cooke proclaimed that in a week's time he had reached out to 800 subscribers through his office ("Their charge of money bags is quite as efficient as a charge of bayonets," he remarked). Cooke also devised new ways to finance bond sales for the people that would become commonplace by the latter part of the war. For instance, 1,000 of the 1,500 employees of the Philadelphia and Reading Railroad purchased 7-30 notes by setting up payroll deduction to ease the purchases for these small-scale investors. Cooke would go on to sell $4,224,050 of the first series and another $1 million of the second series of 7-30 notes in the summer and fall of 1861. Such sales represented nearly a quarter of all sales outside of federal subtreasuries at the time. Even in the early stages of the conflict, Cooke promoted bond sales—and his own brand in the process.[46]

Still, the early war measures relied on a steady stream of credit emanating from the northeastern bankers. Such a task became more complicated when gold reserves declined markedly. In the six weeks from the original agreement in August 1861, the *New York Herald* reported that specie reserves in New York declined from $48 million to $37 million. Such action matched the gold reserves in the New York subtreasury, which in and of itself was a concern because these reserves were not making their way to other government creditors. New York banks dealt in greater volume than their Boston and Philadelphia brethren, and also had greater flexibility because their gold reserve expectations were not statutory. The Associated Banks were in agreement that their specie reserves were not to fall below 25 percent of note circulation even though no statutory specie reserve existed in New York State. Pennsylvania required banks by law to maintain specie reserves that covered 8 percent of notes; in Massachusetts, the state dictated a reserve requirement of 15 percent. Up until September 1861, the various banks held specie reserves well above their required (or agreed upon) specie thresholds, but chinks were already starting to emerge in this financial armor.[47]

Issues emerged in September as certain members of the New York Associated Banks fell below their agreed-upon 25 percent specie reserve threshold. While the banks acted as a single entity and covered one another, the fall in specie reserves grew as not enough gold made its way into the bank coffers. A 10 percent drop in specie reserves in early September alarmed the various banks in New York and this panic spread elsewhere. The fact that Union forces continued to struggle on the battlefield and there appeared no immediate end to hostilities only exacerbated the situation.[48]

At this moment of great despair for the specie reserves of various banks, Europe and California came to the rescue: the greatest influx of gold specie to date from those locales arrived and stabilized financial markets. Despite the outbreak of hostilities, European nations still relied on Northern foodstuffs—a subscription that amounted to $95 million in the year ending June 30, 1861, and $119 million for the following year. The *New York Times* reported on October 8 that western Europe's foodstuffs demand "relates not to the old but the acknowledged deficit of the new crop of wheat in England and France and the reported short supplies in Spain, Belgium, and Holland." The *Boston Daily Advertiser* went so far as to remark that the traffic along the New York Central and Erie railways of said farm materials proved "so enormous that the supply of cars is entirely insufficient for the freight moving toward the seaboard." When coupled with nearly $3 million in gold specie arriving from California monthly, specie reserves exceeded any amount necessary, but Chase's insistence on the gold being transferred from the various New York banks to the subtreasury resulted in a precipitous decline of specie reserves by December 1861.[49]

Specie Suspension

As the federal government converted Treasury notes into 6 percent "1881" bonds (named as such because they were twenty-year coupon bonds that matured in 1881) to compensate bankers, sales picked up. Bureau of Public Debt records provide the clearest evidence as to the nature of the bond sales to

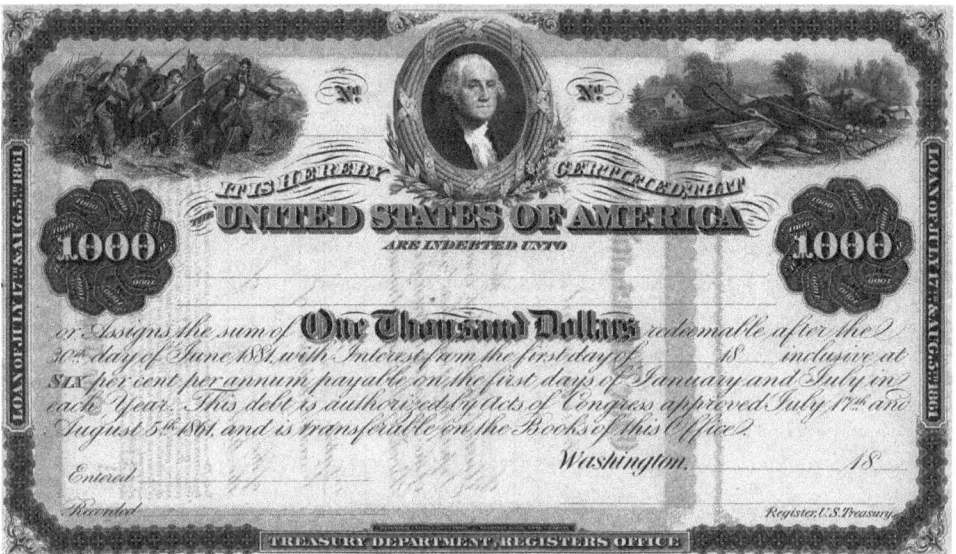

This unissued registered bond was part of a $250 million loan authorization connected to the loan of July 17, 1861. (Courtesy of The Joe I. Herbstman Memorial Collection of American Finance™)

banks and the population at large. The first bonds had interest dating from November 16, 1861, although the government did not deliver the first bond until January 9, 1862, revealing how ill-prepared the federal government was. The bond ledgers at the National Archives for the '81 issue show just how essential the Associated Banks remained to early bond sales. The bond ledgers reveal some $17 million in sales among the first thirty "vouchers" to John A. Stevens on behalf of the Associated Banks. Early sales had an international dimension as well: Schuchardt & Gebhard, a New York–based firm with active business in Amsterdam, purchased some $109,000 of the '81 issue from early November; German-tied firm Marcuse Balzer pocketed $8,500; London-based Morgan & Co. $65,000; and the German-associated Seligman's $10,000. But a closer examination of the bond ledgers portrays a wide assortment of individuals who bought into the Union cause. This represented a noticeable shift in investment marketing and strategies to date. The everyday citizenry answered the call to invest and it previewed future investments during the war.[50]

While the calendar turned to December and the entire North (and for that matter the Confederacy) anxiously awaited war or peace with Britain over the *Trent* seizure, Chase's report to Congress and the fear of specie payment suspension remained ever present. Chase's message to Congress endeavored to place a positive spin on a rather precarious situation. Import duties fell far short of what was necessary owing to mounting expenses ($32 million drawn in versus the anticipated $57 million) and land sales and other sources of income also fell short. Furthermore, Chase could do little to combat the ever-increasing size of the army and navy as the war dramatically expanded and all the associated expenditures connected to the armed forces mounted. Despite Chase's best efforts, the facts remained incontrovertible—expenditures continued to climb for the floundering federal government and the ability to cover said expenses was becoming more and more difficult. While Chase had procured $197 million by borrowing, it fell short of the $250 million authorized by Congress and the $320 million Chase thought necessary to fund the war effort (Lincoln thought the figure $400 million to be more appropriate). In Chase's mind, with the downward revision of revenue from $80 million to $55 million and an increase of expenditures from $318 million to $532 million, the federal government faced a minimum deficit of $200 million through fiscal year 1862 (that is, the end of June 1862). Such a deficit presented great concern to traditional norms of financing the government in the antebellum era. Chase's reticence to endorse taxation further hampered the government's efforts to meet any and all demands. Instead, Chase made a call for a "more absolute reliance, under God, upon American labor, American skill, and American soil." When it came to future loans, Chase hesitated, declining "from making any recommendation concerning the authorities with which it may be expedient to invest him in respect to future loans," rather leaving this decision "to the better judgment of Congress." A call for a national currency as part of the report represented a further evolution in the secretary of the treasury's thoughts on how to pay for the war and operate a functional economy. Although not the full cry for a national banking system that he presented in his 1862 report, it nevertheless represented a deviation from Chase's time as governor of Ohio, when he placed a great emphasis on the state's right to dictate monetary policy.[51]

By late 1861, all signs pointed toward the suspension of specie payment—in other words, American banks refusing to exchange gold and silver specie for their own bank notes. The *Journal of Commerce* reported as early as November 26, 1861, that London bankers held grave concerns over the likelihood of specie suspension. Mounting specie exports to Europe fueled speculation over suspension of specie emanating in London and impacting actions in New York. *The Economist* declared that as of November 25, only $80 million had been contributed by the banks and (to a significantly lesser degree) the public—a far cry from the $600 million *The Economist* deemed necessary for the government to operate a war (or for that matter the roughly $320 million Chase had predicted in his message to Congress that summer). In the mind of *The Economist* (and many other British banking interests of the time) the federal government simply borrowed too much money and did not tax its people enough. This would come to a head in time, they thought, by leading to specie suspension. Such claims led to panic on Wall Street by the middle part of December and the question of specie suspension ran rampant throughout lower Manhattan. By December 18, the *New York Tribune* reported the suspension question taking place "both in and out of bank parlors" and the reality that "the necessity of ultimate suspension was generally conceded, and the question was whether it should take place with full or empty vaults." Chase traveled to New York but could not assuage the concern of most New York financiers who called in their notes—creating a growing specie problem in the city. From December 7 to December 28 specie deposits in New York fell by a third as people tucked away their gold. The point of specie suspension had come. Despite a vote of confidence in continuing payments as recently as December 17, on the evening of December 28, following a seven-hour meeting, the banks voted to suspend specie payment. All this occurred despite the fact that war with Britain appeared to be avoided for the time being with the release of Confederate ambassadors Mason and Slidell, detained during the *Trent* affair. Suspension among Philadelphia and Boston banks soon followed and was subsequently undertaken by banking institutions throughout the North.[52]

The suspension of specie payments in December 1861 placed the Union in a precarious position. To complicate matters, Congress found itself in the midst of a debate on a legal tender—a national currency backed and circulated by the federal government. This stood in stark contrast to the antebellum world of state-issued banknotes that numbered in the hundreds. On the one hand, Secretary Chase hoped that a national banking plan might be implemented to avoid any and all legal tender implementation, expressing such hope to Senator William Fessenden of Maine in early 1862. The prospect of legal tender created "alarm in many minds" according to one financier. However, as the winter progressed, the notion of federal legal tender legislation gained traction as a better alternative to Union financial collapse that surely would carry forward to the military front as well. The *New York Times* called for "prompt action upon some feasible plan," noting that such action would command "the willing consent of the vast majority of the People of the loyal States, who desire to see the sovereign power of the Government asserted and exercised." The hard-money Democrats of New York who championed specie reluctantly supported a legal tender bill in late January and early February, which reinforced the firm belief of the *Times*.[53]

Congress, Greenbacks, and New Bond Issues

By the spring of 1862, the United States teetered on the verge of economic collapse. The stopgap measures undertaken by Secretary Chase following Lincoln's inauguration had followed the time-honored tradition of coordinating war finance through northeastern elites and their respective financial institutions. Early military setbacks for the Union, most notably at the battles of Bull Run and Balls Bluff in July and October 1861, respectively, threw Union finances into complete disarray. The suspension of specie payments in December 1861 posed the challenge of not only funding basic government operations, but also funding a war drastically increasing in scope as it entered its second calendar year. The federal government would now have to step in and put forward some sort of legislation to, at a minimum, stop the bleeding. Beyond that, the exigencies of war required more funds to defeat the Confederacy. Union battlefield success in 1861 perhaps would have ameliorated the concerns of many regarding federal finances. The string of defeats and diplomatic entanglements such as the *Trent* affair, however, inspired greater urgency to "fix" the financial system.

As Congress returned to session in early 1862 amid the suspension of specie payment in the North, the issue of legal tender remained the most pressing matter the legislative branch faced—an issue so important that the Ways and Means Committee had worked through the Christmas holiday in order to devise a new legal tender bill for the House of Representatives. Legal tender marked a shift from late antebellum money policy. No longer backed by gold or silver coin, the government-issued currency only had the backing of the federal government—effectively creating a fiat currency. Shortly after the new year in 1862 a group of bankers, in addition to societies (or boards) of trade and commerce from New York, Philadelphia, and Boston, descended on the capital to discuss with members of the Senate and House Finance Committees the merits or (lack thereof) of legal tender. Despite the concern of more conservative bankers in New York like George Coe, none could refute the financial necessity of legal tender legislation being taken up by Congress. The *Herald* pronounced as much when it declared, "Let there be no hesitation, therefore, about passing the financial bills immediately; and when that business is done let Congress disperse and go home and leave the suppression of the rebellion to the President, the Secretary of War, and General McClellan." While more conservative bankers in New York still disparaged legal tender, others emphasized a need to act to stave off potential economic collapse. For one Buffalo banker, legal tender was "not a debatable question. The struggle is for life. The knife is at our throat. We must strike with the most available weapon, and leave theory for a more convenient season." Such statements made it clear—the urgency of the moment could not be denied and the issuance of a currency to revive the Northern economy was a necessity.[54]

Fears emerged over what could be done in January 1862 to correct the financial situation. Assistant Secretary of the Treasury George Harrington wrote to Chase regarding this problem and the difficulties posed by New York financiers. "Mr. Cisco says there are strong indications of an attempt to make direct war upon the Treasury," declared Harrington. "Mr. Coe's bank even sent in the small amount of $75 for the coin & several times yesterday they called upon him." Harrington concluded his remarks to Chase by laying the blame firmly at the feet of "the dissenters. Gallatin Coe & Co." Shortly after the new year, in the midst of congressional debate on the issue, Congressman Elbridge Gerry Spaulding wrote to financier Isaac Sherman, remarking, "We must have at least $100,000,000 during the next three months, or the government must stop payment. With the Navy and Army of 700,000 now in the field we cannot say that we will not pay." Others remained skeptical that some sort of currency would be necessary. Future New York governor Reuben Fenton, for one, pushed taxation. "We should have a comprehensive scheme of finance, should tax and tax largely as the only means of preserving the public credit. Our people have great capacity for paying taxes and no people are more willing. The platform is, move the army, economy in public expenditure and tax heavy to preserve the credit and to pay." Senator Preston King shared the sentiment: "We must levy taxes and enough to keep our credit good." Another vocal proponent of taxation was Francis Lieber. In the winter months he wrote to Senator Charles Sumner, proclaiming, "Now, my dear Sumner, tax, tax us. Let me state as a positive fact that the people are anxious to pay heavenly taxes, more so than probably ever in history before. Indeed, without a 150 to 200 million tax bill our Legal Tender law will be a ghost enough to frighten the stoutest man." Despite the various opinions that circulated in New York and Washington, few denied the need for fundamental change enacted by Congress to stave off financial collapse.[55]

As the financial situation grew bleaker, press and financiers entrenched on their respective sides. The venerable financiers of New York City—a key group that would be needed to support the legislation—found themselves divided. Not surprisingly, hard-money Democrats opposed this legislation, but so too did more moderate members. George Coe of the American Exchange Bank, Jacob Vermilye of the Merchants' Bank, David Martin of the Ocean Bank, and James Gallatin of the National Bank all came out against the Legal Tender Act. Most of them feared inflation that might come with the greenback issuance but were also concerned over the massive $500 million bond issue and a lack of clarity as to the demand on the secondary market. The *New York Times* refused to fully embrace some form of legal tender but offered support for "prompt action upon *some* feasible plan." The *Times* added that the bill would be observed by a "willing consent of the vast majority of the People of the loyal States, who desire to see the sovereign power of the Government asserted and exercised." Despite such positive sentiments, others remained suspicious of the Union's financial prospects. *The Economist* voiced its doubts regarding Federal finances as word of the North's financial woes reached British shores. "At the outset of the American struggle it was believed that money would be the strong point of the Federal States; it is now believed that it is precisely their weak point. There is an old maxim that war can be made to support itself." The publication went on to state, "There is another newer but often cited maxim that a nation never knows it true strength until it is bankrupt. These dicta would seem to indicate that the war would grow in spite of the apparent ruin of the Federal finances. Yet the almost universal belief of competent men of business is that this ruin will be fatal to the Federal hopes." The challenge the Union faced, therefore, centered on the belief that the financial obstacles ahead required the people to participate.[56]

The finance committees in both houses of Congress drafted the Legal Tender Act. In the Senate this task fell to John Sherman of Ohio. Henry Cooke, brother of bond czar Jay Cooke, commented to Sherman, "You gentlemen of the 'Finance,' and 'Ways and Means' committees now have a splendid chance to establish a national financial policy that will carry the country through the existing crisis, and provide for its permanent prosperity when peace returns." In the House, the task fell to E. G. Spaulding and Samuel Hooper, two men with considerable financial experience in the commercial realm. By late January when the bill came up for debate, it contained a three-pronged approach of $150 million in legal tender, an equal amount raised via taxation, and a call for the creation of a national banking system. The bill reached the floor for debate on January 28, 1862.[57]

After extensive debate on the issue and numerous amendments—both successful and not—the matter passed the House on February 24 and passed the Senate the next day. Even many hard-money proponents with Democratic allegiances such as George Opdyke, John J. Cisco, Morris Ketchum, and others voiced support for legal tender by February 1862. For many legislators (and bankers) the bill came to be viewed as the best option at the time and merely a wartime scenario that did not have any permanent ramifications. Lincoln signed the bill into law on February 25. The legislation authorized the printing of $150 million in United States notes (known as greenbacks) and made these notes lawful currency. Additionally, the Legal Tender Act permitted $500 million in 6 percent interest-bearing bonds. Congress hoped to make the bonds appealing to the population at large and keep war profiteering to a minimum. As one Ohioan purportedly stated, any man who "hawks the credit of the Government in the markets ... to make the best bargains for himself that he can" was merely "dust ... compared to the rights and interest of the people of this country." The bonds were callable by the federal government in five years although they did not mature for twenty (hence their nickname "5-20s"). Importantly, these bonds could be purchased with the newly circulating currency so that a wider array of individuals could purchase the debt. However, the measures did little to dissuade the concerns of prominent bankers—particularly in the vital financial hub of New York. Union victory remained far from certain and doubts loomed with regard to a possible repudiation of the debt. These bankers simply would not commit any further money to "the cause" and sales among their clients and even the larger populace lagged accordingly. The concern over these financial matters pushed Chase to desperate measures and by the summer of 1862, he was looking for someone to step in and make the bond drive a success.[58]

Looking back at 1862 later in his life, Senator John Sherman of Ohio remarked that by 1862 the United States was "physically strong but financially weak ... the problem of this contest was not as to whether we could muster men, but whether we could raise money." By late 1861, Secretary Chase and the Treasury Department confronted a collapsing financial system. Despite such challenges, as the calendar turned to 1862 a new era dawned for U.S. finances. Legislation enacted in the fog of war challenged long-established approaches to American war finance dating back to the Revolution. Into this void emerged a democratic push that tossed out traditional assumptions of war finance and made the Civil War one in which the Union's citizenry found a remarkably vested interest. Jay Cooke and his nationwide army fundamentally upended the war finance method in America. In so doing, the shift was apparent, and Wall Street and American capitalism would never be the same.[59]

CHAPTER THREE

Patriotism and Profit
Jay Cooke and the Democratization of Debt

The history of finance is a history of the rise and fall of values, in other words, of speculations and panics. Wall Street is our temple of Janus. The lust of money is as strong as the lust of dominion, and avarice, like its nobler brother, ambition, "scorns delights and lives laborious days."
—William Worthington Fowler, writer (1870)

Money is God. Gold and Greenbacks and Stock—father, son, and the ghost of same—three persons in one; these are the true and only God.
—Mark Twain, writer and humorist (1871)

The circumstances of the time turned Jay Cooke & Co. to government finance. The power and prestige of the firm were built up through war finance, and, in order to sell government securities, Jay Cooke practically revolutionized the methods of marketing investments in the United States. The Civil War was in a very real way a turning point in the history of our investment banking, a development in which Jay Cooke was the leader.
—Henrietta Larson, Harvard Business School professor and author of Jay Cooke biography (1936)

We fellows in Wall Street had the fortune of war to speculate about and that always makes great doings on a stock exchange. It's good fishing in a barrel.
—Daniel Drew, Wall Street banker (n.d.)

On September 18, 1863, Union spy Spencer Kellogg Brown wrote from his Richmond jail cell to his sister Kitty. On the eve of his trial, Brown relayed to his sister the supreme faith he held in the Almighty. "God has been very kind to me, and for the past twelve months I have tried earnestly to please Him," wrote Brown. Resigned to his fate, Brown attempted to put his house in order regarding "some little trinkets." Brown's back pay owed by the federal government figured prominently in his letter. Brown left no doubt for his sister as to where this money should go. "Tell him to invest in United States six per cent bonds," Brown ordered. He left the purchase of such bonds to his uncle Cozzens in St. Louis, who controlled finances for Brown's wife. This was quite possibly Brown's last patriotic display for his beloved Union, as Confederate forces executed Brown a week later on September 25, 1863.[1]

BY 1862, THE FINANCIAL STRUGGLES of the Union had reached a tipping point. Traditional war financing by elites akin to other conflicts in the nation's history could not meet the needs of the Union war machine growing in size and scope on a daily basis. As Union forces numbered in the hundreds of thousands by the spring of 1862, and moved on multiple fronts against the Confederate armies, their costs came into sharp relief. How would the United States fund this war? Legislation to authorize the issuance of debt proved one thing, but who would buy such debt remained another thorny issue entirely. To sell the debt and to right the financial ship of Union fell to a relative newcomer named Jay Cooke. The $500 million 5-20 bond drive initiated in 1862 would become Cooke's trial by fire on a national stage, and through the successful implementation of his new sales tactics the war took on a new meaning financially for all throughout the North.

The actions undertaken by Cooke and his financial network throughout the North revitalized American war finance, stabilized the American state, energized the role of finance capitalists, and democratized the sale of bonds more broadly. By extending and publicizing bond sales to the general population writ large—sales that crossed gender, racial, political, and regional boundaries—Cooke made the war a people's contest. The entire nation gained ownership in the fate of the Union. By selling this confidence in the Union to the people, Cooke helped not only to sustain a war effort with valuable funds, but he also redefined American war finance. Small-scale investors purchased $50 and $100 bonds in large quantities, marking a stark contrast to antebellum war finance. Such actions linked the nation's investors to the cause of Union. These people quite literally "bought in" to the war on a level unseen in American history—asserting notions of civic inclusion and duty in the process.

Union spy Spencer Brown's decision to invest his back pay in Union war bonds reflected an emerging dynamic by the middle of the war. Patriotic self-interest moved to the forefront of the decision making of many Northern investors as the federal government democratized bond drives. For a spy like Brown, investment in Union war debt at the high interest rate of 6 percent not only served his wife's financial interests, but also reflected an act of patriotism championed and heralded by the Northern press and many in the public as well. Patriotic self-interest became a defining feature of the Union war effort in 1862 moving forward. "Bond czar" and Philadelphia financier Cooke proved central to this shift in narrative and strategy. In stark contrast to notions of shared sacrifice that infused the literature of organizations such as Union Leagues and the Sanitary Commission, Cooke proposed an alternative form of patriotism. In his view, bond investment not only provided material gain for investors, but afforded a notion of citizenship that one historian described as avoiding "the subordination of private interest to the public good." Further examination of the Treasury Department bond registers for the 5-20 sales reveals a disparate group of Americans, including many new immigrant groups, who latched onto Cooke's notion of a newfound sense of patriotism and citizenship, all the while making material gains. Furthermore, this inclusion of marginalized groups, including women, Native Americans, and immigrant groups aided the incorporation of a larger swath of the American public.[2]

In the early days of this popular investment, Cooke and the Treasury relied on antebellum savers—the close to 700,000 Americans who opened and contributed to savings accounts in the decade-plus leading up to the Civil War, usually for a moderate interest return between 4 and 6 percent. The 5-20 loan changed this, however, as investors now viewed the 6 percent interest offered as a financial windfall. With these new bonds, investors saw a way not only to serve their financial self-interest, but the patriotic cause of Union as well. By the spring of 1862, the Bank Commissioners of Massachusetts reported and attributed a decline in deposits to "investment in the national loans." The commissioners went on to opine, "The rate of interest on these securities being higher than that paid by savings banks, has doubtless attracted a large number of those who usually deposit [in savings banks] in considerable sums, and it was specially to attract this class, that the government bonds have been issued in denominations so much smaller than has been customary heretofore." Thus, these purchases in the early days of the 5-20 issue and its predecessor relied on an antebellum notion of saving coupled with marked self-interest in order to facilitate bond sales.[3]

Furthermore, the bond sales also reflected geographic diversity. The 5-20 drive consisted of subscribers across the entire North, border states, West, and even parts of the Confederacy. By spreading the sales literally across the continent, Cooke and his network of financial agents fired a new national imagination of financial civic inclusion that incorporated people previously outside the financial markets. This created a uniquely American identity, defined not by region, religion, race, ethnicity, gender, or political affiliation, but rather by investment. Similarly, the 5-20 bond drive proved instrumental in the development of a class of finance capitalists—an expanding group of financial elites that stood in stark contrast to more everyday investors. These individuals emerged during the war on a scale never before seen—and in doing so redefined financial markets during the Civil War and beyond.

Jay Cooke and the Move toward Popular Investment

By the fall of 1862, Union military fortunes met with mixed results. The once spectacular Peninsula Campaign died on the outskirts of Richmond. Meanwhile, in the western theater the Union military captured New Orleans and controlled large swaths of the Mississippi River with impressive victories over the course of the calendar year. However, it was the small Union victory in Sharpsburg, Maryland, in September 1862 that propelled Abraham Lincoln forward on a war of emancipation. In October 1862, the Lincoln administration issued the Emancipation Proclamation and signaled a significant shift in war aims. Going into effect January 1, 1863, the Emancipation Proclamation declared slaves residing in the Confederacy (with some exceptions) "henceforth and forever free." The war's duration and difficulty necessitated a shift in war strategy, and this also necessitated a longer-term financial system to meet the needs of the expanding conflict. That same month, Secretary of the Treasury Chase formally granted Jay Cooke the exclusive private agency for the federal government's $500 million 5-20 Loan. Cooke enthusiastically embraced his appointment. "I feel greatly gratified & encouraged by your kind appreciation of my former efforts," Cooke declared in response to his appointment, "and I accept your new proposition & orders with the determination & confident belief that I shall be able to prove fully the wisdom of the conclusions you have arrived at & have so plainly stated in your letter." Cooke went on to emphasize the importance in his mind of financial agents and "editorial talent" to enlighten "the whole community" as to the importance of the 5-20 loan issue. From the start of his agency, therefore, Cooke recognized the importance of democratic sales of bonds.[4]

From the outset of his appointment, Cooke intended to sell these bonds in large quantities and to market them through a sales team coordinated around a concerted media effort. Cooke's message centered on the relevance of these bonds, the ease with which the public could procure them, and the patriotic associations that could be made in such purchases by the public at large. Despite this shift, the United States faced fiscal constraints as previous bonds failed to sell at a pace that would fund the government. Cooke's ascension to the role as exclusive agent coincided with these consequential political and military developments, only complicating efforts at messaging a successful sale of the various bonds.

The loans, after all, had been structured to enable a larger swath of the population to purchase the bonds. The 6 percent 5-20 loans had biannual interest payments to the bondholder issued in May and November of a given year. These bonds existed in small denominations—as low as $50—and so afforded an opportunity for "every Capitalist, be he large or small, or Merchant, Mechanic, Farmer" to "invest at once his spare funds." Finally, prospective buyers had the option to purchase the bonds with the controversial new national fiat currency of "greenbacks" (although the Treasury paid out interest in gold specie). To sell the loan, Cooke received a commission of one-half of one percent of the proceeds for the first $10 million, and three-eighths percent thereafter with marketing costs absorbed by Cooke and his colleagues. Within a month, Cooke's efforts received favorable reviews from the secretary of the treasury. Jay Cooke's brother Henry wrote to that effect from Washington in late October. "You have gone into it with a startling energy and vigor," exclaimed Henry, "and we must try to keep up with you, if we can in our humble way ... The Governor [Secretary Chase] is much gratified." The favorable reviews on the part of Secretary Chase of course hinged on a need to maintain a high level of sales to keep the Union's finances afloat.[5]

Success for a loan of this scale on American soil was without precedent and required Cooke & Co. to create from scratch an elaborate national network of agents, subagents, subcontractors, salesmen, and clerks—not to mention an infrastructure at the Treasury Department to meet this new demand. The operational center of this new empire focused on Jay Cooke & Co. on South Third Street in Philadelphia, but Jay's brother Henry conducted the critical political and lobbying work out of their Washington finance house, located across the street from the Treasury building. Henry received the earliest word from Secretary Chase at the Treasury and from congressional allies on Capitol Hill regarding financial matters and then relayed the information via telegraph to Jay in Philadelphia. Even rumors and gossip emanating from the Treasury and the War Department proved speculative fodder for Henry Cooke, which he exploited to the company's advantage. Unconfirmed reports of Union victories (or defeats) played just as much a role in price fluctuations and demands for bonds as anything else. Sometimes the initial reports proved inaccurate and it led to price swings on Wall Street and lowered demand for Cooke's agents. Amid this, Cooke & Co. became the first "wire house" in the country—that is, the first firm that sold securities throughout the country and used the telegraph to confirm purchases and sales.

This image depicts some of the 400 female employees of the Treasury Department during the American Civil War. (*Harper's Weekly* 9, no. 425 [February 18, 1865], courtesy of Lincoln Financial Foundation Collection and The Institute of Museum and Library Services via Archive.org)

Secretary Chase called on Jay Cooke because of the dire financial situation that plagued the Union by the early fall of 1862. The Legal Tender Act issued hundreds of millions of dollars of currency into circulation in conjunction with an emerging income tax that expanded over the course of war. Additionally, Congress intended 5-20 bond sales to solve the financial crunch the Union faced, but by the end of the fiscal year in June 1862, 5-20 sales amounted to less than $14 million. Even with the introduction of Cooke to enact sales on behalf of the government, it took until the spring of 1863 for the operation to succeed. Logistics played a key role in all this. The network of several thousand agents working on Cooke's behalf took time to organize. Additionally, the delay in delivery of the bonds themselves from printers and engravers likewise pushed back the subsequent delivery of the bonds to the public throughout the country. Some of the delays reflected the small stature of the antebellum federal government, unable to meet the demands of a mid-nineteenth-century war. For instance, L. B. Chittenden, the register of the treasury, had to affix his signature personally to every single bond issued by the Treasury. This reflected only a portion of Chittenden's responsibilities at the Treasury Department, and as bond sales passed $1 million daily a significant buildup and delay in the delivery of bonds arose. With additional bond plates produced that increased bond production to nearly $3 million daily, Treasury appointed an acting register of the treasury in order for Chittenden to dedicate his entire energies to signing the bonds—no matter the size of the denomination. Such delays reflected the inadequacies of the federal government to operate a war of this scale, even with something as simple as a physical document. Even with a vast expansion of Treasury staff (including a massive increase in the number of women working in the department), Jay Cooke expressed his frustrations on the delay of bond deliveries to his brother Henry in late May 1863. "The delay of bonds," Cooke bemoaned, "is ruinous and they say it is getting intolerable. It takes all their time to manufacture excuses." On a very basic level pertaining to the execution of the loan and bond issuances, the government proved entirely unprepared.[6]

While Cooke kept the Philadelphia and Washington markets under his direct control, he utilized regional subcontractors or partners to pursue his financial agenda. In New York, Cooke utilized Fisk & Hatch; Clark, Dodge & Co.; Vermilye & Co.; and Livermore, Clews & Co., among other firms. In Boston, he relied on Spencer, Vila, & Co., and in Pittsburgh, Cooke relied on Joshua Hanna. These various bankers and banking houses became responsible for their individual markets and in turn sold a significant number of government securities to the public—and even among themselves in organized off-market arenas. These financial firms represented only a portion of the massive network orchestrated by Cooke that sold his vision of war finance to the American public. In order to sell bonds across the North and beyond, Cooke would come to rely on a vast array of agents. These traveling salesmen, in conjunction with local actors such as post office clerks, played an increasingly important role in selling bonds to Northern residents.[7]

Fisk & Hatch offers just one example of how these large financial firms worked in conjunction with Cooke, the federal government, and everyday investors to achieve the desired investments. Founded by two Vermont natives, the firm borrowed capital in the late antebellum period to build a financial house that could contend with the increasing volume of Wall Street trading. Having capitalized sufficiently, the firm seized upon the opportunity presented by the large-scale issuance of bonds and became a formal partner of Jay Cooke to represent the New York City market. Fisk & Hatch sent out a

Office of JAY COOKE,
Subscription Agent,

At Jay Cooke & Co. Bankers,

114 South Third Street,

Philadelphia, Nov. 1, 1862.

The undersigned, having been appointed SUBSCRIPTION AGENT by the SECRETARY OF THE TREASURY, is now prepared to furnish, at once, the

NEW TWENTY YEAR 6 PER CENT. BONDS

of the UNITED STATES, designated as "FIVE-TWENTIES," redeemable at the pleasure of the Government, after five years, and authorized by Act of Congress approved Feb. 25, 1862.

The **COUPON BONDS** are issued in sums of

$50, $100, $500, and $1000,

The **REGISTERED BONDS** in sums of

$50, $100, $500, $1000, and $5000.

Interest will commence from the **DATE OF SUBSCRIPTION**, and is **PAYABLE IN GOLD**, at the Mint, or any Sub-Treasury or Depository of the United States, on the first days of May and November of each year. At the present PREMIUM ON GOLD, these Bonds yield about EIGHT per cent. per annum. The ample provision made by Customs Duties, Excise Stamps and Internal Revenue, for the payment of Interest and liquidation of the Principal, makes an investment in this Loan safe, profitable and available at all times. In a word, this being the permanent Loan into which the Legal Tender Notes are convertible, it will become the PRINCIPAL LOAN in the market, and a profitable mode of investment for Trust Funds, the surplus funds of capitalists, as well as the earnings of the industrial classes.

Subscriptions received at PAR in Legal Tender Notes, or notes and checks of banks at par in Philadelphia. Subscribers by mail will receive prompt attention, and every facility and explanation will be afforded on application at this office.

A full supply of BONDS will be kept on hand for immediate delivery.

JAY COOKE,
Subscription Agent.

Flyers such as this November 1862 issue became common from Jay Cooke & Co. They laid out some of the basic information tied to bond issues such as the 5-20 bond and encouraged investors to visit the firm's Philadelphia office. (Image courtesy of The Library Company of Philadelphia) circular in the spring of 1862 to bankers nationwide emphasizing the profit opportunities associated with government bonds:

> We are engaged in negotiating the new five-twenty six per cent loan on behalf of the government. We desire the co-operation of patriotic bank officers and bankers in the effort to popularise this loan, and bring it to the attention of the people throughout the country. We are satisfied that if the real facts concerning the extent of the public debt at the present time, the immense resources of the government now being developed ... are properly laid before the people money will flow into the Treasury from the sale of these bonds with sufficient rapidity to supply all its wants, and effectually solve the problem of the national finances.

The firm worked tirelessly on behalf of Cooke & Co. in the vital New York City market. By the close of 1866 the firm had done so well as to raise its capitalization to $400,000. The firm's correspondence revealed the concerted effort to sell bond issues on a mass scale to the "popular" investor and frame such an act in patriotic rhetoric.[8]

While sales reached unprecedented levels in New York, Philadelphia, and Boston (see Appendix) the sales in other regions of the country are perhaps more illuminating. The assistant treasurer in San Francisco, D. W. Cheeseman, negotiated nearly $2.5 million in 5-20 sales alone. Most of these sales were tied to vast shipping conglomerates primarily focused on Far Eastern shipping, such as George Howes and Co.; E. Spicer and Co.; Flint, Peabody and Co.; J. R. Britton and Co.; William Sherman and Co.; Cameron Whittier and Co.; and Simon Kinkelspiel and Adler. This does not include other firms such as the clothiers Neustadter Brothers and the booksellers H. H. Bancroft and Co. (the namesake of UC–Berkeley's Bancroft Library). But the sales also incorporated others living in more rural areas, such as the farmer A. B. Abel, who lived in the San Francisco suburb of Vallejo. The sales on the West Coast did spread beyond the Bay Area and even California. Sales also emerged in Oregon, chief among them being Campbell Chrisman, a farmer who had emigrated from Missouri and purchased $2,500 in 5-20s. The sales listed Chrisman's home as Eugene City, Oregon, although he appears to move around within the state at times. Other 5-20 sales in Oregon took place in Corvallis and Albany.[9]

While major urban centers relied on larger financial institutions, the more rural Northern landscape forced Cooke to enact an alternative plan. Out west, the underdeveloped financial infrastructure enabled traveling agents and subagents as the primary means by which the general populace could get their hands on bonds. By the fall of 1863, Cooke's network of agents had hubs in Pennsylvania, Ohio (two), Indiana, Illinois, Michigan, Wisconsin (two), Missouri, Iowa, California, and Minnesota. In time these agents would take charge of small armies of traveling salesmen within each of the respective states. As the operations scaled up, however, these "agents" essentially functioned as state coordinators for the plethora of traveling agents (salesmen) who worked out of the local offices and traveled through prescribed regions. Cooke detailed the assortment of high-profile traveling agents, those who might be considered state coordinators or co-coordinators, including George A. Bassett (Indiana), Henry C. Storms and W. B. Hubbard (Ohio), C. J. Bradford (Pennsylvania), Thomas F. Shewell (Illinois), William Poulterer (Michigan), F. T. Loes and Paul Jagode (Wisconsin), and Silas Yerkes Jr. (Iowa, Missouri, and Minnesota). Typically traveling agents had a background in sales—former insurance men, real estate agents, and so forth—though many also had been leaders in their community and in a position to persuade. All told, thousands of subagents and traveling agents worked for Cooke & Co. during the initial 5-20 campaign; the number topped three thousand by war's end. Such a sizable enterprise involved a complicated network of borrowing and lending as traveling agents at times extended credit to individuals in order for them to purchase bonds. Such a complicated system of financial exchange foreshadowed the increasing complexity of emerging financial markets, financial instruments, and securitization. And Cooke directed the whole empire, transmitting instructions in a variety of forms from direct letters to subagents to generic circulars from the Philadelphia office. The group of traveling salesmen aided Cooke in spreading the bond message, and perhaps most crucially, bond sales outside of the larger urban centers.[10]

As early as December 1862, Henry Cooke wrote to Salmon Chase of the high hopes Cooke & Co. held in the agents: "We sent, yesterday, an intelligent and energetic agent to the west to push the 5 20 loan; and urged upon him as an important part of his duty, to visit the editors at all leading prints and judiciously enforce your great idea, securing as far as possible, the hearty cooperation of the newspapers." From the earliest days of the agency, the Cooke brothers realized the intricate communication necessary to facilitate bond sales on a national scale.[11]

Robert Clarkson offered one example of a traveling agent in Cooke's army who had migrated to the Midwest in December 1862 to organize bankers as subagents in some of the region's larger cities. Clarkson made his way through Ohio, Indiana, Illinois, and Wisconsin and reported back to Cooke the political situation in each respective state and how to exploit the various conditions. Clarkson at first spoke rather negatively regarding the prospects out west. On one occasion he remarked, "There is a growing disposition to have Ohio take care of herself, and the murmurs are by no means concealed that while the war is employing the machinery and capital of the Eastern states the West is left in the cold." This East/West binary of eastern capital thriving at the expense of a more agriculturally focused West meant Cooke and his team needed to work more creatively to cultivate sales in that region of the country.[12]

But it was not just about money. Like virtually every corporate business culture to come, Cooke encouraged his subagents to believe they were doing "American" work, even God's work. Sales reinforced "the justice of our cause, and, [invoked], we firmly believe, the protection of Divine Providence," declared one subagent. By 1864, similar reports were pouring into Philadelphia "headquarters" from an "army" of subagents who became convinced that their service was as important as any corporal's. They were, after all, "selling" the war, modulating their pitch to figure out which version of the war the public would "buy." True, as one agent complained, selling bonds was a little like "casting pearls before swine." Nevertheless, "while much money may not be invested, a patriotic and loyal feeling has been awakened." Common financial and emotional investment linked citizens of the United States to the solvency of government (and thereby, themselves); Unionism served no longer just a patriotic feeling, it signified a new kind of ownership. In this instance, patriotism did not require supreme sacrifice to the Union cause, but rather a belief in supporting Union war efforts in a way that could also bring investors monetary gain.[13]

Selling the Idea of War Bonds to the American People

In order for the bonds to reach far and wide throughout the North, Cooke implemented a massive advertising and marketing campaign unlike anything the United States had ever seen. Newspapers became the primary medium through which Cooke advertised the bonds. Cooke and one Philadelphia clerk named Sexton undertook the early advertising efforts entirely on their own. Only after more than a year of putting forward their own copy did Cooke enlist New York–based advertising firm Peaslee & Co. to promote the 5-20s. Another outlet that aided the advertising wing of Cooke's endeavors was the newly formed Associated Press. This organization assisted Cooke in disseminating information regarding the loans on a national scale. While many of the advertisements originated in Philadelphia-based newspapers such as the *Inquirer, City Item, Press,* and *Bulletin,* the final leg of the advertising work fell upon the various agents and subagents who marketed the advertisements in local newspapers and periodicals. Local advertising proved challenging, as salesmen attempted to negotiate the best possible advertising rate so as to not cut too far into their own profits. The salesman themselves received a third of Jay Cooke's government commission—in other words, they received one-eighth of a percent of all their sales. Advertising costs, then, had to be kept to a minimum for these commission-driven salesmen.[14]

The power of the telegraph and printing press enabled Cooke to advertise the 5-20 loan on a national scale by targeting an array of readers. Cooke used not only major newspapers, but also religious periodicals and non-English-language publications to target immigrant readers. Cooke often wrote pieces for newspaper editors to merely reproduce. In all cases, however, his language revealed a fervent desire to emphasize a wartime patriotism centered on material self-interest. Robust sales reflected a widespread belief in the bond issues. As Cooke wrote, "No one here heartily loved their country better than their pockets." Such a belief—while counter to notions of Christian sacrifice seen elsewhere in wartime literature—more accurately reflected a patriotic notion of material self-interest. Cooke then took such a notion and fused it with the democratization of bond sales in the 5-20 issue. Thus the advertisements reaffirmed the ideal of small-scale investors. "The Government with impartial wisdom," declared one advertisement, "has not left this loan to rich speculators alone, who would gladly buy up the bonds in vast amounts, but, by taking subscriptions in small sums, has put the permanent advantage of the Loan within the reach of the people." Such editorials and advertisements found their way into a wide variety of Northern publications.[15]

Success hinged on convincing the Northern consumer to dedicate their meager earnings to the cause. Word to that effect quickly spread and the newspapers regaled their readership with the democratic nature of purchases. Cooke utilized these newspapers with great effect as he targeted outlets that supported the Lincoln administration and the war. Papers throughout the North wrote about the "Popular" loan and its resonance among the "industrial classes" as well as "capitalists." One Philadelphia newspaper detailed the numerous sources of bond purchases:

> From Maryland the orders are steadily on the increase, and for Western Virginia and Kentucky sales have been very considerable. An order was received yesterday from Key West, Florida. A soldier in the Army of the Potomac sends to the subscription agent his surplus earnings, with the

As part of the efforts to reach as wide a swath of the Northern populace as possible, bond advertisements were placed in other languages—such as this bond ad in German. (Image courtesy of Rutherford B. Hayes Presidential Library & Museums) remark "If I fight hard enough my bonds will be good." Another "brave defender" sends from Suffolk five hundred dollars to invest in five-twenties, and says "I am much pleased with my purchase. I am willing to trust Uncle Sam. If he is not good, nobody else is." While soldiers exhibit such a spirit there can be no such word as fail. An agent, writing from Louisville, says "I am crowded with applications for five-twenties, and trust the orders I have already foreworded will be speedily filled. I am getting letters from all parts of the State, making inquiries, and look for large sales."[16]

The emphasis on bond sales among soldiers as well as a broad representation of the Northern population only furthered the patriotic sentiment surrounding bond purchases. The conflation of service in the army with investment of one's military salary reinforced this patriotic element by the time of Cooke's ascension to the agency for the 5-20 loan. Another report from Ohio emphasized military service and investment. "Her sons have fought on every battle-field under the inspiration of cheering assurances from their homes," declared one Buckeye State publication, "and now Ohio seals her good works, and glorifies herself by the avidity with which her people subscribe to the Government loan." Service therefore took on many forms during the war and investing in the Union through bond purchases afforded another opportunity to serve the Union on top of enlisting and serving on the front lines.[17]

Such sales also migrated outside of the traditional northeastern financial corridor. Claims from St. Louis declared, "Thus is St. Louis coming up and sustaining the Government—furnishing, thus far, her quote of the 'sinews of war' to pay our brave and faithful soldiers who are fighting the battles of their country." The fact that such claims came from outside the established financial centers of New York, Boston, and Philadelphia reveal the ability of the sales to reach wide swaths of the North. Daily reports noted the various contributions from regions throughout the North, including the border states. In every report that Cooke managed to circulate, a clear message emanated—a strong and vibrant Northern economy composed of strong state economies that ensured the stability of investments and made for a profitable endeavor.[18]

Newspaper reports on the success of bond sales peaked in the spring of 1863 to counter setbacks on the military front for the Union. Many of these reports were initiated from Cooke's office. Such efforts at building confidence emanated from the highest levels of government and made their way down to the everyday citizen. The *Fitzgerald City Stern* spoke of the issue at hand. "We have had two grand uprisings of the loyal people, equally significant," the newspaper reported. "The first was when the first gun was fired on Sumter, and the 'North rose as one man' to defend the honor of the nation. The second is now, when men of all classes, the capitalist and the laborer, are investing their hard earned dollars in Government Securities. . . . The confidence of the people proves the wisdom of his plans. If an American does not know the value of money, who does?"[19]

Confidence was a common theme in newspaper articles. The *Allentown Democrat* detailed daily sales of $2.25 million. "This response," the *Democrat* claimed, "shows immovable confidence in the Government,—and affords most unmistakable and overwhelming proof of the unabating zeal for the right, the sterling integrity, and the undying devotion to the Union, the strong adherence to the Government, the immortal patriotism, and the illimitable resources of the American people." Similarly, the *Philadelphia Commercial Dispatch* remarked, "The enormous weekly investments in the 5-20 loans show the confidence of the people in the stability of our Government." Other newspapers warned the public to procure the bonds while they lasted, one even noting, "The superiority of these bonds over any and every form of investment must be apparent to all and laggards will regret not having procured them whilst they were to be had."[20]

Others spoke to the confidence of border state purchasers close to combat and how that could influence more secure regions of the North. "Probably the most gratifying feature in connection with the subscriptions to this popular loan," the *Philadelphia Ledger* proclaimed, "may be found in the fact, that the amount taken by the border states daily increases, especially is this so in Kentucky and Missouri. In Ohio and Indiana there are also free takers. If capitalists in the immediate vicinity of the war have confidence in the Government, as these subscriptions indicate, those of the North should not doubt nor pause." Such a range of newspaper articles made it clear that the bonds found homes across the North for a variety of reasons. These statements on the part of Cooke and his advertisers reveal what patriotism meant for Cooke & Co. For many, these types of investment imbibed them with a deeper appreciation of sacrifice for the public good, while simultaneously profiting off such acts.[21]

These reports also aimed to educate the Northern population, for your average "common man" in nineteenth-century America had little to no knowledge of investing and needed validation to either shift resources from savings institutions or invest their money in bonds. Jay Cooke stepped into this breach, spreading the gospel of investing to the public through various articles, most notably his famous pamphlet "The Best Way to Put Out Money on Interest." Such articles became commonplace for Cooke as the principal method by which he sought to educate the public to their new financial duties (and opportunities). In this pamphlet, Cooke responded to a letter from a fictitious "Berks County Farmer," who had supposedly written into Cooke headquarters with a series of questions. "What sizes are the bonds?" the farmer asked. "As I cannot come to Philadelphia how am I to get the Bonds? [and] Do you take country money, or only Legal Tender Notes, or will a check on Philadelphia or New York, answer for subscriptions?" In his responses, Cooke answered such nuts-and-bolts questions but also played to patriotism disguised as self-interest and self-interest disguised as patriotism. And the newspapers played along. As one editorial in the *Lane Express* noted, a large subscription "strengthens the nation. These small subscribers . . . will pinch and save and work to buy more, and thus weave themselves into the very life and interests of the Government." Still another newspaper noted, "It has been found by experience that, through private agencies, Government loans could be made attractive to the mass of the public."[22]

Financial manuals aimed at the general populace flooded the market to capitalize on the rise of popular interest in investing. Illuminating the differences between the various types of war-created securities, *Memoranda Concerning Government Bonds for the Information of Investors*, published by New York firm Fisk & Hatch in March 1862, went through multiple printings during the remainder of the nineteenth century. Coupon bonds and registered bonds formed the most popular types of financial instruments for each of the various war bond drives. Coupon bonds (as the name implied) came with perforated redemption coupons attached that could be turned in semiannually for the interest dividend on the bond itself. These coupons could be surrendered at the U.S. Treasury in Washington or at one of several offices throughout the North. Perhaps one of the biggest selling points (and one that made coupon bonds so liable to theft) was the fact that the interest could be collected without the presentation of any sort of identification. Registered bonds, on the other hand, were formally registered with the Treasury Department in Washington, with interest payments issued through various subtreasuries throughout the North. Because of the formal registration of these bonds (and thereby at least their implied sense of security from theft), registered bonds often sold at a higher price compared to coupon bonds. Coupon bonds were often more appealing to citizens because of the fact that one did not have to go through the laborious process of transferring formal ownership of the bond on the occasion of a sale in order to ensure interest collection. Treasury bills and notes as well as certificates of deposit constituted additional instruments that all were shorter term in nature—typically between one and three years. Investors learned to distinguish between the different types of financial instruments, interest rates, time to maturity, and other key factors.[23]

But alongside this world of risk and speculation at a frenetic pace remained the potential for the everyday investor to be involved. Various magazines and journals picked up on this sentiment and regaled the reader with tales of the small investor. "The entire population of the country entered the field," one columnist remarked, "Offices were besieged by crowds of customers . . . Broadway was lined with carriages. The fashionable milliners, dress-makers, and jewelers reaped golden harvests. The pageant of Fifth Avenue on Sunday and of Central Park during the week-days was a bizarre, gorgeous, wonderful! Never were such dinners, such receptions, such balls . . . Vanity Fair was no longer a dream." In essence, the world of finance now ensnared many more in its web. Other writings such as *A Brokers's Office in the 1860s* revealed that Wall Street clientele hailed from all walks of life. Even Horace Greeley's *Tribune* drank the financial elixir, remarking "The intense desire to buy almost any kind of security amounted almost to insanity." Another piece entitled "Wall Street in War Time," addressed the simple fact that "Paper-money brought everyone into Wall Street, and interested every family in the ups and downs of stocks . . . every body seemed to be speculating in stocks. Nothing else was talked of at clubs, in the streets, at the theatres, in drawing-rooms. Ladies privately pledged their diamonds as margin with brokers, and astonished their husbands with the display of gains." By the 1870s tourists flocked to Wall Street to see the financial dramas they read about in newspapers, journals, and novels. Tour guides walked the crowds through this financial maze as all wanted the opportunity to at least come into contact with this newfound world—if not to participate in it directly. One observer perhaps summed up this new world: "The war, which made us a great people, made us also a nation in whom speculative ideas are predominant."[24]

The rising nature of popular investment and the explosion of banking in New York City led to a literary revolution in both fiction and nonfiction portraits of the new economy. A staple narrative thread was the "common man" investors versus Wall Street elites, with one side always favored—depending on the author. "They make money at the start, but in the end they almost invariable lose," commented Wall Street banker William Fowler of the "country bumpkins" who invested in U.S. bonds—although evidence appeared to prove otherwise. Still others described the Main Street investor as a man "uncomfortably stuffed into a business suit with a starched shirt, high collar, and cravat." While the Wall Street narrative often pushed against that of the investor who was new to the game, other novels revealed the flip side of the coin, where the "clueless" investor used his perceived ignorance to his advantage. One of these novels, *The Man from the West*, regaled the reader with the story of Henry Armitage (undoubtedly a play on the word *arbitrage*), hailing from Galveston, Texas, who had recently inherited a sizable fortune from his deceased father. Much of the proceeds stemmed from investments in Civil War bonds. Armitage made plans to deal with a Wall Street firm, Flam & Whipple, who presented to him (and any Main Street patron for that matter) "an appearance of affluent leisure," reflecting an easy existence for those in the know. The twists and turns of the novel reinforced the idea that Main Street could and would get the better of the Wall Street elite.[25]

Cooke's team promoted sales even in regions of the North with decidedly copperhead or "secesh" sympathies. In early May 1863, Cooke & Co. championed $1.5 million in 5-20 sales in Baltimore alone—not terribly distant from the recent Union setback at the battle of Chancellorsville, Virginia. In order to sell such arrangements to skeptics, some marketing emphasized the primacy of government bonds. Per the marketing materials, if the U.S. government could not honor bonds and the biannual interest payments on these issues, no financial instrument would be sacred. In essence, the economy writ large would come under threat. A local newspaper claimed, "The one important idea seems to be forcing its truth upon the people and that is if the government loans are not safe and good no others will be. When the nation goes down all else sinks with it." Another sale of $10,400 in Indiana was, according to the banker sending along the money, "from a Copperhead neighborhood and I doubt if a single person who subscribes for the bonds ever had a real Union pulsation of the heart since the rebellion broke out."[26]

The sales of 5-20s were unprecedented at the time. During the fiscal year ending June 30, 1863, 5-20 sales totaled $175,037,260—a stark contrast to fiscal year 1862 that only totaled $13,900,000. As summer turned to fall, the amount exceeded even the great sales of May 1863. On October 21, 1863, alone, 5-20 sales totaled $2,364,000—rounding out a week of slightly more than $12 million in sales. The work on the part of Cooke and his team revealed the power of marketing and, once more, the power of fusing investment with patriotism.[27]

Countering the Shoddy Aristocracy and War Profiteering

Cooke's efforts to sell bonds to a wider swath of the population had to overcome a healthy suspicion of wealthy Northerners and especially the ever-present threat of war profiteering. "Shoddy" came into usage during the war itself to reference wool clothing (especially jackets) that companies constructed from "shoddy" wool or scraps of wool from older materials. These jackets often did not survive their first rainstorm before disintegrating. Over time, "shoddy" reflected not merely poor craftsmanship, but a sense of what one historian described as "the broadest range of immorality and malfeasance" and "the hypocrisy of selfishness of Republican contractors, and, by extension, the current administration and its supporters." Financiers such as J. P. Morgan provide a prime example. The financier faced criticism early in the war over shoddy rifles sold to the U.S. government. A wealthy financier profiting at the expense of soldiers met with swift condemnation. Democratic newspaper editors increasingly identified war profiteers as a new class of Republicans using the war for their own material gain. As one Pennsylvania editor noted, the "shoddy aristocracy" not only grew rich through war contracts, but also "lucky speculation in stocks." The fact that many contemporary American newspapers and financiers used the terms "stocks" and "bonds" interchangeably meant this could extend to American war debt as well. The challenge, therefore, for Cooke and his marketing team was to find a way to sell bonds to the public while making it a patriotic issue of self-interest, but not abhorrent profit. The challenge to combat these notions of profiteering therefore took on complicated and nuanced understandings as the war progressed.[28]

The emphasis on and criticism of profiteering also made its way into sermons in various houses of worship throughout the North. "Our national character [is] becoming greatly weakened by the prevalence of a spirit of ostentatious and costly self indulgence," declared one Congregational minister. He added, "Long-continued and unusual prosperity has a terrible influence to enervate and unman a people." Other sermons even called on individuals to "lose money for a principal." Religious journals likewise joined in and lambasted the overall "state of moral corruption" that permeated the North. Such statements—which reflected a larger notion of Christian sacrifice—provided all the more reason to distance bond purchases from greed, luxury, and perceptions of selfishness that made the rounds in the Northern press. While one Connecticut Democrat equated Northern excess to "dancing in a graveyard," a poet bluntly stated, "Shoddy . . . is scuttling your ship." Such statements reflected in part what historian Philip Paludan refers to as "corruption of market-driven morals," a great concern among portions of the Northern populace during the war.[29]

Other evidence of shoddy citizenship emerged with the premium placed on gold as a result of the Legal Tender Act. While the New York Stock and Exchange Board (NYSEB) (the precursor to the New York Stock Exchange) passed a resolution banning the trading of gold at the boards (along with shorting government bonds), the trade cropped up by early spring 1862 in the "Coal Hole" on William Street. The "Gold Room," as it became known, operated outside the parameters of the NYSEB and allowed transactions including traditional cash exchanges, margin buys, and contracts for future deliveries. Some practices emerged with catchy names such as "spread eagle" and "twisting the shorts." The aggressive swings in the gold premium—that is, how many greenbacks it might cost to purchase $100 in gold—relied on the political and military fortunes of the war. By the summer of 1864, gold reached 285—as in $285 in greenbacks purchased $100 in gold specie—nearly doubling the depreciation of greenbacks in a year's time. Nevertheless, the Gold Room speculation was a financial barometer of the general confidence of the country. Abraham Lincoln made his thoughts on the Gold Room and gold speculation quite clear when, in a letter to the governor of Pennsylvania, he noted: "For my part, I wish every one of them had his devilish head shot off." Jay Cooke referred to the gold traders disparagingly as "General Lee's left flank" while others referred to the Gold Room members as "Jefferson Davis speculators." The Gold Room figured prominently into the bond question because the value of gold relative to greenbacks had implications for the greenback market and the extent of legal tender in circulation, not to mention ramifications for inflation. Because greenbacks were the primary mode of purchase for bond sales, Cooke & Co. kept a watchful eye on the "Gold Bugs."[30]

Notions of shoddy took on a decisively anti-immigrant tone during the war as well. Immigrants had long been a source of derision and contempt in late antebellum America. While scholarship is rich on "nativist" sentiment in the 1840s and 1850s, culminating in part in the American Party's brief ascension to the national stage, anti-immigrant vitriol flourished during the war itself. Anti-immigrant sentiment leaned on the "shoddy" narrative. In December 1863, *Frank Leslie's Budget of Fun* published the poem "How Are You, Shoddy?" in which Bridget Fitz-Shoddy takes aim at the wife of Irish descent of a war profiteer. A February 1863 *Harper's Weekly* cartoon similarly lambasted an Irishwoman as the wife of a shoddy contractor gaudily displaying her wealth. The Washington-based journal *Old Guard* even went so far as to lament the decline of Washington, the city having been "conquered by hordes of newly civilized barbarians." These xenophobic critiques of immigrants, especially those who recently came into money, reveals the backlash to immigrant investment in Union bonds in various Northern cities.[31]

One of the most infamous pieces of fiction on corruption during the war was Henry Morford's *The Days of Shoddy*. In the story, New York merchant Charles Holt and his clerk Burtnett Haviland take different paths when it comes to the war. While Haviland enlists to serve in the war, Holt not only pursues Haviland's wife, but also endeavors to amass a fortune through war profiteering. Yet, Holt's aspirations are not realized. Captured in the confusion following the first battle of the war at Bull Run, Holt is remitted to Libby Prison in Richmond, Virginia. Haviland, meanwhile, ends his brief enlistment and returns home—disenchanted by the corruption of his former boss and what he witnessed during his brief term of service. Morford's message is clear: true patriots avoided corruption as part of their service and sacrifice to the nation and the cause of Union. This combination of corruption and war profiteering extended to a wide array of army contracts. Within this environment Cooke and the federal government endeavored to sell bonds to as wide a cross-section of immigrants and others as possible.[32]

5-20 Sales among the Masses

Examining bond sales from a consumer standpoint provides a rather interesting account of how these sales played out on a practical level. The vast array of ledger books housed in the records of the Bureau of the Public Debt at the National Archives opens a window into the world of the bond purchaser from the Civil War, and in the process reveals the diversity of individuals (in the millions) who purchased this debt. The accounting from the war bond drives encompasses more than 500 volumes and even this massive record omits some of the data. The bond ledgers reveal sales that crossed ethnic, gender, and socioeconomic lines.

Immigrants were prominent in the portfolio of 5-20 investors, as they embraced some of the marketing put forward by Cooke and his allies in order to stake their claim to a civic identity in the war-torn United States. Immigrant populations in many cities invested heavily as a result. An example is Cincinnati, Ohio: With a population of approximately 161,000 at the time of the 1860 census and home to a diverse economy, bond purchasers ran the gamut of life in the Queen City. Immigrants comprised a large segment of Cincinnati's population and this was no different when it came to the composition of bond sales in the city. Maria Martin, an Irish immigrant and wife of a laborer, purchased $100 in 5-20s. Similarly, Mary Hine, a German immigrant whose German immigrant husband worked as a local carpenter, purchased a

$50 bond for the family. Another German immigrant, Mary Fry, who was most likely a servant, purchased $100 in 5-20s. Other immigrants included Catherine Seybold ($100), a Prussian immigrant and farmer, and Cordelia Andrews ($100), an immigrant from England and wife of a "finner."[33]

Just like in Cincinnati, immigrants contributed to bond sales in Chicago. English immigrant Eliza Davis—married to a clerk—contributed $50, while Scottish immigrant and merchant James Nicol put in $100. Charlotte Varphol, a Prussian immigrant, put $100 in for herself as well as funds for her children, Rudolph and Robert ($100 and $50, respectively). Hungarian (and highly regarded photographer) Alfred Pattoini invested $150. Pittsburgh sales incorporated Austrian immigrant and civil engineer Felician Slataper—a recent transplant from the nation's capital—who purchased $400 in 5-20s. These immigrant investors, including recent transplants and women denied the right to vote, asserted their inclusion in the nation through purchasing bonds.[34]

Further examination of sales reveal the character of bond purchases throughout the North. From Cincinnati, John Besler, a clerk in town, purchased $100 in 5-20s early in the conflict, and he also purchased them for other members of his family, including wife Caroline ($200) and his daughter Louisa ($200). Esther A. Baldwin, a schoolteacher in Cincinnati (and quite possibly a war widow) put $50 toward 5-20s. Cynthia Haughty, a farmer, likewise put down $50 toward 5-20s. Abijah Watson, whose occupation was listed as "stewart" in the 1860 census, invested $100. Further records in Cincinnati reveal the disparate nature of the sales. Sarah E. Owens, a mother of three, wife of a physician, and owner of a boardinghouse, dabbled in the 5-20 market by purchasing a sizable $450. Mary A. Todd, a servant in Cincinnati for a local minister (although originally from Virginia), bought $500 worth. Charles S. Royce, a schoolteacher and father of four, bought $150 in 5-20s, while George Gault, an eighteen-year-old son of a miller (one of six children) who moved to Cincinnati from South Carolina invested $100 toward the drive. Merchant William Drennan purchased a sizable amount of 5-20s for his family during the drive including for his wife Hannah ($500) and children George and Mary ($100 each), as well as most likely his mother Eliza ($500). While William was a merchant at times during the war, it appears he was also the sutler or traveling salesman for the 64th Ohio Infantry, a regiment with several men who invested including Capt. William Sarr ($800). Just as curious were those who invested that leave behind little historical record of their occupation, just a residence in Cincinnati—including individuals such as Roxanna Ross ($100) and Sarah A. Brooks ($600).[35]

Chicago sales likewise covered a wide array of occupations. Cyrus R. Hagerty, a father of two born in Pennsylvania and a carpenter by trade, pledged $200 to the Union cause. Sales also emanated from residents outside of Chicago, including merchant Matthew Griswold ($100) from Peoria and farmers Orren and Sarah Disbrow ($100 each) from Alden, Illinois, and Gerry Battes ($100) from Peoria. Still other investors in Chicago included physician Ephraim Ingals ($150), the Reverend John Woodbridge ($100) of the North Presbyterian Church, Louisiana-born clerk Charles Philbrik ($50), farmer Matthias Loos ($50), physician Franz Mergler ($400), and farmer Virginia Stevens ($150). Finally was Charles C. P. Holden, a ward leader in Chicago as well as veteran of the Mexican War, who picked up $200 in 5-20s during the drive proper.[36]

Other cities contain similar stories, no matter how small the investments might have been. In the old northwest enclave of Detroit, Michigan, there were some investments in the 5-20 drive. While only nine individuals/banks invested in the 5-20 drive via primary sales to Detroit, the number included people like David Cooper, a merchant who resided downtown at 21 Michigan Avenue. Although a Canadian native, Cooper (who at this time was in his early 70s) invested a sizable $5,000 in 5-20s. Heading east to Pittsburgh, further sales emerged. George Ammond, a tailor and father of three, invested $400 in 5-20s. Sophia M. Dean, the wife of a steamboat captain, put down $100 toward bonds. Reuben Miller, a twenty-one-year-old machinist, packaged $150 to put in toward the drive, while a Philip Bentel (occupation unknown) from nearby Freedom, Pennsylvania, invested $500 in 5-20s. Presbyterian minister (and future chaplain of the 102nd Pennsylvania Infantry) Alexander M. Stewart deemed it providential to place $200 in bonds toward the cause.[37]

St. Louis and Baltimore offered similar narratives. Waldemar Strauss, a St. Louis salesman, purchased a $50 bond, whereas Alexander Dienst, a dentist from the Baden region of present-day Germany, purchased $100. Janet Simmons, the wife of a confectioner, bought $100 worth, while a Dr. Lewis Huffell bought a modest $50 bond. Emil Ulrici followed up the signing of his loyalty oath in 1862 by purchasing $1,000 in 5-20s. In Baltimore, a Methodist Episcopal minister named Joseph France purchased $200 in bonds. Dr. Augustine Darlymple, an Irish immigrant, bought $500 while Caroline Rafford, the wife of a "master sailor," bought $200. Finally, Ann Stoner, the wife of a farmer in Frederick, Maryland, bought $100. These sales from a variety of Northern cities and states revealed the changing nature of war finance at this time. In under a year, Union war finance had moved away from solely seeking funds from the established financial elite of New York, Philadelphia, and Boston to incorporating all segments of the population. While some were undoubtedly of the financial capitalist class, a closer examination of these sales reveals just how widespread the sales were becoming—drawing on men and women, native sons and daughters and immigrants alike—to fill the coffers of the Union in order to undertake the war.[38]

Such acts during the Civil War revealed a new strategy for asserting a partnership in the nation, as those people previously denied rights and privileges entered into a new contract with the federal government through purchasing bonds. In a sense, they asserted a national identity defined not by religion, race, gender, ethnicity, language, or political ideals, but by investment. In undertaking such acts, the federal government raised the largest sum by democratic means in the totality of the nineteenth century—a feat that would not be surpassed in the United States until the war bond drives of World War I. From Bangor, Maine, to Derry, New Hampshire, to Cazenovia, New York, to St. Paul, Minnesota, to Detroit, Michigan, to Davenport, Iowa, and beyond, the war truly became one that encompassed the entire Northern populace and drew on a wide range of groups on the margins of society—politically or otherwise. Immigrants, women, African Americans, and Native Americans all invested in the cause of Union.[39]

Quantifying the sales sets them in even starker relief. Take, for example, the registered bond sales of the 1862 5-20 loan scheme (sales ran from May 1862 to January 1864). The total sales of the 5-20s amounted to $514,771,600. The registered portion of these sales were $74,995,150, or 14.6 percent of the total. Because 5-20 bonds were often more expensive (selling well above par at times) the purchaser lists are admittedly a "who's who" of Northern socialites, politicians, and senior military officials. Purchasers included several Union generals (including future president James Garfield), an admiral (David Farragut), cabinet members (Gideon Welles and Salmon Chase), prominent socialites (George Templeton Strong), President Abraham Lincoln, French nobility (Comte de Dion), Cubans, Haitians, and even a future president of Peru (Francisco Calderon). But in addition to these relatively well-heeled purchasers, literally thousands of other individuals purchased at far lower levels. Women comprised a large portion of the purchasers, accounting for 26.1 percent of all registered 5-20 bonds with the average bond purchase amount per woman at $2,400 (about $50,000 in 2020 dollars). (Male subscribers to the 5-20 registered bonds—comprising 73.9 percent of individual sales—had more than double this average amount at $5,500.) Of course, such ledgers cannot answer the question of *why* women were buying bonds in such unprecedented numbers. Perhaps women were inclined to find safe havens for family income. Civil War historians such as Nina Silber, Judith Giesberg, and Matthew Gallman have posited that Northern women asserted their economic role during the war in an attempt to stimulate the economy and contribute to the war effort as they entered previously male domains and spheres. Similarly, some of these women could also have very well purchased bonds from soldier pay making its way home.[40]

Nevertheless, examining the register books for coupon bonds reveals a tremendous amount about some of the purchasers. No fewer than twenty-one members of Congress (from both major political parties as well as some Unconditional Unionists) invested in bonds. Still others included renowned writer Nathaniel Hawthorne, socialite P. T. Barnum, future Mark Twain character Bloodgood Cutter, *Chicago Tribune* editor Joseph Medill, publishers Thurlow Weed and Evert Duyckinck, and prominent businesses such as the clothiers Brooks Brothers and the parent company of the Guinness Brewery of Dublin, Ireland. Still other purchasers included countless army and navy officers as well as rank-and-file soldiers and sailors. Ministers accounted for many purchases in the 5-20 ledger books, as did various Masonic organizations. Other intriguing organizations included the Ebenezer Society—a pacifist group located in upstate New York, but one that provided the government with funds to purchase the arms of war. International firms also waded into the domestic market, including British and Dutch banks, as well as miscellaneous German firms—not to mention other companies such as Dane, Dana & Company and the Chinese Mutual Insurance Company, with its deep ties to the Chinese trade.[41]

While coupon bond sales are significantly harder to track within the records of the Bureau of the Public Debt, on very rare occasions bank ledgers from the period have survived and detail sales. One example of secondary sales for 5-20 coupons can be seen through the surviving accounts of Brown Brothers & Co. out of New York City. While the surviving ledger records are relatively small compared to other New York financial institutions at the time (Brown Brothers' sales in 5-20 coupon bonds come in at just over $100,000 according to the surviving records), they nevertheless offer some invaluable insight into 5-20 coupon sales. In keeping with the registered bond sales, Brown Brothers sold a sizable portion of its bonds to women (38 percent of sales). Additionally, some bonds can be tracked relatively easily through various sales. For instance, a $1,000 coupon bond, no. 48495, originally sold on November 26, 1863, to a Howard Potter Tread. The bond eventually made its way back to the bank on July 15, 1865, via the Ladies Relief Society of Jersey

City, New Jersey. The journey undertaken by such bonds as no. 48495 reveal the fluid nature of such sales in the Civil War era and the wide scope of these who came into contact with bonds.[42]

Critics and Congressional Investigations

Despite Cooke's success selling the debt, his exclusive agency led to bipartisan attacks, and his marketing tactics and commission rates were not without their critics. Cooke's monopoly led some to remain skeptical of his work—even from within President Lincoln's own party. Shortly before Christmas 1862, Republican Charles R. Train moved on the floor of the House of Representatives to initiate an investigation of the Treasury Department:

> *Resolved*: that a select committee of five be appointed to inquire whether any officer or employee in any Department of the government is a partner, or interested directly or indirectly in any banking house, money corporation, or other business firm having contracts with the government, or dealing in stocks or other property; and that said committee have power to send for persons and papers and to employ a stenographic clerk at the rate of compensation usually paid to such an officer; and that said committee have authority to report at any time by bill or otherwise.[43]

While the investigation did not go any further, it nevertheless revealed the desires of some within the administration's own party to undercut Cooke and his success. One newspaper vocal in its criticism of Cooke was the *New York World*. Even in the midst of wild success for the loan in May 1863, the *World* challenged the integrity of Cooke and his larger network. While levying heavy criticism on Cooke & Co., the paper also reserved the right to criticize the Treasury for its "cunning contrivances" that only furthered the struggles the Union faced, confronting a nation "wasted by war, and impoverished by taxes."[44]

Even as the 5-20 loan wound down, renewed calls emerged from Congress to investigate Cooke. Democrat Alexander H. Coffroth introduced a resolution on January 5, 1864, calling for a full investigation of the bond issue and the potential profits if the Treasury had sold bonds itself: "Resolved, that the Secretary of the Treasury be requested to report to this House what have been the services of Jay Cooke and Company to the government in the sale of United States securities and what has been the rate and whole amount of compensation therefore." The resolution also called for a monetary comparison of what it would have cost the Treasury to conduct all sales and advertising on its own. To such inquiries Cooke and Chase were more than willing to present the numbers—revealing a cost of $1.4 million to the federal government (or about .002 percent of the proceeds from the sale), while noting that expenses before Cooke assumed the agency were twenty-five times that number.[45]

Yet even before Cooke and Chase could provide this rejoinder, criticism and calls for investigations also emanated from the Senate. Senator (and future vice president) Thomas Hendricks took to the floor of the Senate on February 11, 1864, to call out Cooke & Co.—which he referred to as the "rich banking firm which has been made rich by the drippings from the Treasury." The senator bemoaned the fact that "perhaps a million dollars has been made by the firm of Jay Cooke and Company by being made the special and exclusive agent of the Treasury Department in disposing of the bonds of the government which might have been disposed of by the ordinary machinery of the Department." Such a stinging critique did, however, afford senator and close Cooke ally John Sherman the opportunity to defend his Ohio brethren. "The firm of Jay Cooke and Company is an old, leading banking house in the city of Philadelphia" proclaimed Sherman—although "old" is certainly open to interpretation since it had been founded less than four years earlier. Sherman continued, "The people everywhere, in all parts of the country, came with their little earnings, some more, some less, and poured them into the Treasury, taking in return the pledge of the government to repay their loans. The money of the people in little streams and rivulets poured into the national Treasury, and thus sustained the national life." Sherman reflected the desire of most Republicans on Capitol Hill to defend the firm working tirelessly to fund the war effort. Indeed, Henry Cooke's allies on the Hill did their best to support the Cooke enterprise.[46]

Despite the defense promoted by Sherman, Cooke's actions did beg the question of what his true motives may have been. Some of Cooke's financial actions proved problematic in conception or execution. Certificates from state or local financial institutions, fractional currency, as well as counterfeit bills, could be tremendously difficult for Cooke to accept in a nation with an established national fiat currency. In addition, the thousands of agents lacked a thorough vetting from Cooke, nor did they face any governmental regulatory control. By far the largest problem that plagued Cooke revolved around securing legal tender to properly make payments to the government. Cooke remained cognizant of the fact that his control of greenbacks could have a devastating impact on the money market of the Union writ large. For one example, on November 21, 1863, Cooke had nearly $17 million in various state banknotes residing in numerous banks throughout the East but not enough legal tender by which it could be relayed to the Treasury at Washington or to the subtreasury in New York. Cooke forever had to walk a fiscal tightrope when it came to his usage and cornering of greenbacks. Despite these challenges, by January 1864 the $500 million subscription had been reached and the 5-20 loan came to a close.[47]

Bond Success

At the end of the 5-20 sales, congratulations flooded into Jay Cooke's office. Cooke's system revealed the power of the 5-20 issue as an unprecedented democratic success. "Never before in the history of this or other countries has any financial emergency so vast in its proportions been so promptly met," Cooke remarked. He added, "I think we may regard the success of this loan as the herald of the approaching day of Peace, Reunion and permanently established Prosperity in which the citizens of every section shall participate." Cooke's agents replied in kind. New York financiers Fisk & Hatch said, "We congratulate *you* on the successful termination of the grandest financial triumph the world ever saw." F. P. Handy, president of the Merchants Bank of Cleveland, similarly replied, "Allow us to congratulate you on the glorious success of the popular 5-20 loan . . . Looking to the future, we join with you in regarding its success as 'the herald of peace and reunion.' Such bonds can never be broken." Similarly, newspapers also praised Cooke and his network. The *Philadelphia Inquirer* declared, "This loan constitutes one of the most remarkable features in the financial history of any country and its success has no parallel . . . No nation on the face of the Earth can boast of success so complete and at the same time so safe and satisfactory to all parties concerned." Cooke's method of selling bonds directly to the American populace reflected a new and successful chapter in American financial history.[48]

The closure of the 5-20 loan led to increased market action on the New York Stock Exchange. Active trades of these bonds on the secondary market had been few and far between while sales out of Cooke's office were ongoing. Even as late as September 15, 1863, only 2,000 5-20 bonds sold on the New York Stock Exchange Board. By January 1864, however, following the formal closure of the 5-20 scheme, sales thrived on the NYSEB as a secondary market emerged. By late February, 19,000 bonds sold on the exchange in the morning session. By mid-May, that number had jumped to 30,000; by mid-June, 54,000; and by July 22, sales on the exchange numbered over 100,000 in the morning session alone. On one morning in January 1865, bonds sales topped 250,000. Not only were more bonds being sold on the exchange, their valuation was progressively on the rise. Bonds selling at par or slightly above par in the fall of 1863 were peaking north of 110 by the summer of 1864. Such a premium on bond sales reflected a confidence in the Union not only to win the war, but subsequently to pay back these loans.[49]

The 5-20 drive marked a seismic shift in the scope of Union war finance, bearing little resemblance to policy in 1861. Chase and the Treasury Department eschewed the northeastern financial elites that had been the bedrock of United States war finance since the Revolution. Under the guidance of Cooke, everyday citizens spanning the country financed the Union cause. These individuals took either current wage earnings or accumulated savings and injected them into the bond effort. The combination of higher yields that spoke to their self-interest and patriotic marketing made the widespread sale of these bonds easier in a brief period. The "people" had spoken with their acts of financial agency and asserted their rights to civic inclusion while also ushering in a new moment of popular financial capitalism. While this was the people's war, make no mistake that the war's financial circumstances also ushered forth a new era of finance capitalists. The war debt forever changed the composition of capital markets, the banking institutions behind the movement, and the role of the federal government in the fiscal operations firmly cemented in New York. Such actions were only enhanced by foreign sales of 5-20s and the subsequent 7-30 drive—both of which played essential roles in dictating postwar finance for the remainder of the nineteenth century. One newspaper article summed it up: "He [Cooke] succeeded in popularizing the great five-twenty loan, and now finds the people so anxious to convert their currency into bonds that it is only with difficulty he can meet the sudden and increasing demand."[50]

Because the sales of Union bonds happened at the various United States subtreasuries, these institutions—in New York, Boston, Philadelphia, Pittsburgh, Cincinnati, Baltimore, Chicago, St. Louis, and San Francisco—became anchor points for future bond sales. Moving beyond the traditional northeastern financial networks of Boston, Philadelphia, and New York and the political network of Washington, the spread of 5-20 bond sales into the Midwest and West Coast truly extended the war's aims from coast to coast. Furthermore, those who purchased the bonds expanded outside of the traditional urban landscape as well, revealing the wide, disparate nature of bond sales across gender, racial, social, and economic boundaries.[51]

The battles in Congress and the tension among Wall Street financiers reveal a different dimension to the struggles over Civil War finance. While northeastern financiers were reluctant to engage fully with the cause of war finance by the end of 1861, leading to specie suspension, the war's evolution led to significant changes. In time, Congress and Wall Street worked closely to broker a financial arrangement conducive to banking activities and bond sales as a whole. Much like the democratic initiatives to broaden investment and couch it in terms of patriotic self-interest, so too were financiers drawn into such an arrangement by the midpoint of the war. Jay Cooke could not only use the banks as vital secondary markets for these bonds, but also sell them on a war wrapped in patriotic bunting in order to finance the increasing scope of operations by 1863. Once again, the "Napoleon of Finance" proved his worth. But the story of Civil War finance expanded beyond the borders of the United States. International sales proved as important, if not more so, in the story of Civil War finance.

CHAPTER FOUR

The Sale of American Stocks Constitutes the Chief Business at the Bourse
Foreign War Finance

On September 12, 1864, the *New York Times* reprinted an article from the *Richmond Examiner*. In the midst of battlefield reports, it contained a detailed assessment of "Yankee Loans" in Europe. In particular, the article zeroed in on bond sales in the Netherlands and the German states. The bonds, purportedly shipped "by the bale" to these regions, found many takers according to the article. "Germany is the most efficient ally of LINCOLN," the article declared, noting that Germans were "the best economists of Europe." The piece likewise emphasized purchases of American Civil War debt at the hands of the Dutch. The "docile and credulous people," the article opined, acted as a ready market for investment. While the primary thrust of the Confederate article centered on possible repudiation of Northern debt—a event that never occurred—the emphasis on the Germans and Dutch is noteworthy. Referring to the Dutch and Germans as "infidels and abolitionists," the article conceded that "money is abundant among the masses." Such statements detailed the intense suspicion on the part of Confederate actors to an openly democratic bond sale. Furthermore, they revealed the intense xenophobia that helped to frame aspirations of a Confederate empire.[1]

International buyers purchased 15 percent of the overall bond market, no small amount, and revealed the validity of and confidence in the Union in European eyes. At the war's outset, longtime financial entities in London and Paris resisted firmly aligning with the Union owing to the deep ties both European countries had to Southern cotton. Defeats for the Union army in the summer and early fall of 1861 only reaffirmed the decisions made by many in England and France. These decisions by European bankers crippled Wall Street. The reticence on the part of these European partners circulated throughout the financial firms in New York and gave them a moment of pause. If international support lagged for the Union cause, what secondary market might these New York firms have among their traditional clients across the Atlantic? Furthermore, what message would a lack of international support send to prospective domestic buyers? In time, European nations came around to supporting Union financial efforts, especially in the Netherlands and the German states. Despite insistence on the part of the federal government that it could function without international support, actions on the ground in Europe told another story. Nonstate actors in finance working in concert with American diplomats aided the Union cause across continental Europe. Among other things, kinship and religious networks on the part of merchants, bankers, emigrants, and others who publicized and championed the Union cause provided the nexus for international investment during the Civil War.

In particular, German investment in American bonds relied heavily on economic and social relationships between merchants on both sides of the Atlantic and immigrants communicating with loved ones in their native German states. The U.S. vice consul in Frankfurt perhaps stated it best when he remarked, "Since the population of the country has become more confident in America, by reading from relations or acquaintances, who have emigrated to our country, the high rate of interest has been exercised more than in any others." Nonstate actors proved critical in selling the war, and by extension Union debt, to the German people. The market in Union bonds stabilized and then accelerated, providing a powerful imprimatur on the Union war effort as an international financial effort. All told, several hundred million dollars' worth of these bonds made their way across the Atlantic and were sold in a vibrant secondary market. While Britain was the primary financial hub for American bond sales in the antebellum period, the underappreciated continental sales in the Netherlands and especially the German states constituted the more critical market during the American Civil War itself. For the German states, the political connections to the revolutions of 1848 and the growth of the capital market in Frankfurt in particular portended a transformation in European capital markets. Frankfurt's reliance on the government bond market and close coordination with Dutch bankers made Frankfurt and Amsterdam the primary markets for American debt during the American Civil War. Frankfurt leaders constructed a privileged financial system within the established market (a market within a market) that played a key role in the sale of Union debt in the city. The financial legitimacy of the United States during the Civil War depended upon the support of the German and Dutch bankers, and critically, the everyday citizens of these regions.[2]

The failed 1848 revolution in the German states led to widespread migration to America. These German immigrants in time gravitated toward the Republican Party and its antislavery and free labor message. When coupled with the anti-aristocratic sentiment of these immigrants from their days in Europe, the antagonism toward the Confederacy was palpable. This hostility for the Confederacy fueled American bond sales abroad and boosted support for the American cause on the Continent. By supporting the Union, Europeans of all classes reinforced the validity of the American political experiment and thereby fueled domestic bond sales as well. Such investments and relationships forged during the war and based on shared ideology, kinship, and faith-based arrangements—coupled with pursuit of profits—also played an important role in the postwar period, when such partnerships fashioned formal syndicates to sell postwar bonds.[3]

Studying international bond sales during the Civil War does not come without significant difficulty. Whereas the ledgers housed at the National Archives carry meticulous records of initial purchases, subsequent purchases on the secondary market become much more difficult to trace. Furthermore, Wall Street financial firms could hold bonds on behalf of international clients, so some physical bonds never traveled overseas. Other bonds made their way overseas to cities like London, Paris, Frankfurt, Amsterdam, Brussels, and Munich. Depending on the country, the sales took place either on the exchange or via informal "off-exchange" markets. Despite the opaque nature of international sales, the mere fact that foreign exchanges quoted American debt—and even came to incorporate midday quotations on the exchanges—reveals an active and dynamic market.[4]

Despite international investment's critical importance in establishing and legitimizing Union bonds as a worthy investment, Americans stateside debated such investment in the American Civil War at length. Secretary of the Treasury Salmon Chase remarked that a foreign loan helped to ensure the sanctity of American credit while simultaneously downplaying the severity of the crisis at hand. "All hopes and all fears that the existing rebellion will result in a dismemberment of the American Republic are alike groundless," Chase stated, "and that whatever else may happen, the good faith of the American people . . . will be hereafter, as heretofore scrupulously maintained." The passage of the July 1861 initial loan bill included a provision for $50 million of the bill in a direct European loan. Chase vacillated on the issue during his tenure and by the summer of 1864 seemed content to support a foreign loan, even though doing so, he told Horace Greeley, "galls me." Chase's successor, William Pitt Fessenden, demonstrated initial interest in pursuing an international loan separate from the Treasury-authorized bond issues, but by the fall of 1864 his opinion on the matter had soured, even leading him to declare in December 1864, "This nation has been able, thus far, to conduct a domestic war of unparalleled magnitude and cost without appealing for aid to any foreign people."

Thus at least publicly there remained reticence to call on foreign investors for a sponsored loan (outside secondary sales) and a belief remained that domestic sales alone would suffice for the sake of the Union war effort.[5]

Civil War general and New York City Democratic Party politician Daniel Sickles also advocated for a foreign loan, but emphasized the power of a widely held bond issue abroad—in essence building on the domestic tactics employed by Cooke. Writing from New Orleans, Sickles exclaimed, "Our bonds should be placed within the reach of our friends in Europe by a popular arrangement that will enable the producing class to buy them in small amounts—by means of pamphlets, friendly journals, and advertisements, the inducement of a fair commission held and to judicious agents—the excellence of the security and ample return in the way of interest would be made apparent to our friends and to all who like a proposition & safe investment . . . The same could be done in Germany and probably in France." Little did Sickles and others know that financial houses abroad were already undertaking such activity. Initially, however, all eyes looked toward England—the nation that had financially supported the United States through the late antebellum period.[6]

England

England served as the first European market of interest, and at the outset of hostilities Northerners viewed it as the market of greatest importance to both financial and diplomatic circles. "English sympathy is very apt to follow English Capital," financier William Aspinwall remarked. "This is one good political reason for placing bonds in Europe." Union officials remained well aware of the fact that any hope of international support on behalf of the Union (or the Confederacy for that matter) remained heavily tied to the financial interests of the City of London. Any efforts on the part of Parliament at Westminster would be linked closely to the actions of the bankers a few miles to the east—and relied upon several key members of Parliament who also comprised the financial elite of London. Additionally, the actions of Britain would have a powerful impact on France and Napoleon III's approach to the war. As far as Washington was concerned, British actions held the key to Confederate recognition and the financial coffers associated with such an action.[7]

In 1861, international investors found the situation compounded because of divided loyalties over their antebellum investments. The firm of Brown Brothers perhaps embodied this most clearly. Brown Brothers, which maintained a partnership house in Liverpool, was one of many American banks with deep transatlantic ties. Baltimore-based Brown Brothers partner Frances A. Hamilton wrote to fellow partner James Brown, located in New York City, in the fall of 1862 pleading for the American houses to restrict their commitments to American securities and emphasizing the importance of collective decision making between partners on both sides of the ocean. Hamilton criticized the American houses for their support of the Union and asked that a "little leniency" be reserved for those who viewed the war as a campaign of "subjugation" against the South. Hamilton also emphasized a desire for "a free and full interchange of thought and suggestions" connected to their partnership. American financial institutions were well aware of the delicate balancing act in the war's early years when it came to demonstrating support for the cause while simultaneously maintaining connections with transatlantic partners.[8]

The famous British banking house of N. M. Rothschild & Sons largely governed the British market. Their American agent based in New York, August Belmont, proved crucial to these negotiations. Having been the Rothschild financial agent in New York for nearly twenty-five years by the time of the Civil War, Belmont's influence over international financial support proved valuable to Secretary Chase. Belmont claimed early on that little interest existed in a formal European loan—in fact it was "not at all propitious." Belmont wanted to support the Union war effort, most especially because, as an active antebellum Democrat, he needed to tack with the political winds if he wished to remain cozy with the administration. Belmont emphasized his comparative advantage of financial diplomacy, particularly on the question of how to forestall foreign recognition of (and thereby loans to) the Confederacy. The May 6, 1861, declaration of British Foreign Secretary Lord John Russell to treat Confederate privateers as belligerents (which opened the possibility of eventual Confederate recognition) provided Belmont with the excuse to begin a lengthy conversation with his London banking associate Baron Lionel Nathan de Rothschild, who also represented the City of London as a Member of Parliament in the House of Commons. "An interference, or one sided neutrality such as foreshadowed by Lord John Russell's speech," Belmont warned, "can only prolong the fratricidal war and entail ruin not only upon both sections of our Country, but upon the material interests and commerce of the world." Belmont was usually at his best when making arguments like these that made the self-interested position seem also the righteous one.[9]

The precarious state of Union finances at the war's outset also weighed on Belmont's mind. An incomplete recovery from the Panic of 1857 and uncertainty over the future of the United States led most investors (foreign and domestic) to shy away from federal securities. Confederate securities ranked higher in the bond market early in the war owing to the power of cotton as collateral. The immediacy of the situation became readily apparent when five days after Fort Sumter the Confederate Congress authorized a $50 million loan raised through a combination of the sale of 8 percent bonds and non-interest-bearing Treasury notes. Belmont immediately went on the offensive with his London counterparts to dissuade them from pursuing such an investment by singling out several Confederate states that had repudiated their debts in the antebellum period. "Who will take a dollar of a Confederacy of States," Belmont exhorted, "of which 4 have already repudiated their debt and the remaining five will in less than three months be in default of their semiannual dividend?" Belmont lambasted the ulterior motives of the Palmerston government to MP Rothschild. "If the cotton supply is at the bottom of this unaccountable policy [of British intervention], then, I must say that it is a very shortsighted one and one which must bring untold ruin and desolation upon the material interests of both hemispheres." Four days later, Belmont reiterated his fears of English intervention further by dangling the moral hazard of slavery. "This cursed poison of slavery," Belmont determined, "will be fostered as a political and social institution upon this continent from the Chesapeake to the Cordilleras if the British Government continues in the course which it has begun." Belmont's concerns over British support for the Confederacy played a large role in shaping his actions in the early months of the Lincoln administration.[10]

The importance of the British market placed great pressure on the United States and partners in the City of London. To facilitate these investments, Belmont opened a dialogue with Secretary Chase and Secretary of State William Seward about the feasibility of a foreign loan to the federal government. Belmont remained highly skeptical of a foreign loan's viability among European banks, and he was certainly aware that Chase could not send a government Treasury agent abroad to test the waters without making the Union appear unsteady, which would have disastrous ramifications on the already shaky American securities market. Obtaining European financial support for the Union without demonstrating desperation on the part of the Lincoln administration became the challenge. Belmont believed himself to be in a position to aid the administration in just such a task. Given his preexisting plans to travel to Europe (for his wife's health), he suggested an arrangement wherein he traveled abroad with the authority to negotiate a foreign loan on behalf of the United States government should the opportunity present itself. Few eyebrows would be raised as travel plans had already been made and the condition of his wife was well known in the inner financial circles. The plan received

A circa 1855 photograph of New York City financier August Belmont. Although prominent in national Democratic Party circles, Belmont initially attempted to assist the Republican Lincoln administration with floating and selling Union bonds in Europe owing to his close connections with the financial house Rothschilds. (Brady-Handy Photograph Collection, Prints and Photographs Division, Library of Congress, LC-DIG-cwpbh-02773)

the approval of Chase and Seward and on June 17, 1861, Belmont boarded the steamer *Persia* out of New York Harbor, bound for England as the voice of an administration he had vowed to defeat just eight months prior.[11]

Belmont's mission on behalf of the Lincoln administration struggled from the outset and revealed the lack of appetite for American debt among British bankers in the early days of the conflict. In London, Belmont secured an hour-long audience with Prime Minister Palmerston, who quickly cut to the chase—"We do not like slavery, but we want cotton." In other words, the British government (and financial institutions) remained wary of Union securities and their potential impact on relationships with Southern cotton firms (both during the war and in a potential postwar Southern nation). Belmont heard the same message as he traveled through France and the German-speaking states. At the end of his tour he made the situation abundantly clear to Chase—the European market (at least in 1861) proved unfavorable for Union securities as long as cotton remained a precious commodity and the South the prime supplier.[12]

The precarious nature of the war across the Atlantic and potential intervention on the part of the British, French, or both powers was not lost on prominent European houses. In a confidential letter from the London branch of the Rothschilds to the Paris house in December 1861, serious discussion emerged over moving all American-held assets to the Frankfurt house. Nathan Rothschild's comment to the head of Paris operations (his brother James) to redirect these assets reflected a desire "to guard against the risk of confiscation in case of war . . . it might be more secure to put the stocks into the name of our Frankfurt house." No other correspondence seems to reflect this shift and regrettably little of the Frankfurt house records survive, but even this single letter reveals the awareness on the part of the Rothschilds of possible intervention by the two major European powers.[13]

Once word of Belmont's efforts leaked, he appeared of little use to the Lincoln administration, having failed to smooth the way for foreign loans. Republican journalists continued to remember him primarily as chair of the Democratic National Committee, and he was swept up in charges of disloyalty that ran the gamut from being a mere copperhead to actively encouraging Confederate bond purchases in Europe. Meanwhile, more moderate Democrats criticized him for his seeming lukewarmness on the question of Union, while Peace Democrats lambasted him for being a "traitor" to his own party. Belmont donned the title of a political "outsider" for more bigoted reasons as well: The *Chicago Tribune* ran an article critical of any "dishonorable peace" designed to "enrich the Belmonts, the Rothschilds, and the whole tribe of Jews." Still another damning anti-Semitic and politically critical remark came from former president James Buchanan. In the midst of the war, Buchanan stated, "What can be expected from a party at the head of which is a speculating German jew." The prominent New Yorker George Templeton Strong offered a stinging critique in his own diary when he remarked that Belmont "well deserves hanging as an ally of the rebellion." The anti-Semitism that permeated the arguments of Belmont's numerous detractors only furthered the general hostility.[14]

Even the patient Lincoln turned on Belmont. Although Lincoln initially appreciated the efforts of Belmont on behalf of the Union cause, he soured on the German financier whose criticism of Union war policy included a barb directed at the president regarding an "intermeddling of civilians in military affairs." Such language ended the correspondence between Belmont and Lincoln, perhaps not coincidently as the North moved toward the midterm elections of 1862. Although the Democratic Party made gains at the state and national levels in the midterms, they failed to unseat Republican majorities in Congress. Such success made Belmont a useful ally for the Republican administration, but Belmont likewise had his own interests at heart.[15]

Belmont's overriding goal always remained the health of his financial house. Interestingly, he had more confidence in the Union than did his superiors, Rothschild & Sons, who refused (as a firm) to underwrite the war effort. Even so, Belmont began to purchase 5-20s on behalf of his own house and Rothschild personal accounts in the spring of 1864 on both the New York and London Stock Exchanges (depending on his location). In a three-week span he purchased $250,000 of 5-20 bonds and by the fall he added to the bond portfolio through purchases from brokers such as Peter Cazenove and Co. of London ($350,000); the Amsterdam banking agent for the Rothschilds, Becker and Fuld ($140,000); as well as smaller purchases from Behrens and Sons, Helbert Wagg and Co., and L. Cohen and Sons. Many of these firms also made sales on behalf of Belmont, especially on the Amsterdam exchange. By the end of 1864, Belmont's investments on behalf of the firm in U.S. government securities had brought in profits of over £5,000 pounds apiece for him & Nathan Rothschild (roughly $50,000 each in 1864 dollars). Despite the inability to convince the London Rothschilds to actively invest in the Northern cause, August Belmont fared much better with Baron James de Rothschild—head of the Paris house—whom Belmont later claimed was one of the most active investors in the Northern cause overseas from the start. By the summer of 1862, Belmont and James de Rothschild engaged in extensive business in United States debt not only for the French house, but for their clients as well.

James de Rothschild even convinced prominent Russian political thinker Alexander Herzen to invest in U.S. securities.[16]

Other financial houses in London invested early in the conflict. In addition to the Rothschilds, George Peabody and J. S. Morgan undertook extensive investment in the Union bond market. The two Americans focused on the potential of these sales in the early months of the conflict while they found themselves separated by an ocean. "It may so happen," wrote Peabody in July 1861, "that you have an opportunity of taking on advantageous terms some of the new loans for which the United States Govt will soon ask." Peabody at this point authorized an initial investment of $200,000 in whatever new bond issue emerged. Once the American expatriate bankers found themselves back in London, Peabody and Morgan's investments escalated in the spring of 1862 (significantly earlier than other international investments in the cause) and carried forward through the course of the war, gradually amounting to millions of dollars' of investment in the 5-20 bonds (not to mention sizable investment in the national loan of 1861 and 7-30 notes). Interestingly, the firm created a personal wire service to provide word from Liverpool regarding events in America as reported by transatlantic ships. Thus, the firm had the edge over other London houses that had to wait for news to be set in type by the London press. Peabody & Co. used its quicker access to information to turn tidy profits.[17]

Peabody wasted little time in making his investments on behalf of the Union. On April 14, 1862, George Peabody's firm purchased $2,000 in 5-20s—a small investment that was followed by a purchase of $5,000 just five days later and a larger investment of $49,000 on May 14, 1862, for a total of $56,000 in 5-20s by mid-May 1862. The firm followed this up with at least $60,000 in additional purchases by year's end. The year 1863 included at least $200,000 worth of 5-20 purchases, and the house bought even bigger in 1864, investing at least $653,500 more in 5-20s in the final quarter of the year alone. The final months of the war and the subsequent years tallied millions more worth of investments in the 5-20s and other American securities. These investments on the part of Peabody and Morgan represented one of the largest, if not the largest, investments in American securities in Britain during the American Civil War. It did, however, represent only a small percentage of the overall 5-20 issue. Such purchases on the part of the firm within three months of the initial bond issue as part of the Legal Tender Act legislation revealed a distinct commitment to, and confidence in, the Union.[18]

Whereas Jay Cooke went out of his way to ensure that American bonds sold at a minimum on par (in some cases legislation mandated this be the

This statue of American financier George Peabody is located next to the Royal Exchange in the City of London. The statue was unveiled in July 1869 shortly before Peabody's death. Peabody played a prominent role in purchasing American debt out of his London house during the Civil War and the early postwar period. A replica of this statue is located in the east garden of Mount Vernon Place in Baltimore, Maryland. (Photo by the author)

case), bonds overseas sold below par on all European exchanges during the war. Amsterdam-based Rothschild banking agents Becker & Fuld wrote daily reports to London detailing 5-20 quotes on the Amsterdam exchange. In 1863, for instance, 5-20 bonds fluctuated between $64\frac{1}{4}$ and $72\frac{1}{2}$—certainly below par (even when factoring in a slightly different valuation owing to bills of exchange) but advantageous for the firm who purchased the securities for their own portfolio as well as for selling to other firms such as August

Belmont and Co. (the name of August Belmont's stand-alone financial firm in New York City). Such below-par sales, however, can be misleading. On a practical level, these bonds issued in dollars involved transactions in local currency and utilized exchange rates that tended to fluctuate on currency, despite a clear exchange rate with gold. Thus, while European quotes of American securities were always below par during the war years, when properly exchanged (based on dollar pegged to gold) they often operated at a premium to New York markets. Nevertheless, European confidence, in whatever form, however below par, helped to create and sustain American confidence.[19]

Domestic financier Jay Cooke made a small overture for foreign sales in Britain in late 1863. William Evans, an English financier, sold a small portion of bonds ($30,000) abroad at the behest of British politician John Bright. For Cooke, such an endeavor was an exception to his otherwise domestic financial pursuits during the war itself. Evans continued to make sales on behalf of the Cookes. In September 1864, following the prompt sale of $100,000 worth of 5-20s, Evans wrote to Cooke to speak of the prospect of further European sales. "Demand on the continent for your gov't securities is wonderful," exclaimed Evans; more tellingly, he ended the letter by telling Cooke, "Perhaps, they [U.S. government] will follow your advice and avail themselves of the offers of the German bankers." Such a statement might reflect a change of heart for Cooke when it came to foreign investment. Initially, Cooke chose not to actively promote foreign sales as a true path of revenue for the federal government, at least not in the war's early years. For the most part Cooke really did restrict his focus domestically, despite any rhetoric otherwise—a stark contrast to his postwar rail career when he hawked bonds in Europe.[20]

Once the benefits and interest in foreign sales became apparent, the Cookes and many others began to heartily endorse such an approach, at least in theory. Corresponding in August 1864 from Paris following travels throughout Europe, Henry Cooke wrote to his brother Jay noting that a massive opportunity for foreign investment had been missed. "There was never a finer opportunity," lamented Henry, "for safe operations on a large or small scale with good margins in gold paid in advance." Henry went on to say that bankers made offers to him for purchases of 5-20 bonds in excess of $20 million, but he only committed to $100,000 in sales up to this point (via the British banking house Barings) and awaited further consultation with his brother upon his imminent return to the States. By 1865, Jay Cooke had been sold on the power of international sales. "If we go into the agency matter," he wrote Henry, "we must at once lay on plans to cover the whole world. France & California included." But by the time he completed his transformation, other banking houses largely headquartered abroad pursued a brisk business in overseas bond sales of Union debt.[21]

Beyond London, the city of Liverpool also proved of great importance to the Union financial cause. The port city, a massive center for slave trading and cotton shipments destined for the mills of Lancashire, served as a key location for the Union and Confederate causes alike, pitting respective diplomats against one another in their attempts to curry favor in the important city. U.S. Consul Thomas Haines Dudley arrived in Liverpool in 1861 and quickly set to work counteracting Confederate efforts, which were already underway. The floating and placement of a Confederate loan in 1863 via the Paris banking house Erlanger was a source of immense irritation for Dudley. In December 1862, Dudley wrote to Secretary of State Seward regarding the early indications of Confederate loans in Britain. "Referring to previous dispatch and the raising of money for the Rebels on Confederate bonds in England I have now to report that there is no doubt about the matter," Dudley solemnly reported. He added, "From what I learn seven hundred thousand pounds sterling have been raised." "Perhaps," Dudley concluded most ominously, "the worst feature about it [the bond issue] is that every man who holds a bond has an interest in the success of the Confederacy. It is just that much stock invested in the concern, if it succeeds the bonds are good, if it fails they are worthless, that is the war, they will regard it and will use all their means and efforts to secure its success." By December 1862, Dudley confirmed that a £3 million bond issue had been successfully placed, thereby raising funds for the Confederacy. Nevertheless, Dudley worked tirelessly with a group of informants (as well as American ambassador to Brussels Henry Sanford) to undercut Confederate financial efforts in England. Police officers and other individuals for hire brought information to Dudley's attention that could then be directed to the British government in an effort to quash the construction of ships for the Confederate cause. While Union bonds did not flourish in Liverpool, the market remained vital to understanding British markets writ large.[22]

Concerns also arose in Liverpool regarding the prospect of counterfeiting of bonds, bills, and Treasury notes that could make their way across the ocean to the United States. Dudley voiced his concerns on the matter as early as January 1862. "A man residing in Liverpool called on me this day and informs me that certain parties in this place and London are now engaged in counterfeiting US treasury bills," reported Dudley. "The business is being conducted upon an intensive scale; and that large quantities of them will be issued here and circulated and also sent to the United States." Dudley wrote of similar concerns in the fall of 1862, this time in regard to counterfeiters working in Dublin, Ireland, who were about to embark for the United States. As aptly demonstrated by Stephen Mihm, the world of counterfeit U.S. bills at the state and now federal level proved a constant thorn in the side of government officials. This world of illicit funds, be they money or specie, reflected additional challenges the government faced in a war that extended beyond the borders of the United States.[23]

The primacy of Britain for bond sales had been the focus of the American government in the first eighteen months of the conflict. The efforts to sell bonds proved fairly widespread—even Karl Marx purportedly purchased bonds in 1864 while living in London. But the stain of enslavement made many firms hesitant to invest heavily in Union debt. Even the Emancipation Proclamation and a shift in war aims on the part of the United States did little to noticeably increase investment before the end of the war. While some firms such as Peabody and Morgan with clear American ties invested in the Union cause, the relative silence on the part of the major financial players in the city spoke volumes. For the United States to meet with financial success during the war, it would need to look elsewhere on the continent of Europe.[24]

France

While a limited market for securities sales, France was invaluable as a source of information for financial machinations on the Continent and evidence of the power of rumor to expose market volatility. Emperor Napoleon III banning the sale of American securities on formal French exchanges only furthered the subversive tactics undertaken by the representatives of the United States. The U.S. Consul to Paris, John Bigelow (himself a bondholder courtesy of George Peabody), wrote regularly to Secretary of State Seward. Confederate efforts to inflate French (and by extension European) markets in their favor through false information or deliberate sabotage of U.S. securities greatly concerned Bigelow. In September 1863, Bigelow wrote to Seward: "There was a lively excitement produced at the Bourse on Saturday by a rumour that the emperor had recognized the South. The agitation was so great that the Minister of Foreign Affairs had to have posters put up contradicting the report. No doubt the report was issued with a view of testing the effect of such a measure upon the public. If so the inquirer seemed to have a received a prompt reply."[25]

The spread of rumors on the part of Confederate agents to inflate their off-market bond sales (and likewise depress U.S. bonds) became a common occurrence in France during the American Civil War. The delicate work behind the scenes of American diplomats and their respective agents therefore proved all the more vital to the success of the Union cause and messaging in Europe. Additional (false) rumors regarding a naval battle between the USS *Kearsarge* and the CSS *Florida* served the purpose of "having the double design of raising the price of American freights and confederate bonds." Bigelow also spoke of counterfeiting concerns. In reference to counterfeiting taking place in France and efforts being made there to combat the problem, Bigelow proposed that the United States invest in patenting a French product that had proven successful as an anti-counterfeiting measure. Such evidence reinforced the power that these bonds held in the international arena and the possibilities that counterfeiting afforded. Reports of agents leaving Paris with millions in greenbacks (real and counterfeit) to upend the American economy were but one of many rumors that Bigelow relayed to Washington. Even if bond transactions on the formal exchange remained illegal in France, the financial underworld proved a whole other matter for Bigelow to counteract.[26]

Bigelow did not act alone in promoting American interests in France during the war. William Dayton, the United States ambassador to France, wrote to Secretary of State Seward in November 1863 regarding what in his mind was a promising opportunity. Penned the night before Seward accompanied Abraham Lincoln to the dedication of a new national cemetery in Gettysburg, Pennsylvania, where the president would make "a few appropriate remarks," Dayton confided in Seward that an American-friendly bank in Paris (Monroe & Co.) was open to selling Confederate bonds on behalf of the Union. Bonds that had fallen into the hands of the U.S. government could be sold in Paris outside of the public exchanges by the "reliable and loyal" bank of Monroe & Co., which had numerous "applications for the purchase of Confederate bonds." "Why not sell their Bonds, as you sell their cotton for what they will bring?" asked Dayton, who envisioned that such sales at prices well below par would further cripple the credit of the Confederate States abroad. While no response from Seward exists in the archival records, this nevertheless demonstrated efforts floated by members of the U.S. government abroad to undermine Confederate financial strength and diplomatic leverage. Indeed, two could play at the disinformation game.[27]

Bigelow took a proactive role with the French press as a representative of the federal government, forming a close relationship with financial writer André Cochut. Cochut, whom Bigelow referred to as "a faithful friend to the United States," wrote extensively on the conflict and the financial repercussions as the financial writer for *Le Temps* (Time) and *Revue des Deux Mondes*

(Review of Two Worlds). *Le Temps* circulated widely throughout Paris and contained numerous pieces written in support of the Union cause. Bigelow seized the opportunity and reach of the newspaper, offering to feed Cochut information—thereby making Cochut an unofficial mouthpiece of the U.S. government.[28]

In one of his most famous pieces in September 1862, Cochut's "Les Finances des Ètats Unis" outlined how the Union had financed the war to that point and the need for a strong North to ensure an economic partnership with France in the years to come. "There is one thing that became as necessary to Europe as cotton," declared Cochut. "They are 'food stuffs,' the *bread stuffs*, as they say in America, and the northern states have the privilege of producing them." The power of Northern wheat and other foodstuffs reflected the intricate and increasingly important ties between the two regions. Cochut also praised the Union bond efforts, noting that early sales of the 6 percent bonds (these could be 5-20s or '81 National Loan) had raised over a billion francs in capital.[29]

In December 1862, Cochut wrote a two-part piece on the respective financial situations of North and South. Entitled "La Situation Aux Ètats-Unis," it provided detailed figures and built on Cochut's broader piece from September of the same year. Perhaps most importantly, the piece foretold an ominous postwar order if the fight did not end soon. In the Northern half of the piece Cochut opined:

> The conclusion if one takes the point of view of European interests is that the Confederates are not a nation, whatever may have been said, but just an army, ably commanded, valiant and patient: the fight extends the army unevenly that his defeat is only a matter of time. Encouraging slavery by semblances of sympathy was a political mistake among statesmen, an aberration of the moral sense of individuals. Industrial prosperity of Europe will not recover, there will be raw cotton factories and selling when the North has taken decidedly top products, when American democracy will be put in this broad way that leads to such great destinies.

The sense of inevitability on Cochut's part regarding a Confederate defeat, coupled with the political miscalculation of maintaining slavery, loomed large in his mind. The economic precarity that also existed informed the decision making of French elites in government as they explored what cotton production may look like in a post-slave South. Cochut's ideas provided a singular view on the matter, but nevertheless impacted larger segments of the French population through the circulation of his articles. The words of

Cochut, aided by Consul Bigelow, undoubtedly impacted French circles as much as rumor and speculation on the part of Confederate agents.[30]

Such remarks on the part of Cochut caught the attention of individuals stateside—perhaps most notably the Cookes. Referring to the work of Cochut, Henry Cooke remarked, "His ideas are clear and comprehensive and I know you would be pleased with him. Should we ever undertake a foreign negotiation he would be of great use to us, as he has the entrée to columns of the leading journals of Paris." American bond sales in France met with significant challenges from both the French government as well as Confederate collaborators in Paris. As Stève Sainlaude has recently demonstrated, Napoleon III sympathized with and even advocated for a Confederate South. While Napoleon III's foreign minister tempered some of the statements coming from the emperor, his actions at home reinforced some of these Confederate sympathies. Napoleon III banned American debt sales in France, but there were ways around it. For instance, Paris financial house Hottinguer & Cie used London-based Barings to conduct purchases of American debt for the bank and its clients. While the Barings registers do not reveal all the various clients of Hottinguer, they nevertheless do demonstrate efforts on the part of at least one prominent French bank on numerous occasions working around government constraints. Still, the issue remained: If Britain and France remained largely out of range for Union bond investment, where could the Union and its allies turn? To that end, the German states became an especially appealing market.[31]

German States

Despite the allure of the London and Paris financial markets, the primacy of Union bond sales abroad centered on the German states. Frankfurt emerged as a financial capital of the mid-nineteenth century and became the sovereign debt market of greatest importance for the United States. In the wake of the 1848 revolutions that swept Europe, Frankfurt became the political and economic capital of the German states at a time when Germany itself was not a unified state. For many Americans, Frankfurt symbolized liberalism and democracy. Such an atmosphere fostered extensive ties between the North and the region by the time of the Civil War. In addition, connections between the regions centered on extensive migration from the German states to the northern part of the United States, especially that emanating from Frankfurt and the surrounding region. Between 1850 and 1860, approximately 1.1 million immigrants arrived from the German states in America. Of those 1.1 million, approximately 25 percent emigrated from Frankfurt and its environs. As historian Patrick Gaul points out, the city of Frankfurt also became a point of interest for Americans traveling abroad: by 1864, 222 Americans called Frankfurt home.[32]

But the true value in Frankfurt for American financial aspirations lay in state actors working in concert with nonstate actors. The commercial and financial nature of Frankfurt facilitated bond sales among the German people. Transatlantic connections that predated the war helped to enable bankers, merchants, and journalists on either side of the Atlantic to build a financial infrastructure that exceeded all expectations for the United States at the outset of the war. The growth in German holding of American debt not only enabled American success during the war, but also fostered financial relations in the postwar period. As historian Benjamin Hein has recently posited, Frankfurt also rose to financial prominence during this time owing to two government bond markets effectively operating separately from one another. The public stock exchange, or *Börse*, served alongside a private arrangement in Frankfurt that morphed over the course of the nineteenth century. By the time of the American Civil War it went by the name *Effecten-Societät*. This private enterprise, accessible only to the wealthiest financiers and their allies, enabled a market to emerge that led to coordination in some of their efforts pertaining to government securities before reaching the more public venue of the Börse. Such actions enabled what Benjamin Hein has referred to as "market segregation" that proved incredibly consequential for bond sales in Frankfurt. In essence, the Effecten-Societät enabled a mechanism wherein Frankfurt financiers colluded on bond sales. These entities operated separate from the infamous alley or curb exchanges located outside of virtually every major European bourse at the time period. The curbside *Winkelbörsen* in Frankfurt mirrored others in London, Paris, Amsterdam, and beyond that tended to attract more lowbrow clientele. The Effecten-Societät in essence operated as a private exchange for the buying and selling of debt. In turn, these financiers and their allies could coordinate actions on the exchange proper.[33]

The decade prior to the Civil War proved one of tremendous economic growth in Frankfurt, and this growth centered in part on a significant increase in the sovereign debt market—of which American debt played a sizable role. The half a billion dollars' worth of American securities that made their way to Europe in the five-year period between 1849 and 1854 led to tremendous growth in the American portfolios of various Frankfurt-based institutions and the profile of Frankfurt as a whole. Such growth generated greater financial awareness within the city—especially as it pertained to foreign investments and the "savings of a new middle class." By the eve of the Civil War, investments in government bonds in Frankfurt had become a phenomenon among particular parts of the educated class of the city. By 1861, 4,000 Frankfurters worked in the world of finance in some shape or form as American securities became increasingly more prominent in the city. *Der Aktionar* (The Shareholder) even remarked, "Without having any benchmarks for the value or worthlessness of these papers, they bought everything that was recommended from New York and sent to their customers by German retailers on this recommendation." Speculation and profit ran in tandem for those in Frankfurt and beyond in the 1850s. By the latter part of the decade, U.S. securities became an attractive investment in the German states, ranging from state debt to municipal debt and beyond. The German ties to New York appeared to deepen. Family members worked in financial firms in New York upon arrival and coordinated with actors across the Atlantic in Frankfurt. Demand for and interest in American stock grew so much that three hundred individuals founded the "Central Committee of American fund owners." This organization relied on prominent Frankfurt bankers to promote American business interests and proved a vital ally of the United States when war broke out in the spring of 1861. The fact that bankers such as Leopold Sonnemann (who also owned the pro-Union newspaper *Neue Frankfurter Zeitung*) served as members of the Committee only reinforced its powerful hold on capital investment moving forward. A May 1861 newspaper column written prior to the receipt of news of Fort Sumter warned that a Civil War "must scare us financially." The war, therefore, had an acute resonance in Frankfurt as military fortunes thousands of miles away would have repercussions on the exchange.[34]

The importance of American representation in Frankfurt seemed lost on Abraham Lincoln as he considered a consul general for Frankfurt. William Walton Murphy, a Michigan-born lawyer, found himself appointed to the position despite having never left the country prior to his departure for Frankfurt. Although Murphy was not well traveled, he did not lack political astuteness. A fellow diplomat referred to Murphy as a "wirepuller" who would be able to adapt to the needs of the federal government in Frankfurt by working his way into the inner circle of the city's financial elite. The free city had distinguished itself from the likes of Berlin and Vienna, which were centered on more courtly arrangements. Frankfurt, by contrast, found itself first and foremost as a commercial center and therefore public diplomacy was conducted through the financiers of the city. Financial support through debt investment was but one way to guide the Union cause.[35]

United States representation in Frankfurt struggled in the early months of the war. Murphy's predecessor, Samuel Ricker, hailed from Louisiana. An avowed Confederate sympathizer, many accused Ricker of providing pro-Confederate articles to local newspapers and more than one consul in another German state called for Ricker's removal. Murphy's ascension to the role of consul still came with a lag time as Murphy crossed the Atlantic to take up his station. Ricker endeavored to send Murphy on a long trip throughout the German states in an effort to undermine his work in Frankfurt itself. Additionally, Ricker purchased and outfitted a blockade runner following his tenure in Frankfurt that brought weapons and gunpowder into the Confederacy. Murphy's arrival in November 1861 ended Ricker's tenure, but Ricker remained in the employ of a Frankfurt bank and would become a thorn in the side of Murphy as he attempted to forge a new identity for the Union's consul general in Frankfurt.[36]

As Murphy assumed his position in November 1861, he came to rely upon a community within Frankfurt of Germans and non-Germans alike that could help him not only bridge a language barrier, but also provide legitimacy to the financial claims that Murphy brought forth. Frankfurt-born emigres to America served as some of Murphy's earliest allies in his new position. When August Belmont returned to his native city in 1861, he expressed at length the financial needs of the Union and the role that prominent German banking houses could play. Belmont spoke with his superiors in the Frankfurt home of the financial behemoth Rothschild and enticed them to be early purchasers of United States debt issued during the war. Belmont also made the rounds of other financial houses in the city.[37]

Gustav Körners served perhaps a more important role in persuading the financial community of Frankfurt. Unlike Belmont, Körners came from a staunchly antislavery background, having been an early member of the Republican Party. He was a close confidant of Abraham Lincoln and was pivotal to Lincoln's ascension to the Republican nomination in 1860. After successfully raising a regiment in his adopted state of Illinois, Körners found himself appointed as the new consul to Spain in the spring of 1862. While in transit to Spain, Körners returned to Frankfurt. Körners had escaped the German states (allegedly in women's attire) following the failed student uprising of 1833 to bring democracy to a unified German state. Nearly thirty years later, Körners returned to his hometown for the first time since evading his arrest for treason. Körners wrote back to the United States in the fall of 1862 to detail his success with Frankfurt's bankers. "I convinced them," Körners wrote in a letter to Lyman Trumball, "that here there is no danger of our defeat, and consequent insolvency." Murphy also relied on August Gläser, his consulate secretary who was a holdover from the previous consul. Gläser would prove invaluable to Murphy's success in Frankfurt on behalf of the Union cause.[38]

Murphy took his charge seriously. Writing to Secretary of State Seward in the winter of 1861–62, he stated, "Our cause is to win and conquer public opinion by its own intrinsic justice, while the Southerners are able to avail themselves of the assistance of the world bewitching medium: cash." Murphy therefore utilized his position as consul in Frankfurt to leverage powerful stakeholders in the city to promote the cause of Union. In order to demonstrate his commitment, Murphy held a series of events to foster support for the United States in the summer of 1862. On July 4, 1862, Murphy invited "all Americans and friends of the United States living in Frankfurt and surrounding areas" to a local inn to celebrate Independence Day. Speakers read the Declaration of Independence in English and German before the crowd consumed the large spread of food and drink made available to the hundred-plus gathered in attendance. Less than two weeks later, a second and even larger event occurred, drawing on individuals from the German states, but also Switzerland and the Netherlands. The Frankfurt Bundesschiessen, or "shooting festival," served as a platform to inform the European peoples on happenings in the United States tied to the "civil dispute." At the festival, Murphy gave a lengthy address to recognize German-born soldiers serving in the Union army and his hopes for a united Germany. The affair certainly had the effect of uniting those present against the Confederacy. "Their opponents are also our opponents" one speaker from Baden remarked. To be sure, the state of affairs in Frankfurt tracked the military fortunes of the Union armies. The incorrectly perceived setback at the battle of Shiloh in April 1862 had as much of an impact on finance as that of the great victory of the capture of New Orleans later that month. By the summer of 1862, as Union forces approached the gates of the Confederate capital of Richmond, Murphy could report, "The feeling in favor of the Union [was] constantly increasing, notwithstanding the agony like efforts of Southern agents to misrepresent the rapid progress of our cause for the restoration of the Union."[39]

By 1863, such actions paid dividends. Murphy reported to Seward that the demand for bonds on the German secondary market proved "so extensive as generally to exceed the supplies in the market." Such interest in the German states accelerated following the Union victories at Gettysburg and Vicksburg in July 1863. "The transactions in U.S. bonds," Murphy reported that summer, "assumed, in fact, an astonishing extent." The activity in Europe more broadly spiked beginning in the fall of 1863, largely owing to the rumor that a large

German bank would float a loan to the federal government—something that would create a snowball effect of further financial support for the North. Such activity led on September 10, 1863, to the official listing of the 5-20 bond on the Frankfurt Stock Exchange following the approval of the Frankfurt Chamber of Commerce. On October 3, 1863, Murphy wrote to Seward regarding the rumored £10 million (slightly under $50 million in 1863) 6 percent loan potentially on offer by the Bank für Handel und Industrie in Darmstadt. The bank was of "good reputation and credit" as far as Murphy had uncovered and had the potential to open the floodgates for European loans to the American government—causing some excitement on European exchanges. While the effort never came to fruition, it nevertheless reflected the changing sentiments within European financial circles on behalf of the Northern cause. In addition, one views the efforts on the part of the French bank Erlanger to finance a cotton loan on the part of the Confederacy in a somewhat different light when one realizes that Erlanger also purchased Union bonds at the exact same time on the Frankfurt Börse.[40]

Union financial pursuits in Frankfurt faced stern competition in the form of the Erlanger bank. Raphael Erlanger had begun as an apprentice at the Frankfurt house of the Rothschilds before opening his own banking business in 1848. However, it was Raphael's son Emil and his connections with the Confederacy in Paris that had wide-ranging repercussions. The Confederate minister in Paris, John Slidell (of *Trent* affair fame), orchestrated with his colleague in London (James Mason) an agreement to float a Confederate loan through Erlanger & Cie in Paris. The £3 million loan bore 7 percent interest and included an astounding 18 percent commission for the Parisian house. Once more, the bonds could be turned in for Confederate cotton as opposed to specie—thereby making the financial instruments worth far more in actual cotton. Despite the best efforts of Consul General Bigelow in Paris to undermine the sale of the loan through his press contacts, the bank found little trouble in subscribing the loan. The Parisian bank along with the family bank in Frankfurt and partners Schroeders in London found the loan oversubscribed in a matter of days. Murphy identified in at least one letter to Secretary Seward Frankfurt banks that participated in the Confederate Erlanger loan, including the Mitteldeutsche Kreditbank and the banking houses of Siegmund and Rudolf Sulzbach and Wilhelm Friedrich Jäger. Such investments placed Murphy on the defensive—and he took an active role in downplaying the bond issue. Murphy worked with Frankfurt publishers to publicize widely the annual report of the Confederate Secretary of the Treasury to lay bare the financial plight of the Confederacy. According to Murphy, there was in part an understanding that the Erlanger loan had been largely avoided by Frankfurt financial houses and deemed as "shameful for the German national character." The *Weser-Zeitung* referred to the Erlanger loan as "the most indecent of all business speculation." Several Vienna-based papers similarly lambasted those in the German states and within Austria for any pursuit of the loan.[41]

The Frankfurt branch of the Rothschild house proved one of the most vocal opponents of the Erlanger cotton loan and actively worked against the Erlanger business in Frankfurt. The Rothschilds were not an explicit antislavery institution (despite Murphy's claims), but did have a long-standing conflict with the Erlangers in Frankfurt after the latter had attempted to move in on much of the business that the Rothschilds and other traditional private banks in the city conducted. This animosity culminated in Mayer Carl von Rothschild's decision as a member of the Frankfurt Chamber of Commerce to not list the Confederate bond issue on the exchange. "We will not allow [the Confederate loan]," began Rothschild's dissent, "to be quoted we do not believe in the loan and ... we do not believe in the cause ... No Jewish house of any character or wealth has touched that loan." Emile Erlanger had significant qualms with the action of Rothschild and other Frankfurt bankers, lamenting their "stupid confidence" in United States bonds.[42]

At all times, Murphy made a concerted effort in emphasizing antislavery sentiment in the German states. Murphy even went so far as to correct a piece when it said otherwise. In an 1863 *Harper's Weekly* piece on German bankers entitled "The Rothschilds and the Union," Murphy remarked, "But here the firm of M.A. Von Rothschild & Son are opposed to slavery and in favor of Union. A *converted Jew*, Erlanger, has taken the rebel loan of £3,000,000 and lives in this city." The clear politics outlined by Murphy reinforced how investment fused with the cause of emancipation in the German states by 1863. Furthermore, Murphy added, "Baron Rothschild informed me that all Germany condemned this act of lending money to establish a slaveholding government, and that so great was public opinion against it that Erlanger & Co dare not offer it on the Frankfurt bourse. I further know that the Jews rejoice to think that none of their sect would be guilty of loaning money for the purpose above named; but it was left, they say, for apostate Jews to do it." The Jewish network in Frankfurt proved instrumental to sales in the city and Murphy stood to reinforce this. Murphy promoted the effort at selling Union bonds abroad as being in the able hands of the financial titans such as the Rothschilds, while downplaying the prospects of Confederate finances abroad and challenging the most successful and widely known foreign financial endeavor for the South in the Erlanger loan.[43]

Murphy's hard work on behalf of the United States government manifested itself in different and, on occasion, amusing ways. Alexander D. White, future cofounder and inaugural president of Cornell University, commented on the success of Murphy and the Union securities during his travels through Germany in 1863. "William Walton Murphy of Michigan," remarked White, "had labored hard to induce the Frankfurt bankers to take our government bonds, and to recommend them to their customers, and had at last been successful." Upon his departure from Germany in late July 1863, White recalled one of his last experiences in Germany being a stroll with Murphy to the Zeil—a busy Frankfurt thoroughfare not far from the Börse (and currently the home to American fast-food restaurants and European chain retail stores) and encountering the vice consul who handed Murphy a newspaper. Murphy "tore it open, read a few lines, and then instantly jumped out into the middle of the street, waved his hat and began to shout. The public in general thought him mad . . . but as soon as he could get his breath he pointed out the headlines of the newspaper. They indicated the victories of Gettysburg and Vicksburg." Such a report echoed cables that reached Secretary Seward's desk in Washington.[44]

As the war progressed, an insatiable demand remained for American bonds in Frankfurt among all classes in the city. Such sales largely made their way through prominent houses such as Seligman & Stettheimer, the Frankfurt Rothschilds, Lazard Speyer-Ellison, and Philip Nicolas Schmidt. One of the key moments for Union finances in Frankfurt coincided with the placement of Union bonds on the Frankfurt Stock Exchange. This act on September 10, 1863, could not have happened without the key support of Carl von Rothschild, who sat on the board of the Börse. The placement of these bonds on the exchange increased the overall volume of sales and word spread about the value of the investment. These actions provided a much-needed boost to Union credit abroad. Murphy reported to Secretary Seward on the increased volume of sales and ads in local newspapers enticed investors towards a promising profit. By the spring of 1864, Consul Murphy even reported that American debt served as the preferred investment "throughout middle and southern Germany, especially in Bavaria, Wurtemberg, and Baden." He added that Frankfurt bankers called on their London and Amsterdam counterparts to help fulfill some of these orders and even then they could not keep up with the demand in Frankfurt.[45]

Within the 1864 Annual Report of the Frankfurt Chamber of Commerce, reports emerged of a "mass import and wear of American Government securities" and references to the fact that the local market in Frankfurt "set the tone for almost all European stock exchanges." One Frankfurt banker proclaimed, "There was probably no citizen in Frankfurt who had some money or savings and had not invested some of their possessions in this paper [5-20 bonds]." Finally, the chamber of commerce in nearby Württemberg noted that 5-20 bond purchases drew from "all classes of society." The cross section of American debtholders in the German states stood in stark contrast to the limited wartime purchases in the financial centers of London, Paris, and Amsterdam. Such democratic purchases reinforced the narrative that the German peoples shared a kinship with their American brethren beyond the immigrant population, and thereby served as a vital financial partner during the war with implications moving beyond. While profits drove these markets, the widespread nature of purchasers reveals this investment existed well beyond the most elite financiers.[46]

Marketing in Germany also escalated in 1864 because of other financial events—such as the depreciation of Austrian securities. By the end of 1864, *Der Aktionär* proclaimed "the amounts invested in United States bonds by way of trade-ins of Austrian securities exceed anything ever seen here in such a short period of time." The bond issues floated in Frankfurt and absorbed by some of the larger houses such as Karl Pollitz, M. A. Gruenebaum & Ballin, Lazard Speyer-Ellison, and Seligman & Stettheimer revealed the reach of American debt. Murphy used the press, such as the *Neue Frankfurter Zeitung* and *L'Europe*, to his advantage to prop up Union bond sales while simultaneously downplaying efforts for a Confederate bond floated by Erlanger. The end result was the claim that "hundreds of millions" of dollars were invested in American securities on the Frankfurt exchanges alone—a claim that seems on the surface to be quite credible. The *New York Tribune* published a piece in the spring of 1865, commenting on reports of counterfeit Union bonds in Germany. Such a report, according to the *Tribune*, "Grew out of the jealousy of the popularity of our bonds, and was resorted to by brokers in their efforts to aid the sale of home securities." The article went on to claim, "There are now held in Germany a loan of about three hundred millions of dollars in our 5-20 bonds, and the demand has been so great that for weeks past exchange has been 1–2 per cent in our favor." The resale market in Frankfurt and elsewhere following initial purchases in the United States proved highly profitable for these German bankers. Charles Wheeler, U.S. Consul in Nuremberg, likewise reported in December 1864 that local investors in the region included capitalists as well as simple workers and craftsmen.[47]

The success of Union sales in Frankfurt impacted the sales of other sovereign debt issues in Europe. The purchase of American securities at the expense of their Austrian counterparts concerned officials in Vienna. In September 1864, the imperial finance minister had to report significant losses on his own bonds due to "mass" sales in favor of the North American bonds. The situation had devolved to the point that the Austrian government banned the sale of foreign securities within the empire—in part to prevent Austrians from purchasing American debt. This did not stop Austrian investors, however. Many continued to invest in 5-20s through Frankfurt bankers. Others ordered to reinvest the freed monies from the sales of Austrian securities in "American." Some argued that financial collapse had, in fact, been avoided in Frankfurt through aggressive swaps of Austrian securities for United States bonds.[48]

While encouragement and support for the Union cause may have been a factor for continental purchases, it was also undoubtedly the case that the incredible discount at which the bonds initially traded played a role in their price. The Frankfurt-based French-language newspaper *L'Europe* often reinforced such sentiments. On February 10, 1865, *L'Europe* remarked:

> But as fast as rising has been on Austrian values, it has not reached the surprising proportions of rising which occurred on the Americans. These funds supported by many orders provoked by the good news and new financial policies of America, or the restoration of peace seemed to finally crown the heroic and generous efforts of abolitionists, mounted a 49 ⅜ closing price on 30 January . . . the funds of the Union, then the reaction that always follows, too sudden recovery, came down to 54, which further gives a very nice difference about them compared to the previous week.[49]

The severe discounts on Union bonds in Frankfurt laid bare the financial bottom line that impacted some of the sales in the German states. At times, American debt simply reflected a good price and an excellent return on one's investment.

The majority of these bonds surely made their way overseas via New York City houses that had German connections. One prime example is that of J and W Seligman Co. Joseph Seligman had emigrated from Germany to the United States in 1837 and quickly built a dry goods empire. By the time of the war, Seligman's company produced a large quantity of uniforms for the Union army. Seligman recognized the potential to become a significant player in international finance. As such, Joseph sent his brother Henry to Frankfurt in 1862 in the hopes of establishing a German house, and Joseph subsequently followed him across the Atlantic, spending a significant amount of time in the region during the war. While the firm did not formally establish a banking house in Frankfurt until 1864, Joseph became active in the securities market during his visit. Seligman conveyed his confidence in American securities early on. In March 1863, Seligman wrote from "Mainz on the Rhine" detailing interest in American securities: "It is of course impossible to foretell the course of events, the fate of our beloved Union is in the keeping of an all wise Providence as clay in the potter's hands, but this much seems self-evident that if our people know their interest and remain loyal to their flag and the country, the seceded states will be forced to listen to reason and rejoin the Union. People in Europe are getting more and more satisfied at this fact, and hence their willingness lately to interest themselves in our stocks."[50]

Furthermore, Seligman commented from Mainz in May 1863, the firm should invest (in New York) more heavily in securities—at this point '81 National Loan issues as 5-20s did not yet have a tremendous market. Despite his calls for investment, Seligman remained not entirely convinced that the market would fully develop. "Respecting investment of US 6's [National Loan]," Seligman opined, "I would say that I am perfectly satisfied what you three brothers may agree upon, but at any rate I would prefer subscribing for 50 m[thousand] in place of 100 m. Still I shall not object to the latter amount if you all think proper." Seligman effectively leveraged the Effecten-Societät. Seligman's registration with the organization as a guest in their surviving logbooks reveals his ability to crack this hardest of networks to access valuable capital and investors in the city of Frankfurt.[51]

Seligman's tune began to change just a couple months later in the summer of 1863. While William Murphy jubilantly celebrated the twin victories of Gettysburg and Vicksburg on the *Zeil* in Frankfurt, Seligman commented from Soden outside of Frankfurt with advance knowledge of the events. Based on word of the twin victories from fellow financier Speyer Ellison, Seligman purchased American debt in Frankfurt in preparation for the increased demand in 5-20s. While not definitive, it is not hard to imagine that such an action could have taken place at the Effecten Societät. The events across the Atlantic deeply impacted sales in Frankfurt and the network within the Effecten Societät merely reinforced these measures.[52]

While the exact total of Seligman sales remains a mystery owing to the loss of pertinent materials some fifty years ago, the firm undoubtedly played a critical role in financing Union bonds in the German states. Furthermore, the firm represented the fundamental essence of what made American sales so successful in the German states. A coordinated effort of German families on either side of the Atlantic tied their religious and kinship networks to the sale and distribution of Union debt and extended these networks within Frankfurt and the world of financial exclusivity. In the process, this not only solidified the overall success of the firms, but tied the American and German economies ever more closely together.[53]

By August 1864, the *New York Times* reported (on the authority of the London *Times*) of "estimates that $150,000,000 of these Bonds [5-20s] have already been taken in Holland and Germany." A piece in the London *Times* also from August proclaimed, "The accounts from Germany show that the demand for United States Bonds has not experienced the slightest diminution. The parcels brought to London by the weekly steamers and transmitted to Frankfort are absorbed as fast as they arrive, at prices which yield a good profit to the importers." Yet another *Times* piece revealed the power of Murphy to swing the market when accompanied by a representative of the Treasury visiting Frankfurt. While the bonds, it was to be noted, were held in the hands of permanent investors of all classes, the "bears and bulls of the Bourse" were reassured by Murphy's presence on the exchange—as his presence alone purportedly increased the value of the 5-20 bonds on the exchange by 10 percent. "The pains taken by Mr. Murphy to keep the German public well informed on the progress of events in the United States," the article proclaimed, "has contributed powerfully to this popularity of American stocks at the leading German Exchange, and we are taught by his efforts how easy it is, with a little well directed and truthful publicity, to keep public opinion in the right track." Once again, media reports made it clear—confidence helped facilitate sales in Frankfurt. Much like Jay Cooke's calming assurances worked stateside, so too did Murphy work similar magic along the River Main.[54]

One financial institution from Frankfurt that provides us with some of the most concrete numbers from this period is that of Bethmann Bankhaus. While more commonly associated with financing the Eiffel Tower in the 1880s, Bethmann actively traded in Union securities throughout the war. Beginning with National Loan '81 bonds, by the second quarter of 1864, the house rapidly advanced their position in 5-20 bonds. All told, the house purchased $620,000 in 5-20 securities on the Frankfurt Börse between April 1864 and June 1865. This does not also factor in some $35,000 in National Loan '81 purchases during this same period and significantly more than that in the previous two years. These records come from just one surviving ledger and do not necessarily indicate that these are the only purchases undertaken in securities by the bank during this period. Regrettably very few records exist for the bank in terms of who purchased these bonds, as they were all tied into a larger indexing system. While a "M. Guntekunust" purchased some '81 Loans in June 1863, and a "Geo Haas" purchased $500 in 5-20s in May 1864, little else remains from the Bethmann index from this period tying individuals to the hundreds of thousands of dollars in purchases. Nevertheless, such activity on the part of the Bethmanns reflects just one house's active involvement in federal securities during the war itself. Examining the Frankfurt stock quotations (known as the Börsen-Kursblatt) for Union bonds reveals the interest in American securities. To demonstrate the volume of trading and general interest of 5-20 sales, by August 1, 1864, midday trading prices for 5-20s were being listed (the only non-German security listed aside from Austrian state securities, which eventually dissipated). A month later, the Kursblatt also listed the price of the 5-20 on the Berlin exchange, one of only six securities being quoted. Thus, by the late summer and early fall of 1864, American securities on the exchange were a remarkably popular commodity, rivaling any German state securities. The appeal of these instruments made Germany the single most important international market for Union securities during the war—a feat that carried over into the postwar period as well. As demonstrated by Patrick Gaul, some of the Bethmann clients who invested in American debt included the likes of Austrian civil servants, doctors, lawyers, and other industrialists, reflecting at the very least a geographic diversity.[55]

Various American government officials in the German states outside of Frankfurt also relayed the interest of the German people in American bonds as the calendar turned to 1864. Vice Consul W. Marsh of Hamburg wrote to Secretary of State Seward in July 1864 to communicate that "I had a call from Mr. Hoffsteadt, The object of his visit was to inform me that he had had a consultation with eminent Bankers on the subject of a Premium Loan of One thousand Million Dollars, as a preliminary step in support of his offer to the United States Government." Marsh similarly relayed the impact of Lincoln's successful reelection in the fall of 1864 and that proposals of international loans had tremendous impacts on international sales. "At any rate I can truly say," remarked Marsh, "that the German Loan which I was the promoter of had the effect here of selling millions of our Bonds." Marsh similarly relayed the faith of German financiers when he remarked in the spring of 1865, just a month before Appomattox, that one group declared, "Only when we hear of Richmond falling you will see your stocks advance to 75 per cent of their value in Hamburg Change."[56]

Sales in the German states reached their height in February 1865, on the occasion of George Washington's birthday and the simultaneous report of the constitutional amendment to ban slavery. This important news arriving on a symbolic holiday for Americans in Germany led to the U.S. flag being flown over the American consulate—an unusual occurrence at the time. While some skeptics were of the opinion that such an action was undertaken to bull the market, an official telegram from the United States confirming the passage of the Thirteenth Amendment and led to a palpable energy permeating the entire exchange. Almost immediately, 5-20s rose 1 percent on the Börse and within two hours over $800,000 of 5-20s had been sold. Additionally, rumors spread that the war had in fact concluded, leading to further sales on the exchange in Frankfurt, as well as in Amsterdam, Munich, and Berlin. In fact, Berlin sales of 5-20s reached a point that stood 8–10 percent above New York City quotations. In the city of Bonn—home to 20,000 Germans—one banker claimed that at least $1 million in 5-20s could be located among investors. By April 1865, Chlodwig zu Hohenlohe-Schillingsfürst, a future chancellor of the Reich, wrote to Queen Victoria in London. In his letter, he claimed the war in America was currently at the center of "the entertainment of politically educated and uneducated people" in Germany. Hohenlohe-Schillingsfürst also emphasized prominent financiers in Frankfurt who "invested their money in American papers" and therefore hoped for a speedy peace. While some publications warned against individuals overextending themselves in American debt, the sizable investments made by countless individuals could not be denied.[57]

Late winter of 1865 found many reports emanating from Frankfurt emphasizing the frenetic pace of sales in the city. One letter reporting in from Frankfurt in February 1865 acknowledged that "It is possible that the Amsterdam bankers buy and import as many American national bonds as this city, but I think not . . . All that comes [to Frankfurt] is absorbed at once, generally sold before its arrival, and still the cry is for more. Within the last week orders have gone to New York for over five million dollars of five twenties for this city alone!" The report continued, "The sale of American stocks constitutes the chief business at the Bourse. Orders arrive daily for large purchases from Brussels, Berlin, Dresden, Munich, and within the last week the bankers have received orders to purchase considerable amounts for Vienna, Geneva, and even St. Petersburg. New fields for purchase seem constantly opening, so that it is impossible to glut the market." The article went on to discuss the situation of U.S. debt in Austria. "In Austria, it is not allowed by law for any person, as I am informed, to buy or sell anything but Austrian funds, yet the Austrian capitalists have caught the mania, and send their Austrian securities to be sold here, and the avails invested in American stocks, which are held in trust for them by the Frankfurt bankers. I hope his imperial highness, the Emperor Franz Joseph will not find out this great breach of Austrian law, so that their five-twenties will not be confiscated!" The article concluded by estimating that Frankfurt and Amsterdam each held $106 million in 5-20s alone.[58]

So what quantity of bonds sold in Germany? A March 1865 *Philadelphia Daily Bulletin* article (ironically about the importance of keeping the loan domestic) stated $200 million of the loan could be found in Germany and nearly $100 million in England, "with a demand so rapidly increasing not only in these countries but in other parts of Europe that it is expected before long the aggregate total will exceed 500 million." In June 1865, former Secretary of the Treasury Robert Walker declared in a letter to Secretary of the Treasury McCulloch, "More than one hundred and fifty millions of our securities were sold, during less than two years in Europe." In 1867 former Secretary of the Treasury Robert Walker wrote of his exploits traveling through Europe to lobby on behalf of the U.S. debt and critiquing Confederate financial plans. Accepting "any call for a loan would be defeated by the machinations of France & England," Walker subsequently visited "nearly every city of Holland and Germany, giving [an] opportunity to discussed the question personally with these bankers ... the result was that in a brief period the people of Germany, emphatically the great masses of the people, took several hundred millions of our loan at the same rates as our own citizens." Similarly, years later, Otto von Bismarck could boast: "It was reported to me that Lincoln could not keep the war going if he did not receive financial aid from Germany. His commissioners stated that they had been rebuffed in London & Paris. We wished the Union to be restored. The North seemed to me to be morally right, but, quite apart from that, we desired a strong prosperous and united Nation on the other side of the Atlantic." Meanwhile the *New York Tribune* declared in 1870 that Germans alone invested "seven or eight hundred million dollars" during the war. All of these various estimates should be taken with little more than a grain of salt, but barring any definite proof of the actual quantity of bond sales they are unfortunately the best that can be done. Nevertheless, such proclamations reveal a clearly liquid and active German market and reinforce the importance of German investment in bonds as an essential market during the war itself.[59]

Netherlands

The Netherlands served as an important market during the war as well. U.S. Minister to The Hague James Pike reported a large amount of interest in government securities. "The money men of Holland have begun to buy our government securities," Pike reported. "There have been no large operations, but each capitalist is taking a moderate sum and laying it away to wait for results." By the spring of 1864, Pike estimated that weekly transactions of Union bonds numbered $2 million in the city of Amsterdam alone. Such investment on the part of the Dutch reflected an attitude that was willing to avoid wartime circumstances and focus on the profit to be had from Union securities. "The Dutch capitalists, unlike many of the English," reported Pike, "have no prejudices against us, and have larger and more liberal view in regard to our resources, and believe in our ability as well as disposition to pay than I have expected to find." However, Pike also warned the United States that one of the biggest stumbling blocks to European investment revolved around the use of greenbacks to discharge debts. "The act of making government paper legal tender raised a general distrust in commercial and financial circles in Europe," Pike exclaimed, "which a promise to pay the interest on Government bonds in coin failed to allay." Pike continued by noting in January 1864, "We have no better friend in Europe than the Dutch, nor any who would be more glad to see our stocks a mile high," while reportedly Jewish financiers purchased the bonds at nearly a $2 million weekly clip by March 1864. By November 1864, as Americans went to the polls to re-elect Abraham Lincoln, U.S. government bonds "commanded an almost unlimited amount of capital" on the Amsterdam exchange.[60]

Just like the American bonds finding their way onto the Frankfurt Börse, so too did American bonds make it to Amsterdam via the New York brokers. One of the largest sellers to the Dutch banks was none other than Cooke ally Fisk & Hatch. In the spring of 1864, the bank wrote to Cooke on the matter. "We have lately been doing a very heavy business with the Foreign Bankers with many of whom we have confidential relations," the New York bank boldly proclaimed. "These 'Dutch' friends of ours are very decided in their preferences for the old agencies, and are waiting to make their subscriptions through us." The firm's work in the Dutch market paid serious dividends, ones that necessitated a unyielding control on the gold exchange to ensure the fluid demand emanating from Amsterdam. The firm concluded its letter by stating, "We have done a magnificent business in Foreign orders during the past month, and sincerely hope for a continuance of the same." Thus, the demand from Amsterdam remained vibrant. Secondary sales in Amsterdam to eager investors, even in the depths of the Union's war campaigns and the uncertainty surrounding Lincoln's election by the fall of 1864, proved the durability of the financial issue and the interest among the Dutch financial populace.[61]

One of the largest banks in Amsterdam, Hope & Co., invested in American bonds during the war and commented on the vibrant market in American securities in Amsterdam to its close partners—Barings of London. In June 1864, Hope noted to Barings, "United States 6 percent 5/20 year bonds are actively dealt in here," while in October that year Hope remarked that the market fell flat—with the lone exception of American sovereign debt. Such commentary on the part of Hope to its London-based partners revealed the centrality of American debt in the Dutch city by 1864.[62]

Some Americans utilized Dutch services while abroad as well. Rowland Gibson Hazard serves as an excellent example. The war years proved fruitful for Hazard. In the winter of 1864–65, the textile magnate invested heavily in Union bonds. Operating in Europe and utilizing the services of the Dutch bank Hope & Co., Hazard invested in both 5-20s as well as '81 National Loan bonds. While Hazard traveled throughout Europe conducting business in England, France, and the German states, Hope & Co. passed word along of its various purchases on the Amsterdam exchange. Word reached Hazard via other financial houses such as Bethmann Bankhaus in Frankfurt, Baring Brothers in London, and Hottingeur & Cie in Paris. All told Hope & Co. purchased some $110,000 worth of bonds on Hazard's account in slightly over a month. While such purchases occurred in Europe, Hazard was in fact American, based out of Rhode Island, and merely traveling through Europe at the time. These travels nevertheless presented an opportunity for Hazard to purchase American securities on the European continent. Eschewing the better-known and well-established financial market of London, Hazard's investments through a Dutch banking house operating on the Amsterdam exchange reflected the increasing importance of continental European sales to the Union cause. Hazard utilized continental banking syndicates to avail himself of American debt wherever he found himself in Europe, ensuring investment opportunities no matter the locale. Such partnerships proved invaluable moving into the postwar period as well.[63]

Unfortunately, detailed information on Dutch purchasers remains elusive. While some widely publicized purchases on the part of R. G. Hazard provide easy evidence on the issue, translating that into hundreds of millions of dollars is no small matter. To be sure, some smaller purchases can be noted. For instance, an Emile Testa purchased $1,000 via Hope & Co. in January 1865. Similarly, the Sillem family purchased $13,000 in stock of the National Loan on December 4, 1861. Even though the material record may not survive to the degree present in other nations, the role of Union securities on the Amsterdam exchange cannot be underestimated.[64]

The Times speculated that the interest in Union bonds in Germany and the Netherlands resulted from devious work on the part of Union agents preying on ignorant investors. That being said, the antislavery sentiment within Germany and close connection that the Frankfurt Börse had with government securities deeply influenced the success of American bonds, especially on such a severe discount. Based on surviving evidence, the confluence of profit, speculation, and the politics of slavery and emancipation all factored into the widespread investment in American debt in continental Europe during the war.[65]

Other Foreign Bond Sales

Bonds also sold outside of Europe. Moses Taylor, owing to his connections with Cuban sugar markets, provides valuable evidence on this front. The New York banker and merchant (who also controlled the National City Bank of New York) had extensive connections to Cuba through his import business Moses Taylor & Co. Taylor purchased bonds (both 5-20s and the National Loan) on behalf of several hundred investors out of Cuba. These sales ranged from as little as $300 to well into the millions. Taylor's ledger book provides detailed accounts of the sales and indicates that his investors, while Cuban residents, may have hailed from across the Atlantic world. A "J.P.C. Thompson" invested some $150,000 while a "Miss Rosa Céspedes" invested a tidy sum of $700. A "Mrs. James Owens de Knight" purchased $73,300 in combined 5-20s and 6 percent National Loan issues and a "Pablo Herrera" likewise dabbled in both securities to the tune of north of $1.2 million. Prominent Cuban residents such as Tomás Terry (himself a native Venezuelan) and Susana Benitez de Parejo each invested close to $5 million in 5-20 bonds over the course of the war. Other investors included presumably Dutch, French, Italian, British, American, and Spanish expatriates. All told the Cuban sales via Taylor amounted to some $32 million. Such a sizable investment from the Caribbean is a testament to the power U.S. securities were able to garner, even among those who traditionally shied away from finance and had stuck to dry goods while living in the middle of a slave economy. Such a commitment on the part of these individuals reflected shifting attitudes toward greater investment in pure finance.[66]

Representatives of the federal government also utilized bonds for diplomatic missions of importance. Such was the case of William Aspinwall and John Murray Forbes. In the spring of 1863, Aspinwall and Forbes traveled to England at the behest of the Naval Department, but under the official auspices of the Treasury Department. This distinction was important, for Aspinwall and Forbes traveled to England in an attempt to purchase Laird rams being constructed in Liverpool to prevent them from falling into Confederate hands. These rams were not "officially" being bought by the federal government, and hence the men were not traveling on behalf of the navy. Aspinwall and Forbes did receive permission to attempt to negotiate a $50 million loan directly with any international bank. In March 1863, Chase wrote to the two Americans. "There are some advantages," Chase said, "in having a portion of our securities held abroad which should not be overlooked; and now that is has been sufficiently proved that a Foreign Loan is not necessary to us, I am quite willing to sanction a limited negotiation, on terms which will place European takers of our Bonds on an equal footing with original takers in New York." Such a loan never came to fruition. They did, however, begin a line of credit with Baring Brothers in London through an initial deposit of $4 million of Union bonds (out of a total $10 million brought with them). Secretary Chase also authorized Forbes and Aspinwall to float a £10 million loan of bonds with a British house should they find one willing to invest. While the mission ultimately failed and the bonds were returned to the United States (where they were subsequently sold by Cooke), this failed mission demonstrated the diplomatic power bonds held as a way of financing more clandestine operations overseas during the Civil War. Forbes and Aspinwall also traveled under the authority to negotiate a $50 million foreign loan with a foreign banking house. This loan consisted of a new issue of the popular 5-20s through public subscription. Yet even a relatively modest loan of $50 million failed to gain traction in Britain, with a large sticking point being the fact that the interest was not paid in sterling.[67]

The U.S. government enlisted another financier, Robert J. Walker, to disparage the efforts of Confederate financiers. Walker did his utmost to undermine Confederate efforts by stressing the past repudiation of state debts within the Confederacy, including Jefferson Davis's native Mississippi. Walker offered a unique position as a former enslaver himself who had freed his enslaved persons in the 1830s prior to serving as secretary of the treasury during the Mexican War. Walker's campaign was enough to irreparably damage Confederate financial efforts in Europe—especially when coupled with failures on the military front. The publication of Robert Walker's *Jefferson Davis, Repudiation, Recognition and Slavery* undoubtedly impacted the subsequent decline in Confederate bonds in the summer and fall of 1863—so much so that Walker could proudly report back to Chase that "slavery and repudiation are identified and all feel now completely that their own hope of ever receiving anything from the repudiated states of Mississippi and Arkansas and Florida is by emancipation and the success of the union."[68]

Walker also traveled to continental Europe to promote Union bonds. While on the continent, Walker distributed a selection of pamphlets entitled *American*

Finance and Resources that espoused the benefits of the Northern economy, governmental fiscal policies, and the importance of Union war bonds. Walker's time in Europe was equally valuable in some of the ideas that he transferred back across the Atlantic to Secretary Chase and others. Specifically, Walker crafted a narrative of Jefferson Davis as chiefly responsible for state repudiation in Mississippi in the 1840s. The association stuck, and possible repudiation became another weapon to attack Confederate debt. Walker could also be credited with pushing for the democratization of bonds that became increasingly more commonplace by the fall of 1864 with the 7-30 issue. Working off a British savings bank model for the working classes, Walker proposed a bond issue through a very large popular loan that encouraged all members of society to get involved. While his mission to Britain met with mild success in discrediting the financial stability of the Confederacy, his work on the Continent revealed the great interest bonds generated in the German states and the Netherlands.[69]

While some of the messaging abroad may have been designed to achieve similar ends to domestic efforts, the results were far different. Utilizing evolving financial techniques and heavily boosted by speculators on the various European exchanges, international bond sales drew upon financial motives compared to the patriotic ones in the domestic work of Jay Cooke and his financial agents. The international bond sales represented an evolving global marketplace driven by politics, speculation, and profiteering. While many had long assumed the financial centers of London and Paris would prove vital to U.S. debt sales abroad, the underappreciated markets of Frankfurt and Amsterdam resulted in large quantities of international sales. While not financial backwaters by any means, the prominent role these two cities held in American debt during the war cannot be understated. These conscious acts on the part of European financiers had an effect on the domestic market. By instilling confidence via their purchases in the Union, they strengthened the crucial domestic market, something that only accelerated in the latter part of the war.

CHAPTER FIVE

Like a Cord Through the Whole Country
Nationalizing the Economy

In March 1865, an article in the *Philadelphia Press* ran with the headline "One Day's Subscription to the Seven-Thirty Loan." The article regaled readers with stories of the frenetic pace in the offices of the clerks who processed requests for the new bond issue. As the article made clear, it was as if the capitalist machine could almost not keep up with the people's patriotism. Not only that, but the article wished to make a point of the diversity of the various subscribers. "They [bond purchasers] are of all classes, and all degrees, and of all colors," declared the release. "There are black men in Jay Cooke & Co's, and they hold money in their hands; and there is a soldier there; and there is an officer, lame, yet with an unmistakable air of command and of guardianship; and there are Quakers, who look annuity, and couple and pace, and goodness all over them; and there is a clergy man, and a woman that sews." Still another article from the same week noted, "The sums do not come from a few cities or heavy firms, nor from speculators and brokers; the people throughout the loyal states, from New England to California, are investing their earnings in this common cause, and pledging themselves by this action to support the common Government." The article detailed the wide cross section of the United States that invested in the Union cause. "The fifty and one hundred dollar notes are the means of bringing into this great Loyal League thousands who would otherwise be unable to share the profit or the responsibility," declared the author. "The less wealthy classes find them the best investment for their slowly accumulated earnings, and are hastening to secure so sure an investment."[1]

Such descriptions informed everyday individuals that they too could afford these newly democratic financial instruments and be part of the larger cause. While such a notion existed in the earlier drives of the war, they received new strength in the 7-30 drive in 1864–65. The 7-30 drive resulted in $830 million worth of Treasury notes sold nationwide. By emphasizing the disparate nature of bond purchasers, the press celebrated the result of the issue: a drive that called on the people, who answered in kind.

Contemporary literature on American political development has placed a greater emphasis in recent decades on institutional relations ranging from customs houses to the postal service as a primary source of connection for individuals with the state apparatus. The Civil War, however, exposed a vital relationship at the individual level with the state. These connections between people and the federal government via bond purchases represented an intimate connection unlike other antebellum arrangements. When the U.S. Treasury, an institution of the state, issued and redeemed war bonds, individuals who purchased this debt during the war connected with the nation as a whole. The people who purchased 7-30 Treasury notes in 1864–65 represented the most widespread investment in American debt to date. Foreshadowing the massive public loan drives of World War I, these investments and the mechanisms that ensured widespread adaptation reflected a notable transition for individuals with the state. The sharing of names within local communities likewise ensured that such investment met with community approval and engagement.[2]

Despite the wild success of the 5-20 movement, political pressures prevented Cooke from immediately assuming the agency for the subsequent 10-40 and 7-30 issues. But the failure of the bonds to sell at levels akin to the 5-20 drive necessitated a return to the expertise of Cooke. With the shortened 10-40 and 7-30 issues, Cooke expanded on the success of the 5-20 issue. Leaning into the notion of patriotic self-interest, Cooke sold the bond issues throughout the United States to an ever-expanding segment of the populace and in so doing further democratized the nature of sales.

Bonds and the National Bank Act

On January 7, 1863, Samuel Hooper introduced HR 656 in the House, the first such national banking bill to come out of the 37th Congress. Several weeks later, Senate ally John Sherman put forward his own version of a national bank bill. Sherman's bill had in fact been put before the Senate as a reaction to President Lincoln's letter to both chambers calling for a national banking system dated January 19. In a speech on the Senate floor on February 10, 1863, Sherman equated the current system of state banks with slavery and a national system with emancipation. "The policy of this country," Sherman declared, "ought to be to make everything national as far as possible; to nationalize our country so that we shall love our country . . . This doctrine of state rights . . . has been the evil of the times." Several senators spoke in objection to Sherman's claims, most notably Senator Jacob Collamer of Vermont—a fellow Republican. Collamer viewed the end of state banks as a "derangement, utterly destructive of the condition of society in which I live." In the House of

Representatives, one of the foremost critics of a national bank, E. G. Spaulding of New York, made an abrupt turn by February 19, when he spoke at length in favor of the measure. "It seems," said Spaulding, "that the present is a propitious time to enact this great measure as a permanent system and that the duty of the government in providing a national currency shall no longer be neglected... The government of the United States ought not to depend on state institutions for the execution of its great powers." Despite some rancorous debate, the measure passed the House 78 to 64 and the Senate 23 to 21. President Lincoln signed the bill into law on February 25, 1863, a year to the day after the Legal Tender Act. The National Bank Act and Legal Tender Act played critical roles in not only boosting a federal monetary structure but also in amplifying the importance of bonds to the national conversation. Between creating a widespread issue of bonds with the Legal Tender Act and using bonds as starting capital requirements for new national banks, the entire financial mechanism found itself enmeshed in bonds.[3]

The National Banking Act also required new national banks to procure U.S. bonds as part of their capitalization; national banks acquired approximately $250 million in Union bonds to fulfill the requirements. The final version of the National Bank Act led to a sliding scale (dependent more on location than overall capitalization) of bonds required by various banks for capital requirements in order for the banks to conduct business. Any extension of credit required the further purchase of bonds. By the time of Chase's report to Congress in December 1863, 134 national banks had been organized with a capitalization of slightly more than $16 million. By November 1864, these figures had increased to 584 national banks with nearly $66 million in capitalization. By December 1865, these numbers had expanded to 1,647 banks and $418 million in capitalization. Bond purchases by the national banks retained by the Treasury to enable circulation of funds only involved a small portion of the billions of dollars in loans sold by the government, but nevertheless reveal the centrality of U.S. debt to the national financial infrastructure.[4]

While the National Bank Act had immediate consequences, the later amendments during the war are just as illuminating. For instance, an 1864 amendment to the bill reflected above all a concession to Wall Street interests by authorizing Wall Street banks to act as depositors for other banks throughout the country. The New York firms retained exclusive rights to offer interest on the western bank balances and further solidified the de facto central banking role of Wall Street firms and New York City as a whole. The ability of New York banks to pay interest on reserves made Wall Street the money center—linking it with congressional policy and Main Street financial interests. An 1865 act that imposed a 10 percent tax on new state bank note issues effectively killed off many of the state banks that were still fighting the national banking system. By the end of the war, the federal government had chartered 700 national banks, opening a new era in American financial history.[5]

The Struggles of a 10-40 Campaign without Jay Cooke

In March 1863 Congress approved a new loan. Known as the "10-40 loan," it contained a minimum 5 percent interest. The new issue took on the name the 10-40 loan because Treasury issued these bonds for a minimum of 10 years but no more than 40. In addition, this new issue did not commence until the completion of the 5-20 issue (far from over in March 1863). In essence, in the midst of the 5-20 drive, Congress began plans to account for future financing of the war. The 5-20 loans failed to reach the cap of $500 million in 1863. The war continued in 1864 with little sense of resolution. Continued military operations across a landmass the size of western Europe required more funds, and the end of the 5-20 drive meant the Treasury needed to start a new drive to refill the coffers. However, once the 5-20 issue ended in January 1864, Chase did not immediately opt to begin the 10-40 issue. As historian Albert Bolles states, "Though he [Chase] had now been at the head of the treasury department more than two years, he had learned but little, and was just as unwilling as ever to listen to an adviser." Chase ultimately opted to issue the bonds at 5 percent (when the law afforded him the opportunity to do so at 6 percent). Unsurprisingly, the public at large, and especially the financial sector, had little interest in a 5 percent loan with the recent completion of a 6 percent issue that could readily be had on the secondary market. Between January 21 and July 1, 1864, only $73,337,750 of the $300 million in 10-40 bonds sold. Chase remained reticent to acknowledge the error of his ways and opted to flood the market with even more greenbacks, increasing inflation. Chase's hope of debasing the currency to garner favor among investors in the 10-40s did little but alarm the market—and without Jay Cooke at the helm to utilize his widespread sales force and marketing genius, the confidence struggled to emerge.[6]

The 10-40 loan drive continued to languish with the 5 percent interest rate being of little interest to financiers. Chase's resignation as secretary of the treasury in June 1864 further upended the world of Union finance. Senator William Pitt Fessenden of Maine, a prominent member of the Senate Finance Committee, replaced Chase and assumed office on July 5. Although not the first choice of the president, nor a person eager to step into the void, Fessenden nevertheless embraced this call. Fessenden assumed his role in July and immediately set to work trying to finance the war with a brand-new loan issue of $400 million (separate from the 10-40 issue), recently authorized by Congress and containing both long-term bonds and short-term Treasury notes. The passage of such an act belied the fact that Union finances were in a precarious situation and Fessenden's early fiscal policies did little to alleviate the concerns of the Northern public.[7]

Fessenden had first entered the Senate in 1854 and quickly rose in Republican circles in the upper chamber. A staunch antislavery man, Fessenden found himself in the thick of the Kansas-Nebraska debate where his star subsequently rose. Reelected in 1860 on the Republican ticket, Fessenden served on the Senate Finance Committee. Although opposed to the Legal Tender Act in 1862, he nevertheless fell in line with the party and labored to maintain a revenue stream for the Union cause. His competent handling of the financial battles on Capitol Hill endeared him to many in the Republican administration and led to his appointment as secretary of the treasury. Fessenden's ascension to the role came as a welcome relief for the Lincoln administration. Lincoln had struggled to deal with Salmon Chase's political machinations as he positioned himself for a presidential run in the fall of 1864 to challenge the sitting president.[8]

Jay Cooke himself did not have the agency for the 10-40 loan and remained reluctant to take on the new loan issue. On one thing almost all were in agreement on: the 10-40 issue should not begin in earnest until the Treasury had accumulated approximately $100 million in bonds to avoid a delay in delivery. While Cooke stressed that the national banks and subtreasuries remained the best avenue for sales—a letter from another financer revealed what Cooke deep down already knew—"I don't believe they [the bonds] will go unless you take hold." For some members of the financial community, sales would not reach 5-20 levels without Cooke's name and reputation attached to it. Despite Cooke not receiving the exclusive agency to sell the issue, he remained actively involved in promoting it. He frequently traveled from Philadelphia to Washington to consult with Chase, his brother Henry remarking "He [Chase] has about concluded to do so [sell the bonds through the National Banks] but will determine upon nothing positive until he has a full and satisfactory talk over the whole matter with you." Cooke's efforts at pivoting between Washington and New York to stabilize financial confidence—back and forth "like a shuttlecock," as he described it—went a long way in the days of financial uncertainty following the end of the 5-20 issue. While Cooke pledged "urging all within my influence to engage in its sale," reality proved far different. The year 1864 represented a presidential election year and Union war prospects remained far from certain. This binary partially accounted for reticence to invest as uncertainty roiled securities markets as a whole at the time.[9]

Reports flooded into Cooke regarding problems with the 10-40 issue. From Baltimore, John Wills reported, "The new ten-forty goes slowly here and simply because it has not been rightly put upon the market. The people have gotten so accustomed to your mode of distributing loans that they can scarcely be brought to anything else." The *Evening Telegraph* in Philadelphia took it one step further:

> We do not think that the plan of taking subscriptions to the new loan of 10-40 at the rate of interest at which it is put upon the market, is wisely done or maturely thought over. Jay Cooke & Co., by their wide-spread business relations, the prestige which is attached to them from their success with the 5-20 loan and the indomitable energy which characterizes the head of that house, would have secured ten millions where the present mode will secure one. To be sure, we do not believe that so sagacious a man as Mr. Cooke would have advised a 5 per cent loan at all, and we can only wonder what pernicious influence has induced the head of the Treasury to try it.[10]

Sifting between press releases produced independently and those authored by Cooke himself remains a challenge, but the numbers themselves do not lie. The 10-40 sales remained slow through the summer of 1864 as military movements and casualty numbers escalated in the eastern theater of the war and a presidential election loomed on the horizon.

10-40 Sales among the Masses

Despite the sluggish sales for the 10-40 issue, the purchasers represented a wide swath of the North and beyond. In keeping with the prior 5-20 issue, Treasury Department registers for this period reveal the sales were completed by an array of purchasers across gender and socioeconomic lines and ranged from the small $50 bond to purchases by individuals in the four- or five-figure range. Immigrants, widows, and middle-class Americans all procured these bonds, albeit at a slower pace compared to the 5-20 campaign. Because of the driving force that national banks became starting with the 10-40 drive, a whole host of such banks across the country sold bonds to the Northern public.

Women in particular played a large role as purchasers by the time of the 10-40 drive. Women purchasing these bonds in larger numbers, however, revealed an evolution or shift in thinking when it came to patriotism on the part of women for the larger war effort. Bonds represented not a form of sacrifice of the like frequently called upon by entities such as Sanitary Commissions, but rather revealed how patriotism fused with self-interest could still merit a "sacrifice" designation. Oliver Wendell Holmes represented one view of women's sacrifice and patriotism in the war, a belief that they should remain stoic in the face of sacrifice. "The woman hides her trembling fear," the poem declares, "the wife, the sister checks a tear." As the war progressed, however, women found themselves being called on to sacrifice and to take a more central role in the crisis. Historian Alice Fahs described such acts as part of a popular culture creation of the "feminized war." Literature composed by female authors often revealed a need for women to engage in proper citizenship during the war by not only sacrificing husbands and sons to the war effort, but supporting the cause of the United States by all means from the home front. To that end, when women purchased bonds they fulfilled this patriotic narrative even when marginalized from formal politics.[11]

Such a mindset helps to explain in part women purchasing bonds throughout the North. In the shipbuilding town of Bath, Maine, schoolteacher Eliza B. Fisher purchased $100 in 10-40s while twenty-year-old Cora Rouse, the daughter of a local pump and block maker, purchased $100 in 10-40s as well. Moving down the mid-coast to Brunswick, Maine, Caroline Weld purchased $100 in 10-40s, most likely from the proceeds of her boardinghouse in town; included among her boarders was Leonard Woods, the president of nearby Bowdoin College. Moving further down the coast to the bustling port of Portland, Maine, Mary Cumpston, a local schoolteacher and Lydia Thayer—most likely a widow in her early 70s—by 1864 had both invested $100 in 10-40s. Lucy Hall, the wife of a Westbrook farmer, invested $200 in the bonds out of Portland. Eliza B. Perkins, the wife of a local merchant in Kennebunk, procured $100 in Portland. Elsewhere in New England, sales thrived among women in various communities. In Barre, Massachusetts, widow Elvira Wood purchased $100 in 10-40s. Maria Ruggles, the wife of a farmer, and Mary B. Grosvenor, wife of a clerk, invested in Barre in $100 worth of the bond issue in 1864. Moving further south to Bristol, Rhode Island, bond sales likewise met with success. Elizabeth Camm, a housekeeper from Bristol, procured $200 in this bond issue. Finally, in nearby Providence, Ruth Anne Simmons, a local "sew factory worker" curiously found the means to purchase $500 in 10-40s despite the fact her wages more than likely did not support such a purchase.[12]

Still, the other purchases of 10-40s reveal the disparate world of purchasers from small towns across the North. Out of the seafaring town of Bath,

Maine, sales accumulated among the merchants, shipbuilders, and sea captains associated with the industry. At the same time, however, sales also found their way to other members of the community. The booktrader Elisha Clark procured $200 in 1864. Other sales in Bath included James Tibbets ($200), a "mariner" according to the 1860 census. Other portions of Maine also included sales from a wide array of individuals. From Bangor, Maine, came a whole host of sales from individuals from in town and beyond. Rufus Gilmore, a farmer from nearby Holden, Maine, purchased $150 in 10-40s. Similarly, Prentiss Allen from Corinna, Maine, put together enough funds for $200 worth. Josiah Crosby, a lawyer from Dexter, Maine, also bought $100 in 10-40s, while Lemuel Bradford, a sailmaker from Bangor proper purchased $300 in bonds. Migrating south to the largest city in Maine, Portland, revealed even more disparate sales. Some higher sales in the Portland area included Sylvan Shurtleff ($1,000), a "boot, shoe, and leather dealer," as well as Neal Dow ($1,000), the former mayor of Portland and "Napoleon of Temperance" who was instrumental in the passage of the 1851 prohibition law in Maine. Other professionals also invested out of the Portland region, including local jeweler Oliver Garrish purchasing $200 worth as a small nest egg for the children of Portland.[13]

Still, because of the importance of Portland to the southern Maine economy, many sales went to individuals from farther afield who traveled to the bustling port to purchase their bonds. Neighboring communities like Westbrook and Gorham saw subscribers coming into Portland. Edward Knight ($50) and Moses Dale ($100) were both farmers from Westbrook who purchased 10-40s in Portland. The wealthy towns of Kennebunk and Kennebunkport also had their fair share of investors in 10-40s. Maria Rounds, the wife of a local farmer, purchased $500 in 10-40s while William Sewall, a lawyer in Kennebunk, bought $300 worth. Other purchasers such as Barnabas Freeman ($400), a lawyer from Yarmouth, and Emery Lombard, a shoemaker from the mill town of Turner, Maine, show how widespread these purchasers were. Indeed, sales during the spring of 1864 reveal a large investment out of the Pine Tree State. Investments in 10-40 sales out of national banks in Maine would total in the hundreds of thousands of dollars in 1864, previewing what was to come in 7-30 sales.[14]

Sales also flourished in Providence, Rhode Island. Ebenezer Richmond, a local miller, invested $150 in the 5 percent issue while local merchant Stephen C. Arnold procured $400 of 10-40s. Local grocer John Remington bought $200 in 10-40s. George G. Hood, a seed gardener in his early 70s, pulled together the requisite funds to buy a $50 bond—the same went for a local wool dealer with the distinctive name Royal Chapin as well as Providence cashier Edwin Knight. Others from the surrounding area also opted to conduct their business in Providence. Augustine Root, a Congregational minister most likely from Middlesborough, Massachusetts, purchased $50 in 10-40s, while Ansel Holman, the town clerk of nearby Smithfield, Rhode Island, purchased $100 himself. David Waldson (or Waldzon depending on a given census over several decades), a manufacturer from Taunton, Massachusetts, purchased $100 in 10-40s. Charles L. Able, a local liquor store owner, bought $250 and Lawrence Van Wyck, a boarder in nearby Niagara, also chimed in with $100 in purchases. From Washington Stonebraker ($200), a blacksmith in Monkton, Maryland, to Isaac Caswell ($200), a farmer from the small upstate New York town of Ridgeway, bond sales permeated most of the Northeast corridor as well.[15]

Much like the 5-20 drives, immigrants also constituted a large segment of bond purchasers in 1864. The faith and confidence held by these immigrants in America proved even something that might be passed down to children through the act of investment. Mary Campbell (age six in 1864), the daughter of an Irish immigrant mother and Canadian steamboat captain father, had $100 purchased in her name by her parents. Moving further west to sales in Peoria, Illinois, a large number of individuals from the surrounding communities bought into the cause. Charles Holtcamp, a Prussian immigrant and clay potter from nearby Decatur, bought $150 in 10-40s. Antonio Baars ($150), a Dutch immigrant and physician, purchased the bonds as well.[16]

Yet, the quantity of sales occurring in "the West," otherwise known as areas west of Pennsylvania, really set the 10-40 drive apart from its predecessors. Small Ohio towns like Columbus, Cadiz, Gallipolis, and Dayton all became fertile grounds for bond sales. Peter Dolan from Kickapoo contributed $50 to the cause. Miles Smith ($500), a merchant from Knoxville, Illinois, and Charles Day ($200), a bookkeeper from nearby Brimfield, also lent their might. Moving into further reaches of the old northwest, James Nobert, a peddler in Detroit, purchased $300 in 10-40s. Milwaukee, Wisconsin, similarly had sales from the surrounding communities including those to the farmer Denison Baker ($150) from nearby Summit and Squire Sackett ($250), a farmer from Wauwatosa whose daughter Sarah ($150) also purchased 10-40s from this northern outpost. Sales also began to emanate in substantive numbers out of the even more remote region of St. Paul, Minnesota (population 10,400 in the 1860 census): Henry W. Towle, a blacksmith living in Dayton, Minnesota, following a move from Maine, put together funds to buy $100 in 10-40s. Likewise, Alfred Foster, a farmer from Ramsey, Minnesota, also put in $100 toward 10-40 bonds.[17]

Finally, sales of 10-40s also made their way into the border states and regions of the Confederacy itself. While the evidentiary gap makes it somewhat difficult to match as many bond sales in places through the border states and Confederacy, especially because many bonds were in fact purchased by Union soldiers themselves, some conclusions can be drawn. In Knoxville, Tennessee, where 10-40 sales amounted to $30,750, some sales could be attributed to individuals such as local farmer Andrew Goodard ($500) as well as Brig. Gen. Davis Tillson, a Maine native and active raiser of United States Colored Troops units. Moving west toward the Mississippi River and Memphis sees sales emerge among the local Irish immigrant population. James Pierce and James Hammon—both local laborers and Irish immigrants—each purchased $100 in 10-40s, contributing to the city's overall sales of $77,650. Finally, moving downriver to New Orleans, there were sales among Union soldiers, including Lt. Jacob Franzman ($400) of the 62nd USCT and Gen. Gordon Granger ($1,500). Other purchasers such as Horace Bell ($200) could also have been soldiers as well. All told, some $1,005,150 in primary sales of 10-40s occurred in the Confederacy and vital border state of Kentucky—to say nothing of the other border state of Missouri as well as secondary sales in these regions that were significantly more. Such sales revealed the migration of purchases beyond the northeastern financial hubs and into the country as a whole.[18]

These sales help to tell a narrative of disparate purchases, but disparate, small-scale purchases did not make for large-scale sums of money for the government. From March 26 to May 7, 1864, only slightly more than $44.5 million in 10-40s sold, and by the end of 1864 fiscal year total sales amounted to $73,337,100. Poor sales also coincided with little progress in the spring and summer of 1864 on the military front. The new overall commander of Union forces, Gen. Ulysses S. Grant, slowly made his way to the outskirts of Richmond and Petersburg, Virginia, by June 1864, accompanied by astonishingly high casualty rates. In the western theater, Gen. William Tecumseh Sherman made slow progress through northern Georgia and toward the heretofore elusive goal of Atlanta. With these military events, coupled with the 1864 presidential election and the uncertainty it caused in the financial markets, it is not terribly surprising to see a reluctance to more fully embrace the 10-40s. The relatively poor performance of the sales drove the decision to end the drive on January 7, 1865. When the books finally closed, $135 million in 10-40s purchases filled the various ledgers—a rather paltry amount considering authorization had been made for up to $900 million in sales by the time of the loan's termination. While the sales did spread across a wide area of the country, the fact that Jay Cooke did not hold the reins undeniably played a role not only in the poor performance of the 10-40s, but in the ultimate decision to bring in Cooke for the future 7-30 drive.[19]

Democratizing the 7-30 Loan Drive

The 7-30 Treasury note issue represented the most democratic issue of the entire Civil War. Fessenden's insistence on solely utilizing national banks to fund the bond sales by mid-1864 failed to gain traction, and once again Jay Cooke & Co. would be called upon to save the Union finances from themselves. Building off the National Loan and 5-20 loan campaigns, this drive, more than any other, solidified the people's stake in the cause. An (ultimately) $830 million drive consisting of 7.3 percent interest Treasury notes (commonly referred to as bonds), this loan signaled the largest attempt to sell the war to the Northern public. Furthermore, the marketing employed and widespread nature of sales across class, racial, and geographic divides bound the people by debt to the Union. The 7-30 loan not only cemented citizens throughout the North and West as part of a larger American nation, they also helped to present a new vision of the Union—one that portrayed a truly American destiny that interlocked the financial strength and very future of the nation with the people writ large. Wedded in debt to the Union cause and the nation, the public and the federal government became entwined to a degree never before seen; such an action contributed to the propagation of bond sales as an extension of state centralization.

Fessenden's ascension to secretary of the treasury came at a dire time for Union finances. By July 1864, the national debt hovered around $1.8 billion with nearly $72 million worth of immediate calls on the Treasury accounts (whose cash accounts numbered a mere $19 million). The $400 million loan therefore proved essential in steadying Union finances and revenue streams. Half of the loan comprised long bonds (5-20s) while the other half consisted of 7-30 Treasury notes. The 7-30 notes could be converted at the end of three years into long-term bonds should the government (or security-holder for that matter) desire. Secretary Fessenden faced a looming deadline of $50 million due to Union soldiers on September 1, 1864—a sizable amount of money growing with the size of the army, which was 1.2 million strong by the summer. Only three weeks into his position, Secretary Fessenden sent backchannel communiqués to Jay Cooke asking for his advice and revealing his concerns over Union finances.[20]

The two men finally sat down in Washington on July 21 to address the financial matters, and Cooke presented six practicable steps to tackle the issue, chief among them being another popular agency run by Cooke. While Fessenden earnestly listened, he strongly opposed any sort of lead role for Cooke owing to the optics and an ethics cloud that followed Cooke in terms of delivery of money to the subtreasury during prior loan issues. There also existed new bipartisan concerns on Capitol Hill over the agency being held by one individual. When Fessenden returned to Maine in August, Cooke received several entreaties from President Lincoln to visit with him and discuss Union finance. Cooke declined, however, because he was of the opinion that fiscal policy should come from the secretary himself, and Fessenden was well aware of Cooke's views on the matter. Likewise, Cooke used his position to leverage the Treasury and government for better terms moving forward. Yet, such support from the president undoubtedly gave Cooke confidence moving into the fall of 1864.[21]

The Treasury faced struggles in the summer of 1864 as it tried to meet the basic operating expenses of the war that were in excess of $2.5 million daily—a war with no end in sight. On August 17, 1864, total sales of the 7-30 notes numbered some $17 million. The 1862 5-20 drive contained some single days that neared this number. Fessenden confided to one of his associates his angst over the present financial situation: "We are not meeting with the hoped for success with regard to the loan ... and I am afraid we shall find ourselves in trouble unless General Grant can help us." While Fessenden hoped positive results on the battlefield would rectify the situation, in reality Jay Cooke and his small financial army would prove instrumental in the dark days of the summer of 1864 in instilling faith in the Union public while simultaneously expanding the government's power and reach across the entire continent.[22]

The Treasury's situation grew so dire that Fessenden opted to put forward a portion of a new 5-20 issue for a direct bankers' bid—akin to the initial act undertaken by Salmon Chase in 1861 with various northeastern banks in New York, Boston, and Philadelphia. While the bond legislation opened the door for the securities to contain a maturation date as far afield as forty years, the success of the 1862 5-20 issue drove Fessenden's decision, hoping name recognition of the previously successful 5-20 issue would be of great help for a subsequent issue under similar terms. Fessenden put out calls to the major northeastern banks on October 1, 1864, for $40 million in 5-20s but found no takers at par or better. Once again, Jay Cooke swooped in. In a rather infamous exchange, Fessenden bemoaned to Cooke his failure to recently sell $10 million of the bonds on terms of his liking on a personal trip to New York. "What do you want for them," Cooke reportedly inquired. "I want par and your commission will be the accrued interest," replied Fessenden. "I will take them myself," Cooke bluntly replied as he once more shouldered the burden of the nation's bond drive through a $10 million investment on the spot. The name of Jay Cooke once more attached to the drive, and when coupled with Lincoln's reelection shortly thereafter, restored confidence to the securities market, albeit briefly. Henry Cooke wrote enthusiastically to his brother as the success of the new 5-20 issue spread. "We need not urge upon you the importance of giving an affirmative response to the option of the whole ten if you can see your way clear," opined Henry. "If this is successful other and more important negotiations will follow. Of this we are assured. We feel now is our chance." Henry followed up these remarks with a longer letter the following day with one sentence getting at the heart of the matter. "If this present undertaking be a success it will be the gateway to other vastly more important successes." Much like the firm's initial work with the 5-20s in the summer of 1862, they hoped their hard work would beget an exclusive agency and simultaneously improve the situation of Union finance.[23]

Not all went along with Cooke's schemes—particularly hard-money Democrats in New York. George Opdyke, John Cisco, and especially Morris Ketchum had little faith in Cooke and questioned the monetary policy of the Lincoln administration. Even as far back as the initial 5-20 loan campaign Ketchum spoke out against any potential increase in bonds for sale, fearing that they might cause "a panic . . . which will sunder the Government powerless." Ketchum had already arranged a separate sale with the federal government of certificates of indebtedness that had gone over very well in 1864, and he hoped to build on this further. By the time the 7-30 agency came around as a real possibility, Cooke viewed Ketchum as a formidable adversary, especially considering Secretary Fessenden's interest in the New York financier. Yet, many questioned Ketchum's ulterior motives. Harris Fahnstock wrote to Jay Cooke describing Ketchum as a "selfish man" who had not acted "as if his heart was in the success of our national finances." Likewise Ketchum made his opinions on Cooke well known to Fessenden's inner circle, including comptroller of the currency (and successor to Fessenden as Secretary of the Treasury) Hugh McCulloch. Ketchum wrote to McCulloch in August 1864, belittling any word emanating from Cooke and his associates, proclaiming, "These men [Cooke & Co] have been so long in a contaminated atmosphere that there is no health in them." Thus, behind the scenes the two camps fed a war of words.[24]

Cooke extended an olive branch to Ketchum, figuring a joint agency better than no agency at all. A series of letters and meetings between Ketchum, Cooke, and Fessenden put forward a real possibility for the $40 million 5-20 agency (and later 7-30 agency). But the joint agency failed to materialize, largely owing to the power of rumor surrounding a concerted effort to depress the market by Ketchum and his colleagues on the eve of a large-scale purchase by his firm and its allies. What resulted was a game of financial chess on the floor of the renamed New York Stock Exchange as Ketchum and the "Exchange House Crowd" positioned for a depression in the valuation of 5-20 bonds to 103–104 while the pro-Cooke firms—spearheaded by Clark, Dodge, & Co.—did everything in their power to keep 5-20 prices at 105 or above. Another Cooke ally, Fisk & Hatch, wrote to Cooke in December 1864, praising Clark, Dodge & Co., remarking that the firm "stood firm as a rock and blocked his [Ketchum's] game." McCulloch (and by implication, Fessenden) could see through Ketchum's ploy. The comptroller wrote to Assistant Treasurer John Stewart in New York: "I regret that our friend Ketchum, who by reason of his great wealth commanding financial influence and intimate personal relations with the Secretary, should be foremost in words and works, in support of the credit of the Treasury, should have been among the lowest instead of the highest bidders. I wish he might be induced to stand where he ought to stand in relation to the Government." The "Exchange Crowd" of Ketchum and his allies had tried to manipulate the market, and in the process made their desires readily apparent to an unsympathetic administration.[25]

Ketchum and Cooke met with Stewart to again discuss a joint agency for the 5-20 loan, which Ketchum flatly refused. Word of such events quickly made its way back to Washington. Furthermore, Ketchum refused to accept the proposed 7-30 commission terms—something that Cooke, at least publicly, agreed to enthusiastically. Cooke wrote to Ketchum criticizing the Treasury on their commission proposals. How much of this Cooke really believed, and how much reflected gamesmanship to push Ketchum away from any further action is certainly up for debate—but his words resonated. Ketchum's refusal to join the loan proved to be the end of the New York movement against Cooke, and Ketchum's firm would lose all credibility when it came out that Morris Ketchum's son, Edward, embezzled over $2.5 million through the firm, leading to its dissolution.[26]

Despite the struggles of the 7-30 loan, Secretary Fessenden's 1864 Annual Report to Congress in December spoke confidently regarding the general public's willingness to shoulder the financial burden. "These negotiations have afforded satisfactory evidence," Fessenden remarked, "not only of the ability of the people to furnish, at a short notice, such sums as may be required, but of the entire confidence felt in the national securities. After nearly four years of a most expensive and wasting war, the means to continue it seem apparently undiminished, while the determination to prosecute it with vigor to the end is unabated." An 1864 circular reinforced this democratic message. "It is *your* war," proclaimed the circular, "you proclaimed it, and you have sustained it against traitors everywhere, with a patriotic conviction unsurpassed in world's history." Perhaps the single most important endorsement came from President Lincoln in his 1864 annual address. "Held, as it is, for the most part by our own people," Lincoln proclaimed, "[the public debt] has become a substantial branch of national, though private, property . . . Men readily perceive that they can not be much oppressed by a debt which they owe to themselves." Even in the midst of sluggish bond performances through the second half of 1864 while the military cause struggled, Fessenden and Lincoln made it a point to emphasize the people's participation in the drive and the crucial power of confidence in the interplay between capital and the Union cause. The slow injection of capital via bond sales proved unsustainable and the Treasury found itself at a crossroads as the calendar turned to 1865. In January, economist Amasa Walker wrote on "men and money," the two elements that Walker believed were "indispensable to war." Walker added, "You may, indeed, have money without men, but cannot have men without money." This quote in *Merchant's Magazine and Commercial Review* laid bare an even larger issue of having enough money to finish the war. Secretary Fessenden knew the stakes, and the remedy—the agency would once more need to find its way to Jay Cooke.[27]

Cooke's 7-30 Agency

On January 9, 1865, Henry Cooke wrote to his brother that total 7-30 sales amounted to $115 million, almost $20 million of which had been given to Union soldiers as payments in lieu of greenbacks. By January 12, daily sales averaged only $500,000 and the certainty of an established agency via Cooke & Co. became more realistic. Cooke's national banks, the First National of Philadelphia and the First National of Washington, processed sales that exceeded all other national banks at the time. Fessenden saw all that he needed, and following a new piece of legislation that opted to shift the remaining burden into 7-30 notes, Fessenden granted Cooke the commission on his last day in office before his return to the Senate.[28]

From his position, Cooke received a commission of three-fourths of one percent on the first $50 million and five-eighths for the subsequent $50 million. Further negotiations continued for the remaining bonds—a quantity that rose to a total of $830 million following an act of Congress on March 3, 1865. Most tellingly, the agreement permitted the Secretary of the Treasury to suspend Jay Cooke's appointment at any time should he deem it to be a necessity. Cooke disapproved of the conditions of his agency and lamented to his brother, "I am not disposed to work my life blood out under such depressing circumstances." Yet despite this apparent attack on Cooke's credibility, he accepted the agency and worked extensively to promote the new 7-30 campaign to reach its goal of $2 million in daily sales. To accomplish this, Cooke utilized methods similar to the 5-20 campaign. In so doing, Cooke fashioned a national vision that utilized bond sales to promote an American empire that could stand alone among the financial and political giants of the world. "The subscription should run like a cord through the whole country," Cooke proclaimed, "tying it tougher, making one interest, removing prejudices and solidifying the nation."[29]

In order to create the most popular loan ever seen, Cooke undertook an unprecedented advertising campaign to raise awareness while organizing his network of agents across the Union. Cooke & Co. brought on board *New York Tribune* writer Samuel Wilkeson on a salary of $6,000 to "be the manufacture of editorials, letters, notices and so forth to be used by other agents, and inserted in the papers etc." An assortment of circulators soon emanated from the Cooke PR machine in New York City headed by Wilkeson and included the remarkably popular circular "Interesting Questions and Answers Relative to the 7-30 U.S. Loan." Much like the "Berks County Farmer" exchange for the 5-20 drive, this circular intended to inform the public by answering such questions as "When and how can they be obtained?" "What other advantage is there in investing in the 7-30 Loan?" and "How does the Government raise the money to pay the interest, and is it safe and sure?", along with several other questions related to the basic logistical procurement of the bonds. The *Constitutional Union* referenced Cooke as the "Napoleon of Finance" and "Our Modern Midas" while the *New Yorker* remarked, "in these financial times, no name has a more metallic ring than that of Jay Cooke . . . Every farmhouse, bank, hotel, counting room and back settlement hears of the loan. The result is, that from a state of languor it springs into intense activity." Others wrote extensively supporting the 7-30 drive: In the *New York Times*, Cooke had a "Mr. Norvell," while the *Brooklyn Union* contained writings from Michael Hennessy and the *Boston Commercial Ledger* those of James W. Simonton. These writers propagated a message of the people's loan wherein all could invest. When combined with the agents spread through the states and territories, it ensured the most democratic measure of war finance to date.[30]

Further examples in various papers reveal a deeper notion of citizenship and the incorporation of those previously marginalized or excluded from civic participation. One article spoke to "German Hans" and the Irishman "Patrick" in an effort to reach out to immigrant communities in the North while ameliorating the lack of understanding on the part of the general public when it came to securities. One 7-30 agent writing from Dubuque, Iowa, commented on German immigrants who frequently crossed the border from Wisconsin having seen the bank's circular to purchase 7-30s. The agent (a bank cashier) commented that this was a frequent occurrence among members of the German immigrant community. He concluded the letter, "Our government was never so strong as today and will be sustained in all the acts by the people who hold its notes." Another article reaffirmed such sentiments. "The investment is certainly the best that an American citizen can make for it is endowed by the whole credit of the nation, and if the United States is not 'good,'—what bank, what corporation is good?"[31]

Cooke had an ingenious way to encourage bond advertising in newspapers far and wide by incorporating options on bonds for newspaper writers and editors. Recognizing that the funds with which he could operate for advertising would not be enough, Cooke approached several newspaper editors and offered them options on bond issues. The terms typically were for an option of sixty days upon some quantity of bonds. The newspapermen would reap the benefits of the transaction minus the interest. If the price did not advance to the agreed-upon rate, the call typically renewed for some period of time. Cooke utilized this approach with newspapermen throughout the North, including rather famously with C. C. Norvell of the *New York Times*. Thus the newspapers themselves had a truly vested interest in the bond sales and consequently worked hard to ensure their success. When Cooke coupled the options with regular wine shipments from his native Ohio to various newspapers and brokers in Washington, New York, and Philadelphia, editors and their allies in finance discovered that loyalty to the cause of bond sales generated ample rewards.[32]

Newspapers regaled the general public with highfalutin tales of purchases and dedication to the Union cause by everyday citizens. In March 1865, the *New York Tribune* related stories of a boy who traveled from the western part of Indiana to Philadelphia with $10,000 in greenbacks (about $164,000 in 2020) and state bank currency to invest in 7-30s. Still another story told of a German man who walked into a national bank in Dubuque, Iowa, having traveled some thirty miles by foot from his farm in Bellevue. Dressed in ragged clothes to give the appearance of a "mendicant," he had purposely dressed as such to avoid being robbed on the road. He arrived in the office to pull out some $13,000 of his own and neighbors' money to invest in the cause. Countless examples such as these reinforced the national scope of these democratic sales as part of a larger American identity.[33]

Newspaper articles targeted the people in various ways, but all ultimately spoke to sacrifice and the power of the people to help maintain the Union through their financial contributions to the cause. The public approval of the loan was a popular refrain in newspapers. Newspapers emphasized the investments of "merchant," next to "brick-layer" and "minister" next to "fishmonger." Additionally, Union widows proved a valuable subject to market the financial sacrifice that had accompanied their sacrifice of a son or husband to the cause. "Among the soldier's wives who have been enabled to lay up some means," one newspaper exclaimed, "it is justly popular." Such pieces often reinforced the providential nature of the drives and the war writ large. "We have no fears of failure," the same article proclaimed. "Our cause is just and a righteous Providence will guide us successfully to the end." An emphasis on the dual struggle of the widow who sacrificed her loved ones on the battlefield and her purse on the home front became an effective example of the ultimate sacrifice by certain members of the Northern public.[34]

Confidence proved key to the success of securities sales during the war and was a topic repeatedly emphasized by the Northern press. "Let us furnish all the means necessary to accomplish this great work," proclaimed one Buffalo bank circular. "Let us show our unshaken and firm confidence in the Government and its credit." The circular added, "All good citizens who desire to aid in achieving this glorious result should now come forward, and make a good investment for themselves, and at the same time discharge a patriotic duty to their country." Such a statement conflated patriotic duty and self-interest—a common theme in some of the bond literature. Still other articles emphasized how financial sacrifice served as one of several ways the people could give to their country and in doing so reassert their confidence in the Union. "So the people have given to their country all that she asked—their property, their individual rights, their lives," one newspaper exclaimed. "By this they show not only their willingness to sacrifice in her behalf, but their confidence in her power to preserve herself." These refrains among the Northern public revealed a collective call to serve through investment, and the larger democratic nature of the financial cause that millions enlisted in.[35]

The sacrifice of the people also afforded an opportunity at emphasizing American exceptionalism on the matters of war finance. Any comparisons made with European war finance often shed a critical eye toward "big bank" finance. "In foreign lands, when a government calls for funds, it sends its requests to the great bankers of Europe," the *Evening Telegraph* declared, "to the ROTHSCHILDS or the BARING BROTHERS; but in our Republic it is to the people, the common source of all governmental power, that the authorities in distress appeal." Still another newspaper remarked, "Whilst European monarchies have their war-loans absorbed by the few rich bankers—the American loan is so tendered that the humblest citizen may become a bondholder." But perhaps Jay Cooke put it best when he remarked, "This loan could easily have been marketed in Germany. But what a political blunder it would have been to have sold it abroad, and what an economical misfortune. The war debt of the United States, due to the people of the United States, can be easily carried and ultimately paid. Two American national debts have been extinguished by payment. The third one will be extinguished in the same way . . . I hold in this fist [telegraph orders for bonds] the guarantee of permanent union between the East and the West, and the centre and the extremes." The distinction between uniquely American loans versus their foreign counterparts became one in which the people shouldered the financial burden of war, and in so doing reflected the very best ideals of the democratic experiment and the burgeoning power of the American state. Although the idea that loan sales did not exist and did not need to exist overseas was a lie, it is true that the 7-30 did not carry with it as much investor interest overseas as other loans, such as the 6 percent '81s issued in 1861 and the 5-20 loan.[36]

Quantifying bond sales among the people became an effective way of reinforcing the democratic nature of sales, proving that such a notion went beyond mere rhetoric. While Philadelphia and New York newspapers often listed daily subscriptions of quantities in the $50 and $100 bonds, in addition to the largest subscriptions of East and West, the political statements made by such purchases were often emphasized. One New Jersey newspaper exclaimed, "How sublime the thought when near *fifteen thousand* persons, with their $50 and $100, come forward to assist the Government with their mites in one week. This number shows how emphatically the people are interested in this loan." Other accounts indicated the political power that the small-savings individual held. Regarding a point in the spring of 1865 when Congress debated the value of the $50 bond issue as part of the 7-30 loan, one newspaper brought to the attention of the general public, "The working women of one of our western counties, [who] came bravely forth and asked for fourteen thousand fifty dollar bonds, thus settling the matter to the entire satisfaction of our lawmakers at Washington." Still another account of the power of the people attested to their political will:

> While Congressmen debated on Thursday last the policy of restricting the issue of new government bonds to sums not less than $100, and knocked back and forth the shuttle-cocks of ancient argument against and in favor of $50 bonds, the needlewomen of the northern and western villages, cities and towns, and the mechanics and apprentices of thrifty habits and patriotic faith stepped forward and settled the question authoritatively and in favor of both issues. Thirteen hundred and fifty of them carried their little earnings to Jay Cooke's agencies and bought $50 bonds, and 1800 of them bought $100 bonds. A telegram communicating this precious fact to the proper committee in Washington was accepted as a decision of the point under discussion. The provision in the bill authorizing the issue of the small bond was retained.[37]

Other reports, such as that of 3,500 subscriptions on March 15, 1865, out of Portland, Maine, reveal the depth to which the people well and truly bought into the cause of Union and by extension the concept of a true American nation. In undertaking such actions, the American people (largely through Cooke and his network) bought into Cooke's attempts to sell their confidence in themselves back to them—a task that reaped Cooke and Co. a handsome profit.[38]

Newspapers cited the effect of bonds to break the will of the Southern people, but also the opportunity such bonds afforded for sectional reconciliation. In keeping with the military-like significance of the bond sales, one newspaper quipped, "The unexampled success in the disposal of this loan is not without its effect on the rebel mind, giving evidence, as it does, not only of the will of our people to see the war through, but of the money strength of the country to render that will effective." A week later, another newspaper heralded the wonderful opportunities bond sales could offer in bringing the nation back together again: "The circle of influences to establish the Seven-Thirty Loan, and to root down deep the credit of the Government on all American territory, disloyal and loyal—to establish it in our armies—to convert and enlist into the service of the union finances what banks the Rebellion has left alive in the South, and to induce the establishment of new ones under the National Law, where banks ought to exist—this circle is rapidly becoming complete. When finished, the nation will be hooped together with material lines of latitude and longitude, stronger than steel." Bonds came to be seen as a measure that not only bound the Union together, but also could possibly serve a purpose in bringing the South back into the fold once hostilities ceased.[39]

Extending the advertisements beyond English-language papers to many immigrant communities also expanded the possible network of investors on the civic margins of society. There was hope that many immigrant communities would invest in the Union cause, and in doing so, make a statement about their own role as future American citizens. The *Freie Presse* in Philadelphia represented one of several German-language newspapers in the North advertising for the Union. The "Sieben-Dreissiger Anleihe" became well known throughout the German speaking community and "Jay Cooke wieder Regierungs-Banquier" became synonymous with bond sales. While claims would be made incorrectly criticizing the lack of contributions of European financiers, the same would not be said of immigrants to the Union. Once more, these investor acts also played a key role in the larger messaging of the bond drives.[40]

Economic matters also made their way into houses of God. New England Baptist minister George Ide famously spoke to his congregation about the omnipresence of "the pillar of God's Providence . . . arranging all, overruling all," a notion that extended to the world of finance. "How signal has been the interposition of Providence," mused Ide, "at the very point in time when the wants of the Government required extraordinary revenues, and the sources were closed from which treasure had been wont to flow in from abroad, the almighty disposer of events . . . caused the tide of wealth to set strongly upon our shores." Ide commented further, "Brought about by divine interference . . . enterprise is active. Business thrives. Labor is in demand, and well rewarded." One subagent wrote to Cooke relaying his efforts to enlist various clergy in New York's Hudson River valley to encourage their congregants to subscribe to the loan scheme. Of the forty-five clergy he purportedly visited, all but two agreed to share this benevolent message. Thus, the rewards of finance and investment made its way into houses of worship all throughout the North, with agents on hand ready and willing to assist those in answering God's call to invest. Cooke likewise connected with the vibrant Quaker populations in Pennsylvania and Ohio and through communication with various meetinghouses convinced their members to support the cause. According to Cooke's recollection in his memoirs, he promised that Quaker funds would not go towards active war instruments, but rather to treat the sick and wounded—a bold promise to make, but nevertheless Cooke leveraged his position to appeal to any and all potential investors.[41]

7-30 Sales among the Masses

While marketing and daily reports for small sales of $50 and $100 are one thing, a more detailed analysis of 7-30 sales records reveals just how democratic these sales became—and how the marketing and wild tales of widespread democratic purchases across the continent and crossing gendered and racial lines did indeed match reality. To be sure, the majority of 7-30s found their way to New York, Boston, Philadelphia, Baltimore, Washington, Cincinnati, and St. Louis. These were the largest urban centers in the country and an overwhelming percentage of these sales at the primary and secondary levels fed through these cities. But the 7-30 sales (in keeping with the shift during the 10-40 drive) represented a true movement towards many more smaller towns throughout the North, as well as more regions of the border states and the Confederacy itself with a large quantity of small-savings individuals purchasing in the $50 and $100 range. From Bangor, Maine; to Concord, New Hampshire; Barre, Massachusetts; to Elmira, New York; Columbus, Ohio; to Galesburg, Illinois; Madison, Indiana; to Norfolk, Virginia; to New Orleans, Louisiana; Vicksburg, Mississippi; and Albany, Oregon, bond sales touched nearly every facet of Northern and Southern life by 1864. In spanning the continent, these sales brought the war directly to the people—exposing the dramatic democratic revolution of bond sales that introduced the federal government to areas that, save the post, had thus far very little interaction with the national government.[42]

Take, for example, sales in the town of Brunswick, Maine. Located some twenty-five miles north of the larger port of Portland, this small seafaring town home to Bowdoin College boasted a population of some 4,700 persons for the 1860 census. Yet, for such a small town, Brunswick contributed disproportionately to the drive. Once more, these sales came from a vast cross section of the town's population (as well as surrounding smaller communities). These purchases ranged widely. On the upper end were individuals such as Stephen Young. A Maine native and 1859 graduate of Bowdoin, Young was a professor of modern language at Bowdoin by August 1864, when he purchased $1,000 in 7-30s from the First National Bank of Brunswick. At the same time, Ira Merryman, a stonecutter residing on Federal Street, purchased $600 in 7-30s. These represented higher quantities, to be sure, but the purchasers were from different walks of life. A deeper analysis of the Brunswick sales reveals other local buyers. Mary Given, a mother of six and wife of a local deacon, purchased several hundred dollars in 7-30s. Likewise, Lydia Pierce, a seventy-one-year-old woman who ran a local boardinghouse, put

$100 toward 7-30 notes. These sales represent just a small portion of the sales through the First National Bank of Brunswick, which totaled some $60,400 in 7-30s alone. All told, 120 purchases came through the First National Bank between August 1, 1864, and February 3, 1865. While the mean average for the purchases was just north of $500, several four-figure purchases skew this data. The median purchase was $300 with the mode, or purchase of greatest frequency, being $100. This snapshot of a single Northern town revealed the efforts to sell bonds to "the people" and an examination of how the reality of purchases matched or synced with the media messaging emanating from Cooke and his public relations machine.[43]

Migrating west from New England with the 7-30 sales reveals the increasing prevalence of immigrants and farmers as investors in the cause—and not necessarily small purchases. German immigrant August Schmidt made his way to Davenport City, Iowa, by the time of 7-30 sales, ultimately purchasing $1,600 of the bonds. Fellow German Peter Schlichting pulled together the necessary funds for $1,000 in 7-30s. Another purchaser in Davenport City, Reverend William Shand, purchased a more modest $250. While these numbers are beyond the $50 and $100 sales so often trumpeted by Cooke, a detailed examination of the sales nevertheless reveals a plethora of small-sales individuals—albeit with less information to go on (oftentimes initials for first and middle names), thus making it far more difficult to follow. Still other areas contain even more variety. Thomas J. Watson, a wagonmaker in Leavenworth, Kansas, purchased $200 in 7-30s. Charles Kuhns, a farmer in Lafayette, Indiana, purchased $200 in 7-30s. A cobbler, Oliver Delancy, purchased $300 in 7-30s in Cooperstown, New York. These examples offer just a small sample of the innumerable actors who engaged in 7-30 sales even before Cooke's agency in 1865. Further examples merely reinforce the fact that these sales took place on a scale never before seen in American war finance, distributed widely among men and women and throughout the Northern states and territories.[44]

Traveling Agents Crisscross the Nation

Despite the widespread marketing campaign enacted by Cooke to push 7-30 sales, the thousands of traveling agents in pursuit of subscribers undertook much of the grunt work. Indeed, the 7-30 drive led to further sophistication of the sales network throughout the country. Mirroring the structure of the 5-20 drive, these traveling agents spanned the entire Union, both states and western territories, to sell bonds and organize offices wherein bonds could be sold—often at the local (and recently organized) national banks. In undertaking such a drastic expansion of the sales network compared to the 5-20 drive, Cooke and his associates increased the geographic and social profile of potential subscribers, and wedded the populace ever more tightly to the Union cause, strengthening the federal government in the process.

Following the requests of Cooke, many of these agents wrote back to report on their actions. Edward Sacket, who canvassed the old northwest, reported in March 1865 from Wisconsin regarding a slew of bond offices that had been set up enticing all walks of life; this included thousands of dollars in bond sales from the Bohemian miners outside of Green Bay. Other agents reported sales from throughout the North: Traveling agent William Gallaway reported from Illinois "a total of $160.000" worth of bonds sold just in three localities in the previous three weeks. Charles Tarwinkel wrote from Romeo, Michigan, relaying bond sales from the month of March: "Cassapolis 8.000, Niles 30.000, Dowagiac 10.000, Albion 18.000." Winslow Souther wrote from Davenport, Iowa, "Have visited nine counties since my arrival and have found the Loan as popular as in some of our eastern cities and there is hardly a farmer but has more or less in his possession." GP Hopkins wrote from Indianapolis, "The loan is popular and finds all the sparse cash in the place." One such report in March 1865 witnessed the aforementioned Sacket humbly proclaim, "I flatter myself that my trip thus far, has tended to stimulate parties to greater exertion in disposing of the loan, and somewhat added to an increased confidence on the part of the investor." Other agents wrote of great success in setting up networks to sell bonds in Kansas and Missouri, while others proudly detailed sales of $20,000 in Detroit. Still another agent, J. E. Zug, wrote from Illinois: "Farmers who live in a little cabin, wear their home-spun clothes and ride to church and town in their two-horse wagons without springs have in many instances several thousand dollars loaned to the government." Likewise, a Mr. DeCoursey wrote that the bonds attracted "People of both sexes, of every age, class and description, and of all colors wishing to secure a first mortgage on the property of the United States." The impact of Cooke and his network remained undeniable. The first series of the loan sold under the orders of the Treasury alone took 169 days. In fifty-five days beginning February 1, 1865, Cooke's network exceeded the first-series performance by some $34 million. These salesmen and the sub-agents they enlisted were a true testament to the ever-increasing scope of the sales throughout the North.[45]

The 7-30 sales marked a geographic expansion as salesmen moved into western territories in pursuit of bond sales. The sales spread from coast to coast as new bank Wells Fargo & Co. pledged to sell the bonds in California,

Oregon, Nevada, and Washington Territory. Transactions west of the Rockies proved considerably more difficult than those in Europe from a logistical standpoint because of the length of time required to reach the West Coast. Wells Fargo & Co. operated over 300 offices in the region to sell the bonds. Many banks in California were still on the gold standard, however, making it difficult to sell 7-30s. There was also the matter of belief in the bond delivery itself, resulting in over $4 million in bonds sent to California in advance of the sales to overcome skepticism. Nowhere else in the Union did such an act take place to reassure a general public. Orders began to come in from California and interest in purchases came from the Colorado and Nevada Territories. Other sales came from Santa Fe, New Mexico Territory, from "cow-punchers and Mexicans."[46]

Detailed sales records out of San Francisco add clarity to western sales. Totaling some $750,000 in 7-30 sales, these were overwhelmingly purchases in the four-figure range among the various business interests in the city. These ranged from established merchants in the region such as William Coleman and Co., and Hickox & Spear, as well as maritime insurance firms such as the Chinese Mutual Insurance Company, and other small business owners; one of these purchasers of note was the aforementioned bookseller H. H. Bancroft. Still others include a manufacturer named Asher Rosenblatt who procured a more modest sum of $150 in 7-30s, while a Congregational minister originally from New Hampshire named Hiram Cummings procured $1,000 in 7-30s. Others purchasers came from outside of San Francisco in the more agricultural regions of the state, including one Amanda Culver, the wife of farmer Willett Culver who had moved the entire family to California from New York. The Culver family invested $650 in 7-30s. Countless other examples from the region illustrate the sales via the San Francisco subtreasury as well as Wells Fargo & Co. and span California and north into Oregon, covering towns in that state such as Albany, Corvallis, and Eugene.[47]

In stretching these sales across the continent, Cooke achieved his (and the government's) goal of unifying the nation and binding purchasers through the promise of Union and financial gain. The subscription rate reflected faith on the part of the general public to shoulder this burden outside the monied and more densely packed Northeast. Cooke's calculations confirm such an assessment. At war's end some $230 million of the 7-30 sales came from the West.[48]

The 7-30 campaign also incorporated night agencies into its marketing repertoire in an effort to cater to the needs of "workingmen" in northeastern cities and their environs. These "workingman savings banks" originated in

Washington and established themselves in drug stores and other businesses where workers, soldiers, and others could speak with a representative and ask questions about the loan sales. As night became morning, the offices even offered coffee and doughnuts to individuals heading off (or returning from) work. One 7-30 advertisement described the scene among a disparate group of workingmen and women from Chinese, Irish, German, and even Native American backgrounds:

> Out of 100 bond-buyers who crowd the office in Bleecker street, each waiting in turn to lend his money out on interest, at least 60 are mechanics or laborers, 20 are saloon-keepers, small dealers and soldiers, and the rest are an almost nondescript condition of venders, clerks, and even boys, mixed in with a number of women in faded calico or mourning—toil, sorrow, wrinkled thrift, or the working-woman's work-a-day written upon their features. In another arrival the proportion of dealers and soldiers is greater, but throughout the evening a tide of labor pours in through the portals of the "Seven-Thirty," amid a confusion of faces, tongues and opinion. Rude finance discussed with homely sense between workman and workman, political prejudice cured or silenced by a witty word tossed over the shoulder, question after question answered across the counter and the whole matter and genius of the 7:30 understood and appreciated.[49]

With such descriptions, Cooke & Co. reinforced the democratic messaging of the bond campaigns in an effort to popularize the loan. New York City had no fewer than eight of these agencies operating by the summer of 1865 and several more could be found in neighboring Brooklyn, Jersey City, and Newark.[50]

The democratic messaging of bond sales via these night agencies became abundantly clear with further advertising. One telling example of 7-30 sales at a Bleecker Street office in Lower Manhattan in July 1865 noted 157 purchasers, drawn from international buyers and blue-collar roots:

> 27 were shop-keepers, 19 were machinists, boiler-makers, foundry men, etc all workers in iron; 17 returned soldiers and sailors; 12 clerks and store-tenders 10 saloon keepers; nine steamboat men, engineers, etc; five bartenders, four hotel servants, five hatters; four saddlers; four cardrivers; two cabmen; two farmers; three stall-keepers; five shoemakers; four tailors; five bookbinders; six store and working women; six barbers; four cigarmakers; one was a telegrapher; one an actor; one a journalist; 13 were

This advertisement for night offices in Manhattan, Brooklyn, Jersey City, and Newark for the 1864 7-30 loan issue illustrates the effort to appeal to ordinary individuals and accommodate their schedules. (*Liberty Loan Committee Second Federal Reserve District: Report of the Publicity Committee on Work Done in Connection with the Flotation of the First United States Government Liberty Loan of 1917* [Palala Press, 2015])

Irishmen; 16 Germans, and Portuguese, Chinese, and one Moor, were part of the curiosity of nationality. These facts give only a glimpse of a world-wide democratic phase of the 7-30.[51]

The 7-30 agents also made their way into the Confederate heartland to sell the bonds as Union forces moved into the Lower South. Traveling agents ventured into Tennessee, Virginia, Georgia, South Carolina, and Louisiana (especially in and around New Orleans) to peddle the commodity. Much like their 10-40 predecessors, these 7-30s found their way into the Confederacy as sales attained high levels. In Norfolk, Virginia, sales reached the military population stationed in the area, but also individuals like twenty-two-year-old James M. Black, the son of a "timber getter," who purchased $350 in 7-30s in September 1864; the Reverend Vincent Palen also partook in the drive. But for the epicenter of sales in the Confederacy, one must look at New Orleans. The city, occupied by Union forces in April 1862, became a large arena for investment by the 10-40 drive and that enthusiasm carried over into the 7-30 campaign. Like other regions in the North, the bond sales covered a wide swath of individuals. Some, like physician Julius Gunther, purchased several thousand dollars in 7-30s. Emilie Collin, a French-born resident of New Orleans and wholesale liquor dealer, picked up $250 in 7-30s. Another liquor dealer, George Underhill, purchased $100 in 7-30s. Catherine Benedict, a Pennsylvanian transplant and a wife of a local "collector," purchased $300 in bonds.[52]

There were numerous soldiers purchasing bonds in New Orleans as well. While some were high-profile officers such as Col. James Grant Wilson of the 4th USC Cavalry, others were rank-and-file soldiers such as free black private Levi Robinson from Company A of the 115th USCT, who purchased a $50 7-30 note in October 1864, only to die the following August. All told, some $118,000 in 7-30s were sold in New Orleans through the First National Bank alone before Cooke took over the agency. Once he did, nearly $1.7 million in 7-30s found their way through New Orleans—although few records exist once you move into 1865 and Cooke's agency took over the city. Similarly, while it is impossible to know the exact composition of all the various purchasers, some certainly were Northern transplants—either from the antebellum years or because of military service—but undoubtedly some of those on the list of purchasers were residents of New Orleans that held Confederate sympathies, at least before the fall of the city to Union forces. Two years of occupation may have changed attitudes—or at least outward perception—

and bond purchases reflected one way of demonstrating loyalty to the federal government.⁵³

The voluminous reports that these agents submitted to Cooke in Philadelphia not only gave him an update as to the sales in various regions, but offered Cooke a chance to take the political and social pulse of a given area. Bond sales in the South took on different forms, from Unionists looking to cement their loyalty to the Union despite their geographic location, to Confederates looking to hedge against the waning chances of their dying cause. Perhaps most importantly, these Southern bond sales offered former enemies of the Union the opportunity to invest in the new realities brought forward by the war. In doing so, one might even argue that it offered an opportunity for sectional reconciliation by means of bond sales. Such an act demonstrated a substantive attachment to the security of the American state, regardless of one's wartime loyalty. The work on the part of Cooke's network revealed the extent to which the democratic messaging of sales knew no domestic bounds.⁵⁴

Southerners found Cooke's sales of incredible interest (even if they did not bother to learn how to spell his name). On February 20, 1865, The *Richmond Examiner* reported:

> The Federal government is now selling large amount of what they call seven-thirty bonds, being hundred dollar bills bearing interest at two cents a day. Under the auspices of an eccentric financier named Jaye Cook, who has established agencies in all the large Federal cities and under which they hold out, these bonds are selling rapidly, and are pronounced a spendied [sic] financial success... The efforts of the Yankees to sustain this explosive and inflated paper system, has so far been marked by great ingenuity, resolution, and success. Whether they will succeed in conquering the South, depends in a great degree upon their success in upholding this paper system.⁵⁵

Such statements demonstrated how Cooke's name truly took on national stature. Confederates knew just as well of Cooke as their Union counterparts, a testament to Cooke's ability to market well and truly in all regions.

The vibrancy of bond sales led to a significant backlog in outstanding bond distribution. By July 1865, $500,000 of 7-30s remained outstanding to the First National Bank of New Orleans alone. According to local agent Richard Randolph, sales of the 7-30 in New Orleans amounted to some $839,350—although mostly to larger financial institutions and not without a significant delay of months that agitated many of the locals and "exhausted the 'fertility'" of traveling agents' imaginations. Even in the former heart of the secession movement, South Carolina, Cooke attempted sales, but met with little success. The total sales only reached $10,000. Still, the subagent requested that the sales be widely publicized in the hopes that more sales in South Carolina (and its neighbor Georgia) may occur. Not all was this promising, however, as one subagent reported of difficulty in the interior of Mississippi where rampant violence on the part of "jayhawkers" and their adversaries still plagued the region despite a significant Union army presence. This, according to the subagent, contributed to a "rather unhealthy" area to attempt bond sales. Another subagent (Cooke's brother-in-law) in Missouri regaled Cooke with tales of guerrillas running amok as late as March and April 1865, making sales difficult to come by, and resulting in him being robbed on at least one occasion. Richard Randolph's continued sojourns through the South included commentary on the assassination of Lincoln and the great amount of mourning on the part of African Americans in Vicksburg, as well as complete disarray in Mobile, where many former rebels still strolled the streets with firearms at their sides. Word of the bond sales spread across parts of the South, and its native sons offered to open their own banking houses and act as 7-30 agents. One agent wrote from Natchez, Mississippi, to report on "many of the freedmen having sums of money who would be only glad to invest in such bonds." In April 1865, mere days after Lee's surrender, Petersburg, Virginia–based Thomas Branch and Sons wrote to Jay Cooke offering to be a banking agent in the impoverished area, although the firm did note that three members were paroled prisoners from Appomattox. Meanwhile the South Carolina Freedmen's Savings Bank, recently established in Beaufort, South Carolina, also offered its services as a new 7-30 agent. The Southern landscape thus afforded an entirely new market for securities as the war began to wind down and many wondered what fate awaited the former Confederate states.[56]

As was the case with the 5-20 loan, struggles emerged with sales to heavily Democratic areas. Copperheads made life in certain parts of the North very difficult for traveling agents. J. E. Zug drew one of the short straws in the sales game for 7-30s as his travels through Delaware proved remarkably difficult. Speaking about a cashier in Milford, Delaware, Zug revealed the difficulties he faced. "I tried to induce him to try the experiment," remarked Zug, "but he was not disposed to take any special pains to sell, or make popular the Loan, the secret of his indisposition is, he is a copperhead." Two days later, Zug vented his frustrations regarding the cashier at the Bank of Georgetown: "He would have nothing to do with me he is a rebel." Alexander Robb shared similar frustrations writing from Parkersburg, West Virginia, in March 1865. "General Jackson of the 2nd National is rather against the government," reported Robb, "[He] talks down its securities &c &c-is in favor of repudiation and talks queer altogether . . . Folks say his sympathies are with the south and call him copperhead." Yet some copperheads did come to see the light eventually. One report to the Philadelphia office mentioned an agent who had "just invested $700 in seven thirties for 'a poor washerwoman,' the savings of seven years which she had until now been deterred from investing by the counsel of a Copperhead friend."[57]

While Zug and Robb met with difficulties, the winner might very well be Julian Brewer. Brewer's circuit involved some pro-slavery regions of Maryland and as a result led to tremendous difficulties in his quest for sales. One April day Brewer reported, "This morning I begun to go out among the people finding them or the most of them violent southern men and as their armies have not been very successful found them in rather a bad [], They don't fancy 7.30 bonds." Two days later, Brewer reiterated his frustrations regarding selling bonds in this pro-Confederate segment of Maryland. "I do not think I have ever been in a place where there has been so little interest shown in relation to the loan, as the majority of the population are strong secessionists; and do not feel any interest in any thing that has relation to the Government as to getting them to invest their negro made money in Government bonds (at present) is out of the question." Brewer's frustrations reached their peak with his arrest as part of the vast sweeps in the wake of Lincoln's assassination. Brewer remained imprisoned in Washington until Cooke's office properly identified him.[58]

Taking a deeper look at the numbers reveals how widespread small-savings individuals contributed to the 7-30 drive. While 5-20 registered bonds contained a total of 7,034 bond purchases of $50 or $100, these numbers would pale in comparison to small bond purchases as part of the 7-30 drive. In the months of February and March 1865 alone, a total of 113,392 bond purchases occurred in $50 and $100 increments. In fact, the small bond purchases of March 10, 1865, exceeded all small bond individual purchasers for registered 5-20 bonds. Small bond sales continued to accelerate. During the first week of May, small bond sales amounted to 28,239 purchases. Likewise, May 9, 10, and 11, 1865, yielded small bond sales of 10,651, 11,928, and 10,752, respectively. May 12, 1865, however, was the single largest day of small-savings subscribers as 21,307 individuals purchased $50 and $100 bonds.[59]

The bond sales also benefitted from the close coordination between Cooke's offices and the Treasury Department. On numerous occasions

Cooke received formal authorization from the Treasury to buy bonds while acting on behalf of the federal government in order to alleviate concern in the market. On March 21, 1865, Secretary of the Treasury Hugh McCulloch (who succeeded William Pitt Fessenden's brief eight-month tenure) wrote to Cooke authorizing him to purchase bonds in large quantities as "may be deemed necessary" in order to stabilize the market. Such actions reaffirmed the role Cooke and his agents played in steadying bond prices and, to a smaller degree, Northern monetary policy.[60]

Not all financiers cooperated with the federal government. The persistent thorn in the government's side, Morris Ketchum, was once again a culprit. Writing from New York, John Stewart bemoaned to Secretary McCulloch, "There is a very uneasy feeling in the community which it will be difficult to allay. It is said Ketchum is a large seller of Governments and the fall in gold, Governments and other securities is attributed in a considerable measure to the operations of a bear party in which his son is understood to be one of the most prominent actors." Cooke worked actively in concert with the Treasury in late March and early April 1865 to allay fears and right the market. Cooke also used money from other bond sales to prop up any and all sales of bonds that might fall below par on the New York Stock Exchange. In doing so, Cooke helped to maintain the inherent value of the bonds and, by association, the federal government. Once more, such actions reveal the interplay between Cooke and the federal government over federal economic policy—foreshadowing more concerted and centralized monetary policy by the first part of the twentieth century.[61]

Democratization also meant the bonds found their way to Union soldiers. Aside from some efforts by the government to compensate soldiers in bonds, agents also followed the various armies to sell the bonds following army paydays in proper greenbacks. Bonds could be held by the soldiers themselves, mailed home with the assistance of the agents, and even held on behalf of the bondholder with the notification of the next of kin should the soldier fall on the battlefield. One soldier even wrote to Cooke about his rationalization for purchasing the bonds—a message Cooke wanted to spread far and wide in the Union armies. "If I fight hard enough," proclaimed the soldier from the Army of the Potomac, "my bonds will be good." Still another soldier, this one from a USCT unit attached to the Army of the James, wrote to Cooke in the spring of 1865 inquiring whether bonds purchased by soldiers could be held by Cooke & Co. until such a time as the soldiers completed their service and in the interim they could ensure the bonds stayed in the hands of reliable individuals. Another letter to publicist Samuel Wilkeson spoke of $7,000 of sales to soldiers at a night agency office on 60 Bleecker Street in New York City, and $16,000 worth of bond sales to soldiers stationed on Hart's Island in the modern-day Bronx, while two other night offices totaled a further $2,000 in soldier sales. Still another subagent in Minnesota noted that thousands of dollars' worth of bonds made it into the hands of troops mustering out in St. Paul, and the bonds likewise found a sizable demand in Wisconsin among troops mustering out. Another traveling agent reported that $30,000 in bonds were taken out by the 5th Kentucky Cavalry while another traveling agent reported that the First National Bank of Davenport, Iowa, placed bonds at a rate of $15,000 a day in the hands of soldiers. A seamen writing from the recovery ship *Princeton* asked how he might invest his wages in bonds. Another letter detailed the efforts to coordinate sales to soldiers at the paymaster level using them as agents to sell bonds in Kentucky and other portions of the western theater.[62]

The publicist John Russell Young worked arduously to sell the bonds to Union soldiers. Opening a shop run by his younger brother on Bleecker Street opposite the army pay department, they received special permission from Gen. John Adams Dix to sell to the soldiers. The 133rd New York Regiment purchased some $27,000 in bonds. The office sold on average nearly $20,000 of bonds to soldiers on any given day and in five weeks sold nearly $500,000 in 7-30s to Union soldiers. One quartermaster in Virginia proudly boasted of nearly $200,000 in bond sales to Northern soldiers and sailors. Still another report in from Jay Cooke's Philadelphia office described an officer coming in to make purchases at the Third Street office and his subsequent exchange with Jay Cooke: "The lame officer comes in," reported the editor, "and takes gold out of his vest pocket, five double eagles, and jingles them. 'One of my men asked me to bring this in' (this officer commands a camp of rendezvous and instruction for colored troops) and put it into 7.30s. 'Tardy repentance, colonel! But the white gold gamblers have been caught in the same way. Better late than never though,' 'And another has given me $300 to invest.' 'Hurrah! Ah, colonel, it is not altogether a white man's war, is it? I am glad to have black soldiers take the Government loan.'" In all these purchases of confidence, Union soldiers opted to share their financial gain with the United States government on unparalleled levels compared to the antebellum years. This in and of itself redefined how these citizens viewed their government, and the mode of financialization employed to achieve that faith. For many men in the Union army, "Union" entailed not only a sectional reconciliation (and for some the eradication of slavery), but also a fiscal commitment to the nation's future.[63]

In certain circumstances, the U.S. government also used bonds to cover vouchers issued for materials to support the Union war effort. The plan as laid out by Jay Cooke to the Treasury and War Departments permitted some $30 million in 7-30 notes to cover War Department vouchers. As part of the condition of accepting the exchange, these notes could not be redeemed for a minimum of four months so as not to disturb the 7-30 market. In putting forth such an arrangement, 7-30s in theory could be absorbed at an even faster rate and then enable the War Department to clear its books sooner. As news emerged on the potential for these voucher exchanges, letters poured in from as far afield as Kansas requesting exchanges of vouchers for 7-30s. The great success of such a movement reflected the ingenuity of Cooke & Co. and the way that bonds increasingly came to define every aspect of war finance during the course of the conflict.[64]

Lincoln's Death

The excitement of Lee's surrender at Appomattox on April 9, 1865, dampened with news of the assassination of Abraham Lincoln on April 14. While sorrow and anger filled the nation's capital and other regions of the North, of critical importance to Secretary McCulloch was the stabilization of the overall credit of the United States. On April 15, Henry Cooke wrote his brother, referring to "A night of horrors and a day of impenetrable gloom!" Henry's letter further authorized Jay to do everything necessary to stabilize the New York markets. However, Jay did not need such permission, for in his mind the task was vital to stabilizing the Northern economy in the wake of the tragedy and uncertainty that followed. Cooke opted to travel to New York personally to take control of the financial situation, writing ahead to his ally houses, "It is important that government securities stand like a rock. . . . Poor Lincoln—a noble soul has gone." Cooke arrived in New York prepared to buy as many bonds as necessary in order to stabilize the market, but the exchange did not open on Saturday, April 17, as financiers and dockhands alike mourned the death of the president. On Sunday, April 18, Jay received a letter from his brother, "You have *carte blanche* to manage the market as you may deem best." Jay Cooke remarked later in his memoir regarding the active days surrounding Lincoln's assassination:

> The first day my agents brought me some three millions and it required the purchase of less than twenty millions in the space of seven or eight days to end the panic. The bonds were resold and the money was replaced in the treasury at a profit to the government, as I had directed an

advance each day of one-eighth on the old issues of bonds, so that the spectacle was presented to the world of a nation with its credit unimpaired and its securities advancing in price while suffering from a terrible calamity. The London *Times* and other influential European journals commented with surprise upon this wonderful exhibition of confidence on the part of the American people. I have always regarded this as among my greatest successes in finance. The world was not informed as to the particulars of this movement until long afterward. I preferred that the national credit should enjoy all the advantages of this action on my part.[65]

In the wake of Lincoln's assassination and the initial fears over a panic having subsided, sales entered a phase of unparalleled success. In the last two weeks of April (including no business on the day of Lincoln's funeral), Cooke's agency procured over $40 million in sales. May's sales then eclipsed the April numbers, with the first six days in May exceeding $40 million in sales. Once more, these sales found their way to the masses, as $50 and $100 subscribers numbered some 28,239 in the period May 1–6, 1865. The result of these small-savings purchases in late April and early May 1865 led to the second series of $300 million in 7-30s being sold in its entirety by May 13, in thirty working days and well in advance of the July 10 deadline. The third and final series took slightly longer owing to some bond supply issues, but it too came to a close rather rapidly on July 26, 1865, for a total of $830 million.[66]

Newspapers throughout the North sang the praises of Cooke and his army of agents. The *Boston Bulletin* proclaimed, "The Treasury people as well as the Loan Agent and his 'subs' all over the country have ample reason to be proud of this extraordinary triumph," while the *Constitutional Union* declared "The fame of Jay Cooke now world-wide will be as enduring as time." The *Philadelphia Inquirer* said, "Let us not forget that among our benefactors we must reckon not only the brave soldiers and sailors who took us through the contest by their courage and devotion, but also the skillful financiers who, through every discouragement, furnished us with 'the sinews of war.'" Lastly, the *Philadelphia Press* exclaimed, "Now that we have come out of the struggle successfully no one who appreciates the genius and patriotism which led us through the fiery ordeal will hesitate to place the great financier of the war alongside its greatest generals." But the praise avoided another matter—Cooke profited enormously over the course of the war. According to R. G. Dun & Co. credit reporting, at the time of the cessation of hostilities Cooke purportedly had a net worth of several million dollars, a reputation "undoubted," in the phrasing of R. G. Dun.[67]

In the war's aftermath, Cooke proclaimed "Out of three million subscribers to our various public loans, over nine-tenths are of the class called *the people*." While Cooke's calculation is impossible to verify, there is no doubt that the people carried a significant burden of the war expenses, and this especially came to be the case with the 7-30 issue. The 7-30 loan drive reflected the march towards democratization of war finance that originated with the National Loan and '81s from 1861. Slow to start, just as the war progressed to become the people's cause, so too did it become tied financially to the people. The various bond drives funded the daily operations of the war at its most basic level. The traveling agents that appeared at doorsteps and tent flaps and advertisements that filled papers and windows far and wide revealed the great breadth of the bond campaign to reconstitute how individuals interacted with the state and a new dimension in American war finance. The widespread purchasing of this debt via Cooke's agency was essential to financing the cause of Union and eventual emancipation. However, just as the postwar period left many questions unanswered surrounding former enslaved individuals and Confederate aggressors alike, so too did there linger questions pertaining to the national debt. The domestic discussions took place, however, in the shadow of a fundamental change in the nature of American investment banking overseas. The levels of American debt held abroad in the postwar period confirmed that the legacy of the debt took on increasingly global dimensions.[68]

CHAPTER SIX

A Permanent National Debt Is Not an American Institution
Postwar Debt

In an 1866 political pamphlet titled *Soliloquies of The Bondholder*, author Brick Pomeroy regaled the reader with tales of the life of the bondholder. "Here I am, a rich, prosperous, loyal man, with nothing to do but to enjoy myself. Egad, what a blessing the war was to me! It killed off my poor relations, and left me in luck." The fictitious bondholder went on to proclaim, "How I love my government! It is the best the sun ever shone on! These bonds average me eight per cent, interest in gold.... And the beauty of it is, I don't have one cent of taxes to pay. Isn't it nice? This is the best government the world ever saw. Rich men hold bonds—poor men pay them." The bondholder emphasized just how bonds and bond policies exploited those who served in the war. "The d—d fools went to war, and came back and work like dogs to pay the interest on the bonds we sold to give them money... They are paying themselves for getting shot at. Bully for us, bondholders!" After detailing the pervasive nature of the income tax in American life and the "fools" who paid such taxes, the bondholder concluded his thoughts by remarking, "And now I sit in my parlor—I smoke my cigars—I drink my wine—I enjoy myself, and have no taxes to pay." *Soliloquies of The Bondholder* represented an emerging line of Democratic propaganda initiated almost immediately after the end of the war.[1]

In post–Civil War America, Democratic members of Congress and their allies in the press attacked bondholders not as part of a population stretching across gender, racial, sectional, and international lines, but as a class of wealthy elites. Jay Cooke's championing of a "People's Contest" during the war gave way to partisan attacks bemoaning the "bondocracy" or "bondocrats"—a class of wealthy financiers no better than the "shoddy" war profiteers targeted in the years prior. Heather Cox Richardson notes how "bondholder" took on the form of "an epithet for very wealthy men" by the 1870s, but one could argue it started just as soon as the guns fell silent. That said, the critique on the part of Democrats did not reflect mere partisan spin. The postwar period witnessed an apparent movement of bonds into the hands of select financiers and financial institutions as the government refunded the debt. While debt ledgers do not answer all our questions, by 1867 the bonds increasingly migrated into the hands of financiers at least by the time of redemption. For many of the popular investors in the war, the retirement of federal debt and the refinancing of the remaining debt at lower interest rates reset their calculus. The higher interest rates of federal debt disappeared and for many this meant a return to their trusted local savings institutions with relatively high interest rates. The "security" of savings institutions from the antebellum period once again became the norm for many. The bonds in some sense had come full circle: after being purchased en masse by Jay Cooke and his network of agents and partner financial houses and sold to the Northern public, they were now back in bondholders' hands, and with it a democratic moment had passed.[2]

Disputes over retirement, repudiation, repayment, and refinancing of U.S. debt defined the postwar period. Owing more than $2.6 billion by the summer of 1865, the United States now faced the challenge of not only paying the debt, but doing so with a Southern population that had no qualms about repudiating such debt—just as they had done at the state level in the antebellum period. The retirement of Civil War debt, therefore, increasingly entwined itself with the perilous threat of repudiation. As Congress debated the terms of repayment in the Reconstruction era, the high interest rates led Congress and the Treasury to reassess possible modes of paying off the war debt. Refinancing of the debt proved essential and successful in the Reconstruction years. In order to help facilitate the sale of this refinanced debt, large-scale transatlantic financial syndicates took center stage, once more proving the international pull of American debt was not just a flash in the pan, but of enduring interest.

While the struggles over debt sparked domestic debate, the story quickly took on a global focus. Much of this postwar debt found its way to continental Europe, and specifically the German states, Switzerland, Netherlands, and even France. U.S. debt represented a favorable investment for wealthy Europeans alongside "everyday" Europeans as well. The rapid growth and dispersion of this debt throughout Europe and beyond reveals the increasing prominence of American debt overseas on a novel level. Furthermore, the refinancing of such debt in the 1870s enabled the debt to spread further and it was American banks, opening for the first time overseas, that played a large role in facilitating this growth. In conjunction with the opening of a United States Treasury office in London, and American banks opening branches in London and Paris, American financiers pursued transnational approaches in a wave of refinanced debt in the early 1870s. Massive foreign investments in the Reconstruction period revealed not an isolated United States, but rather a country deeply connected to and in a certain sense dependent on European capital in order to function. While everyday Americans may have missed this interrelationship in Reconstruction America, the intimate connection of United States finances to a global stage was undeniable.

Once again, Jay Cooke emerged as a central player to help American financial efforts in the postwar period. This time, however, the challenge would be a successful refunding of the debt at a lower interest rate. Working for a truly bipartisan and national resolution, Jay and his brother Henry used their power and influence in Congress, on Wall Street, and with the press to make refinancing and refunding of the debt a reality. In the process, Cooke and Co. created a more sophisticated network, or syndicate, that crossed the Atlantic to various banking houses throughout Europe. Such efforts foreshadowed a truly global integration of capital markets and the proliferation of syndicate practices that came to define the Gilded Age. Furthermore, the syndicate system of Reconstruction finance marked another move toward financial centralization that concerned politicians and laypeople alike following the war.[3]

The Future of American Debt in the Reconstruction Era

The end of the war brought relative stability to the Treasury, but great uncertainty as to the future of American debt. From the standpoint of American debt, the country truly was in unchartered waters. From a public debt that stood at slightly under $65 million in 1860, the war had caused the U.S. debt to balloon to $2.6 billion by June 30, 1865. This debt reached its wartime peak at the end of August 1865, coming in at some $2,757,689,571.43. The public debt skyrocketed from being 1.49 percent of U.S. GDP in 1860 to 27.1 percent by 1865. But as has been pointed out by Franklin Noll and others, a complicating factor beyond the size of the debt remained the structure of said financial liabilities. By the summer of 1865 the debt comprised thirty-two different financial instruments with widely varying interest rates (ranging from 4 to 7.3 percent). Perhaps most alarmingly, some 48 percent of the debt was coming due (either on demand or by maturity) within five years of the summer of 1865. This collection of debt also contained an average interest rate of 6.3 percent. Secretary Chase's approach to financing the war in its early months had finally come to roost. The suspension of specie payments in December 1861 dictated financial policy that cried for short-term solutions—something that now had deep repercussions as the country entered the Reconstruction period. The American economy had drastically expanded during the war, but the end of the conflict brought questions as to what that economy might look like. The fiat currency of greenbacks stood at some $432 million by the summer of 1865, which also wreaked havoc on the money market and had a trickle-down effect upon the bonds themselves—in both secondary markets and the Gold Room. By the summer of 1865, the war may have been concluded, but the financial situation and refunding solution was far from certain.[4]

When Hugh McCulloch ascended to the role of secretary of the treasury in the spring of 1865, he made it clear that a rapid retirement of the debt was his chief objective—part of a long-term strategy to return the country to the gold standard. "My chief aim," declared McCulloch, "will . . . be to provide the means to discharge the claims upon the Treasury at the earliest date practicable, and to institute measures to bring the business of the country gradually back to the specie basis, a departure from which . . . is no less damaging and demoralizing to the people than expensive to the government." Such a prompt retirement of the debt proved easier said than done, however, as serious questions loomed over what revenue sources might be utilized to pay off the debt, how long it might take, and how the debt might be refunded to reduce the total interest owed by the U.S. government.[5]

As documented by historian Gregory Downs, debt played a role in the demobilization of the Union army even before the formal cessation of hostilities. By March 1865, the government struggled to sell bonds as both 7-30s and 10-40s fell below par. The Treasury faced war bills of some $4 million per day and a shortfall of $100 million in its coffers during the crucial moments in late March and early April. Assistant Treasurer John A. Stewart summarized the situation to Secretary McCulloch when he stated, "We are in the midst of a panic which, though not entirely unlooked for, may, unless arrested be productive of most serious consequences to the public and to the government." The situation led to Cooke propping up the securities market at the behest of the government. At points that spring, Cooke and his allies purchased some $4 million worth of securities a day in order to inflate the resale market. The events of March and early April 1865 led the Treasury to push for a decrease in the size of the military even as the war wore on. According to McCulloch, such actions proved necessary in order to avoid "more trouble ahead." One ally wrote to Jay Cooke to summarize these efforts at demobilization even more bluntly. "The payroll of the army should be instantly subjected to unsparing scrutiny" the reporter declared, "and unsparing hewing & chopping." Although it remained more expensive to send soldiers home owing to back wages due, the army demobilized to in part assuage concerns coming out of the Treasury.⁶

Whether such debt reflected a "blessing" or a "burden" for the United States occupied many pages of print for the remainder of 1865 and into 1866. The opinions on the matter ranged widely. The *Commercial and Financial Chronicle* equated war debt with capital improvements that in the long term would benefit the nation. "A national debt," the article stated, "may be so managed as to stimulate productive power and augment the force of inventive genius, to economise capital and open a beneficent reservoir for gathering together and rendering more productive ten thousand little fertilizing streams of national wealth." One of the most prominent pieces in support of the debt was put forward by Jay Cooke's New York–based PR machine. The essay by Samuel Wilkeson entitled *How Our National Debt May Be a National Blessing* emphasized the power of a national debt to act as a "public wealth, political union, protection of industry," and a "secure basis for national currency, the orphans' and widows' savings fund." Furthermore, Wilkeson contended, "We lay down the proposition that our national debt, made permanent and rightly managed, will be a national blessing."⁷

The Cookes worked doubly hard on solidifying their hold on the press to ensure a favorable discussion regarding debt refunding and the need to have the ever-trusted Cooke & Co. at the helm of any negotiations. Gifts to newspapermen, most commonly alcohol, became a frequent occurrence as the financiers tried to curry favor with the press in the northeastern cities. These newspaper editors had a long reach, as their pieces were often picked up for syndication by other newspapers throughout the country. Additionally, the aforementioned options on bond purchases initially offered by Cooke during the war provided another inducement for the press to write favorably on Cooke when it came to the debt question.⁸

Despite many pieces championing the national debt, some critics remained fairly vocal. One opponent, when citing the "preposterous theory which considers a national debt as a 'national blessing,'" reiterated a popular refrain for the anti-debt crowd when he noted "it is capital to those only who hold it and a tax to everybody else." Secretary McCulloch differed sharply from his bond-selling partner Jay Cooke when he flatly stated, "There can be no reasonable doubt that a national debt is a national burden, for which there can be no substantial counterbalancing compensations." He added in a subsequent letter, "It would be foolish to call it a national blessing, it may be so managed as not to be a national calamity." A British economist at the time spoke to the fact that it was an inherently American trait to pay off such a debt. Americans, in the mind of this economist, had a "strong and controlling sense that debt was always and everywhere an evil; that it was a good thing to 'work off' the mortgage, even if it involved working very hard." Thus, a sense of a dire need to pay off the debt permeated many pieces of writing, playing a role in the battle lines drawn between Republican and Democrats on Capitol Hill.[9]

Another question that arose pertained to how long it would take to pay off the debt. In April 1866, the London *Economist* noted, "There is scarcely a provincial town [in the United States] in which some financial person—some banker or stockbroker—has not made and published calculations as to the quickest and best mode of paying off the great debt. Such a diffused interest must soon create real knowledge." Secretary McCulloch predicted in his 1865 Annual Report to Congress that debt repayment would take between 27 and 29 years. Freeman Clarke, McCulloch's successor as Comptroller of the Currency, put forward 32 ½ years. Senator John Sherman predicted it would take longer—no fewer than 35 years. These predictions all revolved around one theme—this would be a substantial task for the government to undertake that would not have an easy solution.[10]

At the heart of the matter remained the essential debate of rewarding work tied to labor and working the land versus the perception of the creation of wealth held by the financial sector and others who did not properly work for a living. "Direct robbery by force could not have obtained this [oppression] so effectually as has been through the creation of a permanent national debt," claimed one critic. The same article railed against "moneyed institutions and heavy capitalists, who have immense sums to invest, and would like to have the nation guarantee the annual interest upon the same to themselves and their successors." Such statements reinforced the increasingly partisan notion of wealthy "bondocrats" holding a vast majority of the debt. President Andrew Johnson even floated the idea of having interest payments count toward payment of bond principal to holders. Still others, as will be discussed in further detail, pushed for the payment of interest not in coin, but in the fiat currency of greenbacks when the legislation was unclear on the matter. Such disparate thoughts on the matter impeded agreement on financial policy in the early days of Reconstruction.[11]

In the immediate aftermath of the war, there stood the pressing issue of a potential run on the national banks. One of the most dangerous liabilities revolved around the high total of certificates of deposit—short-term financial instruments issued by the government and callable in a mere ten days. By September 1865, the certificates totaled nearly $116 million. If all were called immediately it posed a significant problem for the government to meet its obligations. McCulloch, working with Jay Cooke, refinanced this debt into longer-term bond obligations to stave off a potential run on the Treasury and also diminish the need for such a large cash reserve—funds that now could go towards paying down the debt.[12]

Despite resolving the problem of certificates of indebtedness, greater than a third of the debt would come due in the short term. The front-loaded nature of the debt meant the matter needed to be addressed. Secretary McCulloch reiterated his desire to honor and pay off the debt in his annual report at the end of 1866. "The conviction is becoming fastened upon the popular mind," declared McCulloch, "that it is important for economy in the national expenses, for the maintenance of a true democracy in the administration of a government, for the cause of good morals, and of public virtue, that the policy of a steady annual reduction of the debt should be definitely and inexorably established." McCulloch likewise went on to criticize the burden of a national debt as a "severe strain upon republican institutions." The government's position as far as the Treasury was concerned remained clear, but the challenge remained on how the Treasury and Congress could work together to rectify the fiscal challenge ahead.[13]

In the short term, taxation when coupled with custom duties served the purpose of facilitating debt interest payments and instituting a moderate budgetary surplus in the early postwar period to help to pay off some debt while also creating a sinking fund for the debt. Such a fund contained money set aside to pay off the debt in the future. Taxation in and of itself could not enable full debt repayment (nor remain viable for long—especially the income tax, something the general public opposed). Something else needed to be done to address the debt issue. Millions had bought into the war and identified with the nation writ large—at least for a time playing down regional allegiances. According to historian Eric Foner, "Most . . . viewed the sanctity of the national debt as a moral legacy of the war second only to emancipation itself." Yet politicians viewed the staggering wartime debt, at a minimum, as a topic of great concern, and for others, a threat to the very nation's existence. "The National Debt is the subject, above all others, which fills the thoughts and claims the anxieties of every serious mind in the country," stated author J. S. Gibbons in 1867.[14]

Like Brick Pomeroy in *Soliloquies of The Bondholder*, the theme of the taxation of the poor at the benefit of rich tax-exempt bondholders became a repeated trope in Democratic criticism of the debt. The novel depicted individuals such as "the poor farmer," "the poor mechanic," "the soldier's widow," "the returned soldier," and "the freed negro" as victims of the taxation scheme levied on the lower and middle classes to shoulder the interest payments of the national debt. The "poor farmer" took the opportunity in his soliloquy to take some time and explain the financial situation presumably to his wife, Maggy. In his tale the farmer talks about his role as a substitute for "Mr. Bond" in the war, in the process losing an arm while serving. In keeping with the Democratic argument, the poor farmer decries, "Mr. Bond, the bondholder, pays nothing. The government protects him; but it can't protect the poor, one-armed farmer who fought to save the Union . . . It's better to be a bondholder than a soldier. . . . How I wish the good old Democratic times would come again, when the rich bondholder would not be fastened upon poor people for support." In essence, Reconstruction Democrats countered Cooke's visions of bondholders as profit-seeking patriots with images of rapacious financiers fleecing everyday citizens.[15]

Similarly, the widow shared in the struggles the war and bonds had brought upon her. "There is no sun," she begins, "no hope for my life lies buried beneath the sod of a warmer country than this." After detailing the deaths of her husband and son (in a hospital and on the battlefield, respectively), she harps on the burden of taxation. "I am but a women," she says, "I know not much of politics; but I know I am a widow; that my loved ones are gone; that my heart is dark with sorrow; that the taxgatherer is taking all that we earned before the war; that I am called upon to pay taxes, expenses, and even interest money to support the bondholders who were enriched by the blood of my loved ones." Such a notion drew upon the messaging put forward by Cooke during the war. As Melinda Lawson has demonstrated, bonds as a tax haven of sorts served as one of the appeals of bonds during the war. Now on the other side of the war, Democrats twisted this asset to a liability and repeated this message extensively in the Reconstruction period, stoking class tensions in the process.[16]

The debt crisis quickly became a political game in Washington as Republicans and Democrats sought the advantage. Questions emerged in the summer of 1865 as to whether the United States would assume the Confederate debt—which stood somewhere in the neighborhood (when including Southern state debts) of $1.5 billion. While the national government assumed state debt following the Revolution, the Civil War presented a different beast and despite the fact that there were no constitutional barriers to assuming the debt, most assumed the government would not. No one "outside of a lunatic asylum" thought the South would demand and succeed in payment of Confederate debt, claimed Democratic representative Benjamin Boyer. Similarly, the *New*

York Times cited a Republican lawmaker who equated the assumption of such debt as akin to "fighting windmills" or waiting for "the sky to fall." The Confederate debt would not be absorbed and proved a contentious issue—especially among the British government and British creditors in the immediate postwar period.[17]

To ensure the sanctity of the U.S. debt, Republicans included language on the subject in the Fourteenth Amendment: "The validity of the public debt of the United States, authorized by law, including debts incurred for payment of pensions and bounties for services in suppressing insurrection or rebellion, shall not be questioned. But neither the United States nor any State shall assume or pay any debt or obligation incurred in aid of insurrection or rebellion against the United States, or any claim for the loss or emancipation of any slave; but all such debts, obligations and claims shall be held illegal and void."

Even before the movement toward including such language in the Fourteenth Amendment, serious concerns in Washington over the debt issue had led to action. Of greatest issue was the belief held among many Northerners (and reaffirmed by reports out of the South) that former Confederates would not honor the U.S. debt, and thereby would move for repudiation as well as wanting some sort of compensation for their former slaves. Representative Henry Winter Davis reaffirmed such a belief when he remarked, "None of the white population of the Southern States is interested in paying the public debt . . . If the whites be restored to political power, their representatives are interested in repudiating that public debt." The debates that roiled Capitol Hill during this period reflected some of the extreme partisanship of the Reconstruction era. They also, however, took place in the midst of a fundamental transformation of American debt on the international stage.[18]

The Primacy of the German Bond Market

The German states emerged as the most important arena for American debt abroad in the Reconstruction era. The sophistication of the German economy prior to and after the 1848 revolutions led to a more developed banking system within the German states. In particular the decision to streamline the incorporation of German businesses and their listings on public exchanges improved the functioning of the German securities market. While aiding these businesses and German financial institutions, such a system also significantly aided American debt sales. The private banks of the German states still varied based on their geographic location. While merchant banking in Hamburg remained deeply tied to the shipping industry of this vital port, Frankfurt emerged over the course of the nineteenth century as an important European financial hub. In part, this development emanated from the free-city status of the metropolis on the Main River, and the need for an exchange place for different types of currency that flooded the various German states. The city's exchange dated to 1816 (Berlin's dated to 1805); by the mid- to late 1860s, a slew of German banks in Frankfurt invested heavily in American securities—and especially American federal debt.[19]

Almost from the day the war ended, a concerted campaign in public spaces emphasized the growth in German investment in American debt—and its close transatlantic ties. By the summer of 1865, European continental investors, most notably the Germans, pushed foreign investment in the United States well beyond its pre–Civil War levels. Word quickly spread across the United States of the insatiable demand for federal debt in the German states. Just months after the war had ended, the *New York Times* republished a letter that had originally run in a German newspaper. "It is highly gratifying to observe here," the letter said, "a daily increase in the price and popularity of our stocks. While all other securities are depreciating, only United States stocks seem to gain ground. The largest amount of business done in these securities hitherto was last week—one person having bought the enormous amount of five hundred thousand dollars for himself, beside being a permanent holder to the amount of two hundred thousand dollars." The letter went on to conclude, "The Germans are a thrifty and safe calculating people, ever choosing the safest and best marks for their products, whether money or goods, and they seem to be now the war is over, perfectly satisfied to deposit their savings in American securities." Such articles became increasingly common in American papers throughout the North and the South during the early years of Reconstruction. The letters and reports from the German states played a large role in framing a strong German economy deeply entwined with American debt.[20]

Newspapers repeatedly emphasized the preeminence of Frankfurt as a vital financial hub for American securities in the postwar period. An 1868 letter from an American living in Frankfurt explained as much to the Treasury Department: "Really this market controls the European," the letter said. "Here all the great sales are made, and to this point are all the stocks sent from New York, and here the coupons on nearly all the stocks held in Europe are sent for sale and collection. Frankfurt is about the only city which has its branch houses in the United States." The letter went on to note the plethora of German incorporated banks with capital requirements based largely in American securities. Specifically, the American financier referenced the Banks of Meiningen and Darmstadt, which among other banks "hold several millions of our Five-Twenties."[21]

But what accounted for interest in the German states that fed the demand? For some, these purchases reflected an anticipation of European conflict between the French and German states. One report from Germany indicated, "A real investment demand for 5-20s is now setting in from the peasantry and that class of people, especially since the war looks inevitable." For others, bonds took on geopolitical relevance. "These bonds also invite a large immigration," one article proclaimed. "When the people of Europe receive that the great republic meets its interest promptly, and that too of so high a rate ... the emigrant carries with him his bonds, because he feels the confidence that he can realize upon them ... It seems to us that the missionary influence of those bonds in Americanizing Europe, in drawing its people to our government, and in making them as it were the constant watchers of American progress, is indeed boundless."[22]

But beyond financial opportunism and a potential future in the United States driving these sales, there proved a deeper symbolic resonance for German Americans that echoed back across the Atlantic. While Germans divided their votes between Lincoln and Stephen Douglas in the election of 1860, they resented what many of them viewed as a coup by Southern aristocrats set on destroying the American republic. For many German Americans, they saw parallels to the military coups in the German states in 1848 that ended the democratic dream in Europe. One of the exiled revolutionaries, August Willich, wrote after the attack on Fort Sumter that Germans needed to "protect their new republican homeland against the aristocracy of the South." The Germans opposed slavery; during the 1850s, they had formed their own abolition societies and the German-language press railed against the institution. One German American wrote home, confessing, "I've seen it often enough how the poor slaves are sold away from their wives and children and beaten with a whip until their skin hangs in tatters." He swore "death and damnation to the slave traders," whom he blamed for the war as well as for the abuse of the slaves.[23]

The *Illinois Staats-Zeitung* published a piece in August 1870 leading up to the Franco-Prussian War reinforcing some of these sentiments. "A Statement to the People of the United States Issued by the Delegates to the Convention of the German Patriotic Aid Association of the Union," called upon all Americans, but especially German Americans, to support the Prussian cause in any potential conflict. "During the Civil War," the statement declared, "Napoleon ordered that no American bonds be quoted on the stock exchange of Paris; in

Germany even tradesmen and laborers used their pitifully small life's savings to buy them, for they were convinced that right and justice and liberty would finally win." Such tales five years after the end of the conflict emphasized the importance of German investment in bonds during the war, and the cachet it held in the postwar period as well.[24]

Whatever the reasons for the demand in these bonds, German banks continued to rely on their faith- and kinship-based network between New York and Frankfurt in which American houses bought extensively on behalf of their German relatives and then sold them across the Atlantic. One prime example is that of J and W Seligman & Co. By the spring of 1867 (the earliest point in the postwar period with surviving records), Seligman & Co. was sending more than $100,000 in bonds daily overseas. Perhaps most interestingly, Joseph Seligman distinguished in his letters between "small 5/20" orders—that is, those that were bonds of $50 or $100—and other 5-20 orders in larger denominations. In fact, as spring turned to summer in 1867, Seligman's correspondence revealed a decided pattern: For London, the orders were almost always for larger bonds with less of an emphasis on the $50 and $100 bonds. On July 19, 1867, Seligman wrote to the London house to note the New York branch purchased $300,000 worth of 5-20s ($50,000 of which were small 5-20s). The note remarked that the London house required another $500,000 in large 5-20s as well as $40,000 of small 5-20s and $58,000 in '81s. Conversely, Joseph Seligman wrote daily to the Frankfurt house (known as Seligman & Stettheimer) relaying orders that by early August were exclusively for small 5-20s in varying amounts that at times surpassed $100,000 daily. The small bonds making their way to Frankfurt would seem to reiterate the claims of American representatives abroad who emphasized that the issues were wildly taken up in Frankfurt by investors of all classes.[25]

Bethmann Bank in Frankfurt likewise played a substantial role in the postwar period, one that reveals another networking approach—one based on faith. The Bethmanns represented the single largest Christian bank in Frankfurt, an outlier in a city largely dominated by Jewish bankers. From the conclusion of the war through the end of 1865, the firm purchased slightly over $350,000 worth of 5-20s. In 1867, Bethmann upped its investment in American 5-20s to $1,354,100 with additional purchases of '81s and 5-20s from 1865 (for a combined total of some $71,100). In 1868, the stakes grew even higher with $2,134,900 in 5-20s purchased by the Frankfurt house and half a million dollars' worth of additional Civil War bonds. The first two quarters of 1869 totaled some $782,700 in 5-20 Civil War bonds. In the postwar period, the firm's investments went to a wide range of clients; although only some records survive, they list a wide variety of banks in Frankfurt as well as established citizens.[26]

Other financial institutions in locations like Hamburg revealed the expanding scope of American debt into emerging markets for American securities, such as Scandinavia. Although Hamburg was traditionally focused on shipping—and therefore most of its financial operations pertained to the world of merchant banking—proceeds from these operations migrated into the bond market. By the late 1860s, many Hamburg merchants found themselves depositing their profits into American debt. The bank of Herms & Co., for instance, moved into this market and incorporated American debt as part of many Scandinavian portfolios. H. J. Hertz of Copenhagen purchased tens of thousands of dollars' worth of American debt in the late 1860s as part of his portfolio. Herms & Co. went on to purchase American debt for a wide variety of other Copenhagen-based financiers and clients as well as other firms based in Hamburg itself, such as Henry Hartig. Another Hamburg-based bank, Nordeutsche Bank, similarly purchased American debt for a wide array of clients. While the clients' names have been lost to history, the extent of investment numbered well into the tens of thousands and incorporated financial partners from as far afield as Switzerland.[27]

The Rothschilds' reliance on their German partners reflected a significantly greater interest in American bonds purchased through Jewish connections within Europe that were predicated on familial ties across the Atlantic. All of this is to say that while the *haute banque* or "high bank" had expanded into continental Europe in the mid-nineteenth century, this interest in American securities—specifically here in the case of the European financial titans the Rothschilds—marked a new investment opportunity and pattern. The *haute banque* denoted a series of Parisian banks in the post-Napoleonic period typically distinguished by their honor, respectability, financial power, and activities regarding international money markets. Such networks frequently centered on well-financed private banks that often shared religious ties—increasingly moving outside of France itself to include other countries like what would become Germany. Working in arrangements that epitomized *haute banque* ideals, the Rothschilds coordinated closely with German banks in Berlin, Hamburg, and Frankfurt to access American bonds on favorable terms. L. Behrens & Son in Hamburg, Bleichroeder Bank in Berlin, and Warburg Bank in Hamburg all worked in their respective markets on behalf of the Rothschilds.[28]

For the Bleichroeder house, the active market in Berlin proved remarkably fruitful. By the summer of 1865, the firm was making daily purchases for the

Paris house of Rothschild in the neighborhood of close to $100,000 on average. Additionally, the house made purchases for clients either on behalf of the Rothschilds, or their own clients who currently found themselves in Paris, such as Victor Renary. By the latter part of 1866, the Bleichroeders made significant purchases on behalf of the Rothschilds, including a $700,000 purchase in 5-20s in November and $480,000 of the same issue on Valentine's Day 1867. Surviving records indicate that these purchases largely went to clients and were not held on personal accounts. Yet while these large purchases seem to be for fairly well-heeled clients, other correspondence from the Rothschilds affirms that many purchases in Frankfurt and other German localities were destined for "the public." Thus, for the Rothschilds, the postwar period presented a wonderful opportunity to invest heavily in American bonds.[29]

Switzerland

In addition to the German states, Switzerland also afforded an emerging market for American debt that reveals the additional reach of American financial power. The Swiss intervention into the American market is generally understood to date from the late antebellum period, with its center in the city of Geneva. The city had been annexed by the French in 1798 and subsequently blossomed owing to its close connection to the French crown and the financing of French debt, and it evolved as it moved into the nineteenth century and in the wake of the French Revolution. Although still closely tied to Paris banks (despite becoming a Swiss canton), Genevan banks slowly began to explore alternative investment opportunities by the middle of the nineteenth century. Such alternatives included Dutch debt (federal and local), as well as debt tied to Paris, Amsterdam, Vienna, Milan, and other European locales.[30]

It was not until the midpoint of the nineteenth century that Swiss banks explored the United States as an investment opportunity. In the 1850s, James Odier of the famous Swiss banking house Lombard Odier & Cie (LOC) traveled to New York City. While in the United States, Odier made contact with Andre Iselin, a Swiss-born banker who had since set up residence in New York. The Iselin–LOC partnership proved invaluable during the late antebellum period, the wartime period, and beyond. While LOC initially restricted itself to county and state bonds (mostly New York State), by the latter point of the war the firm delved into federal securities, albeit a limited amount. By August 1865, the LOC portfolio in the United States included $11,000 in federal 5-20 bonds purchased via the New York–based Iselin house.

By January 1866, the 6 percent 5-20 bonds were being floated on the Geneva Stock Exchange and widely advertised by Lombard Odier, whose personal portfolio grew to $39,000 in 5-20s by August 1866—approximately one-quarter of LOC's overall American debt held by the house on its own accounts. Such information is vital to understanding one of the earliest Swiss banks to invest in the United States, and there is a safe assumption that additional purchases for an array of clients meant the bank was involved even more in American Civil War debt operations. According to one account, by the end of the nineteenth century, fully one-third of Lombard Odier's portfolio contained American debt as its overall portfolio expanded in the late nineteenth century.[31]

While Lombard Odier invested heavily in American debt and most likely represented the largest firm in Switzerland for American debt in 1865 and 1866, other houses became involved in this market. Another Geneva house, Edward Pictet & Cie, purchased American debt in 1866 for Italian clients. Pictet & Cie worked closely with LOC during the refinancing of American debt in both 1871 and 1873. The firm wrote on several occasions to its Geneva colleagues at Lombard Odier regarding the conversion of old 5-20s into new American debt instruments—in such a way that appealed to their wide array of clients. Basel-based Passavant & Cie also became involved in American federal debt issues and bought and sold these issues from 1868 onward for clients within Basel, but also Geneva-based Reverdin & Cie (precursor to present-day firm Bordier & Cie). Their investments included clients in Meggen, Switzerland; Frankfurt-based Speyer Ellison, Kahn & Co.; Rothschild & Fils; Paris-based A. Vignal & Cie; and London-based Stern Brothers.[32]

But perhaps Marcuard & Co. was the most important Swiss bank as it pertained to American debt. The firm, located in the Swiss capital of Bern, dated to 1746 when a merchant named Johann Rudolf Marcuard opened the house for conducting financial operations. While the firm is best known for its post-1919 life as part of Credit Suisse, in the mid-nineteenth century its work revolved around American Civil War debt. While many European houses remained reluctant to invest before the end of the war, or at least before the final months of the war in 1865, Marcuard & Co. purchased federal debt at least as early as March 1864. Between these purchases in March 1864 and the Panic of 1873 in September of that year, Marcuard & Co. purchased at least $517,900 in federal debt in at least four different bond issues, with 5-20 purchases the most common. Not only were these bonds purchased during this time, but many were held onto for many years—or exchanged for refinanced bond issues of the early 1870s. Thus, these were long-term investments for many of Marcuard's clients (including for its own house) and did not reflect efforts at exploiting an arbitrage market within continental Europe. The firm's records—although lacking correspondence—nevertheless offer one of the more complete archives for a Swiss financial firm that are available to historians. While Marcuard purchased these bonds in large numbers, in reading these ledger books one gathers an even deeper appreciation for the complex nature of financial transactions during this period. Despite being based in Bern (not a financial behemoth in the nineteenth century) the firm purchased its bonds predominantly in New York City or in Frankfurt—although select purchases in 1866 did come via London and Geneva. The decision to purchase bonds primarily in New York and Frankfurt is informative on many levels—first and foremost, that relationships between firms were of greater importance than perhaps the best deal possible, reinforcing a trend seen in the German and French markets of the time period. Secondly, Frankfurt clearly by this point had much closer ties to Switzerland than has been previously discussed. New York purchases frequently went through the houses of De. Rham & Co. and the Swiss bankers of Moran Brothers, who had relocated to New York City. In Frankfurt, the bank primarily used Hauck & Fils (although on occasion it utilized other Frankfurt houses including the venerable Rothschilds). There is also some reason to believe that some purchases occurred in Amsterdam, as a Dutch bank (Goll & Fils) did purchase bonds on behalf of Marcuard at one point in 1871. All told, Swiss investment reflected the larger world of Civil War bond sales beyond European financial centers.[33]

Britain

British financiers maintained their reluctance in the immediate aftermath of the war to invest in large quantities of bonds. Queen Victoria noted in her diary in February 1865 that a victorious Union army may march northward following the end of hostilities and invade Canada. "A war with the United States is inevitable and not distant," proclaimed British financier and Lord Overstone. Still others in Britain feared the Irish American Fenians aspired to invade Canada with the assistance of the U.S. government. Many in the United States believed the British had betrayed the Union—financially speaking—during the war by siding with the Confederates. A *New York Times* article amplified such beliefs in December 1865, when a list of British subscribers to the Confederate cotton loan became public. The article contained the verbose and provocative title of "THE REBEL LOAN.; A More Complete List of British Subscribers. Who Got Their Interest and Who Did Not. Probable Misuse of Respectable Names. The Subterfuge of the Proprietors of the London Times. Some Account of Some of the Subscribers. Newspaper Writers and Their Situations in the Loan." While the article contained a disclaimer that the names listed could not be entirely verified and some listed had denied the claim of subscribing, the list nevertheless included the names of individuals who contributed some £800,000 worth of capital towards the Confederate cause; the article made sure to note that interest had not been paid out since November 1864, and even then for only a portion of the subscribers. Notable names on the list included J. V. "Craford" the British consul to Cuba; "J. Rutter," the British consul to Uruguay; Lt. Col. Arthur Freemantle, a British military observer subsequently made famous by the novel *The Killer Angels* and the movie *Gettysburg*; William Gladstone, British chancellor of the exchequer at the time and later prime minister; and several members of Parliament. Thus, for some investors in Britain there remained a desire to curry favor with Southern partners following the war years themselves.[34]

While some British houses remained reluctant to invest, others took more bullish approaches to U.S. debt. Barings Bank—a firm that dated to the mid-eighteenth century and had long-standing American connections, most notably helping to fund the Louisiana Purchase—invested heavily in postwar American debt. As soon as word reached London of the surrender of the Confederate armies and the end of the war, Barings resumed large-scale bond purchases for its London-based British clients who had held off on investing in U.S. securities while the war still persisted. Once it became clear that the North had emerged victorious, however, these clients clamored for the debt. Not only did British clients request the debt, but other London-based banks used the connections that Barings had in America to procure five- and six-figure sums of 5-20s repeatedly throughout 1865, 1866, and 1867. Even at the height of postwar Anglo-American tensions, these houses purchased large amounts of American debt.[35]

The Barings also represented continental clients who had the bank purchase bonds on their behalf—especially French-based clients who had greater difficulty locating the bonds in France itself. While French aristocrats comprised a large segment of Baring's European investors, other wealthy individuals also had the bank purchase on their accounts. In addition to these wealthy clients, the firm also bought on behalf of large European banks who purchased these bonds not only for their own accounts but those of their clients. For instance, Paris-based Hottingeur & Cie purchased a large amount of American debt following the war through Barings. Other firms included

Brugmann & Fils of Belgium and Hope & Co. of Amsterdam. Americans based in Europe also invested heavily in debt in the postwar period through Barings—including American ambassador in London Charles Frances Adams, and the American consuls in Brussels, Athens, Berlin, Paris, Malaga, and Cadiz. Clients also reached beyond Europe for Barings and included many New York banks and individuals, and extended to other continents to include Brazilian businessmen, Ottoman firms, the French minister to Aleppo, and Robert Gray, the first Anglican bishop of Cape Town, South Africa. Some international firms used Barings to invest their funds in bonds. One great example of this was the Canton-based Russell & Co., which in the late 1860s and early 1870s purchased more than $600,000 in American debt via Barings. At the time Russell & Co. was the largest American commission house in China—a title it would hold into the early 1890s.[36]

While not as quick as its competitor Barings, N. M. Rothschild of London also ratcheted up its involvement in American debt following the end of the war. By the late 1860s, the firm had purchased extensively on behalf of an array of London clients, clients in other parts of England, and select London banks. Similar to Barings, the firm also purchased on behalf of continental European clients. This included firms like Bleichreoder in Berlin, which worked closely with the Paris Rothschild house, as well as Becker & Fuld of Amsterdam and Behrens of Hamburg. But as the postwar period evolved, these purchases took on a much larger and more diverse range of clients. Much like the Barings, the Rothschilds had European clients from the aristocracy and even members of royalty—including modern-day France, Poland, Italy, Belgium, Russia, and even Latvia. The firm's clients in American debt similarly came from other parts of continental Europe, ranging from Nice, France, to Warsaw, Poland, to Berlin, Germany.[37]

Financial institutions across the globe also relied on the Rothschilds and in doing so they shed greater light on the reach of American debt. The Bank of Australasia in Melbourne, Australia, purchased bonds as did the Bank of Constantinople in the Ottoman Empire—more than $500,000 worth. Other financial clients included the Moscow Discount Bank, the Enskilda Bank of Sweden, Thomas J. Heppe & Son of Copenhagen, the Bank of Belgium and Holland, Lombard Odier, Avigdor Paine & Fils of Nice, The Trust and Agency Company of Australia, and the Bank of Alsace Lorraine to name but a few. Such clients throughout Europe reveal the widespread reach of American debt by the latter part of the 1860s. Far from a period wherein the United States retreated into a world of isolation, it instead embraced many of these financial connections that integrated the country on a global scale.[38]

CAUTION.

BANKERS, BROKERS, and Others, are hereby cautioned against accepting, receiving, negotiating, or otherwise dealing with all or any of the under-mentioned Securities of the United States, the same having been acquired by means of Forgery:—

United States Bonds.—6 per Cent. Five-Twenty Bonds, 1867.

Nos. 5603	34247	95913	114868-71	166499	171670-1	193993
6018	36435-8	96240	114873	167139	174595	200232
7113	44639	106660	115666	168484	175362	207847
9431	69024	110202	140959-60	169338	178926	215665
12587	80094	114864-6	143397-8	170643	181750	224944
25385						

47 of 1000 Dols. each = 47000 Dols.

94-7	9282	18417	22160	42558	67414	78684
1491	9612	18545	27711	56611	71681	87519
1904	10091	20676	36775	59143	71787	99189
4877	11921	20685	39325	64017-18	73036	113860
5455	17182	21789	39866	64198	76825	115575
7533						

40 of 500 Dols. each = 20000 Dols.

6717	41451	87300	105285	153080	176451	198379
6850	41453-4	92488	107242-4	167053-4	184364	206189
7170	41459	92490	115315	167057	194941-3	212931-2
11674	44970-1	99830	119513	169037	196041	215579
16184	82521	101271-3	127230	169569	198375	227108
18765	85083-4	104864	127772			

50 of 100 Dols. each = 5000 Dols.

United States 5 per Cent. Ten-Forty Bonds, 1864.

65546	78182-3	87129	88392

5 of 1000 Dols. each = 5000 Dols.

United States Funded Loan Bonds.

7445-9	18590-3	32669	43487-8	53777-80	59944-5	65220
8801-2	25868-70	33451-2	46022-4	53794-6	61027	67623-5
10827	27551	33471-3	49672	54633	62583-7	67739
14513	28616	41863	49971-2	59907	63695	71628
15110-4	29197-209	42705-6	52860-8	59909	63907-8	82725-34
18587-8	31839-62					

125 of 1000 Dols. = 125000 Dols.

1140	4224	8692	11555	12336	13065-9	17949-51
3235	4312	11210-42	12333	12338	17713-27	19342-5

69 of 500 Dols. = 34500 Dols.

10277-84	15618-9

10 of 100 Dols. = 1000 Dols.

In the event of any attempt to deal with all or any of the aforesaid Securities, information is requested to be given to INSPECTOR BAILEY, Police Station, Old Jewry, City, E.C.

London, 1st March, 1873.

While counterfeit issues in the United States tended to center on money, this advertisement circulated by London-based N. M. Rothschild and Sons revealed there were similar concerns across the Atlantic when it came to U.S. bonds. (Reproduced with the permission of the Trustees of the Rothschild Archive)

Netherlands

The postwar period witnessed extensive investment via the Netherlands as well, especially in Dutch markets based in Amsterdam. Examining some of these banks that lay outside the established European syndicates is illustrative in demonstrating just how U.S. bonds were introduced at a transformative time for European markets. The Nederlandsche Credit en Deposito-bank of Amsterdam was one of the most crucial financial actors in Amsterdam at the time. The central bank of the Netherlands, the Nederlandsche Bank (as it became known), received charter approval from the government on February 22, 1863, nominally as a Dutch bank designed to right the flagging Dutch banking industry. But its capital drew largely from Frenchmen, the majority of shareholders were French, and the opening of a Paris branch almost immediately after the granting of its charter demonstrated that Amsterdam would play second fiddle to the larger branch in Paris, and Parisian business quickly overtook the work being done in Amsterdam. Among other things, the Nederlansche Bank worked to underwrite American government bonds from 1864 to 1870.[39]

The financial firm of Hope & Co. was central to the purchase and sales of American debt in Amsterdam. Although originally founded by Scotsmen, the firm originated in Amsterdam and eventually came to open a branch in London as well (Hope & Co. also had very close ties to Baring Brothers in the City of London, as many financiers for the firm apprenticed in London and vice versa). The firm's early eighteenth-century investments were in the realm of the slave trade as well as the transport and financing of Quaker travel out of Rotterdam to the New World. By the early nineteenth century the firm had grown to the point that it helped to underwrite the financing of the Louisiana Purchase. While the firm struggled in the early part of the eighteenth century (retaining a staff of eleven in 1813), its business had grown such that the firm had a staff of 1,500 by the early 1850s. As the nineteenth century progressed the firm moved away from a more traditional merchant approach centered on goods to focus on securities spanning the entire world. Such business came to be conducted by the firm itself, but in the realm of international bonds transactions it was increasingly conducted by close associates Weduwe W. Borski.[40]

A further examination of the records of Hope & Co. from the Reconstruction period reveals an active and dynamic market for American Civil War bonds for a clientele that spanned the Continent. Hope & Co.'s sales represented purchases on behalf of established European families (including royalty) as well as other Dutch financial firms and their extended families. For example, while Hope & Co. executed the aforementioned purchases for American textile magnet Rowland Gibson Hazard, they also undertook sales for Princess Elisabeth van Saxe Weimar Eisenach. Additionally, sales were undertaken on behalf of Prince Frederick Hendrik, Dutch financier J. G. Sillem and his wife Olga Ophie Sillem, and others such as an F. Jameson in Paris as well as Sarah Somers Leckie and Louise von Tappe. Russian interest in the bonds came via Hope & Co. Charles Jutting acted as an agent for Barings and Hope in the Russian financial capital of St. Petersburg, and he began placing requests for 5-20 loans in earnest in 1867. Russian interest in the American federal debt reached a point that by the fall of 1867, Hope was sending an invoice with each letter to Jutting detailing sales of American debt in Amsterdam. Such frequent correspondence between Jutting and Hope & Co. is evidence of interest in American federal debt in the Russian republic—even as Mississippi state repudiation remained a topic of grave concern for Russian investors.[41]

In addition, the papers of Borski and their work on behalf of Hope & Co. also offer insight into the sales of American Civil War bonds in the immediate postwar period. These individuals spanned a wide swath of Europe. The prominent Polish banker Leopold Kronenberg—who helped to establish the Warsaw Credit Association and was one of the primary financiers of the Warszawsko-Terespolska Railway—offers a prime example. He purchased $30,000 in 5-20s through the Dutch house in 1867. The bonds came from a wide variety of primary sales stateside and include a bond out of a $1,000,000 lot purchased by the Metropolitan Bank in New York as well as a $1,000 bond out of a $50,000 lot purchased by the Lowell (Massachusetts) Institution for Savings. Another bond came from a $55,000 lot purchased by Vermilye & Co., while a fourth came from a smaller lot purchased by an individual named Samuel Fowler. The interest and sale of these bonds more than likely helped to underwrite Kronenberg's extensive investment in other Russian railroads in the latter part of the nineteenth century. There were other Russian connections as well. Heinrich VII, Prince Reuss of Kostritz and the first German ambassador to the Russian court at St. Petersburg, also purchased bonds through the house shortly after his appointment in 1871. The diplomat included '81s and 5-20s from 1864 as part of his portfolio, as well as two other issues from 1865 and 1867. Count Ernest Charles de Stackelberg, a Russian career diplomat assigned to Paris at the time of his investment, undertook an investment of $28,000 in 1865 5-20s made shortly before his death in 1870. Prince Nicolas Labanov Rostovsky also invested in Amsterdam. The fact that these bonds were held for such brief periods (averaging slightly over a year) would seem to reinforce the idea that such investments were part of a repo market for these individuals and the firm, although further information would need to be uncovered to verify such claims.[42]

The Borskis also actively invested on their own books, although for many of their purchases their clients were contained to the Netherlands itself. While some clients hailed from Amsterdam, others resided in the Dutch cities of Rotterdam, Haarlem, Arnhem, Beetsterzwaag, and Leeuwarden. These individuals came from a wide array of industries as well. They included Gebr Gratama, part of the Gratama Brothers bank of Leeuwarden, as well as Y. H. Bogaers from Rotterdam, who purchased $12,000 in 1865 5-20s in the fall of 1872 (this after having sold $4,000 of the same security in May of the same year). Another individual, an F. H. Brinkman from nearby Haarlem, also actively traded in securities via the Borskis ranging from 5-20s to refunded 5 percent bonds. The Borskis' personal accounts were also active in Civil War bond sales. Willem Borski, C. A. Borski, and Y. Borski all invested in 5-20s and 10-40s in the postwar period, as well as 5 percent refinanced debt. Willem Borski was perhaps the most actively involved in the sales of bonds, especially the 5 percent refinanced debt in 1872–73: Borski bought and sold over $100,000 of this debt in just over a year.[43]

All told these various Dutch firms and their clients, spread far and wide across the European continent and beyond, helped to further the American financial footprint in the Reconstruction era. While the evidentiary record for the Netherlands in the postwar period leaves something to be desired, the material available affirms the importance of Dutch firms to American debt issuance and the larger networks that permeated the European continent. As European investment skyrocketed in the immediate postwar years, the investors anxiously looked across the Atlantic at the intensifying debate regarding debt repayment that engulfed Congress by the late 1860s.

Waving the Bloody Shirt

When Congress reconvened in December 1865, the body took up the passage of a resolution declaring the debt "sacred and inviolate" that passed overwhelmingly. Yet, the turn to 1866 did little to quell the concerns of the nation as a whole. The *Nation* reported concerns over a combination of Northern Democrats and former Confederates working to repudiate the debt: "It would hardly be a safe thing for the national credit to have such a body of men in Congress, reinforced as they would probably be, by a considerable number of

Northern men ready to go for at least qualified repudiation." Senator Henry Wilson took it a step further by expressing his fears over the debt—an item he viewed "as sacred as the blood of our heroes poured out on the battlefields." The debt issue proved fundamental to Republicans' electoral strategy in the 1866 midterm elections. Former Union general Benjamin Butler warned a crowd in Massachusetts if Democrats were elected "What would your 7:30s be worth?" But perhaps the *New York Herald* stated it best when it remarked, "Herein lies the secret of the astounding popular strength of [the Fourteenth Amendment] ... No man who has a fifty dollar government bond salted down would trust its redemption to the chances of the casting vote in Congress of a Southerner who has lost his thousands in Confederate script." The Republican message that framed the sanctity of the debt as part of the Union cause proved a rallying cry not only on principle, but for the fundamentals of electoral politics of the age.[44]

Questions also lingered over how the government would repay the bonds in the postwar period. Greenbacks, totaling more than $400 million in 1865, remained the lawful currency. Politicians on both sides of the aisle assumed that this currency would be a temporary measure rectified in peacetime. Legislation creating 5-20s in February 1862 made it clear that interest had to be paid out in gold. Beyond that there remained an open interpretation as far as the repayment of the principal—a fund that totaled nearly $607 million in 1865 (slightly over one-quarter of the national debt). Many wished to return to the gold standard owing to the wild fluctuation in greenback valuation (although the fact that gold ran at a premium to greenbacks did mean that the debt could be retired at a relative discount). Nevertheless, the Funding Act of April 12, 1866, gave the secretary of the treasury the ability to contract the greenback supply by $10 million in the first six months following the act's passage and a further $4 million a month from that point forward. This authorization did not lead to the complete retirement of the greenbacks owing to the tightened economic climate of the latter part of the 1860s. As a result, Treasury only pulled $44 million of the greenbacks from the money supply and the country still had not returned to the gold standard. The contraction of the money supply had the effect of propelling gold even higher.[45]

Politics and morality soon merged with the money issue and its repercussions extended to the realm of bonds and repayment. For many, specie held connotations of honor, whereas a fiat currency met with suspicion if not evil undertones. Questions over how to repay bond issues devolved into accusations of theft and swindling of the American people by specie advocates (a bipartisan caucus that was divided more along regional lines). Future president James Garfield weighed in strongly on behalf of hard money. "On the one side," Garfield declared, "it is proposed to return to solid and honest values; on the other, to float in the boundless and shoreless sea of paper money, with all its dishonesty and broken pledges." On another occasion, Garfield reiterated such sentiments when he remarked, "Business men and legislators have taken paper money in such overwhelming doses that they are crazed, and like the lotus-eaters wish to return no more to solid values." John Sherman (in an apparent reversal of his earlier position) reiterated such sentiments: "It [a soft money bill] proposes to pay to the creditor of the Government who now holds the interest-bearing obligations of the United States a note not bearing interest, and compel him to take that note against his will. It thus proposes to confiscate the property of the citizen." With the battle lines drawn, the future remained uncertain over the exact timetable for a return to the gold standard, but for many questions of honor connected to the very question.[46]

Such beliefs marked a deviation from the initial views in Congress following the end of the war. Republican senator Justin Morrill (a bondholder himself) exclaimed in 1866, "A permanent national debt is not an American institution, as our history has already twice proven, and though it may take a number of years to wholly extinguish the present debt, the policy of gradual extinction can and should be steadily pursued." Others reiterated the sentiments of Garfield and Sherman, emphasizing a need and the honor of repaying the loans in specie. Theodore Pomeroy stated, "I am ashamed to have a proposition made at the close of the Thirty-Ninth Congress to pay off the debt of the United States or any portion of it otherwise than by bonds payable, principal and interest, in gold, or else by gold itself." Henry Corbett quipped, "Public credit should be 'like Caesar's wife, above suspicion.'" Timothy Howe likewise complained that greenbacks were "an active and bitter reproach upon the integrity and good faith of the nation, because they constantly flout the business world with promises which are as constantly broken." The press also got wind of the matter and each side's mouthpieces promoted their position—lobbing claims of "bondocrats" and "repudiators" alike. The clash over the legacy of bonds and who they benefitted and exploited became a fundamental political schism in the Reconstruction era.[47]

Proponents and opponents of gold specie waved the bloody shirt of the war to call for a repayment in their preferred medium. For specie proponents like Howe, payment in anything less than gold reflected the ultimate insult. "The cause in which that debt was contracted is one to which three hundred thousand soldiers gave their lives," exclaimed Howe. "Who is he who dares stand by the graves of the patriot dead and say that the cause would warrant the sacrifice of their lives but it not worth the tribute of our money." Conversely, greenback proponents slammed the double standard of debt repayment in gold but soldiers' service pay only in greenbacks. One newspaper remarked, "The soldiers who risked their lives in their country's quarrel could be paid with greenbacks, but the bond holders must have gold."[48]

Many Democrats seized on the "Ohio Idea" championed by George Hunt Pendleton, George McClellan's vice presidential running mate in 1864. Criticizing Republicans for ineptitude and corruption when it came to the public debt, he (and an increasing percentage of Democrats) called for the repayment of principal whenever possible in depreciated greenbacks. Republicans and their allies in the press attacked any such schemes as akin to repudiation of the debt. The Republican Party in 1868 established a plank in its platform denouncing repudiation in any form. Ulysses Grant won the presidential election in the fall of 1868, but still had to contend with the actions of a lame-duck president in Andrew Johnson. During Johnson's annual message in December 1868, he broke with Republicans and called for a repudiation of the debt. In an ironic twist, Johnson equated the continued servicing of the debt as a new form of slavery upon the country. "The borrowers would become the servants to the lenders—the lenders the masters of the people," exclaimed Johnson. Congress responded in kind with a House resolution the following week declaring "that all forms and degrees of repudiation of national indebtedness are odious to the American people." Congress then passed a bill in early March 1869, promising the government's repayment of all bonds in coin. While the bill never became law because of a pocket veto by Johnson, Grant's term began soon thereafter and one of the first pieces of legislation passed during his administration was the Public Credit Act. Passed into law on March 18, 1869, the act pledged all United States obligations paid out "in coin or its equivalent." The crisis over how bonds would be repaid appeared resolved for the time being, and it was no coincidence that a drastic increase in European investment coincided with the Public Credit Act.[49]

Jay Cooke once more entered the fray to champion payment not only in specie, but also a return to resumption in the near future. In the fall of 1869, Cooke proclaimed, "It is plain then, that if we resume—it must be on a basis of *confidence* and not *ability* to pay on demand. If the Government can possess itself of specie enough to inspire Confidence it can resume—but the Treasury must be strong—stronger than the cliques and opposing influences of trade—or confidence will be lost and suspension follow." Cooke called for resumption to begin on January 1, 1872, giving the Treasury enough time to retire greenbacks at a reasonable rate and the accumulation of enough specie to ensure that suspension did not occur in the near future. A variety of factors ultimately worked against these goals (including the devastating fallout from the Panic of 1873) and resumption did not occur until 1879.[50]

Despite the Public Credit Act, serious questions abounded regarding the refinancing of the public debt, especially considering the vast quantity of the debt reaching maturity in the short term. The fact that some $582 million of the outstanding debt was subject to redemption on demand made for a potential run on the U.S. Treasury. Opinions on a general refunding of the debt came down to fundamental disagreements over whether or not the debt should be repaid off the gold standard. Secretary McCulloch championed a retirement of greenbacks before attempts should be made to refund the remaining debt. Senator Sherman—chair of the Senate Finance Committee—pursued the opposite position and believed that any semblance of refunding or refinancing should be attempted while the money market found itself saturated with hundreds of millions in greenbacks. Sherman noted, "The very abundance of the currency obviously enables us to fund the debt at a low rate of interest; and as the debt was contracted upon an inflated currency it is just and right that upon that same currency it should be funded in its present form." Jay Cooke stood as Sherman's biggest advocate in this battle. The two clashed over the issue of whether 5-20s could be paid off in gold or greenbacks. Cooke himself never wavered on the matter, but Sherman believed that the government had the authority to repay the loan in greenbacks. Cooke pushed hard against such a measure, even confiding to his brother Henry in the summer of 1868, "If the Repubn party is to turn repudiators I will desert them. This whole matter must be at once understood before I give any money. The scoundrels deserve hanging for the irreparable injury they are doing to this glorious nation."[51]

As Table 6.1 demonstrates, however, the great uncertainties of the late 1860s did nothing more than to keep the Civil War debt at a relatively stagnant level. All told, during this immediate postwar period the national debt held in bonds declined by a little less than $100 million—not an insignificant number, but certainly a long ways to go with the remaining $2.2 billion in Civil War debt, that while it had been restricted merely delayed pertinent and difficult decisions on how the federal government would tackle paying it off.

Although the Public Credit Act passed in March 1869, it took another year for Congress to seriously take up the issue of refinancing the debt under new Treasury Secretary George Boutwell. Proposed by Boutwell and passed on July 14, 1870, the new legislation gave the secretary of the treasury authoriza-

TABLE 6.1 Public loan transactions of the U.S. Treasury, 1865–1869

Date	Purchase	Sold
October 1, 1865–June 30, 1866	$620,321,725.61	$712,851,553.05
July 1, 1866–June 30, 1867	$746,350,525.04	$640,426,910.29
July 1, 1867–June 30, 1868	$692,549,685.88	$625,111,433.20
July 1, 1868–June 30, 1869	$253,222,718.31	$238,678,081.66
Totals	$2,312,444,654.84	$2,217,067,978.20

Henrietta Larson, *Jay Cooke: Private Banker* (Cambridge, MA: Harvard University Press, 1936), 219. Data compiled from Secretary of the Treasury, *Report on the Finances*, 1866–69.

tion to issue $500 million in 10-year bonds at 5 percent, $300 million in 15-year bonds at 4.5 percent, and $1 billion in 30-year bonds at 4 percent. While the exact quantities of each bond issue were finalized over time, a refinancing of the debt was finally being discussed and had bonds dropping below the 6 percent level that had defined so much debt during the Civil War itself. The passage of the bill did, however, coincide with the outbreak of the Franco-Prussian War in 1870 and general consensus dictated that no refinancing actions would be undertaken until the war terminated or entered its waning weeks. The reliance on German and French banks as parts of future syndicates to sell debt in Europe necessitated a peaceful resolution across the Atlantic. Discussion continued on how to refinance the debt, but the initial political battle was over.[52]

Unsurprisingly, Jay Cooke once more stood at the forefront of Civil War debt. Although the end of the war witnessed Cooke shift his holdings into railroads (something he had begun during the war proper) he nevertheless maintained an interest in the Civil War debt owing to his sway and association regarding the debt. An opportune Cooke realized that money was still to be had in the postwar period. It also was no coincidence that as the United States dealt with the question of refinancing war debt, Cooke also championed a vitally important bill on the floor of Congress pertaining to land grants associated with his Northern Pacific Railroad. Thus, Cooke advocated for two positions at once with old friend John Sherman and other Republicans on Capitol Hill—while contending with a less friendly Secretary Boutwell. Letters received by Cooke reveal the widespread distrust and disdain his financial circle held for Boutwell. "It seems quite useless to try and argue anything into his head," remarked Harris Fahnstock in December 1870. "It is a pity that he ever left the tape business which he managed so successfully in his native town." Much like Cooke's engagement with Chase in the early months of the Civil War, he would need to placate a man in power in Washington who did not hold the faith of the influential investing class in New York City.[53]

As during the war itself, Cooke & Co. benefitted more than anything else from its role as a government depositor—both for bond sales as well as other government accounts. Similar to the wartime period, Jay Cooke made a habit of using federal dollars at his disposal to his benefit. Cooke issued call loans to interested parties in New York City, including other financial institutions who used their funds (proceeds of bond sales) to then purchase more bonds. For collateral, Cooke naturally used government bonds—an entity he knew he could sell easily on the exchange to cover his accounts with the government. Cooke's New York house even lent funds to his other banks in Philadelphia, and especially Washington, D.C. The importance of Cooke as a government dispositor played a role in his efforts to adjudicate between the Treasury and New York elites.[54]

Further examination of redemption of 5-20s as early as 1867 reveals the disparate nature of owners—but at the same time the increasing centralization around larger holders. To be sure, small-scale purchasers did turn in their bonds initially. But as redemption gained more steam, an increasing number of the bonds became concentrated in the hands of national banks as well as various commercial banks that had played a large role in the initial sales. In particular, Jay Cooke and his collection of affiliate banks throughout the North procured increasing amounts of these bonds and redeemed them regularly in the six-figure range. While the bonds passed in the secondary market to other individuals or were purchased outside the realm of commercial banks, it is not possible to know based on the evidence available when these bonds returned to the hands of the larger banks. But one thing is abundantly clear: between the initial redemptions in 1867 and the more concerted efforts by the fall of 1871, larger institutional players secured control of the bonds (at least for redemption purposes).[55]

In the immediate postwar period Cooke & Co. had been called upon to uphold the financial markets through bond purchases on behalf of the federal government. Cooke made his feelings clear on the matter in 1869 when he remarked on the role of government in the economy. "All that can be done," Cooke stated, "should be daily & hourly & watchfully one to relive the market from Panic & to restore confidence & then to keep things in place by the strong hand of Government." Indeed, on numerous occasions in 1868 and 1869 Cooke claimed he intervened in the market at the orders of the Treasury—under the strictest of secrecy so as to keep the rest of the Street none the wiser. Such acts did not go unnoticed by the press and by Congress. Some members of the press remained critical of McCulloch. "If speculative stocks are high it is Mr. McCulloch who is fostering a reckless spirit of speculation," one paper declared. "If they are dull and on a decline, it is Mr. McCulloch who is crippling business and destroying confidence." In Congress Republican John Logan called for an investigation into favoritism regarding the sale of government bonds as it pertained to the Treasury. The *New York Herald* intimated that such an investigation would reveal "how Jay Cooke and others have become enormously rich by doing that which the department itself should have done." A bill to prevent secret sales of gold made it to the Senate floor—a bill that Cooke staunchly opposed. While the bill failed, it more or less had its desired effect, with incoming Secretary Boutwell shifting away from secret gold sales, creating greater competition in New York for gold used in bond sales.[56]

The American Treasury Abroad

International sales continued to increase in the aftermath of the Public Credit Act. To help facilitate this action, the government opened an office in London for investors to purchase bonds and redeem those being called in by the federal government. An examination of the surviving ledgers from the London office reveals the varied nature of sales that made their way through the office. Of the hundreds of transactions through the office, the majority were for British, Scottish, Irish, and French buyers. Purchases also were directed towards individuals from the German states, the Netherlands, Canada, Malta, Puerto Rico, Italy, and Switzerland. The sales, much like those in the war period domestically and abroad, ranged in the class and stature of the individuals although sales through the office certainly scaled to those of higher classes. For instance, Vincenzo Bugeja hailing from Malta was a prominent businessman from the island and noted philanthropist. (His penchant for gambling and cutthroat approach at the tables in Monte Carlo earned him the nickname "the Maltese Matador.") Archibald Maswell, from Avranches in the Normandy region of France, also purchased the 5 percent funded loan through the London office. Purchases outside of the London office did cross the Atlantic and were purchased on behalf of several individuals and firms. Still other purchasers out of the London office came from the U.S. side of the Atlantic. Anne Bullivant, a self-described "spinster" from St. Catharines, Ontario, procured $10,000 in 5 percent bonds. The firm of Skerrett Brothers, based out of San Juan, Puerto Rico, also bought bonds though the U.S. office in London.[57]

The bond purchasers from the U.S. office in London spanned the European continent and beyond. Other investors include Italian royalty such as

Gaetano Filangierri, Prince of Satriano in northern Italy, who invested repeatedly in these bonds in 1871 and 1872. Similarly, Michael Gravina, Prince de Comitini, and residing in Naples also invested. John Pennington Thomasson, a cotton mill owner in Bolton and future member of Parliament; Theodose Achille Louis, the Comte du Moncel and one of the leading French scientists of the nineteenth century; and Reverend William Edensor Littlewood, an English minister and social activist, all invested in U.S. government bonds in 1871–72. The bond sales also crossed gender lines. English novelist Mary Ann Evans, better known by her pen name George Eliot, purchased U.S. government bonds. The same can be said of Jane Sheil, an Irish widow and extensive landowner in Dublin. Maria Alboni, an Italian-born singer and one of the most famous contraltos in Europe, purchased bonds (she resided in Paris at the time of the sale). Eliza Hudson, a widow in Dublin, purchased bonds. Spinsters Harriet Wright and Hannah Sleightholme heralding from South Cliff, England, purchased $1,000 each. Even Helen Maingay and Elizabeth Maingay of the small island of Guernsey in the English Channel invested sums in the bond sales. When coupled with investments by the Chartered Banks of India as well as Australia, the funded loan of 1871 obtained an even wider global reach. From July 1871 to February 1872, the London office sold slightly under $3.7 million to several hundred individuals. Such sales continued through the office with additional refunding efforts in the early 1880s.[58]

As the calendar turned to 1871, conglomerations of domestic and international financial houses moved forward with a more concerted effort to open the sale of refinanced American debt in the United States and Europe. As the spring of 1871 wore on, there was a variety of moves by rival firms to try and take on the issue of these new 5 percent bonds authorized by Congress in the summer of 1870 and the domestic and international markets they afforded. Small commissions on the refinanced loans meant that large quantities would need to be absorbed and then sold if there were any hope of pulling in a profit. The emergence of a legitimate threat to the agency of Cooke and his network complicated matters: Levi P. Morton and his London partner Sir John Rose arrived in Washington and negotiated with George Boutwell to take on an exclusive agency for the sales, and many assumed that by late winter 1871 Morton & Rose had all but sewn up the agency.[59]

Secretary Boutwell's decision to issue refinanced 5 percent bonds at home and abroad with a wide array of houses that included Cooke and his chief rivals Parsons and Rose shocked virtually every financial house. The London branch of the syndicate included Jay Cooke, McCulloch & Company, as well as Morton, Rose & Company, and even London-based Barings, J. S. Morgan, and the Rothschilds to name just some of the firms. The high number of financial houses caused some firms like the Rothschilds to withdraw. Domestically, the Treasury called on a wide array of firms including Cooke and his allies as well as Democratic rivals from the Civil War period. A slow pace defined the sales in March 1871 and led other houses to withdraw. Calls soon came forward for a reinvigorated collection of houses to form a new syndicate on more favorable terms to sell the balance of the $200 million in 5 percent bonds that remained. Through extensive maneuvering, Cooke and his allies led this charge both domestically and abroad.[60]

The original syndicate and those that followed played a crucial role in refunding Civil War debt. Between August 1871 and June 1879, various syndicates sold some $1.4 billion worth of federal bonds. Such an act enhanced the power of American securities abroad, but also the might of the financial houses that undertook such endeavors. The absence of some of the most famous banking houses of the nineteenth century defined the initial syndicate. The Barings Rothschilds, and Morgans (led by J. S. Morgan, J. P. Morgan's father) all declined to be agents as part of the initial syndicate of 1871. Junius Morgan stated in the summer of 1871 that he "did not see any great profit" to be had through participation in the syndicate. Cooke proved his doubters wrong and successfully sold the issue totaling some $130 million—leading Morgan to recognize the fact that Jay Cooke had "established American credit abroad" without "the aid or cooperation of certain firms who have heretofore assumed that nothing could be done without them."[61]

The syndicate did meet with some criticism. By August 1871, *The Commercial and Financial Chronicle and Hunt's Merchant's Magazine* (a lengthy, awkward title following a merger) called on Secretary Boutwell to "make a candid full statement of the details of the arrangement he has made with the syndicate. The light of the publicity must be shed on all the conditions of this contract and on every step of their fulfillment. The arrangement is not one which requires or allows concealment." Acknowledging that the arrangement had "introduced a new word into the vocabulary of finance," the article nevertheless recognized syndicates as merely the latest word to define what had previously been referred to as "'rings', 'cliques', 'combinations', and some of them were so disgraceful in their objects, so dishonest in their methods, that when a clique was formed of an honest sort, the word 'ring,' or 'combinations,' or their equivalents were avoided, if possible . . ." Such sentiment reflected widespread criticism of these financial syndicates, especially by parties left on the outside looking in.[62]

The funds earmarked for the respective syndicates would ultimately rise to $130 million ($80 million of which was for the European syndicate). The successful sales of the syndicate resulted in the decision on the part of Secretary Boutwell to issue a notice of redemption calling in $100 million of the 1862 5-20s with interest ceasing December 1. Bonds could be redeemed, or similarly could be exchanged for the new 5 percent issue of 1871. For those that desired the new 5 percent issue abroad, the U.S. government shipped these bonds in various steamers in $5 million and $10 million increments—the clerks escorting the bonds not having access to the respective safe under their control to ensure proper delivery. The issuance met with great success not only for the government but also both syndicates. So impressive was the triumph of the European syndicate that the mighty Rothschilds agreed to go in with Cooke and Co. on a future $100 million of bonds to sell in Europe.[63]

Records of the efforts of some European banks pertaining to the 5 percents 1871 issue are found at the National Archives and include firms outside of the established syndicate. Such purchases occurred in the slow sales period that preceded the syndicate. Baring Brothers—which declined participation in the syndicate—nevertheless purchased $98,500 in 5 percent bonds. The Rothschilds in London purchased a modest $13,100 for several clients. The Rothschild house in Frankfurt similarly procured $35,200 in April 1871 including nearly half of the bonds for the Bishop of St. Alban. J. S. Morgan in London continued its support of the Civil War debt in the postwar period with $15,000 in purchases. Seligman and Stettheimer purchased $176,000 in 5 percent bonds in the spring of 1871. Clews, Habicht & Co. topped the sales in the spring of 1871, however, by purchasing slightly more than $2 million of the new 5 percent bonds. Such purchases in the spring of 1871 preceding any and all syndicate arrangements—including firms both part of and outside the future European syndicate—reveal initial interest in the 5 percent bonds in early 1871, albeit light compared to future sales.[64]

While the London Rothschild house may have been initially reticent to invest in the refunded loan, this did not stop the Frankfurt house under M. C. de Rothschild. Writing to August Belmont in April 1871, Rothschild made it abundantly clear subscriptions had been opened at the Frankfurt house as well as "all over Germany also Switzerland." Working in conjunction with Seligman & Stettheimer, the firm emphasized all efforts being made to "further the consolidation of the U.S. Securities" through various means including a prospectus published jointly with Seligman & Stettheimer in "all the more important towns of Germany & Switzerland," as well as all "largely circulated newspapers." By March 1871, Seligman & Stettheimer in Frankfurt reported back to Boutwell that $200 million had been subscribed in Frankfurt alone. By July 1871, Barings of London reported to the United States government a total of some $98,000 in 5-20s to exchange for refunded 5 percents. Jay Cooke McCulloch & Co. similarly indicated $186,100 in 5-20s to exchange by the summer of 1871 as part of a request to procure $1.1 million in 5 percents. Seligman & Stettheimer submitted a request for $106,000 in 5-20 exchanges. The issue met with mild success, even with a slow start. The sales had convinced the government to move forward with a refunding of the debt and extended American credit and the reputation of Cooke abroad. Levi Morton wrote to President Grant reflecting this belief. "There is no wiping out the fact," Morton declared, "that it was a wonderful negotiation and will put Jay Cooke & Co. head and shoulders above any American house in Europe, and make them peers of the proudest of the European houses." Such a statement from Morton—a fierce competitor of Cooke's for government bond sales—reveals that even Cooke's enemies could recognize his masterful moves to achieve the agency. These lower-interest-rate bonds reinforced efforts on the part of the U.S. government to repay its debt, but simultaneously recognized how slow the process would be.[65]

But perhaps most critically, the success of this international loan in 1871 demonstrated a new chapter in the world of American investment banking. For the very first time, an American bank had successfully placed an American loan abroad—at least in name without the lead of European financial houses. President Grant praised such an action to one of the partners of Jay Cooke & Co. when he championed the fact that the loan "was established without the aid or co-operation of certain firms who have heretofore assumed that nothing could be done without them," concluding his statement by emphasizing "that the prestige of success was attached to American agents rather than to the Barings and Rothschilds." Even the *Bankers Magazine* declared by late 1871 "It may be said with the exception of England no nation stands higher in respect of public credit than the United States."[66]

The next refunding issue of January 1873 led to a change of heart for several of the larger, more established firms such as Barings and the Rothschilds. Those firms on both sides of the Atlantic saw what success had come from the issue and opted to join if possible. By 1872, the American houses angled for such a position by promoting Grant's reelection within the Democratic enclave of New York City. The firms quickly took sides in the winter of 1872–73 to make a play for the $300 million redemption. On one side, Jay Cooke's firm led a contingent that included the London-based Rothschilds and the Seligman houses. On the other was a group led by Levi Morton and his network in Paris and London, Pierpont Morgan and his transnational house, and London-based Baring Brothers. Pierpont Morgan spent the majority of January 1873 camped out in Washington to curry favor with the outgoing secretary of the treasury.[67]

Ultimately the rival factions saw the advantage of working together on the matter. In late January the two sides joined together, bridging a divide between the two networks to take on the $300 million 5 percent loan. While the firms only accepted $10 million initially, they had an option to buy the balance before the end of the year. The agreement was signed by Cooke & Co., Morton, Bliss, and Drexel Morgan—who all acted on their own behalf as well that as their London associates (Baring Brothers; Jay Cooke, McCulloch & Co.; J. S. Morgan & Co; Morton Rose & Co.; and N. M. Rothschild & Sons). The issue did not meet with as much success as the initial syndicate of 1871. While the blame found its way more generally to the European houses for the failure to issue more bonds (even though European placement outnumbered American bonds $28.5 million to $21 million), the meager sales proved undeniable. European firms divided £105,000 in profit among themselves by the end of the year and realized that the failure of Cooke & Co. opened the door for future investments on a larger scale if they were so inclined.[68]

The attempted refunding in 1873 took place in the midst of a deep economic contraction that threw the United States into a depression and took down the mighty financial house of Jay Cooke. But the Panic itself was remarkably transatlantic—revealing the globalization of financial services. The Panic of 1873 did not itself start in the fall of 1873 in the United States with the fall of Cooke, but rather could be traced across the Atlantic to a colossal crash in the Vienna Stock Market from the previous May. Overspeculation in railroad issues of American companies along with those of European rails brought down this exchange. The close ties between the Vienna exchange and that in Berlin had a crippling effect on that exchange as well. The financial panics spread through continental Europe during the spring and summer of 1873 and finally reached the United States by the fall of that year. Only then did the New York exchange suffer and a panic set in within the United States. But as historians such as Hannah Catherine Davies have recently pointed out, the transatlantic connections regarding this panic were felt and believed much more acutely in Europe compared to the United States. These transatlantic speculations influenced the refunding issues of 1873, which were likewise transatlantic in scope. Financial crisis in Europe (and later the United States) factored into the subsequent difficulty of the European syndicate to place the loan in the fall of 1873 and even into the spring of 1874.[69]

One of the victims of this massive financial collapse was none other than Jay Cooke. Although Cooke had proven integral to the United States during the war and made his modest fortune in federal debt, it was in the postwar period that Cooke set his sights on the world of railroad bonds to a much more significant degree. The illusive transcontinental railroads that would help to define the post–Civil War nineteenth century proved to be Cooke's downfall. By the summer of 1873, a consensus had begun to brew that financial stresses on the market were becoming too much to bear. In anticipation of such an event, the U.S. Treasury began that summer to tighten the money supply and collect large quantities of gold. Cooke's overextension in the stock of the Northern Pacific Railroad proved increasingly problematic as country bankers opted to call and withdraw their funds in Northern Pacific stock. By September 18, 1873, Cooke & Co.'s New York office was forced to shutter its doors and its additional branches quickly followed suit. The Panic of 1873, as it became known, led to a depression that devastated the United States as well as Europe.[70]

The announcement in 1875 that the United States would resume specie payments in 1879 sent further ripples through the market as European financiers envisioned a powerful United States returning to the gold standard. The latest secretary of the treasury, longtime senator (and Cooke ally) John Sherman, coordinated extensively with August Belmont and the Rothschilds from 1877 to 1879 on matters of bond sales abroad. Indeed, if anyone approached the level that Cooke & Co. had held, it was Rothschilds via August Belmont. Pierpont Morgan complained at one point to his father regarding the primary role Belmont had taken at the expense of firms like their own. "So far as we are concerned here," Pierpont mused, "we are entire nonentities. We are never consulted or informed & have no more idea of what is being done than if we had no interest or liability in the matter." Charles F. Conant even was sent abroad to contend with the issue as "the operations of the [banking] syndicate have become so important." By 1879, the government had ushered in a further five refunding issues utilizing transatlantic syndicates with great success. In 1880, as the United States conducted its tenth census, there was an attempt made to determine the ownership of the national debt with distinctions between domestic and international holders of the debt. Estimates came in that some $250 million in American federal debt was located overseas at the time of the census—down from its high of $1 billion some eleven years earlier, but still a sizable quantity of the dwindling Civil War debt. Budget surpluses during the 1880s rapidly dwindled the Civil War debt, to the point that it effectively disappeared by the turn of the century.[71]

Writing many years after the Civil War, the established Frankfurt banker Saemy Japhet told of his introduction at a young age to American securities: "There was hardly an investor in South Germany who did not buy United States bonds ... They all believed in the ultimate victory of those who identified themselves with the cause of liberty ... The profits made in American securities and American trade were one of the stepping stones on which the newly enriched world of Germany could tread." Japhet's commentary is illuminating and places a distinct emphasis on American bonds as a fundamental building block for the German economy. But this point reveals something even deeper—the fundamental arrangements that facilitated these sales. Familial and religious connections along with antislavery sentiment across the Atlantic for many German banks helped to expand the German market while informal partnerships also took advantage of the American bond market. Yet, much of this was predicated on honor and trust—particularly for informal arrangements that came into being during this period of rapid financialization. Despite the perception of government bonds as safe investments, an ocean separated these houses from the U.S. government. This was a nation composed of a collection of states, many of whom had defaulted on state bond issues in the antebellum and immediate postwar period. It was imperative for German and Dutch banks to have close connections via partnerships stateside. It was these German banks that projected *haute banque* ideals (and *haute banque* connections) across the Atlantic—opting to push beyond the fairly conservative notions of "international markets" put forward by their French rivals (or in some cases, partners). It was this bold step on the part of German banks that slowly roped the *haute banque parisienne*, albeit indirectly, into this wider financial market. The prestige and reputation of the *haute banque* when coupled with the more aggressive investment pursuits of German banks fostered new relationships that opened a window into deeper international markets centered on an emerging German financial sector.[72]

Thus American finance had come full circle. The antebellum financial system predicated on British and (to a lesser degree) Dutch financial entities had witnessed a reversal by which American banks projected a new wealth overseas. A national financial transformation facilitated by the Legal Tender Act and National Banking Act had forced American banks to shed the antebellum financial world only to expand a powerful sphere of influence abroad. The United States was not the world's creditor yet ... but it is dangerous to simply attribute American financial preeminence by the end of the nineteenth century to financial capitalism underwritten solely by Civil War debt.

Nevertheless, the financial transformations of the Civil War era enabled Gilded Age finance to propel America in that pivotal direction.

Domestically the question of Civil War debt in the conflict's immediate aftermath became a source of great partisan rancor on the national stage. Republicans and Democrats latched onto the issue in an effort to court voters in the new world of Reconstruction-era politics. Once again, Jay Cooke found himself called upon to aid the government in its quest for fiscal stability and a path forward to gradually reduce the debt, with an eye toward its ultimate retirement. Cooke once again did his duty, but in so doing he found himself stretched too thin—and the Panic of 1873 led to his financial downfall and mired the country in a deep economic depression. But the domestic side of debt retirement only tells part of the story of postwar debt. At least as important was the prevalence of American debt in international circles stretching across the globe by the end of the 1860s. By looking at this international story, one garners a deeper appreciation for the story of American debt and American banks on the world stage after the Civil War.

Conclusion

On a cold, dark, blustery Christmas Eve, the banker Ebenezer Scrooge settled down for his holiday slumber. But even the merriment of the holidays in the City of London did little to improve Scrooge's mood. Frustrated by the fact that his workers (most notably trusty clerk Bob Cratchit) would require Christmas Day off with pay, Scrooge struggled to fall asleep. Shortly after he dozed off, the ghost of his former business partner, Jacob Marley, appeared to warn Scrooge that he would soon be visited by three spirits—those of Christmas Past, Present, and Future.

Most of us know the story of Charles Dickens's *A Christmas Carol*, published in December 1843 and set in nineteenth-century London. Scrooge, through the visits of the three ghosts, comes to appreciate the true meaning of Christmas and the value of family, friendship, and love. While this tale has been adapted to film versions several times over, those who have not read the text itself may not realize the financial reference made by Dickens between Marley's visit and that of the Ghost of Christmas Past. Prior to the visit of the Ghost of Christmas Past, Scrooge had a dream, a nightmare in fact, in which he had slept through an entire day, thereby rendering his investments so worthless to be but a mere "United States security." Dickens, who had visited the United States shortly before writing *A Christmas Carol* and was aware of recent defaults by numerous American states, chose his sole reference to the United States in this work to reflect the general sentiment of many investors in the antebellum period. Many in the United States and abroad met U.S. debt at the state and federal level with great skepticism. This was especially true of Dickens's British audience, which included many investors who found themselves with numerous American investments in default by the early 1840s and expressed grave concern over repudiation. Yet even in this period of great skepticism, the United States utilized the various conflicts fought from its inception through the Mexican War to refine its approach to financing wars, and by extension, the faith and confidence of others in the debt of the United States. The evolution in wartime finance to gradually incorporate longer-term securities became a blueprint for early war finance efforts during the Civil War.[1]

But if the war ignited a public embrace of bonds, it was short-lived. In reality, the financial capitalists of New York (a class that grew nearly tenfold in the 1860s) used the war to champion the cause of Union (and ultimately emancipation) while enriching themselves in the process. The need to conduct and finance a war forced an increased dependence between the state and finance capitalists. As the American state came to rely on these capitalists and the evolving world of American private banking to sell bonds to the Northern people, their financial decisions became deeply entwined with the fate of the nation. The retirement of the debt and a decrease in interest rates led to a large-scale return of everyday investors to savings institutions. As Sven Beckert has noted, the war enabled "a vast realignment of forces in the national economy." At its core, the war and its aftermath enabled a new political economy—one of enlarged state intervention, increasing influence for northeastern banking elites moving into the postwar period, and greater wealth inequality more commonly linked to the Gilded Age. None of this would have been possible if not for the vast financial demands of the United States brought on by the Civil War.[2]

For finance capitalists, the fortunes of the Union armies (and therefore the fate of the Union) impacted their loyalties. As the war transitioned from one of Union to also embrace emancipation, the capitalists too started to embrace this turn in the war's aims. The region of the North that remained perhaps most closely allied with the cotton regions of the South was not one of the first areas to openly support emancipation, but as it became clear that the Republican cause and the Union war aims were shifting in that favor, the financiers came to embrace it. For some, they even spoke of their own "emancipation" from being so closely allied to cotton. The war had afforded an opportunity for these finance capitalists to break ranks with the merchant capitalists and merchant tendencies of their own banking houses. As United States debt numbered in the billions (1860s money), New York City financiers realized that their postwar world was not one that necessarily had to revolve around cotton, but could be based in bond issues and other securities.

For the moneymen on the front line of this fascinating war-born economic boom, the result was a strange surge of faith in capitalism, all inflected through patriotic concepts of Union, democracy, and the rewards (personal and national) of a centralizing economy. Underwriting this frame of thought was an influential group of New York City financiers who had come to view the maintenance of the Union as an economic necessity. Forming the Loyal Publication Society of New York, they published pamphlets like "The Maintenance of Union: A National Economic Necessity," which stressed, among other things, "Separation of the Union is so completely shown to be synonymous with retrogression of general civilization, that at this enlightened period, no one can advocate such a retrograde movement without offending against all mankind." Such sentiments reflected a dominant trope that emerged among the financial elite during the war's years—Union victory did not just unleash freedom but unleashed the American economy itself.[3]

Furthermore, as the United States gradually retired its debt, capital flowed from state securities into the vibrant market of rail securities. While historians traditionally associate the postwar period with the financing of railroads in the United States (and beyond), federal debt and federal debt policy was one of the overriding financial concerns of the Reconstruction era. The question surrounding federal debt consumed politicians in Washington and financial interests in New York City and indeed throughout the country. As numerous historians and economists have demonstrated, Civil War debt and the retirement of such debt led to economic growth that exceeded that of the relatively stagnant period of the Civil War. But the growth of the economy in the postwar period reveals something much deeper—the emergence of a rapidly integrating and far more globalized economy. While the war witnessed federal debt holdings overseas in the range of $320 million, the Reconstruction era saw this debt grow exponentially, reaching $1 billion by 1869. This $1 billion represented slightly under half of the entire national debt of the United States. Finance capitalism in the postwar period also transformed American investment banking. No longer subservient to London banks, American banks (with the aid of the federal government) oversaw unprecedented growth in the United States predicated on the integration of capital markets and increasing globalization. Kinship- and faith-based financial networks were central to this growth and facilitated the flow of credit.

Other exchanges cropped up that specialized in various commodities. The Mining Exchange recovered from its failure in the wake of the Panic of 1857. In 1865, investors founded the Petroleum Board to deal in the relatively new commodity of oil, which had been discovered in Pennsylvania fields and successfully drilled in 1859. The fact that the future uses of petroleum were highly speculative further drove the success of that particular exchange. Other informal or curbside exchanges emerged and disappeared with increasing frequency during the Civil War as well, trading in a volume of as much a million shares a day by 1863. The end of the business day no longer meant the end of trading, as after-hours trading merely shifted uptown to the Fifth Avenue

Hotel on Madison Square. The nonstop business of Wall Street could not be denied by the midpoint of the war. Stocks and bonds traded at all hours, on market and off market, and reflected a changing dynamic within American capitalism.[4]

Between the end of the war and 1870, $500 million in canal and road securities entered the market. Foreign indebtedness in American railroads increased from $100 million in 1866 to $390 million in 1874. The transition from federal bonds to rail securities has been demonstrated by Dolores Greenberg and Richard Bensel. The seventeen most important firms in postwar railroad financing previously marketed some 44 percent of primary bond sales from the war's most infamous 5-20 issue. American railroad securities thrived in London, Frankfurt, and Amsterdam in the decades following the American Civil War. As such, many American firms opened European houses or formalized partnerships with European banks to facilitate the sale of these securities. The intricacies of these partnerships, silent or formalized, revealed the increasing complexity and globalization of financial markets, all dating from prior relationships forged with Union securities from the Civil War. For the first time, American banks opened branches abroad and utilized new technology and financial instruments to transform global markets.[5]

Employing new financial techniques and boosted by speculators on the various European exchanges, international bond sales were driven by the search for profit, unlike the work done at home by Jay Cooke and his financial agents. International bond sales represented an evolving global marketplace—one in which powerful firms relied on faster access to information to make large speculative purchases driven less by politics than profiteering. Such sales opened new doors of opportunity for financiers throughout Europe, and these acts on the part of European firms had an effect on the domestic market. By instilling confidence via their purchases in the Union, they unknowingly strengthened the crucial U.S. market composed of "everyday" purchasers.

The world of global finance entered a new stage in the second half of the nineteenth century. Union securities, new financial syndicates, "silent partners," and evolving financial markets and financial instruments all redefined securities in an increasingly globalized world. While New York cemented itself as the premier financial market within the United States, sales in London, Paris, Amsterdam, Frankfurt, and beyond revealed the global reach of Civil War securities and the new financial world they helped to engender. The seismic shift undertaken in financial markets, spearheaded by Union securities, reveals a larger transformation of capital markets in the nineteenth century.[6]

The United States came out of the war with a debt near $2.8 billion. Through political machinations and the sophistication of international markets powered by syndicates, the United States paid off the debt in rapid fashion.

By 1884, Hugh McCulloch had returned to his position as secretary of the treasury under the Arthur administration. In his annual report of that year, he remarked:

> In the management of its debt the United States has been an example to the world. Nothing has so much surprised European statesmen as the fact that immediately after the termination of one of the most expensive and in some respects, exhaustive wars that has ever been carried on, the United States should have commenced the payment of its debt and continued its reduction through all reverses until nearly one-half of it has been paid; that reduction in the rate of interest has kept pace with the reduction of the principal; that within a period of nineteen years the debt, which it was feared would be a heavy and never-ending burden upon the people, has been so managed as to be no longer burdensome.[7]

The winding down of Civil War debt progressed over the remainder of the nineteenth century—that is, the original Civil War issues and their immediate successors of lower interest rates that emerged in the late 1860s and early 1870s were no longer on the Treasury books. With every annual Treasury report, these numbers dwindled as customs revenue helped to offset some of the government debt. With the tenth census of the United States in 1880, the government did make an effort to determine ownership of national debt. Of the outstanding Civil War debt, $28 million in registered bonds remained in the hands of foreign owners while $221 million in coupon bonds resided with foreign banks that made payments through the New York subtreasury. As was the case in the early 1870s, the U.S. Treasury again opened an office in London to sell refinanced Civil War debt to the European masses in the early 1880s. Some $44.5 million of the 3.5 percent interest bonds sold in Europe, but European possession of the debt continued to drop. August Belmont claimed in August 1881 that European possession hovered somewhere in the neighborhood of $150 million, and within the next three years the figure was less than $100 million. By the 1890s the U.S. Civil War debt had effectively been paid off and European investment in federal securities was minimal at best. While the United States would never return to the 1830s and the complete elimination of the national debt, the Civil War debt had effectively been repaid.[8]

The Civil War bonds sold by Jay Cooke and his army to millions of Americans and the countless foreign investors represented a shift in how the American government financed wars moving forward, but to a larger degree it also shifted American financial markets, their international reach, and the newfound world of investment banking. Cooke & Co.'s lead at syndicate underwriting changed the nature of American investment banking and foreshadowed the efforts of investment banks from the early twentieth century onward. The war created a market of high liquidity that morphed investment banking into a specialized institution, the legacy of which continues to the present day. This specialized business benefitted from war finance and evolved in the postwar period to comprise other avenues of financial pursuit including railroads, mortgage-backed securities, and an ever-growing futures market along with other derivatives. Fisk and Hatch's *A Memorandum on Government Debt* had furthered the investment banking sector by explaining government debt and including a glossary of Wall Street terms for the increasing number of financial institutions opening during the war and beyond. For many, the ideas of shorting the market and a bear versus a bull market were all new items to explore and reflected the rapid growth of the American financial sector (especially surrounding investment banks) as a result of the Civil War.[9]

Of course, by the time the federal government redeemed its bonds, financial institutions that made the initial sales to everyday investors had largely collected all the bonds by purchasing them at favorable rates. With banks promising to take care of the final settling with the government, millions of individuals now had disposable funds to invest in the postwar period. But despite the availability of funds, many banks and brokers on Wall Street made it progressively more difficult to invest by imposing higher margins and one hundred–share minimum transactions. While this suited financial capitalists, it left small-scale investors without viable options. Many had tasted the world of finance but found the door now closed.

In the stead of democratic investment emerged a whole new world of democratic speculation. As various financial firms and brokers on the Street made wide-scale democratic investment prohibitively expensive, the thirst for speculation merely moved into the world of "bucket shops" that emerged throughout the country. The name had its origins in nineteenth-century Britain, as a reference to shops that sold the dregs of the beer kegs thrown out by pubs. By the second half of the nineteenth century the phrase referred to establishments where individuals could wager on the price movement of stocks and commodities. These establishments relied on the new technology of the ticker. Invented in 1867, the ticker was a printing telegraph device that could pass along stock quotations to brokers' officers and thereby allow investors to learn of prices from afar—be it the next street over or across the country. The invention of these financial instruments enabled a centralization of financial power within the exchanges of New York and Chicago while simultaneously having an unprecedented psychological effect. The ticker came to be used throughout the nation as Western Union took a hold of the telegraph market. By 1879 1,514 tickers were in use—a figure that reached 2,200 by 1886. With incredibly small margin requirements, these bucket shops enabled former investors to achieve their speculative fix. But instead of buying bonds or stock, these individuals were betting on stock value movement. Despite the fact that some did not realize they were not actually buying the stocks themselves, the bucket shops numbered in the thousands by the late 1870s and early 1880s and became a new form of speculative investment for the everyday investor. The bucket shop bonanza of the latter part of the nineteenth century revealed that just because democratic investment opportunities had disappeared, it did not mean that the desire to "invest" or to "speculate" had disappeared with them. Shadow investing became the new order of the day—one that challenged the power of the financial capitalists of the New York and Chicago exchanges and raised serious doubts over what constituted legitimate investment. All told, such acts contributed to the redefinition of American financial capital in the nineteenth century. Such a system and the technological developments of the day, notably the telegraph and stock ticker, proved a suitable platform for the next step in the evolution of modern American finance. What had originally begun as a market born of speculation in government bonds and greenbacks soon came to involve greater speculation in the market as a whole.[10]

As the ticker expanded, so too did the incorporation of bucket shops throughout the country. Bucket shops existed in New York by 1877 and were formed in Chicago, Milwaukee, St. Louis, and other northern cities within the year. The Chicago Board of Trade's official historian, Charles H. Taylor, remarked in 1917 that the bucket shops served as "a sort of democratized Board of Trade, where the common people could speculate." Contemporary newspapers reiterated such sentiments. The *Chicago Tribune* described the bucket shop as a place where "no broker is necessary, any person, man or woman, boy or girl, white, black, yellow or bronze can deal directly." The *National Police Gazette* referred to the clientele in a bucket shop as "all classes of men who have been bit by the scorpion speculation." The *New York Times* even declared that by 1884 bucket shops were "thriving in all of the large towns and cities from New York to Chicago." The bucket shops concentrated in the hands of several parent companies. "The Big Four" controlled operations in New York according to the *Times*, while Haight and Freese Company operated seventy branches along the Eastern Seaboard from Richmond to Buffalo. The Coe Commission Company headquartered in Minnesota ran operations from Boston to Spokane, Washington, while M. J. Sage Company operated 200 branches throughout the South. By the mid-1880s the *New York World* proclaimed that the bucket shop operations in New York were as sophisticated in presentation as their neighbor broker's offices.[11]

Haight and Freese's 1899 *Guide to Investors* declared that its operations were "designed for the benefit of THE MILLION" who did not have the capital to conduct business with high-end brokers. The *Wall Street Journal* reporter Sereno Pratt claimed that by the early twentieth century, only 60,000 individuals conducted trades on the NYSE, whereas Haight and Freese alone claimed more than 10,000 accounts. But the prosperity of the bucket shops led financial actors on boards and exchanges to mount legal challenges rising all the way to the Supreme Court. The 1905 Supreme Court case *Board of Trade v. Christie* declared bucket shops illegal via violation of state anti-gambling laws. Justice Oliver Wendell Holmes offered the majority opinion on the case. It took the better part of a decade to effectively shut down the bucket shops, but everyday investors would soon garner greater opportunities with World War I bond drives and the marked increase in corporate stock plans.[12]

The repercussions of Civil War debt and the financial world that it helped to engender on an international scale forced a reckoning. Through the remainder of the nineteenth century American investment banking truly came into its own, culminating in the Panic of 1907 and the role that J. P. Morgan and other New York City bankers took to steady the financial waters. The latter part of the nineteenth century also witnessed the rise of speculation taking over everyday life. A Supreme Court ruling in 1905 against bucket shops declaring them illegal (while simultaneously acknowledging the legality of futures trading) led to a fairly rapid winding down of this democratic "investment." But the die had been cast, and the appetite for everyday investment carried forward into the twentieth century.[13]

War finance too remained tied to the Civil War. While the Spanish-American War called on only several hundred thousand investors, World War I represented an entirely different story. Some twenty million subscribers representing 82 percent of U.S. households and 20 percent of the U.S. population invested in American war bonds of the various campaigns including the four Liberty Loans and the Victory Loan. These campaigns, running from June 1917 to May 1919, raised $21.4 billion. Additional campaigns such as the War Savings campaign brought in an additional $1 billion and involved 34 million Americans. Such actions represented the greatest democratic financing of an American war to date, and certainly relied on practices put forward some fifty years earlier during the American Civil War. The rise of corporate stock programs for employees grew out of World War I and led to a drastic increase in investors among the general public. This pattern continued during the 1920s and contributed to the widespread effects of the Great Depression when the market crashed in 1929. The power of margin trading had permeated everyday life, and whether individuals in the late 1920s knew it or not, such an influence of everyday investing and the lure and power of speculation on such a widespread scale could be traced back in part to Jay Cooke's financial army.[14]

In fact, World War I finance efforts made repeated references to Civil War financing. "The methods which were employed to arouse the country to subscribe to the Liberty Loan," declared the *Tampa Tribune*, "the advertisements, the posters, the speeches, the editorials—had their origin, not in England during the present war, nor in France, nor in Germany, but in the United States, back in the days when the Union was in peril. Then was launched the first great popular war loan. It met with a response that at that time excited the wonder and admiration of the world. There had been nothing like it before in history." Still other newspaper reports cited Jay Cooke's work, repeated by small banks throughout the nation, from a twentieth-century take on Cooke's question-and-answer with the Berks County farmer to the fact that Cooke's grandson had organized the formation of a "crisis club" in Philadelphia to help purchase outstanding Liberty Loans. Others spoke to Cooke's drives and how they "dispirited the South, gave Europe useful evidence of the determined courage and material wealth of the northern people, and was a factor of vast importance in deciding the fate of the Union." Even national loans elsewhere during World War I called on Cooke's expertise. "Jay Cooke was a patriot of sanity, faith and vision," proclaimed one Canadian newspaper. "It is on the principles he enunciated that Canada's new 'Victory Loan' is to be floated, and the Canadian people may be relied upon to make it a great success." All told, the various harkening to Cooke in the midst of World War I reinforced the key role he held in supporting the Civil War and the democratization of debt.[15]

Reflecting on his role as secretary of the treasury during World War I, William McAdoo wrote in his memoirs regarding the wildly successful role of the popular war bond drives of that conflict. McAdoo created a messaging campaign centered on appealing to the masses. "Any great war must necessarily be a popular movement," explained McAdoo. "It is a kind of crusade;

and like all crusades, it sweeps along on a powerful stream of romanticism." He described that such an act or action needed to permeate the entire populace. McAdoo added, "We went direct to the people and that means to everybody—to businessmen, workers, farmers, bankers, millionaires, school teachers, laborers. We capitalized the profound impulse called patriotism." Perhaps most tellingly, McAdoo cited the fact that Secretary Chase did not undertake such actions, a crucial misstep in McAdoo's estimation. While perhaps technically true, this missed a key point: The approach undertaken by McAdoo found its greatest inspiration not in the work of Chase, but that of bond czar Jay Cooke. Cooke's legacy, therefore, lived on and inspired a subsequent generation of war bond drives.[16]

More than anything else, Civil War bond sales and the financial environment that they helped to engender marked a stark transition in the world of American financial capitalism. The marketing and sales approach of Cooke (coupled with his religious ethics) and the financial system born out of the National Bank Act and Legal Tender Act helped to foster a business system in the late nineteenth century that led American businesses to gain national and eventually global power. Civil War bond sales fostered a consumer market for financial securities that would grow in the early twentieth century between employee corporate stock ownership and widespread participation in the World War I bond drives. The language employed to make such sales of war bonds also harkened back to the language and approach undertaken by Cooke and his marketing and sales force. While significantly larger in scope than Civil War bond sales, the marketing and approaches used in World War I drives owe a great deal to Cooke and his operations that helped to fund the Union.

The indices associated with the stock exchange have, for better or worse, become a barometer of economic health for the country, and the vast majority of Americans interact with this world in one way or another—through a 401(k), an E-Trade or Robinhood account, or solicitation of a broker like Charles Schwab to conduct trades on their behalf. The world of the trader has been replaced with that of the coder—writing financial algorithms to facilitate high-frequency trading to make a quick buck on lightning-fast transactions. What lessons might have been learned from the various economic collapses of the twentieth and early twenty-first centuries remain to be seen. That said, the world of Civil War bonds undoubtedly set the nation and its financial markets on a new path forward, one that 150 years later we continue to reckon with.

Appendix

Supplementary Tables

TABLE A.1 New York banks, their operating capital, and their subscriptions to the initial $50 million installment

Bank name	Operating capital	Subscription
Bank of New-York	$3,000,000	$1,547,000
Manhattan Company	$2,050,000	$1,050,000
Merchants' Bank	$2,776,400	$1,423,000
Mechanics' Bank	$2,000,000	$1,025,000
Union Bank	$1,500,000	$768,000
Bank of America	$5,000,000	$1,546,000
Phoenix Bank	$1,800,000	$922,000
City Bank	$1,000,000	$512,000
Tradesmen's Bank	$1,000,000	$512,000
Fulton Bank	$600,000	$307,000
Chemical Bank	$300,000	$154,000
Merchants' Exchange Bank	$1,235,000	$632,000
National Bank	$1,500,000	$768,000
Butchers' & Drovers' Bank	$800,000	$410,000
Mechanics' & Traders' Bank	$600,000	$307,000
Greenwich Bank	$200,000	$102,000
Leather Manufacturers' Bank	$650,000	$307,000
Seventh Ward Bank	$500,000	$256,000
Bank of the State of N.Y.	$2,000,000	$1,025,000
American Exchange Bank	$5,000,000	$2,562,000
Bank of Commerce	$9,148,480	$4,687,000
Broadway Bank	$1,000,000	$512,000
Ocean Bank	$1,000,000	$512,000
Mercantile Bank	$1,000,000	$512,000
Pacific Bank	$422,700	$215,000
Bank of the Republic	$2,000,000	$1,025,000
Chatham Bank	$450,000	$230,000
People's Bank	$412,500	$210,000

(*Continued*)

TABLE A.1 (*Continued*)

Bank Name	Operating Capital	Subscription
Bank of North America	$1,000,000	$512,000
Hanover Bank	$1,000,000	$512,000
Irving Bank	$500,000	$256,000
Metropolitan Bank	$4,000,000	$2,050,000
Citizens' Bank	$400,000	$205,000
Nassau Bank	$1,000,000	$512,000
Market Bank	$1,000,000	$512,000
Saint Nicholas Bank	$750,000	$384,000
Shoe and Leather Bank	$1,500,000	$768,000
Corn Exchange Bank	$1,000,000	$512,000
Continental Bank	$2,000,000	$1,025,000
Bank of the Commonwealth	$750,000	$384,000
Oriental Bank	$300,000	$155,000
Marine Bank	$399,000	$204,000
Atlantic Bank	$400,000	$205,000
Importers' & Traders' Bank	$1,500,000	$768,000
Park Bank	$2,000,000	$1,025,000
Artisans' Bank	$0	$0
Mechanics' Banking Assoc'n	$500,000	$256,000
Grocers Bank	$300,000	$153,000
North River Bank	$400,000	$205,000
East River Bank	$206,525	$103,000
Manufacturers & Merchants	$500,000	$256,000

Bank quotations for the initial $50 million advance, Stevens Papers, NYHS.

TABLE A.2 5-20 Primary sales by subtreasury region

Location	Agent	Quantity
Philadelphia	Jay Cooke	$365,952,950
New York	John J. Cisco	$107,630,350
Boston	Ezra Lincoln	$26,306,450
Washington	F. E. Spinner	$2,589,000
San Francisco	D. W. Cheeseman	$2,478,600
Chicago	Luther Haven	$2,297,050
St. Louis	Benjamin Farrar	$2,241,900
Philadelphia	A. McIntyre	$1,691,250
Baltimore	W. W. Hoffman	$1,387,150
Cincinnati	Enoch F. Carson	$1,250,700
Pittsburgh	C. W. Batchelder	$450,050
Buffalo	C. Metz Jr.	$445,000
Pittsburgh	Joshua Hanna	$293,100
Cleveland	Second National Bank	$141,650
Detroit	H. H. Sanger	$71,000
Philadelphia	First National Bank	$71,000
St. Louis	First National Bank	$51,300
Cleveland	First National Bank	$25,000
St. Louis	First National Bank	$50

"Register of Bids for 5-20 Bonds," UD 48, RG 53, Bureau of the Public Debt, NARA II.

Notes

Abbreviations

AHP	Archives Historiques Pictet, Geneva, Switzerland
ANMT	Archives Nationales du Monde du Travail, Roubaix, France
ANZ	Bank of Australasia, ANZ Group Archive, Melbourne, Australia
BB	Burgerbibliothek Bern, Bern, Switzerland
BING	Baring-ING Archive, London, England
BL	Baker Library, Harvard Business School, Harvard University, Boston, MA
BOW	Bowdoin College, George J. Mitchell Department of Special Collections & Archives, Brunswick, ME
BR	British Records, Kew Gardens, London, England
BUT	Butler Library, Rare Book and Manuscript Library Collections, Columbia University, New York, NY
CAA	Credit Agricole Archive, Paris, France
DA	Diplomatic Archives, Brussels, Belgium
DB	Deutsche Bank Archive, Frankfurt, Germany
HA	Hamburger Staatsarchiv, Hamburg, Germany
HL	Houghton Library, Harvard University, Cambridge, MA
HSBC	HSBC Archives, London, England
HSP	Historical Society of Pennsylvania, Philadelphia, PA
HUN	Huntington Library, San Marino, CA
HW	Hessisches Wirtschaftsarchiv Darmstadt, Darmstadt, Germany
IFS	Institut für Stadtgeschicte, Frankfurt, Germany
JPM	J. P. Morgan Library, New York, NY
LC	Library of Congress, Manuscripts Division, Washington DC
LL	Lilly Library Manuscript Collections, University of Indiana, Bloomington, IN
LMA	London Metropolitan Archives, London, England
LOC	Lombard Odier & Cie Archive, Geneva, Switzerland
NA	Nationaal Archief, The Hague, Netherlands
NARA II	National Archives and Records Administration, College Park, MD
NYHS	New-York Historical Society, New York, NY
NYPL	Manuscripts & Archives Division, New York Public Library, New York, NY
NYSE	New York Stock Exchange Records, New York, NY
OU	Oklahoma University, Norman, OK
PEM	Phillips Library, Peabody Essex Museum, Rowley, MA
RAL	Rothschild Archive London, London, England

RIHS   Rhode Island Historical Society, Providence, RI
SA   Stadsarchief Amsterdam, Amsterdam, Netherlands
SALT   SALT Galata Archive, Istanbul, Turkey
SB   Staatsarchiv Bremen, Bremen, Germany
SHS   Sanford Historical Society, Sanford, FL
SW   Schweizerisches Wirtschaftsarchiv, Basel, Switzerland
UR   University of Rochester Special Collections, Rochester, NY

Introduction

1. Jay Cooke's memoir, 2, Jay Cooke & Co. Records, BL. Also quoted in Lawson, *Patriot Fires*, 40.

2. Lawson, *Patriot Fires*, 40–41. For a recent treatment of public debt spanning time and geography, see Barreyre and Delalande, eds., *A World of Public Debts*.

3. *Harper's Weekly*, May 10, 1863. For a brief overview of financing the Civil War, see Thomson, "Financing the War."

4. Quote from Oberholtzer, *Jay Cooke*, 1:574. I am not implying that Cooke's foray into selling bonds to the American populace was the first time that such investment occurred in American history. Robert Wright, Howard Bodenhorn, Winifred Rothenberg, and John Majewski (among others) have demonstrated that in the antebellum era investments in items such as bonds, but also other stocks, mortgages, and loans, became increasingly common in the United States.

5. For a sampling of the literature regarding state debt default in the 1840s, see Nelson, *A Nation of Deadbeats*, 124–25; Baptist, *The Half Has Never Been Told*, 290–92; and Sylla, Wallis, and Grinath III, "Sovereign Debt and Repudiation." For the foreign bondholders of state debt see McGrane, *Foreign Bondholders*; Sexton, *Debtor Diplomacy*, 26–30; Wilkins, *History of Foreign Investment*, 58–59; Rothman, "The Contours of Cotton Capitalism"; and Randolph, "Foreign Bondholders and the Repudiated Debts of the Southern States." For Jefferson Davis's argument for repudiation, see *The Bankers Magazine and Statistical Register*, November 1849.

6. On the concept of the fiscal-military state, see Graham and Walsh, eds., *The British Fiscal Military States*; and Brewer, *The Sinews of Power*. For a deeper examination of the French fiscal-military state, see Greenfield, *The Making of a Fiscal-Military State*. See also Todd and Yates, "Public Debt and Democratic Statecraft"; Ferguson, *The House of Rothschild*, 1:3–5; Bergeron, *France Under Napoleon*; and Edling, *Hercules in the Cradle*, 187n17. As Edling notes, the French popular loans of 1854, 1855, and 1859 were something well known to Cooke and his team. See *Imlay and Bricknell's Bank Note Reporter*, December 5, 1862, and *Indiana Weekly Register*, March 31, 1863, both located in Jay Cooke's newspaper scrapbook, Jay Cooke Papers, HSP.

7. Desan, "Strange New Music"; Lawson, *Patriot Fires*, 2.

8. Historian Stephen Mihm has beautifully articulated this idea as it pertains to the early republic; see Mihm, "Follow the Money," 783–85. For more on war financing during the American Civil War see Richardson, *Greatest Nation of the Earth*, 8–169; Bensel, *Yankee Leviathan*; Flaherty, *The Revenue Imperative*; Caires, "The Greenback Union"; and Edling, *Hercules in the Cradle*, 178–221. Edling explicitly notes the lack of a dedicated monograph to

Civil War finance that places a great emphasis on bond sales. Economic historians and economists have long studied the war, however: see Goldin and Lewis, "The Economic Cost of the American Civil War"; Cochran, "Did the Civil War Retard Industrialization?"; and Engerman, "The Economic Impact of the Civil War."

9. Self-sacrifice during the war as a sign of patriotism often became associated with the U.S. Sanitary Fairs and the pleas for donations associated with these events. For more on Northern sanitary fairs see Lawson, *Patriot Fires*, 14–39; Attie, *Patriotic Toil*; Gallman, *Mastering Wartime*; and Giesberg, *Civil War Sisterhood*. For more on New York City banking during the war see Gische, "The New York City Banks," and Beckert, *Monied Metropolis*, 109–44.

10. These ideas of political and civic inclusion via bond sales are masterfully demonstrated with World War I bonds in Ott, *When Wall Street Met Main Street*. Quote from Ott, *When Wall Street Met Main Street*, 57.

11. Balogh, *A Government Out of Sight*; Rao, *National Duties*; and Blevins, *Paper Trails*.

12. For more on this capital concentration, see Beckert, *Monied Metropolis*, 145–75.

13. The best book-length overviews of antebellum American banking and finance remain Hammond, *Banks and Politics in America*, and Bodenhorn, *A History of Banking in Antebellum America*. See also Sylla, "Forgotten Men of Money."

14. For a look at U.S. finance and diplomacy during the American Civil War, see Sexton, *Debtor Diplomacy*, 82–133. For more on the sale of bonds in Frankfurt, and the nontransparent nature of bond sales in the city in the nineteenth century, see Hein, "Old Regime in a New World." For additional monographs on the international dimensions of the American Civil War, see Jones, *Blue and Gray Diplomacy*; Doyle, *Cause of All Nations*; Blackett, *Divided Hearts*; and Sainlaude, *France and the American Civil War*.

15. Such a concept was recently posited by Jay Sexton. See Sexton, "International Finance in the Civil War Era."

16. An estimation of three million purchasers of government securities came from a statement made by Senator John Sherman on the floor of the House of Representatives in March 1864. While such a statement was made well before the $800 million 7-30 issue, Sherman's intimate knowledge of the bond sales owing to his relationship with the Cooke brothers is beyond doubt (Sherman's estimation from *Cong. Globe*, March 11, 1864, 1046). Historians such as Melinda Lawson have promoted the figure of 500,000 individuals purchasing bonds. Matthew Gallman, on the other hand, has suggested a figure of one million. James Macdonald put forward a number of two to three million. Only a remarkably detailed assessment of the over five hundred volumes of the Bureau of the Public Debt at the National Archives can bring forward a figure that would be somewhat accurate, although very open to debate—one of the pitfalls of nonregistered bonds and the prevalence of secondary sales of the bonds by major financial institutions in the North.

17. Joseph Seligman Journal, Seligman Family Papers, NYHS; Mihm, *A Nation of Counterfeiters*, 10. This is not to imply that cotton and slaves were not fundamental to the antebellum United States. As recent historians have demonstrated, North and South increasingly worked hand in hand when it came to the commodity of cotton and in the process created a booming industry by the eve of the Civil War. For a sample of works on the antebellum economy in the United States and the close relationship between North and South, see Johnson, *River of Dark Dreams*; Beckert, *Empire of Cotton*; Baptist, *The Half Has Never Been Told*; Schermerhorn, *The*

Business of Slavery; Rothman, *The Ledger and the Chain*; and Rosenthal, *Accounting for Slavery*. For a recent detailed review of Beckert and Baptist, see Rood, "Beckert is Liverpool, Baptist is New Orleans." For a critique of some of these works dubbed the "New History of Capitalism," see Morris, "The Economics-of-Slavery Culture Wars"; Scott Reynolds Nelson, "Who Put Their Capitalism in My Slavery?" Sharon Murphy's forthcoming work on slavery and finance will undoubtedly offer a vital dimension to this literature.

18. The estimation of at least $400 million in international sales is based on the generally accepted 1865 estimate of New York and Leipzig firm Knauth, Nachod, and Kuhne that claimed that Union bonds held in Europe totaled some $320 million. This number has generally been accepted by scholars but some research of my own has pointed to this number potentially being a bit low. When coupled with at least $35 million of bond sales to Cuban investors, a number of at least $400 million is certainly reasonable. For more on international bond sale figures see Oberholtzer, *Jay Cooke*, 1:513–15; Wilkins, *The History of Foreign Investment*, 102–7; and Platt, *Foreign Finance in Continental Europe*, 151.

19. For more on entities like the Loyal Publication Societies, see Lawson, *Patriot Fires*, 98–128. For more on entities such as the Loyal Publication Societies and Union Leagues, see Irwin, May, and Hotchkiss, *History of the Union League*; Mendite, *Union League*; and Whitemen, *Gentlemen in Crisis*.

Chapter One

1. Edling, *Hercules in the Cradle*, 66–104.

2. For more on American Revolution financing see Hogeland, *Founding Finance*, 72–94, and Wright and Cowen, *Financial Founding Fathers*. For more on the Dutch contributions see Veenendaal, *Slow Train to Paradise*. For more on Revolutionary War–era finance see Wright, *Hamilton Unbound* and *The First Wall Street*. Another book on Revolutionary War finance worth examining is Ver Steeg, *Robert Morris*; Holton, "'From the Labours of Others.'"

3. Ferguson, *The Power of the Purse*, 30–40. Ferguson also incorporates a table detailing the rampant depreciation of continentals up to April 1781, when $167.50 in continentals purchased $1 of specie.

4. Ferguson, *The Power of the Purse*, 30–40.

5. Edling, *Hercules in the Cradle*, 141. For more on British debt see Geillier, *The History of the National Debt* and Brewer, *The Sinews of Power*. Albert Gallatin to Thomas Jefferson, March 10, 1812, WAG, 1:517; Edling, *Hercules in the Cradle*, 124–25. For more on financing during the War of 1812 see Kagin, "Treasury Notes of the War of 1812," 34–39.

6. Edling, *Hercules in the Cradle*, 124–36.

7. Quoted in Edling, *Hercules in the Cradle*, 124–25.

8. *The American Almanac and Repository for Useful Knowledge for the Year 1840*, 105; McGrane, *Foreign Bondholders*, 6–7.

9. Wilkins, *History of Foreign Investment*, 58–59. There are several monograph treatments of this topic including McGrane, *Foreign Bondholders*, and Ratchford, *American State Debts*.

10. Sexton, *Debtor Diplomacy*, 25–27. For the essential work on the Panic of 1837, see Lepler, *The Many Panics of 1837*. Others of note include Nelson, *A Nation of Deadbeats*, 117–25; Temin, *The Jacksonian Economy*; and Austin, *Baring Brothers*, 5, 142–48. Also see Campbell, *The Bank War*. Ann Daly's forthcoming dissertation entitled "Minting America: Money,

Value, and the Federal State, 1784–1858," from Brown University, will prove an invaluable contribution to the literature pertaining to the Panic of 1837.

11. Sexton, *Debtor Diplomacy*, 25–27. For more on the much-overlooked crisis in 1839 specifically, see Wallis, "What Caused the Crisis of 1839?" and Roberts, *America's First Great Depression*, 49–84. The frustration of Europeans pertaining to the state debt perhaps could be best illustrated by the experience of Reverend Sydney Smith. Smith—the canon of St. Paul's cathedral in London—had invested £1,000 in Pennsylvania state debt. But the state of Pennsylvania refused to honor its interest and principal payments, an action that had the minister and former editor of the *Edinburgh Review* fuming. The action (or rather inaction) on the part of the commonwealth inspired Smith to compose a petition to the United States Congress. "I never met a Pennsylvanian at a London dinner without feeling a disposition to seize and divide him," Smith proclaimed. "How such a man can set himself down at an English table without feeling that he owes two or three pounds to every man in company I am at a loss to convive; he has no more right to eat with honest men than a leper has to eat with a clean man." Pennsylvania's repudiation even inspired poet laureate William Wordsworth, also a holder of Pennsylvania debt, to write two poems in the 1840s entitled "To the Pennsylvanians" and "Men of the Western World" denouncing what one historian has called Pennsylvania's "financial and moral infidelity"; Smith, *Letters on American Debts*, 15. See "financial and moral infidelity" in Sexton, *Debtor Diplomacy*, 29. American papers criticized Smith, and the *Boston Courier* described his petition as a piece of "impudence, bombast, and impertinence"; *Boston Courier* quoted in *London Times*, August 8, 1843; also quoted in McGrane, *Foreign Bondholders*, 60. William Wordsworth, "To the Pennsylvanians" (1845) and "Men of the Western World" (1842). *Cong. Globe*, 26th Cong. 2nd Sess. Vol. 9 Appendix, 118–19.

12. Sexton, *Debtor Diplomacy*, 27; North, "United States Balance of Payments," 625n81. See also Roberts, *America's First Great Depression*, 49–83.

13. The actions during the Mexican War paled in comparison to the scope of operations during the American Civil War. Whereas many European powers—especially the British—were known for their extensive war debts (one calculation put British war expenses of a single year as equivalent to eighteen years of peace financing), the United States did not share this reputation. Emphasizing this contract, *The American Almanac and Repository of Useful Knowledge for the Year 1847* stated, "The normal condition of Great Britain is one of indebtedness, that of the United States is freedom of debt." Such a statement, however, reflected an earlier and bygone era of debt in the United States. While the United States did pay off its federal debt briefly in the 1830s, by the 1840s a sizable federal debt joined with increasing state debts to define an increasingly indebted nation on many levels. By the time of the Mexican War in the wake of the Panic of 1837 and the default of several states on their interest obligations, the United States entered a precarious position with investors at home and abroad. For more on Mexican War financing see Cummings, *Towards Modern Public Finance* (there is a wonderful chart on page 160 detailing the various bond issues). "Letter to General Taylor on peace from George Beckwith, Secretary of the American Peace Society," *Boston Emancipator and Republican*, December 22, 1848. Edling, *Hercules in the Cradle*, 150–52. See also Greenberg, *Manifest Manhood* and *A Wicked War* as well as Waite, *West of Slavery*. For a deeper analysis of tension between Mexico and the United States over the issue of slavery see Baumgartner, *South to Freedom*.

14. Walker and the Treasury found themselves forced to return to a financing approach from the War of 1812—high-interest long-term bonds. Walker put out an issue in various newspapers for a 6 percent loan of some $5 million with a maturity date of ten years. Walker asked those interested to submit sealed bids within two weeks to the Treasury in Washington, including the quantity they wished to purchase and the respective price any interested parties were willing to pay. Originally published in the *Washington Union*, on October 30, 1846, Walker also asked papers in Boston, New York, Philadelphia, Washington, and Charleston to print the advertisement. Edling, *Hercules in the Cradle*, 154–55.

15. Cummings, *Towards Modern Finance*, 69–70, 73–77.

16. Report of the Secretary of the Treasury, 1847, 107–10. Cummings, *Towards Modern Finance*, 79–80, 85.

17. Edling, *Hercules in the Cradle*, 165–66; Cummings, *Towards Modern Finance*, 159–60.

18. Quoted in Edling, *Hercules in the Cradle*, 176n63 for details.

Chapter Two

1. Quoted in Beckert, *Monied Metropolis*, 113–14. For a strong set of essays on the secession winter see Cook, Barney, and Varon, *Secession Winter*. See also Fuller, *Election of 1860 Reconsidered*.

2. "The Union Forever!" *New York Times*, April 11, 1861. Quoted in Beckert, *Monied Metropolis*, 113–14. Union Square did not derive its name from the Civil War itself and a political sentiment; rather, its name dates to the antebellum period and refers to the union or joining of Broadway with the Bowery Road (now Fourth Avenue)—hence "Union" Square.

3. This most recent estimation of 750,000 wartime deaths (an upward revision from the long-held number of 620,000) was put forward by Hacker, "A Census-Based Account."

4. Edling, *Hercules in the Cradle*, 178–79, 182.

5. Caires, "Greenback Union," 53–77; Flaherty, *The Revenue Imperative*. For a deeper analysis of agriculture in the antebellum North see Ron, *Grassroots Leviathan* and Pawley, *The Nature of the Future*.

6. For a recent synthesis of this era, see Levy, *Ages of American Capitalism*, 94–125. For another recent treatment of the role of slave traders in American finance, see Rothman, *The Ledger and the Chain*. For monographs that explore the role of the enslaved in more detail, see Baptist, *The Half Has Never Been Told*; Rosenthal, *Accounting for Slavery*; and Schermerhorn, *The Business of Slavery*. On the centrality of cotton to the American antebellum economy, see Beckert, *Empire of Cotton*, 98–241. Other works that address this topic can be found in the bibliography.

7. Oberholtzer, *Jay Cooke*, 1:121–23, 1:125–26. For an excellent overview of the Treasury's finances before the war, see Flaherty, "'Exhausted Condition.'" Here, see Flaherty, "Exhausted Condition," 252. Secretary Cobb attempted a $10 million loan in September 1860. The entire loan was successfully subscribed, but Lincoln's election in November preceded the deadline for the submission of the funds by the banks. Some banks as a result were reticent to commit their funds and some backed out entirely. In the end, Cobb obtained $7 million of the original $10 million. See "Report of the Secretary of the Treasury on the State of the Finances, House of Representatives," *Ex. Doc.*, No. 2, 36th Congress, 2nd Session, 8–9; *Cong. Globe*, 37th Congress, 2nd Session., 1018. Quoted in Caires, "The Greenback Union,"

26. For more on the late antebellum financial situation, see Lawson, *Patriot Fires*, 42–43; for a detailed look at the initial $150 million dollar authorization by Congress and the commercial bank response, see Hammond, *Sovereignty and an Empty Purse*, 37–58, 71–86. For more on the currency struggles of the United States from the Revolution until the Civil War, see Mihm, *Nation of Counterfeiters* and Greenberg, *Bank Notes and Shinplasters*.

8. For more on the state of the Treasury Department upon Dix's assumption of the secretary position, see Hammond, *Sovereignty and an Empty Purse*, 32. "An Act Authorizing a Loan, February 8, 1861," ch. 29 12 Stat. 129 (1861); "An Act to provide for the Payment of Outstanding Treasury Notes, to authorize a Loan, to regulate and fix the Duties on Imports, and for other Purposes," March 2, 1861, ch. 68, 12 Stat. 178 (1861); *Newark Advocate* (Ohio), February 22, 1861, quoted in Caires, "Greenback Union," 27n10.

9. Caires, "Greenback Union," 28. As Caires points out, one of the most detailed accounts of the politics behind the Treasury is Arthur Lee, "The Development of an Economic Policy"; Jay Cooke to Henry Cooke, March 1, 1861, Jay Cooke Papers, HSP (also quoted in Richardson, *Greatest Nation*, 31). Quotes about Chase found in Edling, *Hercules in the Cradle*, 185. For the most comprehensive biography on Chase see Niven, *Salmon P. Chase*. See also Blue, *Salmon P. Chase*.

10. Richardson, *Greatest Nation*, 31–32. Salmon Chase to Abraham Lincoln, March 1861, Salmon Chase Papers, HSP. Flaherty, "Exhausted Condition," 264. For more on Civil War finance in a broad context, see Studenski and Krooss, *Financial History*.

11. "Shall We Be Taxed Forever to Preserve Slavery?", *New York Daily Tribune*, December 26, 1861; *Boston Daily Evening Transcript*, September 20, 1861; "Debt Banking in England," *Chicago Tribune*, January 4, 1862 (quoted in Richardson, *Greatest Nation*, 32–33). For more on war profiteering during the Civil War see Wilson, *Business of Civil War*, 149–59.

12. Caires, "Greenback Union," 53–54.

13. Quoted in Caires, "Greenback Union," 56–57.

14. Quoted in Caires, "Greenback Union," 55.

15. Salmon Chase to John Dix, March 12, 1861, Salmon Chase Papers, HSP. Quoted in Richardson, *Greatest Nation*, 33. For more detailed accounts of the negotiations, see Hammond, *Sovereignty and an Empty Purse*. For a more detailed analysis of how many Americans, elite and otherwise, envisioned a future Civil War, see Phillips, *Looming Civil War*.

16. Fowler, *Ten Years on Wall Street*, 46.

17. Beckert, *Monied Metropolis*, 121–23. Richard Bensel likewise has made the claim that the financial arrangements of the Civil War granted more autonomy for American banks from their British counterparts. See Bensel, *Yankee Leviathan*, 364.

18. "From New York," *Philadelphia Inquirer*, April 3, 1861. Quoted in Richardson, *Greatest Nation*, 35–36. Salmon Chase to Abraham Lincoln, April 2, 1861, Salmon Chase Papers, HSP; Salmon Chase to Abraham Lincoln, April 4, 1861, Salmon Chase Papers, HSP.

19. Spaulding, *Cong. Globe*, 37th Congress, 3rd Session, 116. Quoted in Richardson, *Greatest Nation*, 38–39.

20. "Report of the Secretary of the Treasury, 4 July 1861," *S.Doc. No. 2*, 37th Congress., 1st Session, 5–6. Edling, *Hercules in the Cradle*, 186.

21. Edling, *Hercules in the Cradle*, 187. "Report of the Secretary of the Treasury, 4 July 1861," *S.Doc. No. 2*, 37th Congress., 1st Session, 12–14. Also quoted in Flaherty, "Exhausted Condition," 271.

22. "Report of the Secretary of the Treasury, 4 July 1861," *S.Doc. No. 2*, 37th Congress., 1st Session., 6, 8, 13–14.

23. "Report of the Secretary of the Treasury, 4 July 1861," *S.Doc. No. 2*, 37th Congress, 1st Session, 6, 8, 13–14.

24. *Philadelphia Inquirer*, May 28, 1861. Quoted in Richardson, *Greatest Nation*, 41; Lyman quote from Hammond, *Sovereignty and an Empty Purse*, 44–45. New York City financier August Belmont—the agent for the European financial behemoth Rothschilds—even advocated a loan subscription of small denominations "in imitation of Louis Napoleon." August Belmont to Salmon Chase, June 24, 1861 in Belmont, *Letters, Speeches, and Addresses*, 71–73.

25. "Congress and Its Legislation," *New York Times*, July 17, 1861. Richardson, *Greatest Nation*, 41–42. *Cong. Globe*, 37th Congress, 1st Session, 60–61. Also quoted in Caires, "Greenback Union," 60–61. Chase floated the idea of foreign loan sales to New York City financiers; Salmon Chase to August Belmont, July 1, 1861, Belmont Family Papers, BUT. Chase later contacted Belmont with a series of pamphlets on the importance of the National Loan and European considerations for investment; Chase to Belmont, September 13, 1861, Belmont Family Papers, BUT.

26. Quoted in Todd, *Confederate Finance*, 25–26.

27. Todd, *Confederate Finance*, 26–27.

28. Todd, *Confederate Finance*, 27–31. Robert Colby has recently posited that the vibrant nature of the domestic slave trade within the Confederacy during the war reflected one area for investment during the war, perhaps at the expense of the financial investment referenced here. See Colby, "'Negroes Will Bear Fabulous Prizes.'"

29. Salmon Chase to John Cisco, August 7, 1861, Salmon Chase Papers, HSP. *Philadelphia Inquirer*, August 12, 1861. Salmon Chase to John Stevens, August 20, 1861, Salmon Chase Papers, HSP. William Pitt Fessenden to James S. Pike, September 8, 1861, James Pike Papers, LC. Richardson, *Greatest Nation*, 43.

30. For more on the War Loan Association and its successor, the Treasury Note Committee, see Treasury Note Committee Papers, located in the John A. Stevens Papers, NYHS; Caires, "Greenback Union," 67.

31. John Stevens to Salmon Chase, August 15, 1861, John A. Stevens Papers, NYHS.

32. Caires, "Greenback Union," 69n64.

33. "Statement of Proportions of New York Banks in 50 Million Loan 7 3/10 Treasury Notes," John A. Stevens Papers, NYHS; quoted in Oberholtzer, *Jay Cooke*, 1:151.

34. Quoted in Oberholtzer, *Jay Cooke*, 1:152.

35. "The People's Loan," *Philadelphia Inquirer*, August 30, 1861; also quoted Oberholtzer, *Jay Cooke*, 1:153; Hammond, *Sovereignty and An Empty Purse*, 112–13n8. Quoted in Caires, "Greenback Union," 71–72.

36. Salmon Chase to John A. Stevens, August 22, 1861, John A. Stevens Papers, NYHS; *Boston Daily Advertiser*, August 29, 1861; Richardson, *Greatest Nation*, 43.

37. *Indianapolis Daily Journal*, September 6, 1861. Quoted in Richardson, *Greatest Nation*, 43–44. As Richardson rightly notes, the 7-30s were in fact Treasury notes, but were often marketed as bonds to the general populace. This would remain the case with future Treasury note issues, most notably the 7-30 issue of 1864–65 of some $830 million. For more on Cooke's role see H. D. Cooke to Jay Cooke, July 9, 1861, and August 7, 1861, Jay Cooke

Papers, HSP; Jay Cooke to H. D. Cooke May 15, 1861, Jay Cooke Papers, HSP; Salmon Chase to Jay Cooke, September 4 and 5, 1861, Jay Cooke Papers, HSP. To see the official agent arrangement with H. D. Cooke, see Salmon Chase to H. D. Cooke, September 10, 1861, Henry Cooke Papers, HUN.

38. Hammond, *Sovereignty and an Empty Purse*, 109–11.

39. *Daily Evening Transcript*, September 10, 1861; *Philadelphia Inquirer*, October 3, 1861, Jay Cooke Scrapbook, Jay Cooke Papers, HSP; William Pitt Fessenden to J. W. Grimes, William Pitt Fessenden Papers, BOW. Quoted in Richardson, *Greatest Nation*, 44.

40. Oberholtzer, *Jay Cooke*, 1:135–37; Jay Cooke to Henry Cooke, undated, Jay Cooke Papers, HSP; Jay Cooke to Salmon Chase, July 12, 1861, Jay Cooke Papers, HSP.

41. Even Cooke's father, Eleutheros, saw tremendous potential in Civil War finance. Writing to Jay in late March 1861, he commented "I took up my pen principally to say, that, H.D.'s plan in getting Chase into the Cabinet & Sherman into the Senate is accomplished, and that now is the time for making money, by honest contracts out of the govt. In perfecting loans & various other agencies—the door is open to make up all your losses." Quoted in Larson, *Jay Cooke*, 103–6.

42. Quoted in Larson, *Jay Cooke*, 105.

43. Larson, *Jay Cooke*, 107–8.

44. Quoted in Oberholtzer, *Jay Cooke*, 1:159.

45. Quoted in Oberholtzer, *Jay Cooke*, 1:159–60. "Patriotic Promptness," *The Findlay Jeffersonian*, August 9, 1861. In another letter from his father dated August 25, 1861, Jay Cooke received high praise from Ohio. "I hope with such pilots as yourself and Chase the good old financial ship will be able to weather the terrible storm which threatens her destruction. If to have nobly aided in furnishing the sinews of war, without which the most skillfully planned campaigns against the traitors in arms for the overthrow of the government would be in vain, can be truly said of you as we know it can, then indeed you will have achieved an honor more truly substantial than the combined glory of all the heroes in the field who are thus enabled to fight our battles and rescue our country from destruction," Eleutheros Cooke to Jay Cooke, August 25, 1861, Jay Cooke Papers, HSP.

46. Oberholtzer, *Jay Cooke*, 1:160, 164.

47. Hammond, *Sovereignty and an Empty Purse*, 115–16.

48. Hammond, *Sovereignty and an Empty Purse*, 117–18.

49. Hammond, *Sovereignty and an Empty Purse*, 119–21.

50. 1881 loan records cited above located in "Accounts for the Loans of July and August 1861," Vols. 1–3, The Bureau of Public Debt Records, Record Group (hereafter RG) 53, NARA II. These ledgers also indicate the various banks that that would later partner with Jay Cooke & Co. as agents. Firms such as Vermilye & Co. and Fisk & Hatch figure prominently in the early bond sales from November 1861. The China Mutual Insurance Company, based out of Massachusetts but dealing primarily in the Chinese trade, also purchased some $23,200.

51. Hammond, *Sovereignty and an Empty Purse*, 133–35; "Report of the Secretary of the Treasury on the State of the Finances for the Year Ending June 30, 1862," *Sen. Ex. Doc. 2*, 37th Congress, 2nd Session, 13, 23; also *New York Times*, December 2, 1861. Quoted in Edling, *Hercules in the Cradle*, 188–89.

52. Hammond, *Sovereignty and an Empty Purse*, 149–57; "Specie Payments," *New York Herald*, December 31, 1861, and *New York Times*, December 30 and 31, 1861. See also Curry, *Blueprint for Modern America*, 181–84. For more on the *Trent* affair, see Jones, *Blue and Gray Diplomacy*, 83–110, Sexton, *Debtor Diplomacy*, 95–102, and Doyle, *Cause of All Nations*, 76–81.

53. "Crisis of the Treasury," *New York Times*, January 13, 1862 and February 2, 1862. Also quoted in Caires, "Greenback Union," 118.

54. Caires, "Greenback Union," 136; *New York Herald*, January 24, 1862; T. W. Olcott to E. G. Spaulding, January 31, 1862 in Spaulding, *History of the Legal Tender*, 51, also quoted in Caires, "Greenback Union," 138–39.

55. George Harrington to Salmon Chase, December 29, 1861, Chase Papers, HSP; Elbridge Garry Spaulding to Isaac Sherman, Isaac Sherman Papers, HUN; Reuben Fenton to Isaac Sherman, Isaac Sherman Papers, HUN; Preston King to Isaac Sherman, Isaac Sherman Papers, HUN; Francis Lieber to Charles Sumner, February 18, 1862, Francis Lieber Papers, HUN. For more on taxation in the North during the war see Flores-Macias and Kreps, "Political Parties at War."

56. Beckert, *Monied Metropolis*, 121. *New York Times*, February 2, 1862, quoted in Caires, "Greenback Union," 118; "Will the State of the Federal Finances Bring the American Civil War to an End?", *Economist*, February 22, 1862.

57. Caires, "Greenback Union," 140–41, 145–46; on the criticism of the delay, one Northern editorial lamented, "It is high time that Congress dropped the discussion of secondary matters and gave its earnest attention to the settlement of this paramount question of ways and means." In Caires, "Greenback Union," 147. For a more thorough examination of the congressional debate surrounding legal tender see Curry, *Blueprint for Modern America*, 181–206.

58. Sherman, *Recollections of Forty Years*, 1:48.

59. Sherman, *Recollections of Forty Years*, 1:281.

Chapter Three

1. Spencer Kellogg Brown to Cora Brown, September 18, 1863, in Smith, *Spencer Kellogg Brown*, 380.

2. Lawson, *Patriot Fires*, 14–39, 56–62, and 98–128. Despite the credit due to Cooke and his army, his success in the bond market also relied upon close coordination with prominent northeastern elites. For the moneymen on the front line of this fascinating war-born economic boom, the result was a strange surge (especially given the recent panic) of faith in capitalism, all inflected through patriotic concepts of Union, democracy, a centralizing economy, and the belief above all in the basic tenets of free labor ideology. Underwriting this frame of thought were influential groups of financiers and businessmen who had come to view the maintenance of the Union as (above all else) an economic necessity. These men formed organizations (initially Union Leagues) in Philadelphia, New York, and Boston that attempted to assert the authority of the monied interests in the hopes that such ideas would pass down among the larger populace. For more on the Union League see Irwin, May, and Hotchkiss, *History of the Union League*; Mendite, *Union League*; and Whitemen, *Gentlemen in Crisis*.

3. Massachusetts Bank Commissioners, *Annual Report of the Bank Commissioners*, 171–72.

4. Jay Cooke to Salmon Chase, October 25, 1862, Salmon Chase Papers, HSP.

5. Jay Cooke's circular to his agents, November 7, 1862, Jay Cooke Papers, HSP; Larson, *Jay Cooke*, 47; Henry Cooke to Jay Cooke, October 29, 1862, Jay Cooke Papers, HSP, also quoted in Oberholtzer, *Jay Cooke*, 1:221.

6. Oberholtzer, *Jay Cooke*, 1:214–15, 1:231–32. For more on the notion of hiring a full-time signatory for bonds, see George Harrington to Salmon Chase, April 22, 1863, Salmon Chase Papers, HSP.

7. Larson, *Jay Cooke*, 123–24, 166, 168; Fisk, "Fisk & Hatch," 707. For more on the service of Clews & Co. during the Civil War, see Clews, *Fifty Years in Wall Street*, 39–94. Trading occurred with such frequency that during the war there were brief periods when trading went on twenty-four hours a day—something that happened at no other time for close to another century. One broker, E. C. Steadman, referenced the events as a scene where regular work hours no longer defined Wall Street life; rather, these men and women "rushed into the arena from a hurriedly snatched breakfast and shouted and wrestled throughout the day, stealing a few moments to sustain vitality and encourage indigestion at a lunch counter or restaurant, and renewed the desperate tension in the evening, prolonging it till long past the hour when wearied bodies and shocked nerves demanded respite . . . it was a killing pace." While the markets changed, perhaps the greatest impact of the increase in trading volume was in the creation of the modern lunch counter. Trading volume had reached a point that it was no longer possible for traders and brokers to return to their homes at the lunch hour. As such, American "fast food" made its appearance with a legacy that sticks with us to the present day, for better or worse. Needless to say, all such market activity occurred with effectively no government oversight. Such notions transcended genders as women became actively involved in the market. *Leslie's Illustrated*, a publication catering largely to a female audience, remarked at one point, "Ladies have been the wildest speculators"; Gordon, *Scarlet Women*, 116.

8. For more on Fisk & Hatch, see Fisk, "Fisk & Hatch," 706–22. In May 1864, the firm relocated from its offices at 38 Wall Street around the corner to 5 Nassau Street. To commemorate the occasion, the firm promised Jay Cooke that it would have the largest bond issuance to date by a single firm. On May 9, 1864, the firm placed an order for $5,059,400, indeed the single largest order to date. For more on Fisk & Hatch's role, see Fisk & Hatch to Jay Cooke, January 16, 1864, Jay Cooke Papers, HSP.

9. "Records Relating to Issuing, Transmitting, and Registering Coupon Bonds for Loan, 1861–1865," UD 66, RG 53, NARA II; 1860 United States Federal Census Records, Cascade, Butte, California, p. 691, Family History Library Film 803056, ancestry.com, accessed April 26, 2021; 1860 United States Federal Census Records, Fall River, Wasco, Oregon, p. 611, Family History Library Film 805056, ancestry.com, accessed April 26, 2021.

10. Larson, *Jay Cooke*, 124–25, 241. One western bank of note that Cooke did enlist was the California-based Wells Fargo & Co.

11. Henry Cooke to Salmon Chase, December 6, 1862, Salmon Chase Papers, HSP.

12. Robert Clarkson to Jay Cooke, December 7, 1862, Jay Cooke Papers, HSP, also quoted in Oberholtzer, *Jay Cooke*, 1:223.

13. Quoted in Oberholtzer, *Jay Cooke*, 1:605, 1:609, 1:620.

14. S. M. Pettingill to Jay Cooke, December 2, 1863, and December 7, 1863, Jay Cooke Papers, HSP. Pettingill's first task involved submitting an article to more than 200 newspapers in New York State advertising the 5-20 issue; Fisk & Hatch to Jay Cooke, December 3,

1863, Jay Cooke Papers, HSP. For more on the Associated Press see 41st Cong., 2nd Sess., *House Reports*, no. 114, 101–2; for examples of press releases see *City Item*, March 21, 1863, May 7, 1863, and May 16, 1863; *Philadelphia Press*, May 23, 1863; and *North American and U.S. Gazette*, May 11, 1863, all located in Jay Cooke Scrapbook, HSP. In several different sources from the first half of the twentieth century, there are references to a scrapbook in the hands of the United States Treasury that contained articles from eighty-six different newspapers from November and December 1862 advertising the loan. Unfortunately, this scrapbook seems to have disappeared in the interim, as consultation with Franklin Noll at the Treasury reveals that the scrapbook is nowhere to be found; Larson, *Jay Cooke*, 177.

15. Lawson, *Patriot Fires*, 49–52.

16. *Philadelphia Press*, April 28, 1863; Jay Cooke scrapbook, Jay Cooke Papers, HSP.

17. Jay Cooke scrapbook, Jay Cooke Papers, HSP.

18. *The Democrat*, May 16, 1863; Lawson, *Patriot Fires*, 52–53. The profitability of bonds as a shelter from state and municipal taxation also provided a successful advertising mechanism and one that Cooke frequently drew upon.

19. "Popular Support of the Government," *Fitzgerald City Stern*, April 18, 1863, Jay Cooke Scrapbook, HSP.

20. "The Government Loans," *Allentown Democrat*, April 24, 1863; *Philadelphia Commercial Dispatch*, May 26, 1863, Jay Cooke Scrapbook, Jay Cooke Papers, HSP.

21. "The Five Twenties," *State Gazette*, April 4, 1863; *Philadelphia Ledger*, May 13, 1863, Jay Cooke Scrapbook, Jay Cooke Papers, HSP.

22. Larson, *Jay Cooke*, 127–29; *Public Ledger*, March 27, 1863; Oberholtzer, *Jay Cooke*, 1:244, 1:248–49; "A Day at the Agency for the 'Five Twenty' Loan," *Philadelphia Inquirer*, April 9, 1863; *Evening Bulletin*, June 1, 1863; quote from Lawson, *Patriot Fires*, 59; quote from "Financial" *Intelligencer*, February 1, 1864. John Majewski's *A House Dividing* offers some information on antebellum bond investment being more widespread.

23. Fisk and Hatch, *Memoranda Concerning Government Bonds*, 7–17. Examples of bond theft frequently made their way into local newspapers. A typical example from the *Agitator* (PA) noted "Robbed from the Safe of the Tioga Co. Bank, On Wednesday night, May 25, 1864, the following described bonds and notes:

    1 U.S. 5-20 coupon bonds, 4th series, letter C, Nos. 14,719, for $500

    3 U.S. 5-20 coupon bonds, 4th series, letter C, Nos. 36,180,81–82, each $500

    17 U.S. 5-20 coupon bonds, 4th series, letter F, Nos. 73,870 to 73,895, each $100

    14 U.S. 5-20 coupon bonds. 4th series, letter A, Nos. 19,824 to 19,837, each $50

    3 U.S. 5-20 coupon bonds, 3d series, letter A, Nos 5,804-5-6, each $1,000

    4 U.S. 5-20 coupon bonds, 3d series, letter A, Nos. 3,050-51-52-53, each $500

. . . . The public are hereby cautioned against purchasing or taking any of the said bonds or notes," "Robbed from the Safe of the Tioga Co. Bank," *Agitator*, November 23, 1864.

24. Fraser, *Every Man a Speculator*, 85, 86, 93n29; "Wall Street in War Time," *Harper's New Monthly Magazine* 30 (December 1864–May 1865), 615–16. Later in the piece the author reveals some criticism for the world of Wall Street when they remark, "The bulk of the Wall Street operators buy and sell with very little more ground for the faith that is in them than the man who bets on the red, or 'goes his pile' at poker," "Wall Street in War Time," 617.

25. Wachtel, *Street of Dreams*, 107–8. The literature of the time further revealed the convoluted notions of money and morality of the nineteenth century. For more on this see Westbrook, *Wall Street in the American Novel*, 16–30.

26. "Financial and Commercial," Baltimore *American*, May 9, 1863; *Baltimore Clipper*, May 12, 1863; also quoted in Oberholtzer, *Jay Cooke*, 1:250.

27. Statistics drawn from Oberholtzer, *Jay Cooke*, 1:263, 1:279.

28. Nelson and Sheriff, *A People at War*, 243; Smith, *The Enemy Within*, 15–17; Wilson, *Business of Civil War*, 149–59; Luskey, *Men is Cheap*, 73–78; Burrows and Wallace, *Gotham*, 875.

29. Quoted in Smith, *The Enemy Within*, 21–22, 27–28.

30. Fraser, *Every Man A Speculator*, 84. Cooke found himself by 1863 actively manipulating New York City financial markets to prop up the price of bonds (often at the direction of the Treasury).

31. Quoted in Gallman, *Defining Duty*, 105–6, 108.

32. Smith, *The Enemy Within*, 22–27. See also Gallman, *Defining Duty*, 91–93. Wilson, *The Business of Civil War*, 24–26, 159–75.

33. Bond quotations drawn from "Register of Bids for 5-20 Bonds," UD 48, RG 53, Bureau of Public Debt, NARA II. 1860 United States Federal Census Records, Good Hope, Hocking, Ohio, p. 41, Family History Library Film 803988, ancestry.com, accessed April 26, 2021. For all assertions made regarding individuals, professions, and nationalities, these are made with as much certainty as possible. I have avoided common surnames such as Smith when providing examples from various locations, trying to find instances of individuals who are the only one on the census in 1860 in that locale (or surrounding areas). It is possible that I have misidentified individuals here, but the names and purchases amounts do remain valid.

34. Bond quotations drawn from "Register of Bids for 5-20 Bonds," UD 48, RG 53, Bureau of Public Debt, NARA II. 1860 United States Federal Census Records, Chicago Ward 6, Cook, Illinois, p. 659, Family History Library Film 803166, ancestry.com, accessed April 26, 2021. While Felician Slataper's purchases were noteworthy ($400), it was actually his wife—Eliza Lee Slataper—who became better known. Eliza Lee (of the Virginia Lee family) developed a close relationship with Mary Todd Lincoln in the postwar period. In the aftermath of the assassination of President Lincoln, the two corresponded frequently on the topics of loss and mourning and most likely had a connection regarding the deaths of their sons, Tad Lincoln and Daniel Slataper, who were of the same age when they died. For more on the Slataper/Lincoln dynamic, see Turner, "The Mary Lincoln Letters."

35. Bond quotations drawn from "Register of Bids for 5-20 Bonds," UD 48, RG 53, Bureau of Public Debt, NARA II. 1860 United States Federal Census Records, Cincinnati Ward 11, Hamilton, Ohio, p. 273, Family History Library Film 803974, ancestry.com, accessed April 26, 2021.

36. Bond quotations drawn from "Register of Bids for 5-20 Bonds," UD 48, RG 53, Bureau of Public Debt, NARA II. 1860 United States Federal Census Records, Chicago Ward 5, Cook, Illinois, p. 23, Family History Library Film 803166, ancestry.com, accessed April 26, 2021.

37. Bond quotations drawn from "Register of Bids for 5-20 Bonds," UD 48, RG 53, Bureau of Public Debt, NARA II.

38. Bond quotations drawn from "Register of Bids for 5-20 Bonds," UD 48, RG 53, Bureau of Public Debt, NARA II. 1860 United States Federal Census Records, St. Louis Ward 4, St. Louis (Independent City), Missouri, p. 171, Family History Library Film 803649, ancestry.com, accessed April 26, 2021 and 1860 United States Federal Census Records, Baltimore Ward 2, Baltimore (Independent City), Maryland, p. 81, Family History Library Film 803458, ancestry.com, accessed April 26, 2021. "Native Sons and Daughters" could also be taken quite literally; Native American organizations throughout the North purchased 5-20 bonds as investments at varying levels. The Iroquois in particular invested. While the statistics behind the 5-20 registered bond issue offer valuable insight into an attempt at quantifying this large endeavor, a more detailed look at the names of the drive offers an even richer text for analysis. While banks and insurance companies comprised the majority of organizations to purchase bonds, academic institutions (Oberlin, Harvard, and Columbia) as well as historical societies (The Library Company of Philadelphia, Historical Society of Pennsylvania, American Philosophical Society, and the Portsmouth, New Hampshire Athenaeum) comprised a segment of investors.

39. 5-20 sales comprised 22.6 percent of the total sales of Union bonds (and Treasury notes) during the war that amounted to nearly $2.28 billion. Registered bond sales are more worthwhile from an investigative standpoint owing to the far more detailed records associated with the sales. From the first recorded sale of May 1, 1862, to the initial closure of the sale on January 30, 1864, there were 8,825 purchases (or "warrants" in the parlance of the ledger books) and 511 transfers of the bonds. Seventeen percent of the purchases can be traced to organizations of varying sorts, from banks to literary societies to insurance companies, Masonic organizations, and other business and philanthropic entities. Such organizational purchases averaged $26,100 (about $500,000 in 2020 dollars). The remaining 83 percent of purchases can be traced to individuals. For another assessment of nationalism and finance see Sim, "Following the Money."

40. All data compiled from "Accounts for the Loan of 1862," ledger books, Vols. 124–25, Bureau of Public Debt, RG 53, NARA II. For further reading on women as economic actors on the Northern home front, see Silber, *Daughters of the Union*, 41–86, Giesberg, *Army at Home*, and Gallman, *Mastering Wartime*. Likewise, examining coupon sales is interesting. There were 23,295 initial primary sales of coupon bonds. Organizations comprised a larger portion of coupon sales (30.9 percent), which is not terribly surprising considering bank requirements to tie some of their funds to deposits in bonds as a result of the National Bank Act. With a slight deviation from the registered sales, women's purchases (averaging $1,500, or $32,000 in 2020 dollars) represented some 11.9 percent of individual sales. However, factoring in averages for coupon sales is problematic because of the remarkably active and lucrative secondary market that skewed heavily to smaller purchases of $50 and $100. All coupon sales records located in "Accounts for the Loan of 1862," ledger books, Vols. 78–83, The Bureau of Public Debt Records, RG 53, NARA II. For more on national banks, see Gische, "The New York City Banks."

41. All coupon sales records located in "Accounts for the Loan of 1862," ledger books, Vols. 78–83, The Bureau of Public Debt Records, RG 53, NARA II.

42. Securities Ledger, Vol. 106, Brown Brothers & Co. Records, NYPL. One diary of note pertains to New Yorker Caroline Dunstan, who entered into her diary various bond purchases for herself and other family members. See Caroline Dunstan Diary, NYPL. Dunstan's diary

reveals a vibrant market in New York City; one 1864 entry mentioned that she had "cut off the coupons of 6's of 81 but had no one to take them to Treasury for the gold, which was going down every day."

43. *Cong. Globe*, 37th Cong., 1st Sess., 167.

44. *New York World*, May 20, 1863.

45. Quoted in Oberholtzer, *Jay Cooke*, 1:299–300.

46. *Cong. Globe*, 38th Cong., 1st Sess., 1046.

47. Jay Cooke revealed this precarious financial situation to his brother Henry Cooke, November 21, 1863, Jay Cooke Papers, HSP; Jay Cooke to Salmon Chase, January 16, 1864, Jay Cooke Papers, HSP; Larson, *Jay Cooke*, 146–48; Henry Cooke to Jay Cooke, October 3, 1863, Jay Cooke Papers, HSP. For more on currency known as "shinplasters" and other fractional currency of the era, see Greenberg, *Bank Notes and Shinplasters*.

48. Jay Cooke to subscription agents, January 29, 1864, Jay Cooke Papers, HSP, also quoted in Oberholtzer, *Jay Cooke*, 1:293–95. Cooke received a rather interesting piece of mail in June 1865. A man writing from Berlin Heights, Ohio, referenced the fact his wife had given birth fifteen months after, in his words, "submitting my neck to the conjugal yoke." The boy was named Jay Cooke, although the author indicated they at the time were calling the boy by his nickname "Seven Thirty." C. B. Tillinghast to Jay Cooke, June 14, 1865, Jay Cooke Papers, HSP.

49. New York Stock Exchange sales of September 15, 1863, February 24, 1864, May 16, 1864, June 13, 1864, July 22, 1864, and January 20, 1865, New York Stock Exchange, Stock and Bond Sales and Quotations Price Records (Record Group 1–3), 1818–1952, NYSE. For more on stabilization funds see Geisst, *Wall Street*, 56.

50. *Philadelphia Press*, April 8, 1863, Jay Cooke Scrapbook, HSP.

51. 5-20 sales did revolve around the major urban centers even if those who purchased them may have lived outside the cities. Nevertheless, there was a significant shift to smaller national banks by the time of the 10-40 loan in 1864—largely a product of the National Bank Act of 1863.

Chapter Four

1. "OUR SOUTHERN FILES; Financial Condition of the Rebel States. CONFEDERATE VIEWS ON REPUDIATION The German Financiers Warned Against Negotiating Yankee Loans. The Capture of Atlanta—Very Sour Grapes. Rumors and Speculations About Sherman and Grant. THE REBEL FINANCES. ATLANTA BEFORE ITS FALL. ANOTHER OF GRANT'S PROPOSITIONS," *New York Times*, September 12, 1864. For more on notions of a vast Southern Empire (albeit in different geographic directions for each author) see Karp, *This Vast Southern Empire* and Waite, *West of Slavery*.

2. Quoted in Gaul, "Solidarität auf Kredit," 207.

3. For more on the 1848 revolution, see Rapport, *1848: Year of Revolution* and Siemann, *German Revolutions*; David Landes's *Bankers and Pashas: International Finance and Economic Imperialism in Egypt* describes the integrated nature of capital markets within Europe at the time of the American Civil War. I view this work as building on that of Landes and more fully elaborating on this narrative of globally integrated markets and the importance of Germany to this equation. For more, see Landes, *Bankers and Pashas*, 10–23.

4. For a Confederate analysis of why stock quotations and variations reveal an incredibly active market by nineteenth-century capital standards, see Oosterlinck and Weidenmier, "Victory or Repudiation?" See also Weidenmier, "Turning Points in the US Civil War" and Willard, Guinnane, and Rosen, "Turning Points in the Civil War."

5. Salmon Chase to William Aspinwall, March 30, 1863, Salmon Chase Papers, HSP; Salmon Chase to Horace Greeley, quoted in Sexton, *Debtor Diplomacy*, 128; William Pitt Fessenden quoted in Sexton, *Debtor Diplomacy*, 129; Salmon Chase report to Congress, July 1861.

6. Daniel Sickles to Salmon Chase, July 5, 1864, Chase Papers, HSP.

7. William Aspinwall to Salmon Chase, March 21, 1863, Chase Papers, LC. Aspinwall spent part of his antebellum career in other pursuits outside the United States, such as a railroad line across the isthmus of Panama; Waite, *West of Slavery*, 67, 266.

8. Frances A. Hamilton to James Brown, October 2, 1862, Brown Brothers Harriman Papers, NYHS. Tensions had risen between the various Brown Brothers houses in the lead-up to and the Civil War. The Baltimore house famously flew a Union flag in a city with significant Confederate sympathies. The firm did invest in Union debt during the war itself, but mostly for clients and not on their personal accounts. For more on Brown Brothers and their antebellum and Civil War financial career, see Brown, *Hundred Years of Merchant Banking*.

9. Katz, *August Belmont*, 3–6. For the most comprehensive analysis of N.M. Rothschild & Sons, see Ferguson, *The World's Banker*; Katz, *August Belmont*, 100–101; August Belmont to N. M. Rothschild (hereafter NMR), May 21, 1861, RAL.

10. Belmont to NMR, May 21, 1861, RAL; Belmont to NMR, June 7, 1861, RAL; Belmont to NMR, June 11, 1861, RAL. There were also some cryptic letters sent between Secretary of State Seward and August Belmont regarding financial opportunities in Europe for U.S. debt. See, for example, William Seward to August Belmont, June 19 and September 2, 1861, Belmont Family Papers, BUT. For a less favorable letter, see William Seward to August Belmont, May 19, 1863, Belmont Family Papers, BUT. See also Varon, *Armies of Deliverance*, 48–49 and Sexton, *Debtor Diplomacy*, 135–50.

11. Katz, *August Belmont*, 100–01. One of Seward's letters indicated a detailed conversation on the matter between Seward and Abraham Lincoln. William Seward to August Belmont, May 27, 1861, Belmont Family Correspondence, BUT.

12. August Belmont to William Seward, July 30, 1861, William Seward Papers, UR.

13. Nathan Rothschild to James de Rothschild, December 20, 1861, 132 AQ 5686, Rothschild Bank Records, ANMT.

14. Glanz, "The Rothschild Legend in America," 21; James Buchanan to John Blake, December 31, 1863, in Moore, ed., *The Works of Buchanan*, 11:353; Nevins and Thomas, eds., *Diary of George Templeton Strong*, 3:256.

15. August Belmont to Abraham Lincoln, September 4, 1862, Abraham Lincoln Papers, LC.

16. Rothschild & Sons American Accounts, II/3/8, 127b, 140 a, and 140 b, RAL; Glanz, 21. The account books of James de Rothschild, 132 AQ 6335–6343, ANMT; for more on James de Rothschild and Alexander Herzen, see Efford, "The Correspondence of Alexander Herzen with James de Rothschild."

17. For more on Peabody and Morgan from the Civil War era, see Sexton, *Debtor Diplomacy*, 75, 77, 102–3; George Peabody to J. S. Morgan, July 20, 1861, JPM. See also Peabody Ledger Book, George Peabody & Co. Papers, PEM. While some historians have claimed it is not possible to locate Peabody sales records, some at the very least are located at the

London Metropolitan Archives; see George Peabody and J. S. Morgan Co., Ledger of Overseas Banks, LMA, as well as Peabody & Co. Papers, PEM. One point of concern for British financiers—as well as Wall Street bankers—was a belief that the interest on the bonds was to be paid in "greenbacks," the new currency implemented as a result of the Legal Tender Act. However, such concerns, as raised in a January 18, 1862, editorial in *The Economist*, were not reality, as the interest in the bonds was to be paid in gold—a fact that seemed to be lost in translation across the Atlantic. For more, see *The Economist*, March 14, 1863.

18. Numbers are stressed with "at least" owing to the fragmentary financial records that remain. J. S. Peabody & Co Records, LMA. Other banking houses invested solely in Confederate securities during the war itself. Most notably, Samuel Montague bet large on the Confederacy during the war and did not invest in United States securities until the postwar period; Samuel Montague Ledger Book, HSBC.

19. Quotes derived from letters from Becker & Fuld to Nathan Rothschild & Sons, February 16, 1863, and February 28, 1863, XI/38/47b, RAL. For more on exchange rates see David and Hughes, "A Dollar-Sterling Exchange Rate."

20. William Evans to Jay Cooke, September 7, 1864, Jay Cooke Papers, HSP.

21. Henry David Cooke to Jay Cooke, August 19, 1864, Jay Cooke papers, HSP; Jay Cooke to Henry David Cooke and Harris Fahnstock, January 24, 1865, Jay Cooke Papers, HSP. Henry Cooke kept a diary while traveling throughout Europe. See Henry Cooke Diary, Henry Cooke Papers, HUN.

22. Thomas Haines Dudley to William Seward, December 5, 1862, Thomas Haines Dudley Papers, HUN; Dudley to W. Seward, December 8, 1862, Dudley Papers, HUN; Dudley's work with informants to flood the British government with information regarding the Confederate outfitting of ships can be seen in Dudley to William Seward, July 25, December 2, December 5, and December 8, 1862, Thomas Haines Dudley Papers, HUN. For more on the Erlanger loan and the perspective that the Confederacy's defeats on the battlefield and policy on withholding cotton from the European market contributed to its own downfall, see Lester, "An Aspect of Confederate Finance."

23. Thomas Haines Dudley to William Seward, January 24, 1862, Thomas Haines Dudley Papers, HUN; Thomas Haines Dudley to William Seward, October 4, 1862, Thomas Haines Dudley Papers, HUN. On the importance of counterfeit notes, see Mihm, *Nation of Counterfeiters*.

24. Quoted in Wheen, *Karl Marx*, 268.

25. For more on Napoleon III and his aspirations of ties to the Confederacy and the resumption of a French presence in the region, see Baumgartner, *South From Freedom*, 235–48; Doyle, *Cause of All Nations*, 124–30; and Sainlaude, *France and the American Civil War*, 179–89. John Bigelow to William Seward, September 14, 1863, John Bigelow Papers, NYPL.

26. John Bigelow to William Seward, July 15, 1864, and October 15, 1864, John Bigelow Papers, NYPL. John Bigelow to Salmon Chase, February 17, 1862, Salmon Chase Papers, HSP. For a recent overview of France and the American Civil War see Sainlaude, *France and the American Civil War*.

27. William Dayton to William Seward, November 17, 1863, RG 59, NARA II.

28. John Bigelow to Salmon Chase, September 2, 1862, Salmon Chase Papers, HSP.

29. Cochut, "Les Finances des Ètats Unis," *Revue des Deux Mondes* 41 (September 1862), 208, 206.

30. Cochut, "la Situation Aux Etats-Unis" *Le Temps*, December 27, 1862. This Union perspective followed the Confederate-centric portion in the December 13, 1862, issue of *Le Temps*.

31. Henry David Cooke to Jay Cooke, January 23, 1865, Jay Cooke Papers, HSP; General Ledgers, BING.

32. Gaul, "Solidarität auf Kredit," 145–47.

33. Hein, "Old Regime in a New World," 2–14; quote on 6. Ullmann, "Frankfurter Kapitalmarket," 75–92. Gömmel and Pohl, *Börsengeschichte*, 105–10, 83–86.

34. Gaul, "Solidarität auf Kredit," 148–51. State: December 3, 1861; Statistical Department of the Frankfurt Association for Geography and Statistics, ed., "The Population of the Free City of Frankfurt and Its Territory by Occupation, Employment and Nutrition," 1863, 35; Roth, *Die Herausbildung einer modernen bürgerlichen Gesellschaft*, 397–402.

35. Gaul, "Solidarität auf Kredit," 152–53. Nachlass Rudolf Schleiden to the Bremen Senate Foreign Affairs Commission, October 12, 1861, SB.

36. Gaul, "Solidarität auf Kredit," 158–60.

37. Gaul, "Solidarität auf Kredit," 154; Katz, *August Belmont*, 103–4. See advertisements in the *Frankfurter Journal*, July 1, 2, and 3, 1862; Moore, "The Rebellion Record," 36.

38. Gaul, "Solidarität auf Kredit," 155–56.

39. Gaul, "Solidarität auf Kredit," 156–57; *New York Times*, August 24, 1862. For more on Shiloh and New Orleans impacting American securities in Frankfurt, see William Murphy to William Seward, May 5, 1862, RG 59, NARA II; William Murphy to William Seward, May 19, 1862, RG 59, NARA II; William Murphy to William Seward, June 2, 1862, RG 59, NARA II. As early as October 1863, the *New York Times* reported that "about one half [of domestic 5-20 sales] was taken for England and the Continent, chiefly for Holland and Germany"; "Finances from Europe," *New York Times*, October 7, 1863.

40. August Belmont to Salmon Chase, August 15, 1861, August Belmont Papers, LC; for more on Murphy, see Sexton, 121–25; William Murphy to William Seward, July 27, 1863, RG 59, NARA II; Murphy to Seward, October 3, 1863, RG 59, NARA II; Ferguson, *The Cash Nexus*, 5–6; Murphy to Seward, January 20, 1863, RG 59, NARA II; Gaul, "Solidarität auf Kredit," 191; Frankfurt Chamber of Commerce: Minutes of the Frankfurt Chamber of Commerce, HW.

41. Nelson and Sheriff, *A People at War*, 168.

42. Gaul, "Solidarität auf Kredit," 165–70, 173, 177–78, 197.

43. "The Rothschilds and the Union," *Harper's Weekly*, April 25, 1863.

44. Quoted in Sterne, "From Jonesville to Frankfurt on the Main," 256–57. Alexander White famously noted in his autobiography of an instance while in London where he tried to exchange greenbacks for sterling and was sternly rebuked by the cashier. "Don't offer us any of those things; we don't take them; they will never be good for anything," White, *Autobiography of Alexander White*, 1:94.

45. Gaul, "Solidarität auf Kredit," 190, 192; Flandreau and Flores, "The Peaceful Conspiracy," 224; see Minutes of the Frankfurt Chamber of Commerce 1863–1864, 10 September 1863, 3/2160, HW; quoted in William Seward to Salmon Chase, April 4, 1864, General Records of the Department of the Treasury, Correspondence of the Office of the Secretary of the Treasury, RG 56, NARA II.

46. Gaul, "Solidarität auf Kredit," 192–93. Annual Report of the Frankfurt am Main Chamber of Commerce for 1864, 1865, 55, 58, HW; Demuth, *Frankfurt A/M*, 70–71.

47. Heyn, *Private Banking*, 274–75; Korach, *Das Deutsche Privatbankgeschaeft*, 31; Handelskammer Frankfurt, ed., *Geschichte der Handelskammer*, 1141–42. The newspapers are also enlightening in other regards. For instance, a September 1, 1864, ad in the *Neue Frankfurter Zeitung* contains in very large type the word "Verloren" ("lost") regarding $10,000 in 5-20 bonds bound for Amsterdam on the steamer *Scotia* from New York City for the account of a Phillip Abraham Cohen in Frankfurt. The ad appears several times in September 1864 before disappearing. It is worth noting that the $10,000 worth of bonds contained within this group of $1,000 and $500 bonds was initially purchased by Jay Cooke & Co. in May 1863, as part of a batch of $2 million worth of $1,000 bonds; *New York Tribune*, n.d., Cooke Papers, HSP; based on its location within the newspaper scrapbooks, it's reasonable to assume this article was published in May 1865; Gaul, "Solidarität auf Kredit," 203.

48. Gaul, "Solidarität auf Kredit," 206–07; "From Europe," *Boston Daily Advertiser*, March 18, 1865; Börnstein to Seward, November 29, 1864, SB. In an effort to entice German investors, Austrians advised Germans to invest their money in Austrian instead of American securities, since the latter were among the "most dangerous of all assets." *Der Aktionär*, February 1, April 3, and April 24, 1864; Hein, "Old Regime in a New World," 20.

49. "Finances-Commerce-Industrie-Agriculture," *L'Europe*, February 10, 1865. Many thanks to my sister Ellen Thomson for examining the *L'Europe* newspapers at the Library of Congress on very short notice.

50. Joseph Seligman to "My dear brother," February 20, 1863, Seligman Family Papers, NYHS. Joseph Seligman to W. V. Stout, March 5, 1863, Joseph Seligman Letterbook, Seligman Family Papers, NYHS; White, *Republic for Which It Stands*, 243–46.

51. Joseph Seligman to "Dear Bro," May 29, 1863, Joseph Seligman Letterbook, Seligman Family Papers; Hein, "Old Regime in a New World," 20. According to Hein, Seligman's first registered visit to the Effecten Societät was August 21, 1864. Abt. 3, 4773, "Fremdenbuch, 1844–1867," HW.

52. Joseph Seligman to "Dear Brothers," July 19 and 21, 1863, Joseph Seligman Letterbook, Seligman Family Papers, NYHS.

53. The exact quantity of sales on the part of Seligman is a source of great debate. In 1931, journalist Linton Wells completed his institutional biography *The House of Seligman*, in which he claimed that the firm sold $200 million in securities in Germany during the war. Others have subsequently used this number. While Wells appeared to reference material that contained specific numbers, regrettably the Civil War-era material related to the Seligman businesses has largely been lost in the decades following the completion of Wells's work. The only material that exists are a couple of letterbooks (business and personal) that only reach April 1864. Dolores Greenberg's work has also questioned this figure. For more on Greenberg's questioning of the Seligman figure, see Greenberg, "Yankee Financiers."

54. *New York Times*, August 18, 1864; London *Times*, August 15, 1864. An October *New York Times* article even went so far as to describe the scene on the floor of the Börse with the arrival of John Slidell: "John Slidell has been stopping for some days in Frankfort. A few days since Baron Erlanger, of rebel loan notoriety, took him to the Bourse, wishing to introduce him to several prominent men in the city, most of whom, however, declined the

honor. Five-twenty bonds are in demand at 44 1/8 to 44 1/2. The sales are not quite as brisk yesterday as the day before. Coupons, due in November, are bought now at 2 florins 21 kreutzers, without guaranty, and 2 florins 23 kreutezers with guaranty. The par is of course 2 florins 30 kreutzers, which is called a dollar here." "From Germany: American Affairs Abroad," *New York Times*, October 9, 1864; "Our Paris Correspondent: American Bonds in the German Market," *New York Times*, August 6, 1864.

55. Bethmann Bank Collection, IFS; stock quotations drawn from Kursblatt records, Frankfurt Börse Papers, HW; Gaul, "Solidarität auf Kredit," 202, Demuth, *Frankfurt A/M*, 70.

56. W Marsh to Seward, July 30, 1864, RG 59, NARA II; W. Marsh to Seward, RG 59, NARA II, November 23, 1864; Marsh to Seward, December 5, 1864, RG 59, NARA II; W. Marsh to Seward, March 8, 1865, RG 59, NARA II.

57. Oberholtzer, *Jay Cooke*, 1:515; "German Feeling about the American War," *Daily Cleveland Herald*, July 7, 1865; Gaul, "Solidarität auf Kredit," 203.

58. "American Securities in Europe," *Boston Daily Advertiser*, March 18, 1865. Still another *New York Times* article reprinted before news had reached Germany of the end of the war quoted at length a piece circulating in Frankfurt papers: "In addition to this, the Consul-General of the United States at Frankfort, now takes great pains to keep the German public advised of the course of events in the United States, and he has contributed very powerfully to render the American securities popular on the leading Bourses of Germany. From the leading journals of New York he has always procured the best information regarding the finances, and by well-selected articles has made it an easy task to turn public opinion on the right course." Another report in May 1865 also quoted a figure of up to $400 million in American debt held in Frankfurt by "German capitalists" as well as "common people." In all the reports, the message remained clear: German investment spanning a wide swath of the people could find no comparison in the financial behemoths of London and Paris. "American Finance Abroad; AMERICAN FINANCE," *New York Times*, April 10, 1865; "American Securities in Europe—An Immense Amount," *Chicago Tribune*, May 3, 1865.

59. "Finances," *Philadelphia Daily Bulletin*, March 29, 1865; Walker, "Our National Finances—An Open Letter to the American People," November 30, 1867, quoted in Hawgood, "The Civil War and Central Europe" 151; Bismarck quote from Hawgood, "The Civil War and Central Europe."

60. James Pike to William Seward, February 25, 1863, Foreign Relations of the United States (FRUS), 1863, 3, 810; Pike to Seward, March 4, 1863, FRUS, 1863, 3, 811–812; Courtney, "On the Finances of the United States," 173–75; Pike to Seward, January 27, 1864, RG 59, NARA II; Pike to Seward, March 9, 1864, RG 59, NARA II; Pike to Seward, November 2, 1864, RG 59, NARA II.

61. Fisk & Hatch to Jay Cooke, March 25, 1864, Cooke Papers, HSP.

62. Hope & Co. to Barings Bros, June 28, 1864, and October 18, 1864, Hope & Co. Papers, SA. Hope & Co. also commented in June 28, 1864, of the vibrant market for American securities in Frankfurt and the potential role that Bethmann Brothers might play in selling the securities and as a source of information for London-based Barings.

63. Hope & Co to Rowland G. Hazard, December 8, 1864, December 10, 1864, December 12, 1864, December 16, 1864, December 20, 1864, January 5, 1865, January 6, 1865, Rowland and Caroline Hazard Papers, RIHS. I want to offer my sincere thanks to Seth Rockman

at Brown University for making me aware of this particular collection. Hazard wrote several propaganda pieces on the value of the American economy more broadly, that although they did not address American securities directly, nevertheless played an important role in supporting American securities abroad and the overall confidence in such purchases by Europeans. Hazard's pieces in newspapers were combined and published in London and Amsterdam (in English and Dutch, respectively) and were entitled: "Our Resources. A Series of Articles on the Financial and Political Condition of the United States" (Dutch translation entitled "Financien en Hulpbronnen der Vereenigde Staten"). *Amsterdam Courant*, December 8, 1864. The same, in *Jj-en Amstelbode*, December 17, 1864.

64. I was able to procure access to the Amsterdam stock quotations from the Civil War era that have been digitized by the Amsterdam Stock Exchange. Much like the case in Frankfurt and the Kursblatt records, by the summer of 1863 there were quotations for various Union bonds on the Amsterdam exchange and midday quotations similarly emerged. OPC-Database/ Stichting Capital Amsterdam, Netherlands. Another factor in the limited evidence connected to Dutch stock records is the rise in the nineteenth century of the *administratiekantoor*. These administrative offices pooled issues of loans and in doing so made it significantly harder to track some buyers on the secondary market. See de Jong, Jonker, Röell, and Westerhuis, "Reinventing Institutions," 5–7 and Geljon, *Algemene Banken*, 21–31.

65. *The London Times*, November 4, 1863, and July 12, 1864. Also Sexton, *Debtor Diplomacy*, 123.

66. Moses Taylor Ledger Book, Moses Taylor Papers, NYPL. One of Taylor's clients, Joseph Albright, wrote to Taylor in May 1862 inquiring as to whether investing in 7-30 Treasury notes would be of benefit; Joseph Albright to Moses Taylor, May 13, 1862, Taylor Papers, NYPL. Sales occurred in Canada as well, with Toronto-based R. J. Kimball Bankers conducting a sizable trade in government securities. Its investment reached a point that R. J. Kimball requested to become an official subagent—a request that was supported in a subsequent letter by the U.S. consul in Toronto. Even Canadian distiller J. P. Wiser got in on the act by the summer of 1865, asking for $7,000 in the subsequent 7-30 issue. For more on R. J. Kimball's relationship to the sale of government securities, see R. J. Kimball Bankers to Jay Cooke, July 12, 1865, Jay Cooke Papers, HSP. For the letter from the U.S. consul, see David Thurston to Jay Cooke & Co., July 13, 1865, Jay Cooke Papers, HSP. For J. P. Wiser, see J. P. Wiser to Jay Cooke & Co, May 6, 1865, Jay Cooke Papers, HSP. In other regards bond sales within the United States were made expressly for certain foreign clients. Most notably these purchases were made on behalf of future Peruvian president Francisco Calderon, Robert College in Constantinople, Francis Tudor Hall of Bermuda, "AN Sewall" and "AZ Bananae" of Port-au-Prince, Haiti, and the Comte de Dion of France. Such disparate purchases reveal the truly global reach of these bond sales. "Accounts for the Loan of 1862," ledger books, Vols. 124–26, RG 53, The Bureau of Public Debt, NARA II.

67. For more on the Forbes-Aspinwall mission, see Maynard, "The Forbes-Aspinwall Mission." For Chase's instructions on a foreign loan, see Chase to Forbes and Aspinwall, March 18, 1863, and Chase to Forbes and Aspinwall, March 30, 1863, both Salmon Chase Papers, HSP. For more on Walker's take on European continental investment, see Walker to Chase, February 20, 1864, Salmon Chase Papers, HSP, and Walker to Chase, February 26, 1864, Salmon Chase Papers, HSP.

68. Quoted in Sexton, *Debtor Diplomacy*, 120; Walker to Chase, July 18, 1863. and August 5, 1863, Salmon Chase Papers, HSP; Nelson and Sheriff, *A People at War*, 168–69. Walker even allegedly distributed his pamphlet in Britain via hot-air balloon.

69. For more information on Walker's mission, see Taylor, "Walker's Financial Mission"; Walker to Chase, December 9, 1863, Chase Papers, HSP.

Chapter Five

1. "One Day's Subscription to the Seven-Thirty Loan," *Press*, March 13, 1865. The article was originally printed in the *New York Herald*; *Evening Telegraph*, March 9, 1865.

2. For more on examinations of nineteenth-century state development especially as it pertains to institutional relations see Rao, *National Duties*; Balogh, *Government Out of Sight*; John, *Spreading the News*; and Blevins, *Paper Trails*.

3. Bolles, *Financial History of the United States*, 200–25; *Cong. Globe*, 37th Cong. 3d Sess., February 10, 1863, 840. See also James and Weiman, "The National Banking Acts." *Cong. Globe*, 37th Cong. 3d Sess., January 26, 1863, 840. See also "National Banking Act," *New York Times*, February 3, 1863; *Cong. Globe*, 37th Cong. 3d Sess., February 11, 1863, 840, 874, 877; *Cong. Globe*, 37th Cong. 3d Sess., February 12, 1863, 1115. For more on the press reaction to the legislation see Hammond, *Sovereignty and an Empty Purse*, 340–46.

4. National bank statistics drawn from Oberholtzer, *Jay Cooke*, 1:353, 1:359–60.

5. Wachtel, *Street of Dreams*, 110–12.

6. On passage of 10-40 loan act, see Bolles, *Financial History*, 100–4, and Oberholtzer, *Jay Cooke*, 1:380–95.

7. For a concise account of the development of Chase's resignation, see Donald, *Lincoln*, 507–8.

8. For the best work on Fessenden, see Cook, *Civil War Senator*.

9. Oberholtzer, *Jay Cooke*, 1:386–89.

10. Oberholtzer, *Jay Cooke*, 1:392–93.

11. Gallman, *Defining Duty*, 191–95. See also Fahs, *The Imagined Civil War* and Attie, *Patriotic Toil*.

12. Sales figures from "Records of Subscriptions," UD 36, RG 53, Bureau of Public Debt, NARA II. 1860 United States Federal Census Records, Brunswick, Cumberland, Maine, p. 26, Family History Library Film 803437, ancestry.com, accessed April 26, 2021; 1860 United States Federal Census Records, Barre, Worcester, Massachusetts, p. 295, Family History Library Film 803533, ancestry.com, accessed April 26, 2021; and 1860 United States Federal Census Records, Bristol, Bristol, Rhode Island, p. 52, Family History Library Film 805202, ancestry.com, accessed April 26, 2021.

13. Sales figures from "Records of Subscriptions," UD 36, RG 53, Bureau of Public Debt, NARA II. 1860 United States Federal Census Records, Bath, Sagadahoc, Maine, p. 183, Family History Library Film 803448, ancestry.com, accessed April 26, 2021; and 1860 United States Federal Census Records, Portland, Cumberland, Maine, p. 462, Family History Library Film 803436, ancestry.com, accessed April 26, 2021.

14. Sales figures from "Records of Subscriptions," UD 36, RG 53, Bureau of Public Debt, NARA II. 1860 United States Federal Census Records, Yarmouth, Cumberland, Maine, p. 47, Family History Library Film 803437, ancestry.com, accessed April 26, 2021.

15. Sales figures from "Records of Subscriptions," UD 36, RG 53, Bureau of Public Debt, NARA II. 1860 United States Federal Census Records, Providence Ward 6, Providence, Rhode Island, p. 346, Family History Library Film 805209, ancestry.com, accessed April 26, 2021; and 1860 United States Federal Census Records, District 7, Baltimore, Maryland, p. 156, Family History Library Film 803468, ancestry.com, accessed April 26, 2021.

16. Sales figures from "Records of Subscriptions," UD 36, RG 53, Bureau of Public Debt, NARA II. 1860 United States Federal Census Records, Decatur Ward 2, Macon, Illinois, p. 604, Family History Library Film 803203, ancestry.com, accessed April 26, 2021.

17. Sales figures from "Records of Subscriptions," UD 36, RG 53, Bureau of Public Debt, NARA II. 1860 United States Federal Census Records, Kickapoo, Peoria, Ohio, p. 500, Family History Library Film 803217, ancestry.com, accessed April 26, 2021.

18. Sales figures from "Records of Subscriptions," UD 36, RG 53, Bureau of Public Debt, NARA II. Curiously, sales out of San Francisco did not match 5-20 numbers: only $125,000 in primary 10-40 sales came out of the San Francisco subtreasury. 1860 United States Federal Census Records, District 14, Knox, Tennessee, p. 269, Family History Library Film 805259, ancestry.com, accessed April 26, 2021; and 1860 United States Federal Census Records, Memphis Ward 2, Shelby, Tennessee, p. 63, Family History Library Film 805273, ancestry.com, accessed April 26, 2021.

19. Oberholtzer, *Jay Cooke*, 1:393–94. Moving outside of New England, sales continued to emerge. In Buffalo, Levina Dodge, the wife of a physician, purchased $50 in 10-40s. Mary Ann Metz, a farmer in Clarence ($200), contributed through a national bank in Buffalo. In Cadiz, Ohio, a Canadian immigrant named Elizabeth Beck from nearby Rumley purchased a $50 bond. Jane Cutter, the wife of a carpenter in St. Paul, purchased $300 in 10-40s. Women comprised an overwhelming proportion of sales out of the St. Paul national bank, although census records for Minnesota lack significant detail and offer little in the ways of occupations for many individuals. For the records that do exist, immigrants proved active investors in 10-40s. Margaret Hanna, an Irish immigrant living in Stillwater, Minnesota, purchased $100 in 10-40s while Sarah Geisenger, a Canadian immigrant living in Rochester, Minnesota, put down $500 for 10-40s. For such a small and remote region of the North during the war, sales reached high levels. All told, women comprised a sizable component of bond purchasers during the 10-40 drive, once more reflecting an interest and commitment to inclusion in a civic realm that largely excluded them otherwise. Sales figures from "Records of Subscriptions," UD 36, RG 53, Bureau of Public Debt, NARA II. 1860 United States Federal Census Records, Mankato, Blue Earth, Minnesota, p. 121, Family History Library Film 803567, ancestry.com, accessed April 26, 2021.

20. Oberholtzer, *Jay Cooke*, 1:428–32.

21. Oberholtzer, *Jay Cooke*, 1:430–34.

22. Quoted in Richardson, *Greatest Nation*, 61.

23. Harris Fahnstock to Jay Cooke, August, 17 1864, Jay Cooke Papers, HSP; Oberholtzer, *Jay Cooke*, 1:446–49; Henry Cooke to Jay Cooke, November 7, 1864, and November 8, 1864, Jay Cooke Papers, HSP.

24. Harris Fahnstock to Jay Cooke, September 9, 1864, Jay Cooke Papers, HSP; Morris Ketchum to Hugh McCulloch, August 24, 1864, Hugh McCulloch Collection, LL.

25. Oberholtzer, *Jay Cooke*, 1:458–59; Hugh McCulloch to John Stewart, September 16, 1864, Hugh McCulloch Collection, LL.

26. Caires, "The Greenback Union," 135; Oberholtzer, *Jay Cooke*, 1:451–60.

27. Report of the Secretary of the Treasury on the State of Finances for the Year 1864, 21; undated circular, quoted in Cook, *Civil War Senator*, 176; Abraham Lincoln, 1864 Annual Message to Congress; *Merchant's Magazine and Commercial Review*, January 1865, 22; also quoted in Downs, *After Appomattox*, 91.

28. Henry Cooke to Jay Cooke, January 9 and January 12, 1865, Jay Cooke Papers, HSP. Fessenden would be replaced by Hugh McCulloch, an Indiana native and U.S. Comptroller of the Currency.

29. Jay Cooke to Henry Cooke, February 3, 1865, Jay Cooke Papers, HSP, quoted in Larson, *Jay Cooke*, 165–66; quoted in Edling, *Hercules in the Cradle*, 202.

30. Henry Cooke to Jay Cooke, February 6, 1865; Jay Cooke to Henry Cooke, February 9, 1865, Jay Cooke Papers, HSP; Oberholtzer, *Jay Cooke*, 1:483, *New Yorker*, February 5, 1865.

31. *New York Tribune*, July 17, 1865, also quoted in Edling, *Hercules in the Cradle*, 202; H. M. Kingman to Jay Cooke, May 27, 1865, Jay Cooke Papers, HSP.

32. Oberholtzer, *Jay Cooke*, 1:577, 581–82.

33. *New York Tribune*, March 29, 1865, Jay Cooke Scrapbook, Jay Cooke Papers, HSP.

34. *Evening Telegraph*, March 9, 1865; *Richland Observer*, April 9, 1865, both located in Jay Cooke Scrapbook, Jay Cooke Papers HSP.

35. *Circular for The Farmers & Mechanics National Bank*, n.d.; *Erie Dispatch*, March 9, 1865, Jay Cooke Scrapbook, Jay Cooke Papers HSP.

36. *Evening Telegraph*, March 9, 1865; *Village Record*, March 11, 1865; "One Day's Subscription to the Seven-Thirty Loan," *New York Tribune*, March 7, 1865, all located in Jay Cooke Scrapbook, Jay Cooke Papers, HSP.

37. *Chronicle*, March 16, 1865. I take "small savings individuals" from Carosso, *Investment Banking in America*, 13–20. Carosso's work demonstrates not only the transformative nature of Cooke's bond drives from a marketing and investor standpoint, but also goes on to show how they subsequently impacted the formation of a plethora of investment banks that had cut their teeth in government securities during the Civil War and later rose to prominence in the Gilded Age. Many of these firms in one form or another still exist in New York City today.

38. *Morristown Free Press*, March 16, 1865; *Village Record*, March 11, 1865; *New York Tribune*, February 20, 1865, all located in Jay Cooke Scrapbook, Jay Cooke Papers, HSP.

39. *Ledger*, March 13, 1865; *New York Tribune*, March 21, 1865. Another article reaffirmed these sentiments. "Bonds! Bonds! Bonds! These ruled the hour; there constituted the magnet of attraction, drawing the people in and the greenbacks out; these were cementing the citizens to their government with a power and durability of cohesion that challenged the practical application of Spaulding glue. All day long that line of citizen soldiery constantly forming in the rear as it melted away in the front marched up single file to do the nation service." *American* (Media, PA), April 1, 1865, quoted in Oberholtzer, *Jay Cooke*, 1:596

40. *Constitutional Union*, February 15, 1865; Larson, *Jay Cooke*, 169–72.

41. Ide, *Battle Echoes*, 137–38, 141–42, 143; Isaac Stevens to Jay Cooke, July 18, 1865, Jay Cooke Papers, HSP; Oberholtzer, *Jay Cooke*, 1:583.

42. These locations were gathered from "Records of Subscriptions," Vols. 2–7, Bureau of the Public Debt, RG 53, NARA II.

43. "Records of Subscriptions to Various Loans, 1864–1867," UD 36, RG 53, NARA II. 1860 federal census records.

44. "Records of Subscriptions to Various Loans, 1864–1867," UD 36, RG 53, NARA II.

45. Edward Sacket to Jay Cooke, March 8, 1865, Jay Cooke Papers, HSP; William Gallaway to Jay Cooke, March 21, 1865, Jay Cooke Papers, HSP; Charles Terwinkel to Jay Cooke, March 30, 1865, Jay Cooke Papers, HSP; Winslow Souther to Jay Cooke, March 30, 1865, Jay Cooke Papers, HSP; GP Hopkins to Jay Cooke, April 4, 1865, Jay Cooke Papers, HSP; Edward Sacket to Jay Cooke, March 8, 1865, Jay Cooke Papers, HSP; Wells Fargo & Co. to Jay Cooke, March 9, 1865, Jay Cooke Papers, HSP; R. A. Allen to Jay Cooke, March 22, 1865, and March 27, 1865, Jay Cooke Papers, HSP; J. E. Zug to Jay Cooke, April 18, 1865, Jay Cooke Papers HSP; quoted from Oberholtzer, *Jay Cooke*, 1:620; statistics from Oberholtzer, *Jay Cooke*, 1:507–8. Even Cooke's PR man, Wilkeson. reported in news from New York City, "A huge Irish chambermaid was spelling her way through it, her duster and broom resting on her hips. 'Put your money where it is forever safe!' 'Faiks' I shall just put a hundred into that same.'" Samuel Wilkeson to Jay Cooke, April 4, 1865, Jay Cooke Papers, HSP.

46. Oberholtzer, *Jay Cooke*, 1:597–98, 629–31. Henry Alhman to Jay Cooke, May 11, 1865, Jay Cooke Papers, HSP.

47. "Records of Subscriptions to Various Loans, 1864–1867," UD 36, RG 53, NARA II.

48. "One Day's Subscription to the Seven-Thirty Loan" *New York Tribune*, March 7, 1865, quoted in Edling, *Hercules in the Cradle*, 202; Oberholtzer, *Jay Cooke*, 2:47–48. Citing the quantities of 7-30s sold in the West, Cooke noted that $90 million of the 7-30 sales came out of Ohio, while some $70 million originated in Illinois. The telegraph became the chief means by which Cooke's office and government officials in Washington received information of sales. To confuse the telegraph operators (who could not necessarily be trusted) and reduce the cost of telegraph messages, Cooke & Co. employed codes and ciphers.

49. Quoted in Oberholtzer, *Jay Cooke*, 1:586.

50. *New York Tribune*, July 17, 1865, quoted in Larson, *Jay Cooke*, 167; a partial listing of these New York City–area night agencies can be found in John Russell Young to Samuel Wilkeson, June 16, 1865, Jay Cooke Papers, HSP.

51. "The Working Men's Savings Bank," *New York Tribune*, July 17, 1865, also quoted in Edling, *Hercules in the Cradle*, 203.

52. "Records of Subscriptions to Various Loans, 1864–1867," UD 36, RG 53, Bureau of Public Debt, NARA II. The bond sales even extended to those who quite possibly bankrolled their purchases through rather unconventional means. Take for example Julia A. Cottle. Born in Maine, Cottle moved to New Orleans and by the 1860 census listed her occupation as a "washer." However, her laundry services must have been quite extensive and prolific considering she purchased some $2,300 in 7-30s. When this large sum is tied to the fact that she was not reporting income to the IRS (which tracked such money in New Orleans even in 1862) and the fact that she lived with a significant number of other younger females, it's not outside the realm of possibility that Cottle's "washing" may have entailed another profession.

53. "Records of Subscriptions to Various Loans, 1864–1867," UD 36, RG 53. Bureau of Public Debt, NARA II.

54. Edward Rowand to Jay Cooke, May 3, 1865, and May 29, 1865, Jay Cooke Papers, HSP; "The National Finances," *New York Herald*, March 20, 1865; "Finance" *New York Tribune*, March 21, 1865; *Philadelphia Inquirer*, March 24, 1865, quoted in Larson, *Jay Cooke*, 166–67.

55. Unknown title, *Richmond Examiner*, February 20, 1865.

56. A. C. Graham to Jay Cooke, July 5, 1865, Jay Cooke Papers, HSP; Richard Randolph to Jay Cooke, July 3, 1865, Jay Cooke Papers, HSP; J. H. Sears to Jay Cooke, July 12, 1865, Jay Cooke Papers, HSP; Richard Randolph to Jay Cooke, June 27, 1865, Jay Cooke Papers, HSP; Oberholtzer, *Jay Cooke*, 1:604; Richard Randolph to Jay Cooke, April 21, 1865, Jay Cooke Papers, HSP; Richard Randolph to Jay Cooke, May 15, 1865, Jay Cooke Papers, HSP; Richard Randolph to Jay Cooke, April 24, 1865, Jay Cooke Papers, HSP; Thomas Branch and Sons to Jay Cooke, May 2, 1865, Jay Cooke Papers, HSP; South Carolina Freedmen's Savings Bank, April 6, 1865, Jay Cooke Papers, HSP. Evidence would seem to indicate that in May 1865 the South Carolina Freedmen's Savings Bank purchased $80,000 in 7-30 notes on behalf of freed people; Robinson and Ogden (NYC) to Jay Cooke, May 10, 1865, Jay Cooke Papers, HSP. For a recent assessment of the Freedman's Bank, see Traweek and Wardlaw, "Societal Trust and Financial Market Participation: Evidence from the Freedman's Savings Bank."

57. J. E. Zug to Jay Cooke, March 6, 1865 and March 8, 1865, Jay Cooke Papers, HSP; Alexander Robb to Jay Cooke, March 13, 1865, Jay Cooke Papers, HSP; Oberholtzer, *Jay Cooke*, 1:597.

58. Julian Brewer to Jay Cooke, April 4 and April 6, 1865, Jay Cooke Papers, HSP. For the ordeal pertaining to Brewer's imprisonment, see Julian Brewer to Jay Cooke, April 15, 1865, Jay Cooke Papers, HSP.

59. "The United States Can Carry a Bigger War Debt Than Britain," undated newspaper article, Hugh McCulloch Papers, Lilly Library, Indiana University; 5-20 statistics for May 1863 drawn from Bureau of Public Debt Records, RG 53, NARA II.

60. Hugh McCulloch to Jay Cooke, March 21, 1865, Jay Cooke Papers, HSP.

61. John Stewart to Hugh McCulloch, March 22, 1865, McCulloch Collection, Lily Library. The Treasury did not always act through Cooke—such as on April 3, 1865, when Stewart purchased $13 million in a variety of bonds and coin in order to stabilize the 7-30 market. For more on this act see John Stewart to Hugh McCulloch, April 3, 1865, McCulloch Collection, LL; D. Crawford to Jay Cooke, March 22, 1865, Jay Cooke Papers, HSP; Michael Hennessy to Jay Cooke, March 24, 1865, Jay Cooke Papers, HSP.

62. W. M. Clark to Jay Cooke, March 30, 1865, Jay Cooke Papers, HSP, quoted in Lawson, *Patriot Fires*, 167–68; *Philadelphia Press*, April 31, 1863, Jay Cooke Scrapbook, Jay Cooke Papers, HSP; for more see Paludan, *A People's Contest*, 116–18. "From the Army of the James," *Daily Evening Bulletin*, March 22, 1865; J. R. Young to Samuel Wilkeson, June 21, 1865, Jay Cooke Papers, HSP. W. W. White to Jay Cooke, July 6, 1865, Jay Cooke Papers, HSP.

63. Edward Sacket to Jay Cooke, July 21, 1865, Jay Cooke Papers, HSP; E. S. Rowland to Jay Cooke, May 15, 1865, Jay Cooke Papers, HSP; William White to Jay Cooke, June 29, 1865, Jay Cooke Papers, HSP; John Jumen to Jay Cooke, April 4, 1865, Jay Cooke Papers, HSP; Edward Rowand to Jay Cooke, April 6, 1865, Jay Cooke Papers, HSP; W. M. Clark to Jay Cooke, March 30, 1865, Jay Cooke Papers, HSP; Bleecker Street night office quotations from Oberholtzer, *Jay Cooke*, 1:528–29; "One Day's Subscription to the Seven-Thirty Loan," *New York Tribune*, March 7, 1865.

64. For more on the initial arrangement see Jay Cooke to Henry McCulloch, March 15, 1865, Jay Cooke Papers, HSP; for more examples of voucher exchange requests see A Ives & Son to Jay Cooke, March 13, 1865, Jay Cooke Papers, HSP; S. E. Jones to Jay Cooke,

March 13, 1865, Jay Cooke Papers, HSP; A Beattie & Co. to Jay Cooke, March 15, 1865, Jay Cooke Papers, HSP; A Caldwell to Jay Cooke, April 6, 1865, Jay Cooke Papers, HSP; Edward Rowand to Jay Cooke, April 22, 1865, Jay Cooke Papers, HSP. For a detailed account of nearly $200,000 of vouchers paid off in the Louisville area, see E. W. Clark & Co. to Jay Cooke, March 27, 1865, Jay Cooke Papers, HSP. See also Edward Rowand to Jay Cooke, April 6, 1865, Jay Cooke Papers, HSP.

65. Henry Cooke to Jay Cooke, April 15, 1865, Jay Cooke Papers, HSP; Oberholtzer, *Jay Cooke*, 1:532; Henry Cooke to Jay Cooke, April 18, 1865; quote from Jay Cooke Memoir, Jay Cooke Papers, BL.

66. Oberholtzer, *Jay Cooke*, 1:538–42. As word crossed the Atlantic of Lincoln's assassination, it likewise impacted the market there. For some, there was a belief that such news had been falsely relayed to undermine the London market. Per one account upon receipt of the news of Lincoln's assassination, "In the progress of this unhappy struggle of Federals & Confederates we have been accustomed to false reports designed to affect the markets and further the ends of dishonest speculators, and it was hoped that this might be an instance of the same kind," "The assassination of President Lincoln," *The London Review of Politics, Society, Literature, Art, & Science* 10 (April 29, 1865), 445. Many thanks to John Handel for bringing this article to my attention.

67. Oberholtzer, *Jay Cooke*, 1:572–74. Even General Grant allegedly got in on the compliments directed towards Cooke. In the spring of 1864, Cooke's son visited the Union front and met Grant. Upon identifying himself and his relation to Jay Cooke, Grant purportedly said "Tell your father I appreciate his message and his services. Tell him that he is doing more than all the generals in the army; for without his aid we could not do any fighting" (quoted in Oberholtzer, *Jay Cooke*, 1:495); Pennsylvania, R. G. Dun & Co. Credit Report Volumes, BL.

68. The concept of the war as one closely tied to empire has recently been posited by Heather Cox Richardson, *Greatest Nation of the Earth* and *West from Appomattox* as well as Ari Kelman, *A Misplaced Massacre* and Kevin Waite, *West of Slavery*. Similarly, the United States as part of larger international upheaval and revolution can be seen in Gregory Downs, *The Second American Revolution* and Aaron Sheehan-Dean, *Reckoning with Rebellion*. Only six American railroads at this time had foreign ownership that exceeded 10 percent.

Chapter Six

1. Pomeroy, *Soliloquies of The Bondholder*, 3–4.

2. Richardson, "North and West of Reconstruction," 76. On the same page of the work, Richardson calls for a detailed examination of bond sales and purchasers during the Civil War. It is my hope that this study in part helps to fill this gap identified by Richardson; Osbourne, "Little Capitalists," 97–98. For more detail on bond redemptions, see "Coupon Bonds Redeemed, 1862–1907 (Loan Division)," UD 87, Bureau of Public Debt, RG 53, NARA II.

3. In part, this difference of perception versus reality is inspired by William Cronon's work *Nature's Metropolis*. My sincere thanks to Aaron Sheehan-Dean for helping me make this connection.

4. *Annual Report of the Secretary of the Treasury on the State of the Finances, Statistical Appendix*, 61; *Annual Report of the Secretary of the Treasury on the State of the Finances, 1867*, iii–iv; *Annual Report of the Secretary of the Treasury on the State of the Finances, 1865*, 50–55. Noll, "Repudiation!", 2–3.

5. *Banker's Magazine* XIX (April 1865), 783. Quoted in Unger, *The Greenback Era*, 41. The postwar fiscal policy of the United States government centered, above all else, on the retirement of Civil War debt. The practice of debt retirement was a centerpiece of peacetime debt policy over the course of the nineteenth century for the United States. The Reconstruction era proved no different. Interest-bearing debt by war's end hovered around $2.3 billion and as one economist has put it, was "several orders of magnitude the highest figure in U.S. history to that point." Not only was this debt unlike any other with which the federal government had previously contended, it also represented a sizable portion of government expenditures. The ratio of federal debt outstanding to GNP in 1865 was equivalent to that under Lyndon B. Johnson's administration a century later, when the debt ballooned due to military spending on the Vietnam War and domestic spending on Great Society programs.

6. Downs, *After Appomattox*, 92–94. John A. Stewart to Hugh McCulloch, March 21, 1865, Vol. 1, Hugh McCulloch Papers, LC. Samuel Wilkeson to Jay Cooke, April 11, 1865, Jay Cooke Papers, HSP.

7. For vocal opposition to debt repayment during the war see A. Campbell, *The True American*. For more on the backlash to Wilkeson's publication see Oberholtzer, *Jay Cooke*, 1:638–44.

8. Larson, *Jay Cooke*, 201–2. In addition to currying favor with the press, Cooke & Co. also acknowledged the power of political friends. Henry Cooke had long held a grasp on many in Washington, and the political situation surrounding Andrew Johnson's impeachment trial only made it more important for friends to be had. Jay Cooke put significant money into Republican politics (certain candidates, but not the party itself) for the election of 1868, not only for Grant but also congressional candidates and allies such as Schenck, Logna, Bingham, and several others. The bank's financial records indicate that some $17,825 went into the "political account" in support of favorable candidates. Henry Cooke to Jay Cooke, January 7, 1869, Cooke Papers, HSP. For more on criticism see Secretary of the Treasury, *Report on Finances*, 1867, xiii and 39th Cong. 2nd Sess. (1866–67), *House Reports*, no. 14. For more on the argument that Jay Cooke met with great financial gain as a result of his Civil War exploits, see *Harper's Weekly*, April 4, 1866.

9. *Commercial and Financial Chronicle*, August 19, 1865, 226. Samuel Wilkeson, *How Our National Debt May Be a National Blessing*. Several states did, however, default on state debt in the Reconstruction period. For a good general overview, see McGrane, *Foreign Bondholders*, 282–381.

10. Patterson, *Federal Debt Management*, 54; Barreyre, *Gold and Freedom*, 54n42.

11. "Conversion of the National Debt into Capital," *Lippincott's Monthly Magazine* I (June 1868), 641, 639, quoted in Patterson, *Federal Debt Management*, 57. Some have even contended that the relative thoughts on debt for British and German economists impacted the larger investment practices of these respective nations in the postwar period. For more see Holtfrerich, "Government Debt in Economic Thought."

12. Patterson, *Federal Debt Management*, 62.

13. *Annual Report of the Secretary of the Treasury on the State of the Finances, 1866*, 40.

14. Foner, *Reconstruction*, 22–24. Gibbons, *The Public Debt of the United States*, 1. Quoted in Noll "Repudiation!", 8. Eric Foner claims that some one million Northerners purchased bonds during the war largely via Jay Cooke, who "invoked God, country and manifest destiny" to sell the bonds among his sales network. Foner goes on to say that most bonds "were held by wealthy individuals and financial institutions."

15. Pomeroy, *Soliloquies*, 5–7.

16. Pomeroy, *Soliloquies*, 8–10. She went on to add, "I am a poor widow; I do not understand politics, but I want some one to tell me what I have gained, and why I must bear all the taxation as I have borne all the sorrow?" In another portion of the pamphlet entitled "Why Support Bondholders? The East and the West," the author lays out a detailed assessment of population and square mileage of respective states of the East and West before reminding the reader that "all this country is controlled by the devil of New England radicalism; New England aristocracy; New England protection; New England narrow-mindedness; and New England bondocracy." The critic added further, "New England nabobs hold United States bonds, by a New England Congress exempt from taxation . . . While we in the West are at work, New England bondholders are riding in their easy carriages, sitting in the shade, reveling in wine dinners, sporting in creek and jungle, their wealth secured and in United States bonds, by a New England controlled Congress exempted from taxation," Pomeroy, *Soliloquies*, 21–22; Lawson, *Patriot Fires*, 40–64.

17. James, *The Framing of the Fourteenth Amendment*, 24. Quoted in Noll, "Repudiation!", 11. One of the more eventful stories of Confederate debt in the immediate postwar period features Jim Fisk. Originally from Vermont, Fisk had no qualms with working both sides of the coin during the war —conducting war contracts with the Union army while smuggling cotton out of the Confederacy. In his final act of the Civil War, Fisk made plans to short-sell Confederate bonds by exploiting the arbitrage opportunity that existed between New York and London. For more on this saga, see Thomson, "Jubilee Jim Fisk" and Swanberg, *Jim Fisk*, 20–21.

18. Beale, *The Critical Year*, 333–34. Quoted in Noll, "Repudiation!", 13.

19. For more on this particular dynamic, see Ziegler, "German Private Banks."

20. "Five-Twenties Abroad," *New York Times*, April 2, 1867.

21. "American Securities in Germany," *New York Times*, April 26, 1868. European periodicals also supported these assessments. In November 1868, a report from a Belgian financial paper made its way into the *Atlanta Constitution*. The report from the "Echo de Bourse" proclaimed, "The Germans have a most complete knowledge of the resources of the United States. They have placed a great deal of money in the American bonds . . . The daily sales which are made at Frankfurt, Hamburg, Berne, and Berlin can be almost compared with the sales and transactions of Wall Street." Efforts to ally these German and Swiss markets more closely with American financial brethren in New York reinforced the strong financial bond that cut across the Atlantic; "American Securities," *Atlanta Constitution*, November 28, 1868. Other financial institutions in the German states accrued significant amounts of Union securities for various clients. Schaffhausen in Cologne purchased tens of thousands of dollars' worth of American securities by the spring of 1865.

22. "American Bonds Hoarded Abroad," *Gettysburg Sentinel*, June 26, 1866. "Our Bonds Abroad—A Powerful American Missionary," *Semi-Weekly Wisconsin* (Milwaukee), February 28, 1866. Another letter written from an American in Germany reinforced this sentiment

of the power of bonds on immigration. "These bonds are the most powerful and influential emissaries you could have sent over to the Old Continent to convert the masses in republican principles. They never before heard so much talk about America; your means and resources, your future and your prospects, are discussed everywhere, and in such favorable terms that emigration is the leading topic among the sturdy masses; and the next year will bring you for every $1,000 of your bonds taken in Germany, at least one of her sturdy sons." Quoted in *Semi-Weekly Wisconsin* (Milwaukee), February 28, 1866.

23. For a comprehensive look at German forty-eighters and their ties to Republican politics in the United States, see Fleche, *Revolutions of 1861*, 8–43.

24. "A Statement to the People of the United States Issued by the Delegates to the Convention of the German Patriotic Aid Association of the Union," August 25, 1870, *Illinois Staats-Zeitung*. The gusto with which Germans purchased bonds was not lost on members of Congress when debating arms shipments to France during the Franco-Prussian War in 1870. Senator William Stewart from Nevada remarked during the debate, "Allow me to call the attention of the Senator from Tennessee to the fact which he must recollect, of the amount of our bonds that were taken in Germany at the time we needed that they should be taken, and when they were prohibited from the Exchange in London and from the Bourse in Paris, and not allowed to be on the markets there at all on account of the state of public opinion there, while Germany alone came in and took five or six hundred million dollars at a time when we needed money." The infamous German-American Carl Schurz followed this statement by remarking on the floor that, "I do not think there were on the face of this globe Governments who expressed their sympathy with the cause of the Union during our civil war as straightforwardly and emphatically as the Government of Prussia and the German Governments generally . . . in no country were more of the bonds of the United states taken." Republican senator Charles Sumner perhaps said it best in the same debate when he remarked, "France contributed to national independence; Germany to national strength and life . . . we owe infinitely to Germany." These connections between the two nations born out of the Civil War proved instrumental in this immediate postwar period. *Cong. Globe*, 41st Cong., 3rd Sess., 955–56. The Prussian government even went so far as to sell 5-20s that were in their portfolio in order to cover some of the costs of their war against France in 1870 and 1871; Gaul, "Solidarität auf Kredit," 207–8.

25. American Ledgers, Seligman Co. Papers, OU. Another example of familial ties involved Speyer Ellison. New York City–based Speyer & Co. represented the interests of its partner institution L. Speyer Ellison—a bank with decades of ties to Frankfurt. Speyer & Co. purchased heavily for the Frankfurt house accounts who then proceeded to sell their bonds far and wide in the German states. Much like Seligman, the familial ties of the Speyers enabled a healthy exchange of securities across the Atlantic to meet the growing demands of the German public and citizens of the neighboring countries. While the exact sales on the part of the Speyers have been lost to time, surviving correspondence for the firm and its rivals reveals an intense interest and pursuit of American bonds. Such was the legacy of Civil War sales for Speyer that in 1932 while testifying in front of Congress, James Speyer noted the level of bond sales the firm participated in within Europe. He colorfully added, "The international banker, some people think of as having horns and hoofs, has performed some useful function in the world, and that this country would not have been built up after the Civil War without the international banker getting the money from

Europe over here." The Speyers, much like the Seligmans, relied on familial networks through banking partnerships to facilitate the transfer of American federal debt overseas into the hands of German citizens and clients from throughout Europe and beyond. U.S. Senate Committee on Finance, *Sale of Foreign Bonds or Securities in the United States*, 643.

26. Bethmann's clients went far beyond Frankfurt itself—and even nearby suburbs of the town such as Wiesbaden—to Hamburg, Berlin, Munich, Leipzig, and smaller locales such as Aachen, Heidelberg, Marktheidenfeld, Wildenberg, Freiberg, Friedburg and Miesbach. Additional purchases via the Frankfurt house could also be found in France, Austria, Switzerland, Ukraine, Italy, Russia, Greece, and Romania. The source of bonds for the firm stems from a wide variety of Christian New York City houses—many of which had ties to Jay Cooke & Co. All of these locales drew on a wide array of clients. Some of these clients were established financial institutions like the Norddeutsche Bank of Hamburg (an early house to join Deutsche Bank) and Marcuard & Co. of Bern, Switzerland. Individual buyers included the Greek ambassador to Austria, who came to run the Austrian National Bank, as well as lesser-known individuals whose records have been lost to history such as a "Frau Von Owen" of Frankfurt and as George Kerua of the same city. Bethmann Bank Collection, IFS.

27. Herms & Co. Records, HA; Securities Ledgers, Nordeutsche Bank Records, DB. I am especially grateful to Martin Mueller of Deutsche Bank for his assistance in navigating these financial records and for suggestions on additional archives and secondary sources of great value to my project.

28. Stoskopf, "What is the Parisian 'Haute Banque?'"

29. W. C. Rothschild uttered the following statement frequently in his reports back to the London house, "The small capitalists invest their money in 5/20 bonds." Additionally, he remarked, "There is a great demand for 5/20 bonds which are bought in large amounts by the public." Such statements—of which these are just two—reinforce a common sentiment that emerged by the late 1860s that the American debt had found its way into the hands of many small-scale investors, in marked contrast to other localities. July 8, 1865, July 22, 1865, July 24, 1865, August 23, 1866, November 23, 1866, and February 14, 1867, Bleichroder to James de Rothschild, Bleichroeder Bank Correspondence, 132 AQ 2 P 097–103, Rothschild Co. Papers, ANMT; W. C. Rothschild to Rothschild London, May 4 and May 6, 1867, 1867 Private Correspondence Sundry: Jun—Mar 1867 XI/109/90, RAL. For the Hamburg houses of Warburg and Behrens, it was much more of the same. For Behrens in particular, the daily purchases averaging some $50,000 became a regular occurrence by 1866 for House Rothschild accounts. Likewise, the Rothschild house based in Frankfurt and run by Mayer Rothschild also coordinated with the Paris house. By 1869 the Frankfurt house made daily purchases (alternating between house purchases and those for individual clients) numbering in the range of $50,000. January 18, 1866, April 13, 1866, April 20, 1866, and August 10, 1866 Behrens Co. to James de Rothschild, Behrens Co. Correspondence, Rothschild Co. Papers, 132 AQ 2 P 0275, ANMT; May 12, 1869, May 18, 1869, August 30, 1869, and October 28, 1869 Mayer Rothschild to James de Rothschild, Frankfurt House Correspondence, Rothschild Co. Papers, ANMT.

30. A very succinct and thorough writeup of Geneva banking structures along with a lengthy bibliography can be found in the unpublished work by Laurent Christeller, "The Pictets: banking and finance activities of a patrician family of Geneva (1707–1926)." My sincere thanks to Laurent for sharing this with me.

31. Securities Listing, Lombard Odier Collection, LOC. My special thanks to Sabrina Sigel and Hugo Bänziger for opening this archive to me. As the first of what I hope are many researchers into the archive, this truly was an invaluable examination of Swiss banking records.

32. Archives Historiques Pictet AHP 1.1.8.2; Securities Ledger, Passavant & Cie Collection, SW.

33. Securities Ledgers, Marcuard & Cie. Records, BB. An examination of Marcuard's clients also provides some insight into Swiss financial houses from the time period. While family members, both involved with the firm and not, were some of the clients associated with these federal debt purchases between 1864 and 1873, most were not. On rare occasions names also included occupations. For instance, a "Monsieur Hebler" who was a local appellate court judge purchased American debt through the firm in 1866 and a "C. Jenner" purchased bonds while living in Bern as an architect. Others included the French politician Gabriel Louis of Saint Victor. Still other clients included locations—like the Swiss town of Schöftland. Many of the identifiable clients reveal a network that extends from Bern to other elements of Switzerland. Thus, Swiss banks utilized financial nexuses like New York City and Frankfurt to help expand the web of American finance into the financial peripheries of Europe (by 1860s standards). This close coordination between the Swiss and Germans in particular reveals the larger financial networks at work to help expand American debt holdings abroad in the Reconstruction era. Securities Ledgers, Marcuard & Cie. Records, BB.

34. Wilkins, *History of Foreign Investment*, 108. For more on the Fenians, see Sim, "Following the Money."; "THE REBEL LOAN.; A More Complete List of British Subscribers. Who Got Their Interest and Who Did Not. Probable Misuse of Respectable Names. The Subterfuge of the Proprietors of the London Times. Some Account of Some of the Subscribers. Newspaper Writers and Their Situations in the Loan," *New York Times*, December 9, 1865. See also Sim, "Following the Money."

35. Barings General Ledgers, BING.

36. The Baring clients were located in an assortment of ledgers located in the general ledgers, BING.

37. Clients drawn from American Client Ledger Books, RAL. Furthermore, war claims would impede on any and all attempts at a foreign loan placement in Britain. Shortly after war's end, the federal government began proceedings to place claims on the British government. Initially these claims focused on "recovering" Confederate property in Europe— most notably cotton. While successful in the British court case *U.S. v. Prioleau*, subsequent claims in British and French courts did not meet with such success. Ultimately, the American government pursued larger goals—reparations for damage caused by Confederate warships built in British boatyards. Known as the *Alabama* Claims, these demands put forward in 1869 called for the British government to pay compensatory damages for merchant shipping losses incurred at the hands of Confederate warships such as the *Alabama* and *Florida*. The United States made claims amounting to $2 billion, although it was open to the ceding of Canada in lieu of monetary compensation. A joint British-American delegation signed the Treaty of Washington in 1871 that put the ruling in the hands of an international arbiter in Geneva. The United States received $15.5 million for its troubles. These political machinations and fears over potential warfare went a long way toward halting British investment

in American government bonds in the late 1860s, despite their wild success on the Continent. But the cooling of hostilities and the signing of the Treaty of Washington in May 1871 afforded the placement of a loan abroad. What set this loan apart from previous issues was the fact that American banks were now located overseas. Questions surrounding the *Alabama* Claims permeated European diplomatic circles. For more, see correspondence of Belgian Minister of Foreign Affairs, March 1, 1871, and June 1, 1871, DA.

38. American Client Ledger Books, RAL. Another London-based bank invested heavily in American debt—that of George Peabody & Co. (later J. S. Morgan & Co.). While under the leadership of George Peabody—an American—the London-based bank mirrored some elements of other financial behemoths like Barings and Rothschilds. While this bank invested prior to the war's end and contained many clients in New York, Boston, and Philadelphia, it did include its fair share of European clients. Numerous London banking houses made their bond purchases through J. S. Morgan & Co. and other individuals and banks based in France and Belgium followed suit. The Bank of Australasia had extensive communication between its Melbourne office and London offices. On two different occasions (June 12 and July 28, 1873), the London office received authorization to sell previously purchased securities by the Australian bank; Bank of Australasia Minute Books, ANZ.

39. For more on Nederlansche Bank investment in U.S. government bonds in this period, see Cameron, *France and the Economic Development of Europe*, 177–78. Another bank, the Algemeene Maatschappij voor Handel en Nijverheid (General Company for Commerce and Industry), also worked extensively in American government bonds. Known more commonly by its French name, Crédit Néerlandais, it took a French approach to its investments—much like those of the Crédit Mobilier—and invested in U.S. government stocks, although with a greater interest in railroads and state debt. One example that did emerge for the Algemeene Maatschappij voor Handel en Nijverheid was the purchase of $5,000 in 5-20s in August of 1866 on behalf of the Amsterdam Kassa from the Parisian bank Robinot. A third bank, Amsterdamsche Bank, a conglomerate comprising the Bank für Handel und Industrie in Darmstadt; Wertheim and Gompertz; Becker & Fuld; Lippmann, Rosenthal and Company; and others also invested extensively in U.S. government bonds during this period. Thus, even the financial market of Amsterdam played an integral role in the placement of U.S. government debt. For more on Dutch investment in U.S. government bonds in this period see Veenendaal, *Slow Train to Paradise*, 17. Archief van de Algemeene Maatschappij voor Handel en Nijverheid N.V. Records, Box 27, SA.

40. Jonker, *Merchants, Bankers, Middlemen*, 65–67.

41. Archief van de Firms Hope & Co., Hope & Co. Papers, 1576, SA. Hope & Co. to Charles Jutting, October 31, 1867, SA; Charles Jutting to Hope & Co., March 8, 1867, March 25, 1867, April 8, 1867, October 14, 1867, Hope & Co. Papers, 392, SA.

42. Hope & Co. Papers, 3220, SA. I would like to extend my sincere thanks to Łukasz Wilinski at the Kronenberg Foundation at Citi Handlowy (Warsaw) for his assistance in providing some background information on the Kronenbergs that is not available elsewhere. Others for the firm including several refunded 5 percent bonds of 1871 for Arthur Desjardins—a future advocate general for the French Supreme Court. Also, Emile Robin, the noted French financier and philanthropist, invested through Hope & Co./Borski, albeit for a modest $4,000 initially. His stake ultimately doubled to $8,000 to incorporate refunded 5 percent of 1871. Also, there was an investment made on behalf of one Monsieur

Kakoschkine, the Russian minister to the Italian court. The investments made through the widow Borski's accounts likewise reveal deep and sustained sales in American debt. Hope & Co. Papers, 3221, SA.

43. Hope & Co. Papers, 3229, SA. The prominent Dutch house Insinger also invested heavily in the immediate postwar period from 1865 to 1872. While the firm bought on behalf of some Dutch clients—such as J. Ringeling from Breda—the majority of clients were found outside the Netherlands. These included two American clients/partners (Boonen, Graves & Co. as well as James G. Kings Sons), presumably through arbitrage transactions. However, a more substantive portion of these transactions took place with German firms that up to this point had not made an appearance in the available Dutch records pertaining to Civil War finance. Hundeiker & Abegg of Hamburg and G. Kinder of Dresden both began to figure prominently. While little remains in terms of a history of Hundeiker & Abegg, surviving evidence of G. Kinder points to a Dutch partnership centered in Dresden that invested heavily in Java. This active investment in Civil War securities (to the total of some $50,000) marked a stark deviation from their portfolio writ large. While Insinger invested heavily in this seven-year period, the records beyond 1872 show no interest in these bonds—perhaps a reflection of a shift in their investment portfolio of the conducting of business solely through Hope & Co., with whom Insinger held a close relationship. Insinger Papers, 1166–1167, SA.

44. Beale, *The Critical Year*, 333; *Cong. Globe*, 39th Cong., 1st Sess. (1865), 701. Quoted in Noll, "Repudiation!", 13–14. James, *Framing of the Fourteenth Amendment*, quoted in Noll, "Repudiation!", 15. For a succinct overview of monetary issues in the Reconstruction era, see Levy, *Ages of American Capitalism*, 205–14.

45. Dewey, *Financial History of the United States*, 340–43. Also see Schell, "Hugh McCulloch and the Treasury Department," 408. While many called for the contraction of the currency, others questioned the rash nature of undertaking such an action, especially at the possible expense of repaying the debt. Frederick Pike, a Republican from Maine, lamented, "Is it worthwhile in the present condition of affairs, when the tendency of things is all right, to interpose, and for the purpose of avoiding a supposed catastrophe run the risk of hurrying the country into commercial difficulties that may be serious?" Barreyre, *Gold and Freedom*, 49, 52.

46. *Cong. Globe*, 39th Cong., 2nd Sess., 1499; *Cong. Globe*, 39th Cong., 2nd Sess., 1870. Both quoted in Barreyre, *Gold and Freedom*, 50, 52.

47. Barreyre, *Gold and Freedom*, 54n42. Ultimately, the national debt would never zero again and would never drop below $900 million. Barreyre, *Gold and Freedom*, 55. For more on media coverage see Barreyre, *Gold and Freedom*, 56n46. Secretary of the Treasury McCulloch reiterated such concerns and their subsequent impact on the New York financial market. "Nothing can be more damaging to our national credit," exclaimed McCulloch, "than the openly-expressed opinion by leading men, that there may arise contingencies in which the national debt will be repudiated." For more on ministers and the religious/moral arguments surrounding the national debt, see Barreyre, *Gold and Freedom*, 63–64.

48. *Cong. Globe*, 41st Cong., 2nd Sess., 701; *Jonesboro Gazette*, October 5, 1867; *Cincinnati Enquirer*, March 14, 1867. Quoted in Barreyre, *Gold and Freedom*, 56.

49. McPherson, *Political History of the United States*, 386–88; Noll, "Repudiation!", 18–20.

50. Jay Cooke to Henry Cooke, November 23, 1869, Cooke Papers, HSP.

51. Dewey, *Financial History*, 338; Larson, *Jay Cooke*, 207–8. Jay Cooke to Henry Cooke, July 6, 1868, Jay Cooke Papers, HSP.

52. The Philadelphia *Ledger* proved to be one of the largest critics of the refunding bill and remarked on one occasion "Any one familiar with these transactions knows that there are enormous incidental profits growing out of such operations, as with the control of fluctuating money, foreign exchange, gold, and United States bond markets, values may be raised or depressed at pleasure, the new bonds sold and the proceeds of sale in money held for use and profits to the agents, before transmission to the Treasury, and for the purpose of affecting market values. The country would thus be constantly in peril of perturbations and excitements destructive to all legitimate trade, and these reacting on the public revenues would impair national credit, and prevent the accomplishment of the object proposed by the bill." Quoted in Larson, *Jay Cooke*, 317. *Ledger*, February 14, 1870.

53. Oberholtzer, *Jay Cooke*, 2:266–67.

54. Larson, *Jay Cooke*, 224–28, esp. n68. The brothers also used funds in other "creative" ways. Henry Cooke rose to prominence with the Freedman's Bank (which stipulated in its charter that the bank had to invest significantly (roughly two-thirds) in government securities. Cooke purchased said securities from his brother's firm and ultimately came to take the other third of the bank's assets and tie them up in Northern Pacific Rail Stock—also via Cooke & Co. The entire enterprise came tumbling down with the failure of Jay Cooke & Co. in the leadup to the Panic of 1873. For more see Levy, *Freaks of Fortune*, 104–49. For more on the Freedman's Savings Bank see Fleming, *Freedman's Savings Bank*; Osthaus, *Freedmen, Philanthropy, and Fraud*; and Traweek and Wardlaw, "Societal Trust."

55. "Coupon Bonds Redeemed, 1862–1907 (Loan Division)," UD 87, Bureau of Public Debt, RG 53, NARA II.

56. Larson, *Jay Cooke*, 219–22. Jay Cooke to Henry Cooke, September 24, 1869, Jay Cooke Papers, HSP; 39th Cong. 22nd Sess., *House Reports*, no. 14; 40th Cong., 2nd Sess., 1072; Henry Cooke to Jay Cooke, February 21, 22, 25, and March 5, 1868, Jay Cooke Papers, HSP; Jay Cooke to Henry Cooke, February 24, 1868, Jay Cooke Papers, HSP.

57. "Register of Bonds Issued and Exchanged from the London Office, 1872–1881", Vol. 1, UD 148, RG 53, Bureau of Public Debt, NARA II. The Bank of England also permitted the U.S. government to open a "personal account"; George Forbes to William A. Richardson, January 17, 1872, "Correspondence Regarding the Alabama Claims and the Geneva Award," UD 554, RG 53, Bureau of the Public Debt, NARA II.

58. "Register of Bonds Issued and Exchanged from the London Office, 1872–1881", Vol. 1, UD 148, RG 53, Bureau of Public Debt, NARA II. The material contained in volumes two and three deal with purchases in 1881 that still tie into the refinancing of Civil War debt. In both cases, these volumes draw from individuals in the same geographic areas as they did in 1871; these include British, French, Dutch, Swiss, and German investors. Even when the bonds were not necessarily being directly traded in certain overseas countries, their impact could be felt in subsequent currency and bond issue design. For instance, in the early 1870s the newly open country of Japan sent a slew of representatives to Washington; among other things, they worked on a new currency system for the country modeled after American greenbacks and 5-20 bonds. They even worked out a design for American greenbacks and

bonds that would work their way into circulation in Japan; "Japanese Finances: The New Coin of the Country—How Japanese Bonds are Made in New York—The American Financial System in Japan," *New York Times*, February 10, 1872.

59. Oberholtzer, *Jay Cooke*, 2:269–70.

60. Oberholtzer, *Jay Cooke*, 2:272–84.

61. Carosso, *The Morgans*, 175–78.

62. "The Syndicate," *The Commercial and Financial Chronicle and Hunt's Merchant's Magazine* 13, no. 321 (August 19, 1871), 229.

63. Oberholtzer, *Jay Cooke*, 2:282, 287–88.

64. Records of Subscriptions," Volume 13, UD 36, RG 53, NARA II; J. S. Morgan was very active by British house standards in late 1860s pre–*Alabama* Claims. In February 1871, N. M. Rothschild wrote (presumably to August Belmont, the house's American agent, although the letter is unsigned) as to efforts made to bring the firm in as part of a European syndicate. "We had a visit today from Mr. Cooke (of Jay Cooke & Co) who has received a telegram from the United States Secretary to know whether we would join Barings, Morgan, Rose & other London houses in effecting the conversion of the 6 pr cent Bonds. We replied that it would always give us pleasure to do business with the Government of the United States & to receive any ordered it would do us the honor of confiding to us, but that it was contrary to our custom to place our house by the side of others in negotiations such as the one proposed to us." N. M. Rothschild to unknown, February 10, 1871, "Correspondence Regarding the Alabama Claims and the Geneva Award," RG 53, UD 554, NARA II. Other banks also invested in the syndicate—such as Credit Lyonnais. This French bank previously had bought and sold $250,000 worth of 5-20s in 1866–67 and operated through exchanges in Paris, Frankfurt, Geneva, London, and Lyon. By 1871, the bank put in a stake for $70,000 in the 1871 foreign syndicate. The surviving records of the Credit Lyonnais that date to this time also reveal clients who asked to have their 5-20 purchases converted into various French stocks and bonds and vice versa; Credit Lyonnais Papers, CAA. Some of these French banks had incredibly close ties with financial institutions elsewhere in Europe—perhaps none closer than in the Ottoman Empire. These arrangements were not always of the utmost integrity—one of the most egregious examples being a French bank selling $100,000 worth of Confederate debt to the Imperial Ottoman Bank in Constantinople; SALT.

65. M. C. de Rothschild to August Belmont, April 2, 1871. Later that year a letter from the editor of the *German American Economics* to Assistant Treasurer William Richardson reiterated Rothschild involvement in American securities. For more on the struggles of placing the refunded loan in Germany, see Edward Taussig to William Richardson, August 21, 1871, "Correspondence Regarding the Alabama Claims and the Geneva Award," UD 554, RG 53, Bureau of the Public Debt, NARA II. For a firm that met with success, see Seligman Brothers to William Richardson, July 18, 1871, "Correspondence Regarding the Alabama Claims and the Geneva Award", UD 554, RG 53, Bureau of the Public Debt, NARA II; Barings Bros to John P. Bigelow, July 29, 1871; Jay Cooke to McCulloch & Co to William Richardson, June 29, 1871; illegible to William A. Richardson, October 20, 1871; all letters located in "Correspondence Regarding the Alabama Claims and the Geneva Award," UD 554, RG 53, NARA II. According to Richardson, by July 1, 1871, of the original $452,913,900 in 5-20 coupon bonds, $383,000,050 remained outstanding. The remainder had either been exchanged

for 5 percent bonds or absorbed by the Treasury. William Richardson to Clews, Habicht & Co, December 18, 1871, UD 554, NARA II; George Boutwell to J. S. Morgan & Co., February 28, 1871, Morgan Papers, LMA; quoted in McElroy, *Levi Parsons Morton*, 53.

66. Sexton, *Debtor Diplomacy*, 220–21. *Bankers' Magazine*, September 31, 1871, 789–91.

67. Corosso, *Morgan*, 178–79, A. J. Drexel to J. S. Morgan, January 14, 1873, Morgan Papers, LMA.

68. Committee of Management, "United States Five per Cent. Funded Loan," February 3, 1873, Morgan Papers, LMA. One notable omission from the subscription was Hope & Co. of Amsterdam, which declined an invitation from Baring Brothers. Such a fact is somewhat curious considering Hope's active participation in American securities as demonstrated earlier in the chapter. Hope & Co. to Baring Brothers, February 3, 1873, BING; J. S. Morgan & Co. to Drexel, Morgan & Co., October 23, 1873, Morgan Papers, LMA; J. P. Morgan to J. S. Morgan, Morgan Family Papers, JPM. Corosso, *Morgan*, 179–80.

69. Davies, *Transatlantic Speculations*. Other works that tackle the Panic of 1873 include Nelson, *Nation of Deadbeats*, 161–63 and White, *The Republic for Which It Stands*, 260–73. For a great historiographical overview see, Nelson, "A Storm of Cheap Goods," 447–53.

70. White, *Railroaded*, 82–83.

71. U.S. Department of Treasury, *Specie Resumption and Refunding of the National Debt*, 46th Cong., 2nd Sess., 1880, H. Exec. Document 9, 2–15. Historian Rondo Cameron similarly has argued that there was a sizable shift of American government debt from England to the Continent in the late 1870s—specifically France. By his estimation, some $400 million in US Civil War–era debt was in France by 1877, "French Foreign Investment," PhD diss., University of Chicago, 1952, 74; John Sherman to Conant, October 4, 1877, in Treasury, *Specie Resumption*, 162. John Sherman to Conant, May 12, 1877, in Treasury, *Specie Resumption*, 38. Sherman, *Recollections*, 2: 638–42; U.S. Secretary of the Treasury, *Annual Report*, 1879.

72. Quoted in Chapman, *The Rise of Merchant Banking*, 46.

Conclusion

1. Dickens, *A Christmas Carol*, 17; Richardson, *Greatest Nation*, 42.

2. Beckert, *The Monied Metropolis*, 119.

3. "The Maintenance of Union," Vol. 14, New York Publication Society, 1863.

4. Fraser, *Every Man a Speculator*, 85, 86, 93; For more on the rise of American oil in the nineteenth century, see Zallen, *American Lucifers*, 214-55.

5. Wilkins, *History of Foreign Investment*, 117–19; Bensel, *Yankee Leviathan*, 251–52, and Greenberg, *Financiers and Railroads*, 33, 38–41; Sexton, *Debtor Diplomacy*, 236.

6. Sexton, *Debtor Diplomacy*, 252; Wilkins, *History of Foreign Investment*, 147, and Zeigler, *The Sixth Great Power*, 215.

7. Bolles, *Financial History*, 339–40.

8. Wilkins, *History of Foreign Investment*, 185nn165–70; Sherman, *Recollections*, 2:638–42.

9. Larson, *Jay Cooke*, 216–18; Fisk and Hatch, *A Memorandum on Government Debt*. For more on the importance of an underwriter's reputation, see Flandreau and Flores, "Bonds and Brands"; for more on the evolution of global finance in the nineteenth century see Bersch and Kaminsky, "Financial Globalization in the 19th Century."

10. Hochfelder, "Where the Common People Could Speculate," 335–40.

11. Hochfelder, "Where the Common People Could Speculate," 340–43; Taylor, *History of the Board of Trade*, 565–85, 1218–22.

12. Hochfelder, "Where the Common People Could Speculate," 349–55; Pratt, *The Work of Wall Street*, 71.

13. Pak, *Gentlemen Bankers*, 20–27.

14. Ott, *When Wall Street Met Main Street*, 56–57.

15. "How Jay Cooke Made the People Want to Buy Bonds During the Civil War," *The Tampa Tribune*, November 11, 1917; "Dollar Dialogue on Thrift Bonds," *The Morning News* (Wilmington, DE), May 2, 1917; "Form 'Crisis Club' to Insure Success of Liberty Loan," *Philadelphia Inquirer*, October 17, 1918; "How Jay Cooke Financed the Civil War," *Fennimore Times* (Wisconsin), June 27, 1917; "Jay Cooke's Inspiration," *Nanaimo Daily News* (Nanaimo, British Columbia), November 6, 1917; "Liberty Loan Sacrifices Far Outdone in Civil War," *New-York Tribune*, January 6, 1918.

16. McAdoo, *Crowded Years*, 374. Quoted in Mehrotra, *Lawyers, Guns & Public Monies*, 204n80. See also Kennedy, *Over Here*, 105.

Bibliography

Primary Sources

MANUSCRIPT COLLECTIONS

ANZ Group Archive, Melbourne, Australia
    Bank of Australasia Records
Archives Historiques Pictet, Geneva, Switzerland
Archives Nationales du Monde du Travail, Roubaix, France
    Rothschild Bank Records
Baker Library, Harvard Business School, Harvard University, Boston, MA
    Jay Cooke & Co. Records
    R. G. Dun Credit Volumes
Baring-ING Archive London, England
    Annual Accounts
    General Ledgers
    House Correspondence
    Letter Books
Bowdoin College, George J. Mitchell Dept. of Special Collections & Archives, Brunswick, ME
    William Pitt Fessenden Papers
British Records, Kew Gardens, London, England
Burgerbibliothek Bern, Bern, Switzerland
    Marcuard & Cie Papers
Butler Library, Rare Book and Manuscript Library Collections, Columbia University, New York, NY
    Belmont Family Papers
Credit Agricole Archive, Paris, France
    Credit Lyonnais Papers
Deutsche Bank Archive, Frankfurt, Germany
    Nordeutsche Bank Records
Diplomatic Archives, Brussels, Belgium
    Diplomatic Records
Galata Archive, Istanbul, Turkey
    Ottoman Bank Papers
Hamburger Staatsarchiv, Hamburg, Germany.
    Herms & Co. Papers
Hessisches Wirtschaftsarchiv Darmstadt, Darmstadt, Germany
    Frankfurt Börse Papers
    Frankfurt Chamber of Commerce Records
    Effecten Societät Records

Historical Society of Pennsylvania, Philadelphia, PA
    Salmon Chase Papers
    Jay Cooke Papers
HSBC Archives, London, England
    Samuel Montague Papers
Huntington Library, San Marino, CA
    Henry D. Cooke Papers
    Thomas Haines Dudley Papers
    Francis Lieber Papers
    Isaac Sherman Papers
Institut für Stadtgeschicte, Frankfurt, Germany
    Bethmann Bank Papers
Library of Congress, Manuscripts Division, Washington DC
    Abraham Lincoln Papers
    Salmon Chase Papers
    Hugh McCulloch Papers
    James Pike Papers
    Robert Walker Papers
Lilly Library Manuscript Collections, University of Indiana, Bloomington, IN
    Hugh McCulloch Collection
Lombard Odier & Cie Archive, Geneva, Switzerland
    General Correspondence
London Metropolitan Archives, London, England
    J. S. Morgan Co. Papers
Manuscripts & Archives Division, New York Public Library, New York, NY
    John Bigelow Papers
    Brown Brothers & Company Records
    Moses Taylor Papers
National Archives and Records Administration, College Park, MD
    The Bureau of Public Debt Records (Record Group 53)
    General Records of the Department of Treasury (Record Group 56)
    General Records of the Department of State (Record Group 59)
New-York Historical Society, New York, NY
    Brown Brothers Harriman Papers
    Seligman Family Papers
    John A. Stevens Papers
New York Stock Exchange Records, New York, NY
    Stock Exchange Sales Reports
Phillips Library, Peabody Essex Museum, Rowley, MA
    George Peabody & Co. Papers
Rhode Island Historical Society, Providence, RI
    Rowland and Caroline Hazard Papers
Rothschild Archive London, London, England
    American Accounts
    Belmont Correspondence

    Correspondence Department
    General Ledgers
Sanford Historical Society, Sanford, FL
    Henry Sanford Papers
Schweizerisches Wirtschaftsarchiv, Basel, Switzerland
    Passavant & Cie. Collection
Staatsarchiv Bremen, Bremen, Germany
    Senate Papers
Stadsarchief Amsterdam, Amsterdam, Netherlands
    Borski Papers
    Hope & Co. Papers
    Insinger Papers
University of Oklahoma, Norman, OK
    Seligman & Co. Papers
University of Rochester Special Collections, Rochester, NY
    William Seward Papers

PUBLISHED PRIMARY SOURCES

Bayley, Rafael. *History of the National Loans of the United States from July 4, 1776 to June 30, 1880, in Report on Valuation, Taxation, and Public Indebtedness in the United States, as Returned at the Tenth Census (June 1, 1880)*. Washington: Government Printing Office, 1884.

Bellows, Henry Whitney. *Duty and Interest Identical in the Present Crisis*. New York: Wynkoop, Hallenbeck & Thomas Printers, 1861.

———. *Historical Sketch of the Union League Club of New York: Its Origin, Organization, and Work, 1863–1879*. New York: Press of G. P. Putnam's Sons, 1879.

———. *Unconditional Loyalty*. New York: Anson F. Randolph, 1863.

———. *The War to End Only When the Rebellion Ceases*. New York: Anson F. Randolph, 1863.

Belmont, August. *A Few Letters and Speeches of the Late Civil War*. New York: Privately printed, 1870.

Bigelow, John. *Lest We Forget: Gladstone, Morley, and the Confederate Cotton Loan of 1863*. New York, 1905.

Boker, George. *A Memorial of the Union Club of Philadelphia*. Philadelphia: J. B. Lippincott and Co., 1871.

Bolles, Albert. *The Financial History of the United States, From 1861 to 1885*. New York: D. Appleton and Company, 1886.

Brown, John Crosby. *A Hundred Years of Merchant Banking: A History of Brown Brothers and Company, Brown Shipley & Company, and the Allied Firms*. New York: Privately printed, 1909.

Campbell, A. *The True American System of Finance and The Common Sense Way of Doing Justice to the Soldiers and Their Families: No Banks: Greenbacks the Exclusive Currency*. Chicago: Evening Journal Book and Job Print, 1864.

Clews, Henry. *Fifty Years in Wall Street*. New York: Arno Press, 1973.

Daly, Maria Lydia. *Diary of a Union Lady, 1861–1865*. New York: Funk and Wagnalls, 1962.

Dennett, Taylor, ed., *Lincoln and the Civil War in the Diaries and Letters of John Hay*. New York: Dodd, Mead & Co., 1939.

Dickens, Charles. *A Christmas Carol in Prose, Being a Ghost-Story of Christmas*. London: Chapman & Hall, 1843.

Donald, David, ed. *Inside Lincoln's Cabinet: The Civil War Diaries of Salmon P. Chase*. New York: Longmans, Green, 1954.

Fessenden, Francis. *Life and Public Services of William Pitt Fessenden: United States Senator from Maine 1854–1864; Secretary of the Treasury 1864–1865; United States Senator from Maine 1865–1869*. 2 vols. Boston and New York: Houghton Mifflin and Company, 1907.

Fisk & Hatch. *Memoranda Concerning Government Bonds for the Information of Investors*. New York: 1879.

Fowler, William Worthington. *Ten Years on Wall Street; or Revelations of Inside Life and Experience on 'Change*. Hartford, CT: Worthington, Dustin & Co., 1870.

Freidel, Frank, ed. *Union Pamphlets of the Civil War, 1861–1865*. Cambridge: Belknap Press of Harvard University Press, 1967.

Geillier, J. J. *The History of the National Debt, from the Revolution of 1688 to the Beginning of the Year 1800*. London, 1800.

Gibbons, J. S. *The Public Debt of the United States: Its Organization: Its Liquidation: Administration of the Treasury: The Financial System*. New York: Charles Scribner & Co., 1867

Hughes, Sarah Forbes, ed. *Letters and Recollections of John Murray Forbes*. New York: Arno Press, 1981.

Ide, George. *Battle Echoes or Lesson from the War*. Boston: Gould and Lincoln, 1866.

Kettell, Thomas. *Southern Wealth and Northern Profits, As Exhibited in Statistical Facts and Official Figures: Showing the Necessity of Union to the Future Prosperity and Welfare of the Republic*. New York: George W. & John A. Wood, 1860.

Lathrop, George Parsons. *History of the Union League of Philadelphia, from Its Origin and Foundation to the Year 1882*. Philadelphia: J. B. Lippincott and Co., 1884.

McPherson, Edward. *The Political History of the United States of America during the Period of Reconstruction*. 2nd ed. Washington DC: Solomons & Chapman, 1875.

Merrill, Walter M., ed. *The Letters of William Lloyd Garrison, 1861–1867*. Vol 2. Cambridge, MA: Harvard University Press, 1971.

Moore, John, ed., *The Works of Buchanan, Comprising his Speeches, State Papers, and Private Correspondence*. 12 vols. Philadelphia: J. B. Lippincott, 1911.

Nevins, Allan, and Milton Halsey Thomas, eds. *The Diary of George Templeton Strong*. New York: Macmillan, 1952.

New York Loyal Publication Society. *Pamphlets Issued by the Loyal Publication Society*. Vols 1–3. New York: The Society, 1864–66.

———. *Proceedings at the First Anniversary Meeting of the Loyal Publication Society*. New York: The Society, 1864.

Niven, John, ed. *The Salmon P. Chase Papers*. 5 vols. Kent, OH: Kent State University Press, 1993.

Norton, Charles Eliot. *The Soldier of the Good Cause*. Boston: American Unitarian Association, 1861.

Norton, Sara, and M. A. DeWolfe Howe, eds. *Letters of Charles Eliot Norton*. Boston: Houghton Mifflin, 1913.
Pomeroy, Brick. *Soliloquies of The Bondholder, The Poor Farmer, The Soldier's Widow, The Political Preacher, The Poor Mechanic, The Freed Negro, The 'Radical' Congressman, The Returned Soldier, The Southerner and other Political Articles*. New York: Van Evrie, Horton & Company, 1866.
Pratt, Sereno. *The Work of Wall Street: An Account of the Functions, Methods, and History of the New York Money and Stock Markets*. New York: 1912.
Proceedings of the Meeting in Relation to the Establishment of a Large National Bank in This City. New York: William C. Bryant, 1863.
Russell, Charles. *Memoir of Charles H. Russell, 1796–1884*. New York: n.p., 1903.
Sherman, John. *Recollections of Forty Years in the House, Senate and Cabinet, An Autobiography*. 2 vols. New York: The Werner Company, 1895.
Smith, George Gardiner, ed., *Spencer Kellogg Brown, His Life in Kansas and His Death as a Spy, 1842–1863, As Disclosed in His Diary*. New York: D. Appleton & Co., 1903.
Spaulding, Elbridge. *History of the Legal Tender Paper Money Issued during the Great Rebellion Being a Loan Without Interest and a National Currency*. Buffalo, NY: Express Printing Company, 1869.
Stille, Charles. *The History of the United States Sanitary Commission*. New York: Hurd and Houghton, 1868.
Taylor, Charles H. *History of the Board of Trade of the City of Chicago*. 3 vols. Chicago: Robert O. Law Company, 1917.
Union League of Philadelphia. *Chronicle of the Union League of Philadelphia, 1862–1902*. Philadelphia: Fell, 1902.
White, Alexander. *Autobiography of Alexander White*. 2 vols. New York: Century, 1905.

NEWSPAPERS AND PERIODICALS

Agitator
Der Aktionär
Allentown Democrat
All The Year Round
American
American Gazette
American Whig Review
Amsterdam Courant
Atlantic Monthly
Baltimore Clipper
Banker's Magazine and Statistical Register
Boston Daily Evening Transcript
Boston Emancipator and Republican
Brooklyn Union
Chicago Tribune
Chronicle
Cincinnati Enquirer
City Item
Columbia Spy
Commercial and Financial Chronicle
The Commercial and Financial Chronicle and Hunt's Merchant's Magazine
Constitutional Union
The Democrat
The Economist
Erie Dispatch
L'Europe
Evening Bulletin
Evening Telegraph
Fitzgerald City Stern
Frankfurter Zeitung
Harper's New Monthly Magazine
Harper's Weekly
Illinois Staats-Zeitung
Independent
Indianapolis Daily Journal

Intelligencer
Jj-en Amstelbode
Jonesboro Gazette
Ledger
Lippincott's Monthly Magazine
The London Review of Politics, Society, Literature, Art, and Science
Morristown Free Press
The Nation
Neue Frankfurter Zeitung
Newark Advocate
New York Daily Tribune
New Yorker
New York Herald
New York Times
New York Tribune
New York World
North American Review
North American and U.S. Gazette
Philadelphia Commercial Dispatch
Philadelphia Inquirer
Philadelphia Ledger
Press (Philadelphia)
Public Ledger
Revue des Deux Mondes
Richland Observer
Richmond Examiner
State Gazette
Le Temps
The Times
Village Record

GOVERNMENT DOCUMENTS

1860 United States Federal Census [database online]. Provo, UT: Ancestry.com Operations, 2009.

U.S. State Department. *Foreign Relations of the United States.*

Secretary of the Treasury Reports, 1861–1865.

The War of the Rebellion: A Compilation of the Official Records of the Union and Confederate Armies. 128 vols. Washington, DC, 1880–1901

United States Congress. *Congressional Globe.*

Secondary Sources

BOOKS

Attie, Jeanie. *Patriotic Toil: Northern Women and the American Civil War.* Ithaca, NY: Cornell University Press, 1998.

Austin, Peter E. *Baring Brothers and the Birth of Modern Finance.* New York: Routledge, 2016.

Balogh, Brian. *A Government Out of Sight. The Mystery of National Authority in Nineteenth-Century America.* New York: Cambridge University Press, 2009.

Baptist, Edward. *The Half Has Never Been Told: Slavery and the Making of American Capitalism.* New York: Basic Books, 2014.

Barreyre, Nicolas. *Gold and Freedom: The Political Economy of Reconstruction.* Charlottesville: University of Virginia Press, 2015.

Barreyre, Nicolas, and Nicolas Delalande, eds. *A World of Public Debts: A Political History.* Cham, Switzerland: Palgrave Macmillan, 2020.

Baumgartner, Alice. *South to Freedom: Runaway Slaves to Mexico and the Road to the Civil War.* New York: Basic Books, 2020.

Beale, Howard. *The Critical Year: A Study of Andrew Johnson and Reconstruction.* New York: Frederick Unger, 1958.

Beckert, Sven. *Empire of Cotton: A Global History*. New York: Knopf, 2014.
———. *The Monied Metropolis: New York City and the Consolidation of the American Bourgeoisie, 1850–1896*. New York: Cambridge University Press, 2001.
Beckert, Sven, and Seth Rockman. *Slavery's Capitalism: A New History of American Economic Development*. Philadelphia: University of Pennsylvania Press, 2016.
Bensel, Richard. *Yankee Leviathan: The Origins of Central State Authority in America, 1859–1877*. New York: Cambridge University Press, 1998.
Bergeron, Louis. *France Under Napoleon*. Princeton, NJ: Princeton University Press, 1981.
Birmingham, Stephen. *Our Crowd: The Great Jewish Families of New York*. New York: Harper & Row, 1967.
Blackett, Richard. *Divided Hearts: Britain and the American Civil War*. Baton Rouge: Louisiana State University Press, 2001.
Blevins, Cameron. *Paper Trails: The US Post and the Making of the American West*. New York: Oxford University Press, 2021.
Blue, Frederick. *Salmon P. Chase: A Life in Politics*. Kent, OH: Kent State University Press, 1987.
Bodenhorn, Howard. *A History of Banking in Antebellum America: Financial Markets and Economic Development in an Era of Nation-Building*. New York: Cambridge University Press, 2000.
Bouvier, Jean. *Le Credit Lyonnais de 1863 a 1882: les annees de formation d'une banque de depots*. Paris: S.E.V.P.E.N., 1961.
Brewer, John. *The Sinews of Power: War, Money and the English State, 1688–1783*. Cambridge, MA: Harvard University Press, 1990.
Burrows, Edwin G., and Mike Wallace. *Gotham: A History of New York City to 1898*. New York: Oxford University Press, 1999.
Cameron, Rando E. *France and the Economic Development of Europe, 1800–1914*. Princeton, NJ: Princeton University Press, 1961.
Campbell, Stephen. *The Bank War and the Partisan Press: Newspapers, Financial Institutions, and the Post Office in Jacksonian America*. Lawrence: University Press of Kansas, 2019.
Carosso, Vincent. *Investment Banking in America: A History*. Cambridge, MA: Harvard University Press, 1970.
———. *The Morgans: Private International Bankers, 1854–1913*. Cambridge, MA: Harvard University Press, 1987.
Censer, Jane Turner, ed. *The Papers of Frederick Law Olmsted. Vol. 4, Defending the Union, 1861–1863*. Baltimore: Johns Hopkins University Press, 1986.
Chapman, Stanley. *The Rise of Merchant Banking*. London: George Allen & Unwin, 1984.
Cimbala, Paul, and Randall Miller, eds. *An Uncommon Time: The Civil War and the Northern Home Front*. New York: Fordham University Press, 2002.
Cook, Robert J. *Civil War Senator: William Pitt Fessenden and the Fight to Save the American Republic*. Baton Rouge: Louisiana State University Press, 2011.
Cook, Robert J., William L. Barney, and Elizabeth R. Varon, eds. *Secession Winter: When the Nation Fell Apart*. Baltimore: Johns Hopkins University Press, 2013.
Cummings, James. *Towards Modern Public Finance: The American War with Mexico, 1846–1848*. London: Pickering & Chatto, 2009.

Curry, Leonard P. *Blueprint for Modern America: Nonmilitary Legislation of the First Civil War Congress*. Nashville: Vanderbilt University Press, 1968.

Dewey, Davis Rich. *Financial History of the United States*. 9th ed. New York: Longmans, Green and Co., 1924.

Donald, David Herbert. *Lincoln*. New York: Touchstone, 1996.

Downs, Gregory P. *After Appomattox: Military Occupation and the Ends of War*. Cambridge, MA: Harvard University Press, 2015.

———. *The Second American Revolution: The Civil War-Era Struggle over Cuba and the Rebirth of the American Republic*. Chapel Hill: University of North Carolina Press, 2019.

Doyle, Don. *The Cause of All Nations: An International History of the American Civil War*. New York: Basic Books, 2014.

Edling, Max. *A Hercules in the Cradle: War, Money, and the American State, 1783–1867*. Chicago: University of Chicago Press, 2014.

Fahs, Alice. *The Imagined Civil War: Popular Literature of the North and South, 1861–1865*. Chapel Hill: University of North Carolina Press, 2001.

Ferguson, James. *The Power of the Purse: A History of American Public Finance, 1776–1790*. Chapel Hill: University of North Carolina Press, 1961.

Ferguson, Niall. *The Cash Nexus: Money and Power in the Modern World, 1700–2000*. London: Basic Books, 2001.

———. *The World's Banker: The History of the House of Rothschild*. New York: Penguin Books, 1998.

Ferris, Norman B. *The Trent Affair: A Diplomatic Crisis*. Knoxville: University of Tennessee Press, 1977.

Flade, Roland. *The Lehmans: From Rimpar to the New World a Family History*. Würzburg, Germany: Konigshausen & Neumann, 1999.

Flaherty, Jane. *The Revenue Imperative*. London: Pickering & Chatto, 2009.

Foner, Eric. *Free Soil, Free Labor, Free Men: The Ideology of the Republican Party Before the Civil War*. New York: Oxford University Press, 1970.

———. *Reconstruction: America's Unfinished Revolution 1863–1877*. New York: Harper Collins, 2002.

Fraser, Steve. *Every Man a Speculator: A History of Wall Street in American Life*. New York: Harper Collins, 2005.

Fuller, A. James. *The Election of 1860 Reconsidered*. Kent, OH: Kent State University Press, 2013.

Gallman, Matthew. *Mastering Wartime: A Social History of Philadelphia during the Civil War*. New York: Cambridge University Press, 1990.

———. *Northerners at War: Reflections on the Civil War Home Front*. Kent, OH: Kent State University Press, 2010.

———. *The North Fights the Civil War: The Home Front*. Chicago: I. R. Dee, 1994.

Geisst, Charles. *Wall Street: A History from its Beginnings to the Fall of Enron*. New York: Oxford University Press, 2004.

Giesberg, Judith. *Army at Home: Women and the Civil War on the Northern Home Front*. Chapel Hill: University of North Carolina Press, 2009.

———. *Civil War Sisterhood: The U.S. Sanitary Commission and Women's Politics in Transition*. Boston: Northeastern University Press, 2000.
Gordon, John Steele. *The Scarlet Women of Wall Street: Jay Gould, Jim Fisk, Cornelius Vanderbilt and the Erie Railway Wars & the Birth of Wall Street*. New York: Grove Press, 1988.
Graham, Aaron, and Patrick Walsh, eds. *The British Fiscal-Military States, 1660–c. 1783*. London: Routledge, 2016.
Greenberg, Amy. *Manifest Manhood and the Antebellum American Empire*. Cambridge: Cambridge University Press, 2005.
———. *A Wicked War: Polk, Clay, Lincoln, and the 1846 US Invasion of Mexico*. New York: Alfred A. Knopf, 2012.
Greenberg, Dolores. *Financiers and Railroads: A Study of Morton, Bliss & Company*. Newark: University of Delaware Press, 1980.
Greenberg, Joshua. *Bank Notes and Shinplasters: The Rage for Paper Money in the Early Republic*. Philadelphia: University of Pennsylvania Press, 2020.
Greenfield, Jerome. *The Making of a Fiscal-Military State in Post-Revolutionary France*. Cambridge: Cambridge University Press, forthcoming.
Hammond, Bray. *Banks and Politics in America from the Revolution to the Civil War*. Princeton, NJ: Princeton University Press, 1957.
———. *Sovereignty and an Empty Purse: Banks and Politics in the Civil War*. Princeton, NJ: Princeton University Press, 1970.
Handelskammer Frankfurt, ed. *Geschichte der Handelskammer zu Frankfurt am Main: (1707–1908)*. Frankfurt: Joseph Baer & Co,1908.
Hess, Earl J. *Liberty, Virtue, and Progress: Northerners and their War for the Union*. New York: Fordham University Press, 1988.
Hodas, Daniel. *The Business Career of Moses Taylor: Merchant, Finance Capitalist and Industrialist*. New York: New York University Press, 1976.
Hogeland, William. *Founding Finance: How Debt, Speculation, Foreclosures, Protests, and Crackdowns Made Us a Nation*. Austin: University of Texas Press, 2012.
Hyen, Udo. *Private Banking and Industrialization: The Case of Frankfurt Am Main, 1825–1875*. New York: Arno Press, 1981.
Hyman, Harold, ed. *Heard Round the World: The Impact Abroad of the Civil War*. New York: Knopf, 1969.
James, Joseph B. *The Framing of the Fourteenth Amendment*. Urbana: University of Illinois Press, 1965.
Johnson, Walter. *River of Dark Dreams: Slavery and Empire in the Cotton Kingdom*. Cambridge, MA: Harvard University Press, 2013.
Jones, Howard. *Blue and Gray Diplomacy: A History of Union and Confederate Foreign Relations*. Chapel Hill: University of North Carolina Press, 2010.
Karp, Matthew. *This Vast Southern Empire: Slaveholders at the Helm of American Foreign Policy*. Cambridge, MA: Harvard University Press, 2016.
Katz, Irving. *August Belmont: A Political Biography*. New York: Columbia University Press, 1968.
Korach, Ernst. *Das Deutsche Privatbankgeschaeft*. Berlin: n.p., 1910.

Landes, David. *Bankers and Pashas: International Finance and Economic Imperialism in Egypt.* London: Heinemann, 1958.

Larson, Henrietta M. *Jay Cooke: Private Banker.* Cambridge, MA: Harvard University Press, 1932.

Lawson, Melinda. *Patriot Fires: Forging a New American Nationalism in the Civil War North.* Lawrence: University Press of Kansas, 2002.

Lepler, Jessica. *The Many Panics of 1837: People, Politics, and the Creation of a Transatlantic Financial Crises.* Cambridge: Cambridge University Press, 2013.

Levy, Jonathan. *Ages of American Capitalism: A History of the United States.* New York: Random House, 2021.

———. *Freaks of Fortune: The Emerging World of Capitalism and Risk in America.* Cambridge, MA: Harvard University Press, 2012.

Luskey, Brian. *Men is Cheap: Exposing the Frauds of Free Labor in Civil War America.* Chapel Hill: University of North Carolina Press, 2020.

Maggor, Noam. *Brahmin Capitalism: Frontiers of Wealth and Populism in America's First Gilded Age.* Cambridge, MA: Harvard University Press, 2017.

McElroy, Robert M. *Levi Parsons Morton, Banker, Diplomat and Financier.* New York: G. P. Putnam's Sons., 1930.

McGrane, Reginald. *Foreign Bondholders and American State Debts.* New York: Beard Books, 2000.

Mendite, J. Robert. *The Union League of Philadelphia: 125 Years.* Devon, PA: Union League of Philadelphia, 1987.

Mihm, Stephen. *A Nation of Counterfeiters: Capitalists, Con Men, and the Making of the United States.* Cambridge, MA: Harvard University Press, 2007.

Nagler, Jörg, Don Doyle, and Marcus Gräser, eds. *The Transnational Significance of the American Civil War.* Cham, Switzerland: Palgrave McMillan, 2016.

Nelson, Scott Reynolds. *A Nation of Deadbeats: An Uncommon History of America's Financial Disasters.* New York: Vintage, 2012.

Nelson, Scott Reynolds, and Carol Sheriff. *A People at War: Civilians and Soldiers in America's Civil War, 1854–1877.* New York: Oxford University Press, 2008.

Niven, John. *Salmon P. Chase: A Biography.* New York: Oxford University Press, 1995.

Oberholtzer, Ellis Paxton. *Jay Cooke: Financier of the Civil War.* 2 vols. Philadelphia: G. W. Jacobs and Co., 1907.

Osthaus, Carl. *Freedmen, Philanthropy and Fraud: A History of the Freedmen's Savings Bank.* Urbana: University of Illinois Press, 1976.

Ott, Julia. *When Wall Street Met Main Street: The Quest for an Investors' Democracy.* Cambridge, MA: Harvard University Press, 2011.

Pak, Susie J. *Gentlemen Bankers: The World of J. P. Morgan.* Cambridge, MA: Harvard University Press, 2013.

Paludan, Philip. *A People's Contest: The Union & Civil War, 1861–1865.* Lawrence: University Press of Kansas, 1988.

Patterson, Robert T. *Federal Debt Management Policies, 1865–1879.* Durham, NC: Duke University Press, 1954.

Pawley, Emily. *The Nature of the Future: Agriculture, Science, and Capitalism in the Antebellum North.* Chicago: University of Chicago Press, 2020.

Platt, D. C. M. *Foreign Finance in Continental Europe and the United States, 1815–1870, Quantities, Origins, Functions and Distribution.* New York: Routledge, 1984.
Rao, Gautham. *National Duties: Custom Houses and the Making of the American State.* Chicago: University of Chicago Press, 2016.
Rapport, Michael. *1848: Year of Revolution.* New York: Basic Books, 2010.
Richardson, Heather Cox. *The Greatest Nation of the Earth: Republican Economic Policies during the Civil War.* Cambridge, MA: Harvard University Press, 1997.
———. "North and West of Reconstruction: Studies in Political Economy." In *Reconstructions: New Perspectives on the Postbellum United States*, edited by Thomas J. Brown, 66–90. New York: Oxford University Press, 2006.
Roberts, Alasdair. *America's First Great Depression: Economic Crisis and Political Disorder after the Panic of 1837.* Ithaca, NY: Cornell University Press, 2013.
Ron, Ariel. *Grassroots Leviathan: Agricultural Reform and the Rural North in the Slaveholding Republic.* Baltimore: Johns Hopkins University Press, 2020.
Roos, Jerome. *Why Not Default: The Political Economy of Sovereign Debt.* Princeton, NJ: Princeton University Press, 2019.
Rosenthal, Caitlin. *Accounting for Slavery: Masters and Management.* Cambridge, MA: Harvard University Press, 2018.
Roth, Ralf. *Die Herausbildung einer modernen bürgerlichen Gesellschaft 1789–1866.* Ostfildern, Germany: Thorbecke, 2013.
Rothman, Joshua. *The Ledger and the Chain: How Domestic Slave Traders Shaped America.* New York: Basic Books, 2021.
Sainlaude, Stève. *France and the American Civil War: A Diplomatic History.* Chapel Hill: University of North Carolina Press, 2019.
Schermerhorn, Calvin. *The Business of Slavery and the Rise of American Slavery.* New Haven, CT: Yale University Press, 2015.
Sexton, Jay. *Debtor Diplomacy: Finance and American Foreign Relations in the Civil War Era, 1837–1873.* Oxford: Oxford University Press, 2005.
———. "International Finance in the Civil War Era," in *The Transnational Significance of the American Civil War*, edited by Jörg Nagler, Don H. Doyle, and Marcus Graser, 91–106. London: Palgrave McMillian, 2016.
Siemann, Wolfram. *The German Revolutions of 1848–49.* London: Palgrave Macmillan, 1998.
Silber, Nina. *Daughters of the Union: Northern Women Fight the Civil War.* Cambridge, MA: Harvard University Press, 2005.
Studenski, Paul, and Herman E. Kroos. *Financial History of the United States.* New York: McGraw-Hill, 1952.
Swanberg, W. A. *Jim Fisk: The Career of an Improbable Rascal.* New York: Charles Scribner's Sons, 1959.
Temin, Peter. *The Jacksonian Economy.* New York: W. W. Norton, 1969.
Thomson, David. "Financing the War." In Vol. 2 of *The Cambridge History of the American Civil War*, edited by Aaron Sheehan-Dean, 174–92. Cambridge: Cambridge University Press, 2019.
Todd, Robert Cecil. *Confederate Finance.* Athens: University of Georgia Press, 1954.
Unger, Irwin. *The Greenback Era: A Social and Political History of American Finance, 1865–1879.* Princeton, NJ: Princeton University Press, 1964.

Varon, Elizabeth. *Armies of Deliverance: A New History of the Civil War*. New York: Oxford University Press, 2019.

———. *Disunion!: The Coming of the American Civil War, 1789–1859*. Chapel Hill: University of North Carolina Press, 2008.

Veenendaal, Guus. *Slow Train to Paradise: How Dutch Investment Built American Railroads*. Stanford, CA: Stanford University Press, 1996.

Ver Steeg, C. L. *Robert Morris: Revolutionary Financier*. Philadelphia: University of Pennsylvania Press, 1954.

Wachtel, Howard. *Street of Dreams—Boulevard of Broken Hearts*. London: Pluto Press, 2003.

Waite, Kevin. *West of Slavery: The Southern Dream of a Transcontinental Empire*. Chapel Hill: University of North Carolina Press, 2021.

Westbrook, Wayne W. *Wall Street in the American Novel*. New York: New York University Press, 1980.

White, Richard. *Railroaded: The Transcontinentals and the Making of Modern America*. New York: W. W. Norton & Company, 2012.

———. *The Republic for Which it Stands: The United States During Reconstruction and the Gilded Age, 1865–1896*. New York: Oxford University Press, 2017.

Whitemen, Maxwell. *Gentlemen in Crisis: The First Century of the Union League of Philadelphia, 1862–1962*. Philadelphia: Union League of Philadelphia, 1975.

Wilkins, Mira. *The History of Foreign Investment in the United States to 1914*. Cambridge, MA: Harvard University Press, 1989.

Wilson, Mark. *The Business of Civil War: Military Mobilization and the States, 1861–1865*. Baltimore: Johns Hopkins University Press, 2010.

Wright, Robert. *The First American Wall Street: Chestnut Street, Philadelphia, and the Birth of American Finance*. Chicago: University of Chicago Press, 2005.

———. *Hamilton Unbound: Finance and the Creation of the American Republic*. Westport, CT: Greenwood Press, 2002.

———. *One Nation Under Debt: Hamilton, Jefferson, and the History of What We Owe*. New York: McGraw-Hill, 2008.

Wright, Robert E., and David J. Cowen. *Financial Founding Fathers: The Men Who Made America Rich*. Chicago: University of Chicago Press, 2006.

Zallen, Jeremy. *American Lucifers: The Dark History of Artificial Light 1750-1865*. Chapel Hill: University of North Carolina Press, 2019.

ARTICLES

Cochran, Thomas. "Did the Civil War Retard Industrialization?" *Mississippi Valley Historical Review* 58 (September 1961): 197–210.

Colby, Robert. "'Negroes Will Bear Fabulous Prices': The Economic of Wartime Slave Commerce and Visions of the Confederate Future." *Journal of the Civil War Era* 10, no. 4 (December 2020): 439–68.

Courtney, Leonard H. "On the Finances of the United States, 1861–1867." *Journal of the Statistical Society of London* 31 (June 1868): 164–221.

David, L. E. and J. R. T. Hughes. "A Dollar-Sterling Exchange Rate, 1803–1895." *Economic History Review* 13 (1960): 52–78.

Efford, Derek. "The Correspondence of Alexander Herzen with James de Rothschild." *Toronto Slavic Quarterly* 19 (Winter 2007): 39–47.
Engerman, Stanley. "The Economic Impact of the Civil War." *Explorations in Entrepreneurial History*, Second Series, 3 (Spring–Summer 1966): 176–99.
Fisk, H. E. "Fisk & Hatch, Bankers and Dealers in Government Securities, 1862–1865." *Journal of Economic and Business History* 2 (1930): 706–22.
Flaherty, Jane. "'The Exhausted Condition of the Treasury,' on the Eve of the Civil War." *Civil War History* 55, no. 2 (June 2009): 244–77.
Flandreau, Marc, and Juan Flores. "Bonds and Brands: Foundations of Sovereign Debt Markets, 1820–1830." *The Journal of Economic History* 69, no. 2 (September 2009): 646–84.
Flores-Macias, Gustavo A., and Sarah E. Kreps. "Political Parties at War: A Study of American War Finance, 1789–2010." *American Political Science Review* 107 (November 2013): 833–48.
Freidel, Frank. "The Loyal Publication Society: A Pro-Union Propaganda Agency." *Mississippi Valley Historical Review* 26, no. 3 (December 1939): 359–76.
Gische, David. "The New York City Banks and the Development of the National Banking System, 1860–1870." *American Journal of Legal History* 23 (January 1979): 21–67.
Glanz, Rudolf. "The Rothschild Legend in America." *Jewish Social Studies* 19, no. 1 (January–April 1957): 3–28.
Goldin, Claudia, and Frank Lewis. "The Economic Cost of the American Civil War: Estimates and Implications." *The Journal of Economic History* 35, no. 2 (June 1975): 299–326.
Greenberg, Dolores. "Yankee Financiers and the Establishment of Trans-Atlantic Partnerships: A Re-Examination." *Business History* 16, no. 1 (1974): 17–35.
Hacker, J. David. "A Census-Based Account of the Civil War Dead." *Civil War History* 57, no. 4 (December 2011): 306–47.
Hein, Benjamin. "Old Regime in a New World: Frankfurt's Financial Market in the Nineteenth Century." *The Journal of Modern History* 92 (December 2020): 1–39.
Hochfelder, David. "'Where the Common People Could Speculate': The Ticker, Bucket Shops, and the Origins of Popular Participation in Financial Markets, 1880–1920." *The Journal of American History* 93, no. 2 (September 2006): 335–58.
Holtfrerich, Carl-Ludwig. "Government Debt in Economic Thought of the Long 19th Century." School of Business & Economics Discussion Paper, Free University of Berlin, 2013–2014.
Holton, Woody. "'From the Labours of Others': The War Bonds Controversy and the Origins of the Constitution in New England." *The William and Mary Quarterly* 61, no. 2 (April 2004): 271–316.
James, John. "Public Debt Management and Nineteenth-Century American Economic Growth," *Explorations in Economic History* 21 (1984): 192–217.
James, John A., and David F. Weiman. "The National Banking Acts and the Transformation of New York City Banking During the Civil War Era." *The Journal of Economic History* 71, no. 2 (June 2011): 338–62.
Kagin, Donald. "Treasury Notes of the War of 1812." *The Numismatist* (February 2013): 34–39.

Laughlin, J. Lawrence. "Political Economy and the Civil War." *Atlantic Monthly* 55 (April 1885): 446.

Lester, Richard. "An Aspect of Confederate Finance during the American Civil War: The Erlanger Loan and the Plan of 1864." *Business History* 16, no. 2 (1974): 130–44.

Maynard, Douglas. "The Forbes-Aspinwall Mission." *The Mississippi Valley Historical Review* 45, no. 1 (June 1958): 67–89.

Mihm, Stephen. "Follow the Money: The Return of Finance in the Early Republic." *Journal of the Early Republic* 36, no. 4 (Winter 2016): 783–804.

Morris, Christopher. "With 'The Economics-of-Slavery Culture Wars,' It's Déjà Vu All Over Again." *The Journal of the Civil War Era* 10, no. 4 (December 2020): 524–57.

Nelson, Scott Reynolds. "A Storm of Cheap Goods: New American Commodities and the Panic of 1873." *The Journal of the Gilded Age and Progressive Era* 10, no. 4 (October 2011): 447–53.

Oosterlinck, Kim, and Max Weidenmier. "Victory or Repudiation? The Probability of the Southern Confederacy Winning the Civil War." National Bureau of Economic Research Working Paper 13567, November 2007.

Patterson, Robert T. "Government Finance on the Eve of the Civil War." *Journal of Economic History* 12 (1952): 35–44.

Randolph, Bessie C. "Foreign Bondholders and the Repudiated Debts of the Southern States." *American Journal of International Law* 25, no. 1 (January 1931): 63–82.

Saunt, Claudio. "Financing Dispossession: Stocks, Bonds, and the Deportation of Native Peoples in the Antebellum United States." *The Journal of American History* 106, no. 2 (September 2019): 315–37.

Schell, Herbert, S. "Hugh McCulloch and the Treasury Department, 1865–1869." *The Mississippi Valley Historical Review* 17, no. 3 (December 1930): 404–21.

Sim, David. "Following the Money: Fenian Bonds, Diasporic Nationalism, and Distant Revolutions in the Mid-Nineteenth-Century United States." *Past & Present* 247, no. 1 (May 2020): 77–112.

Smith, George Winston. "Broadsides for Freedom: Civil War Propaganda in New England." *The New England Quarterly* 21, no. 3 (Sept. 1948): 291–312.

Sterne, Margaret. "From Jonesville to Frankfurt on the Main: The Political Career of William Walton Murphy, 1861–1869." *Quarterly Review of the Michigan Alumnus* 65, no. 18 (Spring 1959): 251–61.

Sylla, Richard. "Forgotten Men of Money: Private Bankers in Early U.S. History." *Journal of Economic History* 36, no. 1 (1976): 173–88.

Taylor, Amos. "Walker's Financial Mission to London on Behalf of the North, 1863–1864." *Journal of Economic and Business History* 3 (February 1931): 296–320.

Thomson, David. "Jubilee Jim Fisk and the Great Civil War Score." *Boston Globe Magazine*, April 26, 2020, 14–21.

Turner, Justin. "The Mary Lincoln Letters to Mrs. Felician Slataper." *Journal of the Illinois State Historical Society* 49, no. 1 (Spring 1956): 7–33.

Wallis, John Joseph. "What Caused the Crisis of 1839?" National Bureau of Economic Research Historical Paper 133, April 2001.

Weidenmier, Max. "Turning Points in the US Civil War: Views from the Grayback Market." *Southern Economic Journal* 68, no. 4 (April 2002): 875–90.

Willard, Kristen, Timothy Guinnane, and Harvey Rosen. "Turning Points in the Civil War: Views from the Greenback Market." *American Economic Review* 86, no. 4 (1996): 1001–18.

THESES, DISSERTATIONS, AND UNPUBLISHED PAPERS

Bersch, Julia, and Graciela L. Kaminsky. "Financial Globalization in the 19th Century: Germany as a Financial Center," September 2008.

Caires, Michael. "The Greenback Union: The Politics and Law of American Money in the Civil War Era." PhD diss., University of Virginia, 2014.

Daly, Ann. "Minting America: Money, Value, and the Federal State, 1784–1858." PhD diss., Brown University, 2021.

De Jong, Abe, Joost Jonker, Aliisa Röell, and Gerarda Westerhuis. "Reinventing Institutions: Trust Offices and the Dutch Financial System, 1690s–2000s." EABH Paper 20-04, November 2020.

Desan, Christine. "Strange New Music: The Monetary Composition Made by Enlightenment Quartet." Harvard Public Law Working Paper No. 18-49, July 21, 2018.

Geljon, P.A. "De Algemene Banken en het Effectenbedrijf 1860–1914," PhD thesis, NIBE, 2005.

Gibson, Guy. "Lincoln's League: The Union League Movement During the Civil War." PhD diss., University of Illinois, 1957.

Lee, Arthur. "The Development of an Economic Policy in the Early Republican Party." PhD diss., Syracuse University, 1953.

Migliore, Paul. "The Business of Union: The New York Business Community and the Civil War." PhD diss., Columbia University, 1976.

Silvestro, Clement. "None but Patriots: The Union Leagues in the Civil War and Reconstruction." PhD diss., University of Wisconsin, 1959.

Smith, George Winston. "Generative Forces of Union Propaganda: A Study of Civil War Pressure Groups." PhD diss., University of Wisconsin, 1940.

Traweek, Virginia, and Malcolm Wardlaw. "Societal Trust and Financial Market Participation: Evidence from the Freedman's Savings Bank." SSRN Working Paper 3164418, October 2020.

Index

Adams, Charles Francis, 174
Adams, John Quincy, 3
African Americans, 5, 78, 121, 150, 153
Alabama, 15, 34
Alabama Claims, 240n37, 243n57, 244n64
Allentown Democrat, 69
American Exchange Bank, 36
American Peace Society, 18
Amsterdam: as a financial center for debt, 3, 7, 15, 86, 102, 170; Civil War debt sales, 48, 87, 93, 95, 108, 114, 116, 117, 120; Reconstruction Era debt sales, 172, 174, 177, 178, 197
Antietam, Battle of, 58
Anti-Semitism, 17, 93
Army of Northern Virginia, 2
Army of the Potomac, 1, 66, 152
Aspinwall, William, 88, 118–19, 224n5, 229n67
Associated Banks. *See* War Loan Association
Associated Press, 65
Austria, 76, 107, 109, 110, 113, 114, 227n48, 239n26

Balls Bluff, Battle of, 51
Baltimore, 27, 72, 77, 83, 89, 126, 142, 224n8
Bancroft, H.H., 63, 145
Bank of Commerce, 36
Bank of England, 3, 15, 243n57
Bank of North America, 19
Bank of the Metropolis, 19
Bank of the United States, 14; And the Second Bank of the United States, 17
Baring Brothers, and antebellum state debt, 15; and Civil War debt, 96, 101, 116, 117, 119, 139; and Reconstruction era Debt, 173–74, 176, 177, 186, 187, 188, 189, 190

Becker & Fuld, 93, 95, 174, 225n19, 241n39
Beckwith, George, 18, 213n13
Beekman, James W., 23
Behrens & Sons, 93, 169, 174, 239n29
Belmont, August, 91, 191, 198; and British financial intervention in the Civil War, 89, 90; mission to Britain in 1861, 92, 93; Civil War investing, 93, 96, 104; Reconstruction-era investing, 188, 191
Bennett, James Gordon, 41
Benton, Thomas Hart, 17
Berlin, 103, 114, 169, 174, 237n21, 239n26; and its stock exchange, 113, 166, 190
Bethmann Bankhaus, 112–13, 117, 168, 228n55, 239n26
Bigelow, John, 98–99, 100–1, 106, 225n25, 225n26, 244n65
Bismarck, Otto von, 115
Bleichroeder Bank, 169–70, 239n29
bondholders, 157, 158, 163, 164
Bonn, 114
Borski, 176, 177–78, 241n42
Boston, antebellum United States, 9, 15, 18, 19; early Civil War finance, 24, 27–28, 30, 36, 40, 41, 43, 50, 51; sales under Jay Cooke, 61, 63, 68, 83, 132, 142; bucket shops, 201
Boston Daily Advertiser, 28, 40, 47
Boutwell, George, 182, 183, 185, 186, 187, 188
Bowdoin College, 127, 142
Bright, John, 96
Britain, 6, 13, 14, 15; Civil War finance, 48, 50, 86, 88, 94, 96, 97, 98, 101, 119, 120; Reconstruction-era Finance, 172, 173, 199
Brown, James, 89
Brown, Spencer Kellog, 55
Brown Brothers, 79, 88–89, 222n42, 224n8
Brussels, 87, 97, 114, 174

Buchanan, James, 25, 26, 27, 93
bucket shops, 199–200, 201
Bull Run, Battle of, 8, 24, 33, 35, 36, 39, 51, 75
Bureau of Public Debt, 47, 75, 79, 126, 142–43

California, 36, 47, 63, 64, 96, 121, 144–45
Cameron, Simon, 27, 28
Canada, 172, 185, 202, 229n66, 240n37
Chancellorsville, Battle of, 2, 72
Chandler, Zachariah, 25
Chase, Salmon P., 8, 24, 183; and early efforts at financing the Civil War, 26, 29–30, 31–47 passim; and specie suspension, 48–49, 50, 52; and bringing on Jay Cooke, 54, 55, 58, 59, 60, 64, 80; as a bond investor, 78; and international investment, 87, 89, 90, 92, 117, 119, 120, 173; and the 10-40 issue, 123, 124, 125, 132; and the 7-30 issue, 159, 170
Chicago, 26, 76, 77, 83, 200
Chicago Tribune, 79, 92, 200
Chinese Mutual Insurance Company, 79, 145
Cincinnati, 41, 75–76, 83
Cisco, John J., 52, 54, 133
Clark, Dodge, & Co., 61
Clark, E.W., 19, 42
Clarkson, Robert, 64
Cobb, Howell, 25, 214n7
Cochut, André, 99, 100–1, 225n29
Coe, George S., 36, 51, 53
Coffroth, Alexander H., 80
Coinage Act of 1834, 15
coins. *See* specie
Collamer, Jacob, 122
Confederacy: and bond issuance, 33–34; and U.S. Debt sales, 148–49, 150; and sales abroad, 172–73
confidence, 39, 40, 50, 74, 83, 85, 129; as a factor in investing, 2, 7–8, 9, 24, 26, 56, 68–69; in international investing, 93–94, 96, 107, 111, 112, 120, 124, 125, 138, 144, 153, 155, 167; in investing in United States during Reconstruction, 181, 184–85, 197

Congress, 12, 17, 22, 25; and Mexican War Loan Negotiations, 18–19, 20; and Early War Finance Struggles, 26, 27, 28, 31, 32, 34, 35, 36, 38, 39, 48, 49, 50; and the legal tender debate, 53, 55; and Henry Cooke, 44, 59, 60; investing in bonds, 79; and investigations, 80; and national banking system, 122, 123, 124; subsequent Bond Issues, 134, 126, 140; Reconstruction, 157, 158, 159, 162, 163, 178, 180, 181, 182, 185, 186
Connecticut, 73
Cooke, Henry, 61, 135, 182; and early war finance, 42, 44, 53; lobbying efforts, 59, 81, 125, 133, 159; and international finance, 96, 101; Lincoln's death, 154
Cooke, Jay, 2, 4, 8; reminiscing on war, 1, 156; selling Mexican War bonds, 20; early war finance, 37, 40, 42, 44–45, 46; efforts to popularize loans, 53, 56–57, 136–38, 139–40, 141; and extension of exclusive 5-20 agency, 58–75 passim; and congressional investigations, 80–81; and international finance during the Civil War, 96, 101, 112, 116, 119, 120; and additional loans, 121–149 passim; and selling bonds after Lincoln's assassination, 151, 152, 154–55; and Reconstruction-era bond sales, 160–61, 163, 164, 181–97 passim, 199; and the Panic of 1873, 191, 193; and World War I, 202–3
Cooke, Pitt, 44
Copperheads, 150, 151
Corcoran & Riggs, 18, 19
Cotton, 7–8, 195; antebellum America, 14, 17, 24, 25, 29; Confederate Congress and, 34, 35; Europe, 85, 90, 92, 97, 99, 100, 106, 172, 186
counterfeit, 81, 97–98, 99, 109
Crommelin & Sons, 15
Cuba, 9, 78, 118, 173
Curtin, Andrew, 44
customs duties, 27

Dallas, Alexander, 13
Dane, Dana & Co., 79

Davis, Henry Winter, 165
Davis, Jefferson, 3, 44, 119, 120
Dayton, William, 99
debt: and antebellum state debt issuances, 14–15, 17; and the debates over full assumption, 11; and retirement of the debt, 158
default, 3, 12, 16–17
Delaware, 150
Detroit, 77, 78, 144
Dickens, Charles, 22, 194
Dix, John, 26
Dixon, James, 23
Douglas, Stephen, 167
Drexel & Co., 18, 44, 190
Dudley, Thomas Haines, 97, 225n22
Dutch investors. *See* Netherlands

Ebenezer Society, 79
Economist, 49, 50, 53, 162
Edward Pictet & Cie., 171, 240
Election of 1860, 25, 167
Election of 1864, 113, 116, 125–26, 130, 133
Election of 1868, 181
Emancipation Proclamation, 58, 98
Erlanger, 7, 97, 106, 107, 109, 225n22
Europe, 3, 7, 14, 16, 17, 36, 49; and Confederate investment, 34; And European Foodstuffs, 47. *See also* Britain; France; Germany; Netherlands; and Switzerland
Evans, William, 96
exchange rates, 96

Fahnstock, Harris, 133, 183, 225n21
Fenton, Ruben, 52, 218n55
Fessenden, William Pitt, 40, 50, 87, 124–25, 131–32, 134, 135, 152, 216n29
fiat currency, 12, 13, 51, 59, 81, 160, 179
First Report on the Public Credit, 11
Fisk & Hatch, 61, 63, 70, 82, 116, 134, 199
Fitzgerald City Stern, 68
Florida, 17, 66, 119
Forbes, John Murray, 118–19
Fort Sumter, 22, 29, 30, 34, 42, 90, 103, 167

France: and Revolutionary War financing, 12–13; and general United States investment, 6, 8, 158; Civil War bond sales, 85, 88, 92, 96, 98, 99, 100, 101, 115, 117; post-war debt, 158, 169, 173, 174, 185, 202
Frankfurt: as a center for sovereign debt, 7, 17, 86, 92; and Civil War debt sales, 101–2, 103, 104, 108, 109, 110, 112, 120; and Reconstruction era debt sales, 166
Frankfurt Chamber of Commerce, 106, 108
Frankfurt Stock Exchange, 106, 108, 112, 114, 116, 117
fraud. *See* counterfeit; shoddy; war profiteering
Frederick Huth & Co., 15

Gallatin, Albert, 13, 14, 24
Gallatin, James, 53
Garfield, James, 78, 180
Garland, James, 15
Geneva, 114, 170, 171, 172
Germany, 85, 86, 139, 158
Gettysburg, 99, 105, 108, 111
Gladstone, William, 173
Gläser, August, 105
gold: antebellum use of, 15, 29; early war finance, 36, 40, 41, 46, 47, 49, 50, 51, 55; and the 5-20 loan, 59, 71, 73, 74; and international bond sales, 96, 116, 145; post-war debates, 152, 153, 157, 160, 179, 180–81, 182, 185, 191
Grant, Ulysses, 130, 181, 189
Greeley, Horace, 71, 87
greenbacks, 2, 4, 6; legislation, 54, 55, 59, 74, 81–82; international implications of, 99, 116, 124; and later bond drives, 135, 137, 152, 160, 162, 179, 181, 182
Gurney & Co., 15

Hamburg, 113, 165, 169, 174
Hamilton, Alexander, 11, 17, 33
Hamilton, Frances A., 89
Hammond, James Henry, 34
Hanna, Joshua, 61

Harrington, George, 52
haute banque, 169, 192
Hazard, Rowland Gibson, 117, 177
Hendricks, Thomas, 81
Hooper, Samuel, 53, 122
Hope & Co., 15, 116–17, 174, 176–77
Hottinguer & Cie, 101, 117, 173

Ide, George, 9, 141
Illinois, 64, 77, 104, 129, 142, 144, 167
Illinois Staats-Zeitung, 109
immigrants: as a group of investors, 75, 128–29, 137–38, 143; English immigrants, 76; German immigrants, 67, 75, 76; Irish immigrants, 75
Indiana, 64, 69, 72, 137, 142, 143
investment, and civic inclusion, 5; as a patriotic endeavor, 4–5, 30, 55–56, 65; as a popular notion, 2, 4, 32, 41; religious connections, 65
Iowa, 64, 78, 137, 143, 144, 153

Jackson, Andrew, 15, 16
Johnson, Andrew, 162, 181
Jutting, Charles, 177

Ketchum, Hiram, 23, 54
Ketchum, Morris, 133, 134, 152
kinship, as a factor in investing, 7, 86, 109, 111, 168, 196
Körners, Gustav, 104

Lazard Speyer Ellison, 108, 109, 111
Legal Tender Act, 53, 54, 60, 73, 94, 123, 125, 192, 203
Lieber, Francis, 52
Lincoln, Abraham, 1, 78, 80, 132, 133; and his initial funding call, 12, 22, 23, 24, 25, 26, 27, 33; and other early war finance, 38, 39, 49, 51, 54, 58, 66, 74, 122, 123; and international finance, 85, 91, 92, 93, 99, 103, 104, 113, 115; and his death, 150, 151, 154–55
Livermore Clews & Co., 61
Liverpool, 88, 94, 97, 118
Lombard Odier & Cie., 170–71

London, as a financial center for debt, 3, 7, 16, 17, 87; and specie suspension, 49; and Civil War bond sales, 48, 85, 87, 88–98, 101, 102, 106, 108, 112, 117, 119, 120; and Reconstruction era bond sales, 158, 162, 168, 171–76, 185–90, 194, 196, 197; and the local treasury office, 185–86
London Stock Exchange, 93
Louisiana, 77, 104, 142, 148, 173, 176
Loyal Publication Societies, 9, 195–96
Lyman, George, 32

MacAlester, Charles, 19
Maine, 9, 50, 78, 124, 127–28, 129, 130, 132, 140, 142
Marcuard & Cie., 171–72
Marcuse Balzer, 48
market segregation, 102
Martin, David, 53
Marx, Karl, 98
Maryland, 58, 66, 77, 95, 129, 151
Massachusetts, 47, 57, 127, 129, 142, 179
McAdoo, William, 202–3
McCulloch, Hugh, 115, 133, 134, 152, 154, 160–63, 182, 185, 186, 198
McNutt, Alexander, 17
Memminger, Christopher, 34–35
Mexican War, 11, 18, 20, 21
Mexico, 18
Michigan, 25, 64, 77, 78, 103, 108, 144
Mihm, Stephen, 8, 98
Minnesota, 64, 78, 129, 153, 201
Mississippi (river), 58, 130
Mississippi (state), 3, 17, 58, 119, 120, 142, 150, 177
Missouri, 17, 63, 64, 69, 130, 144, 150
money. *See* greenbacks
Monroe & Co., 99
Morgan, J.S., 48, 94, 98, 187–88
Morris, Robert, 12
Morton, Levi, 186
Morton, Rose, & Co., 190
Munich, 87, 114
Murphy, William, 103–4, 105, 106, 107, 108, 111, 112

Napoleon III, 88, 98, 101
Nash, John Simon, 41
National Bank Act, 122, 123, 203, 222n40
National Banking System, 53
National Debt, 7, 8, 13, 15, 20, 21, 23, 25, 27, 131, 156, 161, 163–64, 179
Netherlands, 8, 12–13, 85, 86, 105, 115, 117, 120, 158, 176, 185
Neue Frankfurter Zeitung, 103, 109
New Jersey, 79, 80, 139, 146, 147
New Mexico, 145
New Orleans, 9, 15, 58, 88, 130, 142, 148, 149
New York City, 5, 8; and antebellum debt, 15, 18, 19; and initial Civil War response, 22, 26, 29, 30, 36, 39; as a center for 5-20 debt, 71, 83; Cooke and his relationship with, 42, 45, 42, 61, 63, 71, 79; and international ties, 89, 91, 96, 110, 114, 123, 170, 172, 184; and the 7-30 drive, 146, 153
New York Herald, 41, 46, 185
New York Stock Exchange, 22, 73–74, 82–83, 134, 152
New York Times, 23, 28, 33, 47, 50, 53, 85, 112, 136, 137, 165, 166, 172, 200
New York Tribune, 50, 109, 115, 136, 137
New York World, 80, 201
night agencies, 145–46, 148, 152–53
North Carolina, 22, 76
Northern Pacific Railroad, 183, 191

Ohio, 53, 81; and Chase, 24, 26, 41, 49; and Cooke, 42, 64, 65, 68, 69, 75, 76, 129, 137, 141, 142, 181
Opdyke, George, 54, 133
Oregon, 63, 142, 145

Panic of 1837, 15, 29
Panic of 1857, 20, 25, 27, 29, 89
Panic of 1873, 190, 193
Panic of 1907, 201
Paris, 7, 85–102 passim, 106, 109, 115, 117, 120, 158, 167, 169, 170, 173
Peabody, George, 94, 95, 98
Peaslee & Co., 65
Pendleton, George Hunt, 181

Peninsula Campaign, 58
Pennsylvania, 44, 47, 64, 73, 77, 99, 129, 141, 196
Philadelphia, 1, 8, 18, 24, 27, 28, 36, 37, 41, 202; and Cooke, 42, 44, 45, 50, 51, 57, 59, 61, 64, 68, 70, 78, 83; and the 7-30 drive, 125, 132, 135, 137, 139, 142, 151, 153, 184
Philadelphia Bulletin, 66
Philadelphia City Item, 66
Philadelphia Commercial Dispatch, 69
Philadelphia Inquirer, 30, 32, 39, 46, 66, 82, 155
Philadelphia Ledger, 69
Philadelphia Press, 66, 121, 155
Pierce, Franklin, 20
Pike, James, 115, 116
Pittsburgh, 61, 76, 77, 83
Polk, James, 18, 20
Produce Loan, 35
Public Credit Act, 181, 182, 185
Puerto Rico, 185

Quakers, 141
Queen Victoria, 172

railroads, 14, 177, 183, 191, 196, 197
Reconstruction, 1, 6, 7, 158, 159, 162, 164, 165, 166, 178, 180, 193, 196
religion, as a factor in investing, 86, 107, 111
Republican Party, 5, 22–44 passim, 73, 80, 81, 86, 92, 93, 104, 125, 162, 163, 165, 167, 179, 180, 181, 183, 185, 193, 195
repudiation, 3, 17, 18, 85, 119, 151, 158, 165, 178–79, 181, 194
Revolutionary War, 11, 12, 13
Revolution of 1848, 86, 167
Richmond, 55, 58, 75, 85, 105, 113
Ricker, Samuel, 104
Rose, John, 186
Rothschild, James de, 93–94
Rothschild & Co.; and antebellum state debt, 15, 17; and Civil War debt, 89, 104, 139; and the Frankfurt house, 107, 188; and Reconstruction era debt, 169–70, 174, 175, 186–87
Russell, John Lord, 89

Sanford, Henry, 97
San Francisco, 63, 83, 145
Sanitary Commission, 57, 127
Schroeders, 106
Schuchardt & Gebhard, 48
Seligman, Joseph W., 8, 48, 108, 109, 110–11, 168, 188, 189
Seward, William, 26, 90, 92, 97, 98, 99, 105, 106, 108, 113
Sherman, John, 53, 54, 81, 122, 162, 180, 182, 183, 191
shoddy. *See* war profiteering
Sickles, Daniel, 88
Slavery, 18, 22, 24, 26, 86, 122, 125, 151, 153, 167, 181; and the international ramifications, 90, 92, 100, 104, 107, 113, 117, 118, 119, 192
Sonnemann, Leopold, 103
South Carolina, 148, 150
Spaulding, E.G., 52, 53, 123
specie, 8, 11, 12, 15, 29, 34, 35, 36, 39, 40, 46, 47, 49, 50; and the bond issues, 59, 74, 84, 98, 106, 159, 160, 179, 180, 181, 182, 191; and reserves, 47; and suspension, 47, 49, 52–53
Specie Circular, 15
Stevens, John Austin, 36, 38, 39, 48
Stevens, Thaddeus, 33
Stewart, John, 134, 152, 160
St. Louis, 55, 68, 77, 83, 142, 200
Strong, George Templeton, 78, 93
Sumner, Charles, 52
Switzerland, 8, 105, 158, 169, 170, 171, 172, 185, 188

tariff, 25
taxation, 2, 4, 13, 14, 18, 23, 27, 31, 33, 49, 52, 53, 163, 164
Taylor, Moses, 118
Tennessee, 148
Thompson, John, 19
Train, Charles R., 80
Tread, Howard Potter, 79
Treasury Department: and the limitations of elite financial support, 24; and Revolutionary War financing, 13–14; and the Mexican War Loan of 1847, 18–19; and early war reactions, 25–42, 46, 47, 51, 54, 57, 58, 59, 60, 61, 63; and international operations, 87, 90, 97, 106, 115, 118, 119, 166; and 7-30 drive, 121–26, 131, 133, 134, 135, 136, 144, 145, 151, 152, 154; post-war debt, 158, 159, 160, 161, 179, 181–87
Treasury Notes, 28, 125; and pre–Civil War financing, 13; and early Civil War financing measures, 25, 27
Treaty of Guadalupe Hidalgo, 20
Trent Affair, 48, 50, 51, 106
Twain, Mark, 79

Union Leagues, 57

Vallandigham, Clement, 33
Vermilye, Jacob, 53, 61
Vermont, 61, 122, 237n17
Vicksburg, 105, 111, 142, 150
Vienna, 103, 107, 110, 114, 170, 190
Virginia, 22, 66, 72, 75, 76, 77, 130, 142, 148, 150, 151, 153

Walker, Robert J., 18, 19, 115, 119–20
Wall Street, 24, 26, 59, 84, 85; and Early War finance, 29, 30; and popular culture, 6, 29, 71, 72, 197; and specie suspension, 50; and national banking, 123
Warburg, 169
War Loan Association, 35, 36, 37, 39, 47, 48
War of 1812, 11
war profiteering, 72–73, 74, 75
Welles, Gideon, 78
Wells Fargo & Co., 144, 145
Weser-Zeitung, 107
White, Alexander D., 108
Wilkeson, Samuel, 136, 152, 161
Williams, John E., 39
Wisconsin, 64, 129, 144, 153
World War I, 5, 6, 78, 122, 201–2

Young, John Russell, 153